SUGAR AND CIVILIZATION

SUGAR

AND CIVILIZATION

American Empire and the
Cultural Politics of Sweetness

APRIL MERLEAUX

The University of North Carolina Press
CHAPEL HILL

This book was published with the assistance of the Thornton H. Brooks Fund of the University of North Carolina Press.

© 2015 The University of North Carolina Press

Designed by Alyssa D'Avanzo
Set in Utopia by codeMantra, Inc.
Manufactured in the United States of America

The paper in this book meets the guidelines for permanence and durability of the Committee on Production Guidelines for Book Longevity of the Council on Library Resources.

The University of North Carolina Press has been a member of the Green Press Initiative since 2003.

Cover illustration: "Cuba's Opportunity" by Udo J. Keppler (1902). Courtesy of Library of Congress (LC-DIG-ppmsca-25603)

Library of Congress Cataloging-in-Publication Data
Merleaux, April.
Sugar and civilization : American empire and the cultural politics of sweetness / April Merleaux.
pages cm
Includes bibliographical references and index.
ISBN 978-1-4696-2251-4 (pbk : alk. paper) — ISBN 978-1-4696-2252-1 (ebook)
1. Sugar trade—Political aspects—United States—History.
2. Sugar—United States—History. 3. United States—Foreign economic relations. 4. United States—Foreign relations. I. Title.
HD9106.M46 2015
338.4'7664150973—dc23
2015003750

Portions of chapter 1 appeared in different form in "The Political Culture of Sugar Tariffs: Immigration, Race, and Empire, 1898–1930," *International Labor and Working-Class History* 81 (Spring 2012): 28–48. Copyright © 2012 International Labor and Working-Class History, Inc. Reprinted with the permission of Cambridge University Press.

The Photograph is violent: not because it shows violent things, but because on each occasion *it fills the sight by force*, and because in it nothing can be refused or transformed (that we can sometimes call it mild does not contradict its violence: many say that sugar is mild, but to me sugar is violent, and I call it so).

—ROLAND BARTHES, *Camera Lucida* (1980)

There's a violent scent of sugar in the air.

—AGUSTÍN ACOSTA, *La Zafra* (1926)

CONTENTS

ILLUSTRATIONS AND FIGURES

FIGURES

ACKNOWLEDGMENTS

A wonderful group of scholars supported this book in its initial phase. Steve Pitti trusted me to follow my instincts and offered timely advice as I made my way through the mountain of sugar. Mary Lui was particularly helpful in the revision process and has guided me as I acclimate to faculty life. Glenda Gilmore and Jean-Christophe Agnew offered their thoughts and assistance throughout the process. Other faculty at Yale and beyond have also helped me along the way. Alicia Schmidt Camacho made it possible to attend a memorable conference in Lubbock, where I got useful feedback on an early version of Chapter 4. Victorine Shepard made brownies and good sense. Deborah Fitzgerald at MIT and Pauline Peters at Harvard persuaded me that I really didn't have any choice but academia. Deborah generously traveled to New Haven to participate in my oral exams. Willie Lockeretz at Tufts, besides being a model of an interdisciplinary scholar, gave me a solid kick toward commodities. He might not like this book, but his influence is here nonetheless. The kernel of this project was born at Reed College through my work with Chris Lowe and Jackie Dirks, exemplary scholar teachers.

I am indebted to many archivists and librarians, notably those at Yale University's Sterling Memorial Library and the former Seeley G. Mudd Library. Yale's Manuscripts and Archives, especially its director, Christine Weideman, and archivists Bill Landis and Tom Hyry, helped me in countless ways, professional and personal. Always hang out with the archivists if you have the chance. Jenny Gotwals donated her own time tracking down sources for me and recommended a great research assistant, Ivel Posada, who helped me find Puerto Rico in the microform version of the ACLU papers.

Portions of this research were supported by the Lamar Center for the Study of Frontiers and Borders, the John F. Enders Fellowship and Research Grant, the Program in Agrarian Studies, and the Yale Center for International and Area Studies. Additional research was funded by Florida International University's Summer Faculty Fellowship.

Thanks to Jeffrey Newman, executive director/president of the National Child Labor Committee for permission to reprint images from the *American Child*.

I have taken sustenance from the friendship and intellectual companionship of my graduate school friends. Naomi Paik, Amina El-Annan, Monica Martinez, Simeon Man, Julie Weise, Rebecca Tinio McKenna, and Lisa Covert all helped with this project at one time or another and have been good company besides. The members of the Yale Asian American Studies Working Group, the Ethnicity Race & Migration Fellows, the Esquina Latina, and the Latina/o Studies Working Group commented on portions of the manuscript at earlier stages.

Colleagues at Florida International University have helped me bring this project to completion. Rebecca Friedman, Kirsten Wood, Bianca Premo, Alex Cornelius, Jenna Gibbs, Tovah Bender, and Michael Brillman have encouraged, edited, laughed, kvetched, walked, and otherwise helped make FIU a great place to be. Okezi Otovo and Elizabeth Heath read the entire manuscript and provided useful comments. Elizabeth went above and beyond, reading many chapters more than once and talking me down from various precipices. I am grateful for her excellent advice and her love of commodities. An earlier draft of Chapter 2 benefited from excellent comments by Rod Neumann, Gail Hollander, Andrea Queeley, and Caroline Faria. Everyone should read Gail's wonderful book on the Florida sugar industry, a topic not covered here at all. As department chair, Ken Lipartito helped me carve out time for research and writing. I also had the pleasure of co-teaching a graduate course on commodity cultures with him, a great experience. I worked with Jon Mogul to curate an exhibit for the Wolfsonian-FIU on U.S. food history. That project helped me think about the big stories I have tried to tell here. I've also appreciated the sage counsel of Victor Uribe Uran, Darden Pyron, and Brian Peterson. Though they have moved on, I count Alex Lichtenstein and Lara Kriegel among FIU's treasures, and I thank them for their gracious help and friendship.

Mark Simpson-Vos has been a pleasure to work with at the University of North Carolina Press. Jason Colby and one anonymous reviewer through UNC Press provided generous and thought-provoking feedback on the manuscript. Tom Rogers commented on several chapters and offered sound advice in the early stages of moving from dissertation to book. Participants in conference panels too numerous to mention have given me extensive feedback and cheered me on. Martha Schulman and Kody Hersh helped me revise the prose for clarity.

Beyond academia, friends and family have watched this book unfold and helped distract me from it. Jenny Gotwals and David Milton have been my friends since before I even thought of writing a dissertation, let alone revising it into a book. I am glad for their friendship, legal advice, and archival expertise. Among many others, Eleanor and Anton Elbers, Heatherjean MacNeil, Jen Weintraub, Nicci Vieira Biernat, and the Hersh family have periodically summoned me back to something akin to the real world. Or at least the version of it that I can tolerate. The Miami Friends Meeting and the Southeastern Yearly Meeting of Friends have helped me feel a little less strange in Miami and Florida.

My family has been fantastic through this long process. My father and stepmother, Mark and Susan Heideman, hosted us on several combined research/grandparent trips. My in-laws, Sheridan and Rod Price, have unfailingly towed the line of "wholesome grandparents" by providing many boxes of homemade cookies and jam, camping trips, and tag sales. Hopefully the next project will involve more trips to Oregon to see them. My grandfather Dr. Kenneth Beatty keenly followed my development as a historian. He was kind enough to share his memories of eating candy as a child in the early 1920s, which crystallized my thinking on a few key issues. I am sorry that he did not live to see this book in print. My grand-mothers, Eleanor Heideman and Mary Catherine Carter Beatty, lived through the same history. I wish that I could have asked about their experiences and shared with them the delight of finishing the book.

My greatest gratitude is reserved for those people whose gifts leave me feeling least capable of expressing my thanks. My mother, Lucy Beatty, is the best mom any person could hope for. Every daughter should be so lucky. She will understand better than anyone that I have felt a little like Jane Moffat trying to read all the books in the library. In the end I fear that rather than skipping it for more interesting fare, I've *written* the dreaded *Story of Sugar*!

My husband, Derek, and my children, Ezra and Leo, have been with me through this and many other adventures. In their obsessive quest for dessert, Ezra and Leo have pushed me to disentangle the sociocultural roots of the association between childhood and sweetness. They make me laugh and constantly remind me that this project is not actually all that important. I mean, really. Who else but mom can make *candy* boring? If you find anything rude accidentally printed in these pages, all I can say is . . . I tried to find it before you did. Parents should always lock their computers before they leave the room. And Derek. What could I possibly say that would cover it all? His attitude toward this project has been a perfect balance of unflagging support and calm disinterest. He has read more of it than he probably cared to and deserves special thanks for help assembling the images. In-house tech support, digitization consultant, chef, best friend, fabulous father, tinkerer, and all around weirdo. Derek wins the prize for herculean homemaking and for keeping us all alive through my research, writing, and teaching. I owe you a magazine and some bonbons. To say the least.

A NOTE ON TERMINOLOGY

Readers may notice that I occasionally use the term "U.S. Americans" to designate people from the United States. I do so because residents of South and Central America and Mexico have rightful claim to the word "American." To them "American" is neither a specific nor a judicious way to describe people from the United States. Because of my own long-entrenched habit of speech, and because the book is ultimately about the boundaries of nationhood, I have not omitted "U.S. Americans" entirely from the text. I know that this may be unfamiliar or unwieldy for those outside of the field of Latin American and Caribbean Studies, and I beg those readers' patience. I have tried to vary my usage, however. I have occasionally left "American" as is, especially in places where it was used by the people about whom I am writing.

I use the term "policymakers" to indicate congressional representatives or people in executive branch agencies who made policy decisions or did research that influenced policy. When I write about "administrators," on the other hand, I generally mean people charged with carrying out policies. Though such people did not make policy per se, their job was to make it work on the ground. Their actions were sometimes more important than the intentions of those who designed the policies. "Colonial administrators" refers to people living in the island territories and governing them through whichever institutions the U.S. Congress had created for each place. Such positions were held by both whites from the mainland and natives of the islands, typically elites educated in the United States or Europe.

SUGAR AND CIVILIZATION

INTRODUCTION

In August 1898, mere weeks after the conclusion of the Spanish American War, people across the United States celebrated victories in Cuba, the Philippines, and Puerto Rico and rallied to support wounded soldiers. One such event near Denver, Colorado, featured, among other attractions, a "candy battleship," a replica of the destroyed battleship *Maine*. Young women nurses sold candy "over the sides of this ship" to the nearly 15,000 people gathered at the event. People staged similar tableaux over the next decade. For example, one candy store in Iowa used candies to build a "large candy battleship, a replica of the Maine," for its Christmas display. When prominent citizens in Oakland, California, feted the new secretary of the Navy, they decorated the banquet tables with "candy battleships [which] floated on a blue sea of sweets, surrounded by hills of pastry." The battleships on display were likely glass candy dishes modeled after the USS *Maine*, a novelty that people displayed in their homes and shops in the decade after the war. Through such events and objects, U.S. Americans memorialized the war but also revealed that they understood sugar to be one of the key spoils of victory, since each of the new island possessions was poised to expand its sugar production. As the United States made sense of its new role overseas, the commodity had a starring role in the ongoing spectacle of empire, which played out in newspaper headlines, on dining room tables, in the sugar barrels and candy counters of neighborhood stores, and on the political stage of Washington, D.C.[1]

Sugar and Civilization tells the story of sugar from the Spanish American War through the New Deal of the 1930s. Along the way, the book describes workers and consumers in multiple locations in order to uncover how people in the United States came to eat so much sugar, and what it meant for them. The book argues that the cultural logic connecting imperial, trade, and immigration policies was the same one that facilitated new habits of sugar consumption within the United States and its territories. Categories of race, articulated through discourses of civilization and nationalism, provided a vocabulary through which people

"Candy Battle-Ship," *Harper's Weekly*, September 17, 1898.
Courtesy of the Beinecke Rare Book and Manuscript Library, Yale University.

made sense of the new geographies of sugar and empire after the turn of the twentieth century. The United States annexed Hawaii in 1898, retained Puerto Rico and the Philippines as territories, and occupied Cuba until 1902, when it achieved nominal independence under a U.S. protectorate. Sugar could be produced either from cane raised on these newly acquired islands or from sugar beets grown in domestic temperate climates. At the very same time that leaders in the United States extended colonial policies through the Caribbean and Pacific, others in the government and private sector busily promoted a domestic sugar beet industry in the arid West. Policymakers thus considered the relative merits of Puerto Rico, Cuba, the Philippines, and Hawaii alongside those of Colorado, California, Michigan, and Louisiana. Their calculations hinged at every turn on the racial characteristics of the people who worked the land, together with their assumptions about the natural advantages enjoyed by each place. Lobbyists on behalf of each region added to the debate, assuring that any discussion of sugar—and by extension of empire—would be contentious. As one writer later put it, sugar had "the power of stirring more political devils in Washington than any other elixir not compounded of oil."[2]

"Small Three-Roller Water-Driven Mill," *Handbook on the Sugar
Industry of the Philippine Islands* (Manila: Bureau of Printing, 1912).

In theory, refined beet and cane sugars are virtually indistinguishable.
Chemical analysis notwithstanding, commentators in the early twentieth century belabored the apparent differences. They proposed that
each type of sugar carried with it the characteristics of the place where
it was produced. Observers often described beet sugar as more civilized,
the natural product of the temperate climates where civilized white
people supposedly thrived. Images of sugar beet production typically
showed white farmers using advanced agricultural machinery, together
with modern factories whose smoking chimneys stood as an emblem
of prosperity in an otherwise arid western landscape. By contrast, cane
sugar was a product of the tropics, an environment that had negative
connotations of indolence, decay, and racial inferiority.[3] According to
common stereotypes, fertile tropical landscapes provided an adequate
living even for those who preferred sloth to hard work. The long-term
consequence was that residents of the tropics had not achieved the
same high level of civilization as whites in temperate climates. Building
on this logic, some critics suggested that white people ought to avoid
cane sugar since it brought the impurities of the tropics into civilized
homes. Resources ought to be devoted to achieving self-sufficiency in

Introduction 3

"Six-Roller Mill with Crusher and Hydraulic Jacks," *Handbook on the Sugar Industry of the Philippine Islands* (Manila: Bureau of Printing, 1912).

beet sugar, and the tropics should be left to its natives. By contrast, advocates of overseas expansion responded that white men could civilize the tropics by bringing modern machinery, science, and agricultural methods to the cane industry. Expansionists explained their reasoning in part through images—widely reprinted in reports and magazine articles—of "native methods" of cane production juxtaposed with images of modern sugar-manufacturing equipment. Why should U.S. Americans not use their ingenuity to profit from the bounty of the tropics? Either way, those who advocated cane or beets agreed that sugar was a modern necessity, and that its production ought to be encouraged for the benefit of white civilization.

The relative merits of cane and beet sugar came up repeatedly during political deliberations over the legal and fiscal foundations of empire in the years after 1898, often serving as a metaphor for broader concerns over who and what should be classified as in- or outside of the nation. Would each island territory be treated as if it were an intrinsic part of the domestic United States? Or would it be considered foreign? In making such calculations, policymakers struggled with opposing tendencies toward expansion and exclusion that had already shaped the nation. The United States had been expansionist from its founding as settlers pushed westward to claim new farmland. In many ways, the acquisition of the new island territories in 1898 was consistent with decades of Manifest Destiny and U.S. Americans' aspirations to control the entire continent. But enthusiasm for overseas expansion was tempered by an equally long history of exclusionary politics, premised on the idea that the benefits of national growth should accrue only to white men. The tendency toward exclusion was exemplified by race-based restrictions on the rights of citizenship and immigration, which primarily affected African Americans, Chinese, and Native Americans. At the turn of the twentieth century, many people in the United States agreed that U.S. democracy was predicated on racial homogeneity. In their view, overseas expansion presented new racial complications. Many people—those who favored U.S. expansion overseas and those who opposed it—worried that the non-white residents of the new island territories were irredeemably foreign and would never be fit for U.S. citizenship. The tensions between these two inclinations—expansion and exclusion—were nowhere more obvious than in debates over the sugar trade with the new territories.[4]

Whether the United States classified a territory as domestic or foreign had significant consequences for how much tariff each island would pay on sugar and whether any particular island would benefit from the tariff levied to protect domestic sugar producers. For states and citizens within the continental United States, uniformity is the rule under the U.S. Constitution. Since 1868, when Congress passed the Fourteenth Amendment, citizens of the United States have been promised equal protection of the law regardless of their race or place of residence, in law if not always in practice. Likewise, Congress has the power "to regulate Commerce with foreign Nations, and among the several States, and with the Indian tribes." But the so-called uniformity clause constrains this power since "all Duties, Imposts and Excises shall be uniform throughout the United States." During the first several decades of the twentieth century, Congress asserted—and the Supreme Court repeatedly affirmed—the right to treat the island territories and the people living in them differently. Based on their plenary power over territories derived from Article IV, Section 3, of the Constitution, Congress declared the right to govern the territories as if they were *not* a part of the United States. Hawaii, Puerto Rico, and the Philippines were possessions or "appurtenances" to the United States, attached but subordinate and thus not intrinsically domestic. Neither the uniformity clause nor the Fourteenth Amendment need apply; Congress could specify different trade, tax, and citizenship policies for each of the territories, and none of those policies had to be consistent with those for the states. While in practice there were often very similar trade policies enacted for the states and for the island territories, it need not have been the case. The trade privileges that the island territories sometimes enjoyed were always contingent on the judgment and goodwill of mainland leaders.[5]

After extended debate, the United States ultimately created a protected sugar market that favored both producers on the mainland and territorial producers in Hawaii, Puerto Rico, and the Philippines. These places all benefited from the high sugar tariff enacted in 1897, which limited competition from foreign sugar. Cuba was the only foreign nation to benefit from a reduced sugar tariff through the Reciprocity Treaty of 1903, thus guaranteeing that its industry would grow to fill the U.S. market. The new territories, Cuba, and the states that produced beets and cane on the mainland make up what I call the U.S. sugar empire. Sugar tariffs were a crucial component of the imperial repertoire through which U.S. policymakers and investors formed the U.S. sugar empire. Encouraged by U.S. tariff preferences, investors from the United States took a major role in expanding and modernizing cane and beet industries in Puerto Rico, Hawaii, the Philippines, Cuba, Colorado, California, Michigan, and elsewhere in the U.S. West after the turn of the twentieth century.

Sugar, Tariffs, and Empire before the U.S. Sugar Empire

When U.S. policymakers and investors created a sugar empire after 1898, they drew on precedents set by their European and English predecessors. Leaders on the other side of the Atlantic had built their empires over previous centuries by creating unequal relationships between themselves and their far-flung territories. They promoted worldwide trade, investment, and migration in order to spread profit and civilization for their own benefit. Goods, workers, and capital moved across borders, their pace guided by preferential trade agreements and bilateral treaties crafted by imperial leaders. The U.S. approach to tariffs in the nineteenth century was forged in the crucible of democratic revolutions, debates over slavery, and legacies of European colonialism. Private investors strategically negotiated the international trade system during the nineteenth century, and their actions set the stage for the later formation of the U.S. sugar empire.

England and continental Europe were at the center of the world economy from at least the seventeenth century through the early twentieth century, in large measure because enslaved Africans assured them power and profit in the new world. Scholars have long recognized the critical role played by trade and labor policies—including those related to slavery—in state formation and imperial expansion for England and

Europe.[6] Virtually every major sugar-producing and sugar-consuming nation since the seventeenth century used tariffs and customs laws to stimulate the industry, and they all relied on enslaved labor to produce that sugar. Mercantilist policies in Great Britain, France, Spain, and Portugal during the seventeenth and eighteenth centuries were crucial to their overseas expansion. Under mercantilism, these nations monopolized trade with their own colonies, admitting items—especially sugar—at reduced rates of duty, while restricting other nations' rights to participate in their colonies' trade. Colonies could neither buy nor sell from foreigners, except at the cost of high trade duties, paid to the colonial power. European leaders saw their colonies as a source of raw materials, including sugar, and as an outlet for goods produced by the colonizing nation. They were restricted to producing goods that would not compete with products of the metropole. As Sidney Mintz memorably put it in *Sweetness and Power*, "Slave and proletarian together powered the imperial economic system that kept the one supplied with manacles and the other with sugar and rum."[7] Tariffs and excise taxes on colonial products were a major source of government revenue, and they were crucial in stimulating plantation agriculture in the colonies, establishing sugar refining in England and Europe, and, ultimately, increasing the quantity of sugar available for consumers everywhere.

The United States emerged from its former status as an English colony in the shadow of mercantilism. The American Revolution was, among other things, a revolt by colonists against mercantilist tariffs and taxes levied by Great Britain. According to the logic of liberal egalitarianism that guided their thinking, it was unjust to treat colonial residents differently in trade and taxation. As was the case for other liberal revolutions of the late eighteenth century, colonists rejected restrictive British trade policies as undemocratic, instead lobbying for greater equality and access to foreign trade.[8] Most European colonial powers eventually moved in this direction. In 1776, the Regulation of Free Trade between Spain and the Indies opened freer trade between Spain, its colonies, and select other countries.[9] Likewise, France enacted free trade between itself and its colonies over the course of the nineteenth century. Though they increasingly offered their colonies free trade, the European powers nonetheless sometimes found it useful and necessary to treat them differently, in large measure because of the presumed racial inferiority of colonial residents. As historian Josep Fradera argues, the result was "the formation of exceptional imperial regimes."[10] He continues: "Political rights and equality before the law, in many cases promised to all the inhabitants of a single political entity, could not be guaranteed in overseas possessions. Neither could the metropolitan tax regulations, increasingly formalized and systematic as they were, be extended to the colonies." The United States became a nation in this period of colonial instability and renegotiation of the relationship between liberalism and trade.

Much of Spain's empire achieved independence in the early nineteenth century. Spain treated its few remaining colonies—Puerto Rico, the Philippines, and Cuba—as an exceptional imperial regime, as Fradera puts it. Spanish leaders did not offer colonial residents equal political status, nor did they enact consistent policies in each colony. Tariffs and taxes varied among Spain's three colonies, though all three were subject to duties that privileged Spanish ships and goods.[11] Spain admitted sugar-manufacturing equipment duty-free. In the Philippines, Spain consistently levied low duties for all countries. Puerto Rican import duties on food were high for all countries except Spain, assuring that Puerto Ricans would eat Spanish olive oil and salt cod transported in Spanish ships. Cuban trade duties varied widely. Fearing slave uprisings, Spain stationed troops there in the early nineteenth century. Spain taxed Cuban planters heavily to fund these encampments. They loosened restrictions on the slave trade and land tenure, enabling Cuban planters to expand sugar production to pay these new levies. Spain also lifted restrictions on Cuba's foreign sugar trade in 1818. These liberal changes opened new markets, especially in the United States.

The U.S. market was highly competitive, and Cuban sugar had to sell low to maintain its place against Louisiana sugar.[12] Commercial treaties between Spain and the United States governed Cuba's trade, but the overall rate of the U.S. sugar tariff also affected the industry. In the first decades of the nineteenth century, a high tariff had protected U.S. mainland planters, who produced sugar with slave labor, primarily in Louisiana. Sugar producers in Louisiana increased output during the War of 1812. Congress raised the sugar tariff, which sustained this growth and encouraged Louisiana planters and manufacturers to invest in the most modern technologies.[13] In the 1830s, Louisiana planters regularly imported the newest equipment from Europe, including vacuum pans, steam-powered mills, and advanced methods for crystallizing sugar. European sugar experts facilitated such improvements, which planters saw as the apogee of civilization. For example, in 1848, Judah P. Benjamin, a New Orleans lawyer and sugar planter, extolled the "advanced civilization" possessed by French scientists who had mastered the "delicate and beautiful process by which a darkly colored and impure fluid is converted into a chrystaline product of snowy whiteness, sparkling grain and perfect purity."[14] Such expertise, he reasoned, could rescue "the indolent or ignorant colonial Planter" and promote an enlightened agrarian capitalism in the United States even if planters lost tariff protection.

In the antebellum period, Louisiana planters competed with Spain's sugar colonies under terms set by the U.S. tariff. To meet this competition, Louisiana planters depended on the sugar tariff, which remained high between 1816 and 1832. When Congress lowered the sugar tariff for a decade beginning in the 1830s, Cuban sugar producers swiftly took advantage of the less-restricted market, investing in much of the same new technology used in Louisiana. With a lower tariff opening the market for their product, Cuban manufacturers increasingly adopted steam-powered mills, vacuum pans, and advanced sugar chemistry. The United States bought much of Cuba's sugar in this period, primarily through British merchants, who also bought U.S. cotton. But then the U.S. Congress again raised the sugar tariff in 1842. The new tariff levied a different, higher rate of duty on refined versus raw sugar. Producers in the United States increasingly specialized in higher grades of sugar, explaining that the "metropolis" possessed the requisite science "in a much higher state of advance than in colonial workhouses and estates."[15] In the meantime, Louisiana defended its tariff protection against northerners' complaints about enslaved labor. Abolitionists repeatedly tried to eliminate the sugar tariff in their efforts to impede slavery; they called for moral consumers to abstain from slave-produced sugar. Congress lowered the sugar duty in 1857, partly for this reason, again opening the market for Cuban producers. Ironically, after the Civil War and the abolition of slavery in the United States, Louisiana planters called for tariffs to protect their investments from cheap Cuban sugar, still produced with slave labor until the 1880s. Because Congress raised and lowered the sugar tariff repeatedly through the nineteenth century, the sugar market was uncertain for planters in Cuba and Louisiana. They responded by doing all they could to keep their production costs low, including investing in efficient technology and seeking low-cost labor, whether it was slave, indentured, or free. Lower production costs and greater efficiency—products of doubt about U.S. sugar tariffs—contributed in the long run to higher world sugar production and lower prices.[16]

Tariffs were crucial for the United States in the nineteenth century, stimulating investment by protecting new economic activities against foreign competition. Thomas Jefferson, who articulated a vision of agrarian democracy in the early nineteenth century, had advocated international trade and territorial expansion as means to protect independent farmers, whom he saw as the core of American political institutions.[17] Jefferson recognized the value of a worldwide geographic division of labor to protect the American body politic from the problems brought by industrialization and urbanization. Jefferson abhorred the European factory system and the wage laborers it employed. He worried that industrialization along these lines would undermine American democracy. Instead, by trading for goods manufactured abroad, people in the United States could focus on agriculture, which promised to nurture democracy. Jefferson's approach to trade complemented his view of territorial expansion. New lands in western territories would allow American men to be independent farmers and democratic citizens despite population pressure in the coastal regions.

International trade was politically important as well, because import tariffs were the main source of government revenue in the early United States. Historian Robin Einhorn argues that this was the result of political compromises between northerners and southerners in the early republic.[18] Import tariffs did not call slaveholding into question because, unlike other forms of taxation, tariffs did not require legislators to decide whether slaves were taxable property. What was more, the federal government lacked the administrative capacity to survey property holdings, which meant they could not effectively assess or collect property taxes. Collecting customs duties at the port solved these dilemmas through simplified, centrally located assessments. Later in the nineteenth century, southerners complained vociferously about the tariff, arguing that it had subsidized northern industrialization at the expense of poor southern farmers. Most tariffs were levied on manufactured goods, and southerners argued that this made for higher consumer prices. Southern farmers received no protection for their produce but nonetheless paid higher prices for the manufactured goods they purchased. Tariffs, they argued, were undemocratic and ought to be lowered. Louisiana planters, of course, recognized that their industry depended on sugar tariffs. For most southerners, sugar tariffs were the exception.

Edwin Atkins, a sugar planter, merchant, and political advisor, had been an early U.S. investor in the Cuban sugar industry and later played a key role in shaping sugar trade policy. In his memoir, *Sixty Years in Cuba*, published in the mid-1920s, Atkins described his experiences on the island under Spanish rule. Framed in paternalistic terms familiar to many U.S. Americans, Atkins showed his own civilizing and modernizing influence in Cuba. The Atkins family had arrived well ahead of any state-sponsored projections of U.S. power, and they were at the forefront of a new U.S. commercial empire later exemplified by the United Fruit Company in Central America and the Caribbean.[19] But, Atkins noted, their profits depended in crucial ways on trade and labor policies enacted by both the United States and Spain. Terms of labor and trade, legislated not on the island but in the metropole, framed Atkins's business prospects in Cuba. Investors like Atkins set the stage for later formal U.S. expansion in the Caribbean.

Over the decades Atkins spent in Cuba, the industry changed dramatically. In the mid-nineteenth century, sugar was made by boiling cane juice in open kettles. After boiling to the point of crystallization, the syrup was dried in shallow pans. Workers then loaded it into casks, called hogsheads, from which the molasses drained, leaving a somewhat lighter-colored sugar. "The hogsheads were then packed hard with dry sugar trodden down generally by the fattest of negro women with their bare feet," Atkins recalled.[20] This and other "primitive customs" that brought black workers' bodies into contact with the sugar were the "impurities" that were eventually removed through refining on the mainland. Shipping merchants who owned wharves and warehouses were crucial intermediaries in the sugar business. Such merchants charged planters for storage and advanced them money to finance their next crops. They shipped raw sugar in hogsheads, from which they extracted more molasses. This spelled extra profit for merchants. Over the nineteenth century, merchants replaced this system with a more economical one in which they shipped highly processed raw sugar in 100-pound cotton bags. Molasses, separated from the sugar crystals in the factory, was shipped separately in tanks.

When Atkins first went to Cuba in 1868, the world sugar industry was in disarray. Before he arrived, sugar prices in Cuba had collapsed, banks had stopped financing crops, and Spain had imposed a new round of taxes. The industry had surged briefly, despite Spain's restrictive trade policies, after the lower U.S. sugar tariff in 1857 and the U.S. Civil War reopened a market for Cuban sugar. This prosperity was short lived. At the very same time, the European beet farmers expanded their output dramatically, stimulated by bounties paid by France and Germany governments. The world sugar market was larger and more competitive in the 1860s. Cuban planters and merchants barely kept pace with the new competition, and they demanded reform from Spain to protect them from the vagaries of the international market.[21] In fact, Atkins arrived at the beginning of Cuba's Ten Years War, when insurgents sought independence—or at least reform—from Spain. For Atkins, this looked like a risky—though potentially quite lucrative—business opportunity. Atkins hoped to profit from Cuban political instability and planters' frequent bankruptcies. Atkins began actually growing sugar in 1882 after decades of operating a commission house specializing in sugar warehousing and financing. The confluence of an increasingly competitive sugar market and arcane Spanish trade policies resulted in Cuban planters losing their land and mills. Atkins acquired land by foreclosing on planters indebted to his commission house. The arcane Cuban legal system made it relatively easy for Atkins to leverage foreclosures to his advantage.[22]

Atkins's father had cautioned his son about lending too much money to failing planters, assuming that the Cuban sugar ship was sinking. But Atkins took a fabulous gamble, investing in the ruins of a crumbling empire on the assumption that the new model of "free trade" would eventually triumph. In nineteenth-century imperial economics, "free trade" did not mean that there were no trade duties. The most common form of free trade in the 1870s and 1880s was the bilateral reciprocal trade treaty, which guaranteed trade privileges between two nations. In fact, as Atkins points out, "there had been much discussion as to the possibility of a reciprocity treaty between Spain and the United States," which would have benefited Cuba's sugar industry. But Spain seemed bent on preserving its "repressive policy," maintaining high tariffs and never making much progress on a reciprocity treaty.[23]

Like Atkins in Cuba, U.S. businessmen preceded the U.S. government in Hawaii, but they did so in large measure by negotiating tariff privileges for their sugar. At the behest of American businessmen, the United States signed a reciprocity treaty with Hawaii in 1876, which offered free trade in sugar, to the great benefit of U.S. investors there. As tariff historian Frank Taussig later explained, this bilateral reciprocity treaty gave Hawaiian producers a bounty over full-duty importers.[24] Since Hawaii could not supply the entire U.S. market, substantial quantities of full-duty sugar had to be imported in addition to the Hawaiian product. The price of full-tariff sugar set the price for all other sugar in the U.S. market. The difference between that price and the tariff accrued as extra profit for Hawaiian planters. Increases in sugar production and investment in Hawaii after 1876 were important precursors to the U.S. annexation of the

islands in 1898. Private business interests spearheaded all of these negotiations, and they did so because without such treaties they had no assur-
ance that their investments would be profitable. Nation-states' trade
policies were thus crucial to private overseas investment.

In the 1880s, Atkins helped draft a reciprocity treaty between Spain
and the United States that would have eased trade with Cuba. His efforts
finally succeeded in 1891 when the United States and Spain signed the
Foster-Cánovas Treaty granting tariff reductions to U.S. American products entering Cuba. Together with the 1890 McKinley Tariff, which eliminated the tariff on raw sugar, Atkins hoped that Cuban planters were
about to "wake from their long sleep."[25] To soften the loss of tariff protection for cane and beet farmers, the McKinley Tariff offered them a 2
cent per pound bounty, following the precedent set by major European
beet-producing nations. Beet sugar production boomed in the United
States in the 1890s, and Cuban sugar production also increased to take
advantage of this newly opened North American market. Cuban planters
and millers invested in new machinery and sought new sources of labor,
including from China.

But tariff winds do not blow steady. The 1894 Wilson Tariff ended free
trade in sugar. Spain retaliated by reimposing tariffs on American goods.
According to Atkins, the resulting economic chaos was the immediate
cause of the insurgency beginning in 1895, which eventually led to Cuba's
independence from Spain in 1898.[26] Atkins argued that Cuban "insurrec-
tions coincide with the changes in the economic conditions brought
about largely by tariff legislation in the United States."[27] Atkins was generally unsympathetic with the Cuban independence fighters, whom he
characterized as unpropertied, illiterate former slaves whose motives
could not be trusted. He compared the insurgents' alleged brutalities to
those committed by "Geronimo the Apache," another savage he believed
had recently been subdued by civilization. Atkins complained that
insurgents repeatedly burned his cane fields. The destruction wrought
by cane fires, together with the virtual cessation of trade, bankrupted
even more Spanish and Cuban planters. "The estates," he wrote, "must
pass into new hands with fresh capital," and the United States must
reduce or eliminate its import duties.[28] Once again, as had been the
case in the early 1880s, Atkins's unparalleled access to North American
capital enabled him to not only survive the crisis but also expand his
holdings. Atkins acquired more land from his less-well-capitalized neighbors during and after the insurgency. The United States intervened

in 1898, bringing an end to Spain's empire and a new start for the U.S. American one.

Recalling these events in the 1920s, Atkins pointed out that "the old-time planter is disappearing" as corporate plantations replaced private ownership. Along with that old-time planter, he implicitly cautioned, the old-style system of restrictive tariffs should also be abandoned. The old-time planter was an emblem of inefficiency, waste, and impurity. The new plantation system brought efficiency, hygiene, and greater public good. The new system, he suggested, was built on reciprocal trade between the two nations. Ultimately, without tariff concessions from the United States and Spain—and without ample labor from slaves and later Chinese migrants—Atkins would never have invested in plantation agriculture in Cuba. The crux of the matter was the sugar tariff. While other observers offered more complex analyses of Cuba's problems, Atkins's lesson from the nineteenth century was simple: restrictions on the sugar trade had only ever led to disaster. The major mistake made by the United States after occupying Cuba had been the long delay in passing a reciprocity treaty—it took five years to negotiate and implement it. In the meantime, duty-free sugar from Hawaii and Puerto Rico began flooding the U.S. market. Ultimately, Atkins reasoned, stable government in Cuba was impossible without protected access to the U.S. market.[29]

Atkins's experience in Cuba encapsulates one of this book's overall aims, which is to broaden our understanding of which nation-state actions we interpret as imperial in the U.S. context. Formal annexation and military occupation are not the only ways that nation-states have engaged in imperial action. Trade policies are also crucial elements of empire.

The U.S. Sugar Empire after 1898

After 1898, the United States took over Spain's role in the Philippines, Puerto Rico, and Cuba and, in the same year, annexed Hawaii. At the very same time, farmers and investors in the U.S. West were busily expanding beet sugar production. Together these places make up what I call the U.S. sugar empire. Conditions on the ground in each place varied across the U.S. sugar empire, of course. But investors and policymakers organized labor, land, and capital in each place in remarkably similar ways, in part because expansion of the U.S. sugar empire happened on the cusp of significant capitalist transformations. Workers migrated in increasing numbers to work sugarcane and beets, millers and refiners upgraded their milling equipment, investors formed ever-larger corporations, and consumers adopted new habits of sugar consumption. These factors played out across the U.S. sugar empire.

Sugar planters grew cane on a plantation scale in the island territories and Cuba, as they had for decades. Cane planters had long exchanged ideas, engaging in experimentation and research that shaped similar agricultural and labor practices on the ground across the colonial world. Wage laborers worked large-scale landholdings to produce cane, which huge central sugar mills processed. In many regions, sugar mills administered their own land. In other areas, plantations and mills were owned and operated separately. While plantation-scale production was the most common system, in parts of Cuba, Puerto Rico, Louisiana, and the Philippines small-scale landowners or sharecroppers also produced cane. Workers harvested cane using machetes and then loaded it onto oxcarts or railcars, which hauled it to the mill. The heavy harvest labor requirements meant that planters needed to maintain a large, mobile workforce. Laborers usually only found year-round work in regions with extensive irrigation or periodic frosts. Beginning in the mid-1800s, planters in the Caribbean and Hawaii brought contract laborers to meet their labor needs. At various times, for example, the Hawaiian Sugar Planters' Association recruited Chinese, Japanese, Korean, Puerto Rican, and Filipino workers. Cuban planters recruited Chinese and later Jamaican and Haitian workers. Cane growers in Louisiana hired workers from China, Mexico, and the British West Indies, in addition to African Americans, who had long worked the crop there.[30]

The mill was the point where agricultural and industrial processes met and the product of the land—cane—emerged unrecognizable as sugar. The sugar technologists who oversaw mill production were an itinerant lot, moving frequently among sugar-producing regions. Together with corporate managers, they brought increasingly standardized management practices with them as they moved across the U.S. sugar empire. Corporations—many of them U.S.-owned—controlled the middle phases of the production process, where much of the money was made. The pinnacle of technological modernity and civilized capitalism, the mill emblematized the corporate captains who headed the industry. After milling the cane into raw sugar, workers in the central mills packed it into 100-pound sacks, and stevedores loaded it on ships and sent it to New York, Boston, Baltimore, New Orleans, or San Francisco. Gantries unloaded the sacks, often at docks designated just for sugar. Immigrant workers and native-born supervising engineers then ushered the sugar through the refining process at one of several large urban sugar-refining corporations. From those major seaport refineries, wholesalers distributed refined sugar to grocers and salesmen in nearby cities and states, who then sold it to their customers.

The sugar beet industry played a crucial role in the economic and political development of the irrigated West, just as cane reshaped the island territories. Farmers did not grow sugar beets on large-scale plantations, but instead small-scale family farmers typically produced beets together with other crops. Beets required reliable irrigation and plentiful seasonal workers to perform the tedious hand labor. Most important, beets had to be processed quickly so as not to lose their sugar content. Beets were a bulky crop, so investors built sugar factories in rural areas in order to reduce transportation costs. Independent farmers negotiated a contract price for their beets with the local sugar factories at the beginning of the season. Sugar companies, because they were usually the only customer in the area, often had the upper hand in negotiations with farmers over contract terms. On the other hand, because a beet sugar factory represented a substantial capital investment that could not be used for anything else, sugar companies were vulnerable to individual landowners' decisions. Farmers might abandon the crop entirely if they did not like the contract terms. Sugar companies thus offered a variety of services to encourage farmers to grow beets, including crop research, technical support, and assistance with recruiting field laborers. Field workers thinned the young plants by hand in the spring, weeded them in the summer, and harvested them in the fall. Work stretched from early spring to late fall but was punctuated with slack periods. During the winter, beet workers sought work in cities, in mines, on railroads, or they returned to Mexico, Texas, or southern Colorado. Though farmers technically employed the seasonal workers, sugar companies sometimes aided farmers by recruiting, housing, and negotiating with laborers. In the early years, sugar companies recruited European immigrant beet workers, as well as Filipinos and Japanese. By the mid-1910s, Mexicans and Mexican Americans were performing a significant share of the contract beet labor in the United States.

In contrast to those who performed field labor and managed the farms, the men at the head of the nation's beet and cane sugar processing companies made extravagant profits. Building on new state and federal incorporation laws, sugar refiners in the late nineteenth century formed highly capitalized, horizontally integrated firms, which controlled most of the refined sugar industry in the United States. Sugar refining had been one of the first industries to incorporate when the American Sugar Refining Company (ASRC) formed as a holding company under New Jersey corporation law in 1891.[31] Shortly after the turn of the century, the ASRC became the sixth-largest industrial corporation in the United States. Sugar refiners were repeatedly the subject of antitrust investigations by the Department of Justice and muckraking journalists. The ASRC and a few other refiners—collectively referred to as the "Sugar Trust"—exerted remarkable control over the terms of the sugar trade. Refiners were in an especially strong position to profit from expansion in Puerto Rico, Hawaii, Cuba, and the Philippines, where they invested in plantations and mills that could produce raw sugar for their refineries. As they expanded into raw sugar production, the Sugar Trust integrated vertically, controlling all phases of the production process from seed to sugar cube. By the 1910s, the ASRC had also invested heavily in beet sugar factories. The trend in the industry was toward ever-greater integration, both horizontal and vertical.

The dominance of large-scale, integrated corporations like the ASRC obscures the industry's unspoken dependence on smaller-scale businesses on the margins of the corporate revolution. Local and regional networks of trade supported corporate expansionism as workers adjusted to the new economies of scale. New workers across the U.S. sugar empire participated as consumers in burgeoning mass markets as they earned wages in the sugar industry. As wage earners who worked to eat, people were often both producers and consumers of sweets. They made meaning of these sometimes-conflicting roles by purchasing goods through merchants from their own ethnic groups. Mexican, Chinese, and Japanese businessmen in particular played a key role in both recruiting new workers for the fields and provisioning them with familiar foods. Small businessmen built niche markets among ethnic, working-class consumers who chose to eat familiar ethnic foods when they could. In assessing what I call the "significance of the numerically insignificant," I track how and why small-scale merchants made and sold less-refined forms of sweets even as manufacturers churned out more and cheaper refined white sugar.

New meanings for sugar consumption were shaped by changing patterns of migration. During the 1910s and 1920s, people within the United States migrated to an unprecedented degree, arriving in cities, where they bought much of what they ate. People moved from countryside to city, South to North, East to West, and everywhere in between.[32] Intensifying disenfranchisement and socioeconomic segregation encouraged many African Americans to leave the Jim Crow South. They left southern plantations in search of better conditions, often finding low-wage jobs in the industrial North and southern cities. At the same time, Congress enacted race-based immigration restrictions and intensified control over the borders to limit the arrival of working-class people from abroad. A cadre of immigration inspectors at U.S. ports enforced limitations on migration from China, as they had since 1860s, and extended those restrictions to encompass all laborers from Asia and most laborers from Eastern and Southern Europe by the 1920s. Yet, to the chagrin of nativists who would have preferred to seal the United States off from anyone who was not white, workers from the Philippines and Mexico continued to arrive.

Sugar fed a growing immigrant and native-born working class at low cost. People viewed sugar as a necessary, healthful, and inexpensive part of their diets. Many nutritionists and physicians insisted that sugar in moderation was healthy "fuel-food," necessary to proper nutrition and crucial for people performing heavy labor. The fact that people craved sweetness seemed to support the idea that it was a natural desire. But sweetness cannot be interpreted merely as a natural human craving. Consumers' preferences emerged from their encounters with ever-expanding supplies of the commodity, which was the result of political economic forces beyond their control. Powerful businesses, in conjunction with the state, used new technologies and economic practices to foster cravings for sweets. Songs on the radio and in the parlor, in kitchens and candy shops, and in the fields and factories, reinforced such cravings right where people produced sugar and candy. Sweetness made the inequalities of power inherent in imperial capitalism seem both natural and tolerable because it was gratifying and pleasurable. Whether in Mississippi, Hawaii, or New York, sweetness was a reward for people whose pace of work was synched to a globally integrated marketplace.[33]

Sugar consumers did not always attribute the same meanings to their eating habits as did policymakers and businessmen. Through their choices of sugar, people sometimes resisted their integration into global capitalism. Working-class people attributed value to a wider range of sugars, including those homemade and unrefined varieties that were not the province of modern corporations. For example, Mexican American sugar beet workers bought *piloncillo*, an unrefined cane sugar from Mexico, even when it cost them significantly more than refined sugar. Likewise, Chinese American consumers used unrefined sugars imported from Asia in their recipes. And African American laborers produced cane and sorghum syrup and molasses as a way to assert autonomy in a labor system that worked to their disadvantage in most other respects. Women, widely assumed to be the main consumers of sweets, spoke out in particular on what it meant to eat sugar. Women were politically active as managers of their household economies, as labor and social welfare advocates, as workers in beet fields and candy factories, and as figures in national politics. People from a variety of backgrounds spun their own stories about how they fit into the global sugar economy, sometimes accepting and sometimes rejecting the roles into which political and economic leaders had cast them.

By the late 1930s, a wide variety of standardized goods—including candy, jam, canned fruit, and packaged baked goods—were cheap and within reach of working-class consumers. In the midst of the Great Depression, New Deal policymakers insisted that working-class people had the right—perhaps even the obligation—to eat these foodstuffs as part of the process of national economic recovery. Policymakers began to classify less-refined sweeteners as marketable products, recognizing both their economic and their nutritional value to working-class consumers. Ironically, as unrefined sweeteners gained mainstream recognition in the 1930s, working-class consumers increasingly could not afford to buy them because the price of mass-produced refined white sugar was comparatively so much lower. Nutrition reformers began to question the decades-old assumption that refined sugar was a healthful source of calories, increasingly complaining that refined foods were weakening civilization. Yet those very foods were the only ones poor, working-class people could afford. At the end of the 1930s, just as in the 1900s, sugar and sweetness reinforced hierarchies of civilization and race.

Empire, the Nation-State, and Capitalism

Sugar and Civilization examines crucial, if uneven, roles played by the nation-state in expanding global opportunities for capital investment and creating divisions of labor that privileged some producers and consumers while disadvantaging others. The nation-state made and protected markets by assembling and stabilizing currency and banking, by financing and building transportation infrastructure, and by regulating the movements of both workers and goods across its borders. The nation-state enabled, adopted, and occasionally regulated new corporate forms and business practices that, in turn, facilitated a transition from a purely industrial to a finance mode of capitalism. Limited liability corporations, trusts, franchises, and holding companies, for example, were all state-sanctioned sovereigns, authorized by the public power to exercise their own private economic power. Most crucially for this book, the nation-state levied tariffs and strategically negotiated exceptions to those tariffs in order to privilege some trading partners over others. While there are many examples of private business interests blazing the path toward empire in advance of formal U.S. government occupation or intervention, private actors almost always made their moves in the shadow of nation-states. The United Fruit Company in the Caribbean, Edwin Atkins in Cuba, and the Big Five sugar companies in Hawaii were all important private investors that built sugar industries in advance of U.S. occupation of those territories. But in each case, private expansion was predicated on privileged access to U.S. markets, guaranteed by commercial treaties and preferential tariffs. In short, because of the nature of the global trade system, private investors *needed* the nation-state.

I define "empire" as an arrangement in which political sovereignty is exercised unevenly across space and in which some people and geographies are differentiated as being outside of the law or subject to an alternate set of legal arrangements. While much of the evidence presented here shows the nation-state asserting sovereignty, there are also examples of private corporations exercising sovereignty and generating new imperial practices. Indeed, there was a close connection between the new practices of empire developed by U.S. administrators after 1898 and those pioneered by private corporations in the preceding decades. More broadly, I use "imperial" as a category of analysis to show how modes of exceptionalizing difference took a variety of forms, including material, legal, and discursive practices.[34] There were close, mutually reinforcing relationships among cultural formations, business practices, and the state. The same ideas, habits, and assumptions that informed imperial policymakers also informed the choices people made about what to eat, how to advertise their products, what to write or sing about, and where to invest. Exceptional states of territoriality and citizenship promoted modern markets, capital investment, wage labor, and expanded infrastructure among the supposedly backward populations in supposedly undeveloped places. In particular, states of exception—legally codified, racially authorized, spatially distinct—lent themselves to efficiently producing raw commodities through a colonial division of labor. Raw materials came from the colonies, while the mainland reserved the right to produce higher-value finished goods. All of these factors fit within my conceptualization of empire, and, using this framework, I interpret the actions of both state and nonstate actors as imperial. Nonetheless, the analysis that follows shows that, through a range of policies, nation-states have long framed the possibilities for global trade, migration, and investment, even when they did not project power formally or militarily.

My approach builds on Sidney Mintz's foundational work, *Sweetness and Power*. Mintz showed how imperial, trade, and labor policies reshaped the meanings of sugar consumption as the British working classes ate more and more of it through the seventeenth and eighteenth centuries. Plantation slavery and British industrialization, he argues, were opposite sides of the same coin. Britain initially offered its sugar colonies preferential tariffs under a mercantilist system that stimulated the slave trade and new investments in the islands. In turn, plantation slavery provided crucial inputs—both capital and caloric—which supported Britain's industrial revolution. As Mintz put it, the colonies balanced "the accounts of capitalism" by cheaply feeding Britain's low-wage industrial laborers. Mintz shows that the most significant explosion in British working-class sugar consumption—and the proliferation of meanings associated with it—emerged *after* Britain dismantled its protective tariffs beginning in the 1830s. Free trade brought the price of sugar down so that even the poorest industrial workers could afford sweetened goods as their main source of calories. As a cheap and pleasurable food, sugar eventually displaced other foods as the mainstay of British working-class diets. Workers acquired the "sugar habit" as they accommodated "the factory world and machine rhythms." Cheap sugar—and, by extension, free trade—thus freed British workers to participate in new labor markets at ever-lower wages.[35]

I share Mintz's interest in the parallel development of agricultural and urban modernities, and I examine international and imperial trade policies as a crucial link connecting workers and consumers across oceans and continents. I find that sugar helped "balance the accounts" of U.S. imperial capitalism as new territories and workers began participating in the U.S. economy. In contrast with Mintz's British example, however, the most significant increase in U.S. sugar consumption occurred during a period of extreme trade protectionism. Tariff protection for U.S. island territories and mainland producers contributed to the remarkable explosion in sugar production and consumption in the first four decades of the twentieth century. Yet the territories never enjoyed unfettered access to the U.S. market, and in times of crisis mainland producers always came first. As a result, people living in the U.S. island territories also became prodigious consumers of sweets as they ate their way through the trade surpluses that resulted from their unequal access to the U.S. market. For colonial consumers, sugar consumption had different meanings than it did for working- and middle-class consumers on the mainland.

Commodity Cultures

Workers harvested cane in Cuba, Puerto Rico, the Philippines, Hawaii, and Louisiana. In nearby mills, other workers milled that cane and processed it into raw sugar, which they then put in sacks, loaded on ships, and sent to mainland refineries for further processing. Refiners bought raw sugar based on its total sugar content, color, and quality—characteristics that together determined raw sugar's value. At that point, a sack of sugar that originated in Cuba's cane fields was indistinguishable from one that came from Hawaii, Puerto Rico, or the Philippines. There would be no way to trace the sugar back to its point of origin since it had been commodified and was now unrecognizably disconnected from the producers of the cane from which it was made. Even after refiners put it into their own branded packaging, refined sugar from one company was indistinguishable from that made by other companies. Refiners might work hard to distinguish their products, but, short of some adulteration or novel innovation, refined sugar remained refined sugar. The fact that the end product was indistinguishable from other goods of the same kind was crucial to modern market exchanges because it guaranteed value across time and space. A buyer could order 50 pounds of refined white sugar sight unseen and be quite sure about what they would receive.

Commodities are standardized, mass-produced goods that are interchangeable with others of the same grade. To make a commodity is not merely to combine sweat, soil, and machinery into a final product. A commodity does not exist without the categories and standards by which it is defined. The standardized categories by which commodities were defined made it possible for buyers and sellers to negotiate a price even if they did not actually have the sugar in front of them at the moment of purchase. Commodities have exchange value precisely because they reflect the criteria—including the cultural values—buyers use to decide what they want and how much they will pay. The process of making those categorizations is fundamentally a cultural one. Popular culture, business practices, and technological innovations all influenced how people created commodity categories. The schemas by which people recognize and classify the world around them are refracted through market transactions. In the early twentieth century, bureaucrats, businessmen, scientists, policymakers, and consumers participated in this process. Together they facilitated the movement of products of local effort into global networks of trade.

The process of commodification has typically been worked out through private market exchanges, reinforced by a rising class of technical experts, and then codified in law by state actors. People have to not only agree on categories of difference; they must also share a common method for measuring those differences. In the early twentieth century, merchants and customs agents assessed the value of sugar by two measures: the polariscope test and the Dutch Color Standard. The polariscope, developed in the 1800s by European scientists and adopted worldwide soon after, measures the amount of light refracted through a sugar solution, which correlates with the sugar content percentage. The Dutch Color Standard was an older method, developed by private sugar brokers in Amsterdam, for evaluating sugar based on the appearance of the sugar. The standard consisted of a set of eighteen "clear, glass bottles numbered from 8 to 25, which are filled, respectively, with sugar of various shades. The sugar in No. 8 is very dark, being scarcely above a molasses . . . and so on up to No. 25, which is not quite as white as a refined sugar."[36] Sealed and certified annually (sugar changes color as it ages), the bottles were "packed in a neat wooden case" and sold "to the sugar trade of the world at $20 per set." These two methods—polariscope and Dutch Color Standard—coexisted for many decades. But as sugar milling technology improved, the Dutch Color Standard became increasingly unreliable. Millers could produce brown sugar with a high sugar content and white sugar with comparatively low sugar content. Bureaucrats worried that they were being cheated of customs revenues and that consumers were being cheated of their rightful sweetness. They were concerned as well that the racial impurities of the tropics were sneaking in to the United States. In 1909, Congress officially eliminated the Dutch Color Standard and determined to levy tariffs on the value of sugar as determined only by the more scientific polariscope test. When they made this decision, policy-makers drew on ideas about the racial hierarchies of civilization.

Karl Marx asserted long ago that commodities are critical to the accumulation and reproduction of capital and that they are surrounded by "magic and necromancy."[37] Commodities embody capitalist social relations, he noted, but, as material objects, they hide the actual conditions of their own production. As if by magic, their materiality obscures the divisions of labor within which they are made and circulated. The point of refining is, after all, to remove the last remnants of sweat and soil from the sugar so that its consumers are unaware of the product's natural and human history. The industrial process aims to eliminate all physical and imaginative connections between producers and consumers. I assert, however, that, as cultural productions, commodities are actually not so good at covering their own tracks, especially in the archives. One of this book's key methodological interventions is to suggest that an examination of commodity cultures can illuminate the comparative politics of race and economy. I use the term "commodity cultures," like "racial formation," to signal a historically situated interplay among state initiatives, socioeconomic practices, cultural productions, and social movements. I argue that commodities were crucial nodes for the articulation and contestation of social imaginaries.[38] Many of the administrative, regulatory, and legislative tasks done by the nation-state were organized around particular commodities. Tariffs were debated one commodity at a time. Congress made immigration policies, or, more often, exceptions to the overall immigration policy, in response to demands from groups of commodity producers. Commodities guided the day-to-day work of border inspectors and customs administrators and the growing cadre of federal bureaucrats assigned to serve the nation's businesses. Policies about selling land and water built on assumptions about the value of the commodities they could produce. Finally, as diverse consumers used sugar, they attributed to it their own meanings and their own assessments of its worth, sometimes at odds with dominant standards.

Another methodological premise of this book is that the political power of language and images comes from repetition and recirculation across a broad discursive field. Thus, I uncover recurring images, tropes, metaphors, and frameworks in published and unpublished sources. Photographs were one register of the overlapping politics of empire, trade, and migration, particularly photographs printed in informational brochures and bulletins, newspapers, and magazines. In

W. A. Rogers, "A Sugar-House on the Bayou Teche, Louisiana,"
Harper's Weekly, April 14, 1900. Courtesy of the Beinecke Rare Book
and Manuscript Library, Yale University.

cial reports—both government and corporate—photographs gener-
\ narratives of progress and modernization in the colonial context. I
particular attention to the visual culture of sugar's racial formation.
During the years between 1898 and the beginning of World War II, the
emblem of the cane mill and its rolling grinders fascinated artists, journalists, activists, and politicians, who saw it as an unstoppable force, not
always for good. The mill stood in comparison with images of ostensibly
less modern forms of consumption, such as chewing raw cane. While I
join those observers in using sugar to narrate changes in U.S. policy, I
have also sought out ruptures in the narrative, which casts sugar as an
all-powerful and hegemonic force of imperial expansion. Real people
made and contested the public policies, cultural formations, business
practices, and social movements that supported the growth of the sugar
industry in the first four decades of the twentieth century, and it is their
stories that I aim to tell.

Sugar and Civilization is organized chronologically and topically.
The first three chapters describe the cultural politics of sugar in the early
decades after the Spanish American War. First, I examine overlapping
debates about trade, migration, environmental, and imperial policies
between 1898 and 1913. Next, I explore how diverse consumers, including
white women, male soldiers, and African American and Asian American
political commentators grappled with the meanings attributed to sugar
and sweetness during these crucial years before World War I. I then pivot
to the World War I era, a period when sugar policies changed dramatically as the United States took control of the Western Hemisphere's sugar
supply. At the same time, policymakers realized the importance of different ethnic groups as sugar consumers.

In the 1920s, people in the United States began to eat dramatically
larger quantities of sugar. To explore how people learned to eat so much
sugar, I trace the consumer cultures of working-class people in different
parts of the United States, focusing in particular on the consumption
habits of workers who actually produced sugar and candy. I begin by
describing how Mexican businessmen imported low-grade handmade
sugars from Mexico to sell to Mexican and Mexican American sugar beet
workers in the United States. Moving from the West and Southwest to the
rural South and urban areas in the North and West, I go on to explain
new mass markets for candy that catered to an increasing number of
migrants from rural to urban places. Rural African Americans continued
to choose low-grade homemade sweeteners even as they encountered

to today's cheap, shitty food culture

cheap mass-produced candy. African American and Mexican American workers worked out the contradictions of integration and exclusion within mainstream labor and consumer markets in part through their choices of sweets.

The remainder of the book tracks the cultural politics of sugar during the sustained crisis of the 1920s and 1930s. For a variety of reasons—many of which are attributable to U.S. imperial policies—the sugar market by the mid-1920s was desperately oversupplied and prices were sharply declining. In the early 1930s, policymakers recognized that the sugar tariff no longer protected mainland farmers. In fact, the sugar tariff had confused the boundaries between domestic and foreign in the U.S. sugar empire. I trace the politics of this crisis through contentious debates over the sugar tariff during the 1920s, which were informed by anti-Mexican sentiment in Congress and by labor reformers concerned over child labor in the beet fields. The 1930 Smoot-Hawley Tariff, which took effect as the nation plunged into the Great Depression, was the highest sugar tariff yet. Its failure to improve the plight of sugar producers caused many policymakers to reconsider protectionism. Leaders in the early 1930s responded by developing nontariff methods to control the sugar market and redefine who could have full access to the U.S. sugar market. They tested their theories after the election of President Franklin D. Roosevelt, who took office in 1933. The New Deal sugar programs used marketing quotas and benefit payments to support mainland farmers and prevent radicalism at home and abroad.

I end by describing the ongoing debates over the political status of the island territories which took place through the New Deal sugar programs. Policymakers embraced a more liberal approach to citizenship and the territories, focusing on workers' rights as economic citizens, entitled to eat the very sugar they worked to produce. At the same time, a new generation of reformers began to argue that, rather than bolstering civilization, cheap, refined sugar was actually degrading it. Policymakers and consumers attributed different meanings to sugar and civilization than had their counterparts in the early twentieth century. But in the 1930s, much as had been the case for the previous four decades, when people ate sugar and candy they also participated in a complex web of imperial culture and politics.

required a bunch of intervention + lowered wages + quality of life

CHAPTER ONE

SUGAR'S CIVILIZING MISSION

Immigration, Race, and
the Politics of Empire, 1898–1913

Standing on a hilltop in Puerto Rico in 1901, U.S. cavalryman William H. Oliver Jr. looked out over cane fields and saw a world in miniature, a vast landscape engineered to produce sugar. "The red brick chimneys of the sugar refineries, emitting threads of silvery smoke, looked like fire-crackers," he noted, "and the laborers in the fields seemed to be moving specks, while the irrigating ditches, which had been dug crosswise at intervals" gave the land "a peculiar appearance."[1] Standing at an elevation, Oliver projected himself—and by extension, the United States—as a gargantuan sovereign, capable of overseeing a richly productive territory. It "seemed almost possible to jump from the middle of one plantation to the middle of another," he observed. Oliver evoked an experience that would have been familiar to troops fighting in Puerto Rico, Cuba, and the Philippines, since the battles of the summer of 1898 took place on a landscape dense with sugarcane. Soldiers' heroic tales, widely reprinted, were replete with references to the cane fields, as they recognized the connection between U.S. military action and the potential growth of the island sugar industry. Although the war had devastated the islands' cane mills and fields, military and political leaders saw their promise, which legitimated their aspirations for reconstruction. By rescuing the islands from Spanish tyranny and convincing the natives to abandon their tropical laziness, proponents of expansion imagined they could extend civilization while satisfying the U.S. American sweet tooth.

Despite different histories of the islands that came under U.S. rule in 1898, sugar cultivation was something the islands had in common. Policymakers and the general public shared a broad consensus that sugar was an ideal crop to foster economic and political modernization, although they disagreed about whether this development ought to occur on the islands or the mainland. While military officials and investors saw prospects for expanded production of cane sugar in the new island territories, businessmen and policymakers in the U.S. West envisioned an irrigated landscape that could produce beet sugar. Should white investors export their ingenuity and machinery to the tropics, where they would use the natural advantages of soil and climate to produce cane sugar? Or should sugar production shift increasingly to the continent, where white farmers could grow beets? The challenge of regulating the flows of sugar and the labor required to produce it thus forced policymakers to consider Puerto Rico, Hawaii, Cuba, and the Philippines in relation to each other and to the continental United States.

Advocates for cane sugar and those for beet sugar had more in common than their disagreements might suggest. Boosters of beet sugar and cane sugar shared a worldview that privileged white men and white sugar, and they claimed authority to include and exclude people and places from the law as necessary to promote economic development. Sugar, they hoped, could stimulate markets for land, labor, and goods where these had been lagging, whether in the U.S. West or the new island territories. At the time that the United States embarked on its overseas civilizing mission, the process of asserting hegemony across the contiguous United States was not yet complete. In the West, beet sugar was crucial to policymakers' strategies for wresting control over land, water, and labor from Native Americans, Mexicans, and Asian Americans. Beets made it possible for them to commodify land and water, assign them a market value, and simultaneously measure people's fitness for citizenship. In much the same way, colonial administrators for Puerto Rico, the Philippines, and Hawaii put cane sugar production at the heart of their "civilizing mission." Thus an interrelated set of colonial policies, implemented simultaneously on the mainland and in the island territories, set the stage for dramatic growth in sugar production across the new U.S. sugar empire.[2]

Policymakers in the United States did not begin with an overarching imperial vision that united policies for each of the territories. After acquiring the islands in 1898, Congress spent the next several years debating precisely how to govern them and whether or not they should be considered part of the domestic United States. Should the territories and their residents be treated uniformly, much as territories destined for statehood would be? Could democratic institutions survive if the nation owned territory that would never be eligible for statehood because its residents were racially unfit for citizenship? Many observers insisted that it would be a fundamental break with American tradition if the United States held noncontiguous territory. Others were alarmed at the expansion of monopoly capitalism, suspecting that powerful sugar corporations were secretly behind the United States' overseas ambitions. Anti-imperialists believed that U.S. investors would degrade the islands by creating vast corporate-controlled plantations that would inevitably employ "imported cheap labor," by which they typically meant Chinese contract workers. In response, those who believed that the United States should keep the islands insisted that U.S. administration would modernize the territories. Anti-imperialists' fears would not be realized, proponents argued, as long as immigration and land laws restricted the growth of plantation agriculture. As it became increasingly clear that the United States would retain the islands, anti-imperialists took an aggressive approach to questions of labor migration and landholding as a strategy to maintain the integrity of U.S. democracy. Ultimately, Congress made policies to govern each of the territories that were not the same as those for the rest of the nation. These new imperial policies were the culmination of extended debates—often centered on sugar—about land, labor, and monopoly.

Though readers now glaze over at the mention of tariffs, voters and politicians passionately debated the issue in the late nineteenth and early twentieth centuries. The tariff was grist for partisan politics, regional alliances, newspaper headlines, and high-paid lobbyists. Republicans viewed tariffs as a way to encourage capital investments in new industries, arguing that "infant industries" needed protection as they grew toward self-sufficiency. Democrats, on the other hand, saw tariffs as a burden to consumers and a boon to the wealthy.[3] Low tariffs, Democrats conceded, could be used to raise revenue, as long as they did not increase consumer prices or stimulate industries that could not survive outside of the tariff "hot house." Given the federal government's budget surplus in the late nineteenth century, southern Democrats viewed tariffs as an unfair boon to northern industrialists and the Union Civil War veterans whose pensions were funded by this surplus. But the sugar tariff—which forced politicians to think about domestic concerns within the context of imperial politics and global markets—had a discombobulating effect on party lines. Normally protectionist Republicans lauded free trade in sugar, while low-tariff Democrats were some of the loudest proponents of high sugar tariffs. In some cases, politicians' approaches reflected their constituencies' interests. Often, however, their ideas about race and empire were as crucial as either constituent demands or party politics.

Immigration restriction was closely tied to the tariff issue and was a subject for equally passionate opinion. Tariff and immigration debates often overlapped (sometimes quite literally) because both invited comparisons of laborers in the United States and abroad. Common sense at the turn of the century held that foreign competition came in two forms: goods produced by "cheap labor" *living* abroad, and goods produced in the United States by "cheap labor" *from* abroad. Whether the goods or the workers crossed the border, the outcome was the same: the erosion of living standards, declining wages, and the degradation of white civilization. Anti-imperialists used these arguments to oppose preferential tariffs for the new island territories. They argued that goods produced in those places by "cheap tropical labor" held an unfair advantage in comparison with goods made by workers earning higher wages in the contiguous United States. Beet sugar, they argued, should enjoy tariff protection against cane sugar from the territories. If the territories did not receive tariff protection, there would be no new sugar plantations, and thus no worrisome migration of Asian workers into the territories. If the territories *did* receive preferential tariffs, strict immigration restrictions would be imperative.

As policymakers sought to influence how U.S. sovereignty would be exercised in the movement of commodities, people, and capital across borders and within the nation, the sugar tariff emerged as a site of an imperial racial formation.[4] The addition of the island territories had the potential to expand the boundaries of what was considered to be within the domestic United States. Expansion of the domestic realm conflicted with a strong urge to exclude nonwhites from the boundaries of national belonging. To reconcile these opposing tendencies between expansion and exclusion, policymakers in the 1900s mapped a hierarchically differentiated landscape through a range of new laws. Sugar—cane and beet—played a key role in the overlapping debates over tariff, immigration, colonial, and irrigation policies between 1898 and 1913. The resulting landscape produced sugar and imperial subjects with remarkable efficiency.

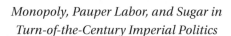

Monopoly, Pauper Labor, and Sugar in Turn-of-the-Century Imperial Politics

Senator Francis G. Newlands (D-Nevada) encapsulated many of the concerns and contradictions about race, empire, and development that motivated turn-of-the-century policymakers. Newlands was a key figure in debates over overseas empire and sugar policy, and he connected these topics to Asian immigration exclusion. His thinking on expansion and immigration was inextricably tied to questions of economic development in the arid West. He articulated a populist anti-imperialist vision and condemned immigrant workers and plantation agriculture in equal measure. Born in Mississippi in 1848, Newlands came of age before the Civil War, and he understood race relations within the paternalist framework of plantation slavery. His faith in white supremacy and Manifest Destiny carried him west, first to San Francisco, where he married the daughter of a silver mining magnate, and then to Nevada, where he served first as a pro-silver representative and then as a senator. Newlands believed that democracy required racial homogeneity and that white civilization was destined to control North America. To this end, he sponsored legislation to create a federal irrigation system to make western dry lands suitable for white farmers, and he advocated immigration restriction and segregation and was a vocal critic of the U.S. role in the Philippines. Newlands's thoughts on race informed his approach to all of these issues. Merging the segregationist ascendency of the Jim Crow South with the anti-Asian politics of the Pacific coast, Newlands used the issue of overseas expansion as an opportunity to build new white supremacist coalitions between southerners and westerners. Indeed, he later made headlines when he proposed a plank for the Democratic platform of 1912 that would have disenfranchised African Americans and barred Asian immigration in one swoop of constitutional revision. Newlands's agenda thus provides a lens for examining how policymakers negotiated the conflicting goals of internal and external empire.[5]

Newlands seized the remnants of antimonopoly populism as an ideological common ground for westerners and southerners in the reinvigorated Democratic Party. Building on a legacy of Jeffersonian agrarianism, populists imagined that farming by smallholders was the ideal basis of American political traditions. From the early 1800s forward, Jeffersonians had seen westward expansion as key to social equality, because it opened new land for settlement and ensured that all hardworking white men could be property owners. Independent property owners, unlike dependent wageworkers, could participate as equals in a democratic polity. The small farm—measured by the yardstick of the 1862 Homestead Act's 160-acre allotment—figured large in the populist anti-imperialist agrarian imagination.[6]

By the 1890s, however, farmers saw themselves as unable to achieve this ideal because of the growing economic and political control by modern

Francis G. Newlands and family, n.d. Newlands Papers,
Manuscripts and Archives, Yale University Library.

capitalists, embodied in corporate monopolies and trusts.[7] Railroads'
power over land sales and shipping rates and bankers' control of finance
were key issues that ignited populists in the 1890s. Southerners and westerners saw themselves as subordinated semi-colonies struggling against
eastern monopoly capital. For many people, the American Sugar Refining Company (ASRC), commonly known as the Sugar Trust, symbolized
corporate monopolies' excesses. Boosters pointed out that the ASRC did
not yet control beet sugar production and that the industry might offer
struggling farmers a crop through which to achieve their agrarian ideals.
With tariff protection, the beet sugar industry would thrive, and white
farmers would gain an advantage against eastern monopolies.

Newlands embraced the budding beet sugar industry at the turn of
the century because it fit with his vision for a civilization of white settlers in the arid West and because it was an emblem of opposition to
monopoly capital.[8] Newlands's advocacy in favor of the beet industry
was not because he or his constituency had vested interests in it. He had
not voted in favor of the 1897 Dingley Tariff, intended to stimulate the
beet industry. He had not fought for bounties on sugar beets, a popular

measure in the 1890s aimed at luring farmers to plant the crop. In fact, his district did not even have a sugar beet factory until 1911. Newlands developed his taste for sugar beets because it let him focus his concerns over race, economics, the silver question, and overseas expansion around one issue. Grown in publicly funded land reclamation and irrigation projects, beets offered white farmers a way to battle corporate dominance and other forces corroding democracy. Public irrigation and land reclamation projects attached value to land and water and put that value in the hands of small-scale farmers. By attracting a sugar factory, towns could further boost market values for land and water, thus reasserting the founding fathers' vision of agrarian democracy while embracing the newest technologies and industries.

Newlands, like many of his contemporaries, associated the power of monopolies with overseas expansion and labor migration into the United States. He believed that imports and immigrants undermined U.S. sovereignty and that the acquisition of the island territories would bring more of both. That beet sugar might compete with tropical cane sugar from the island territories crystalized Newlands's and others' complaints about overseas expansion, which included concerns over land monopoly and "cheap labor" from Asia. From Newlands's perspective, overseas expansion was yet another way that monopoly capitalists like the ASRC disadvantaged small white farmers. Expansion was the outcome of capitalists' drive to monopolize more land and to exploit racially inferior workers. To Newlands, imperial expansion was incompatible with a republican form of government. American political ideals could only flourish when white smallholders' autonomy was guaranteed by limits on monopolies. Monopolies, he argued, ought to be regulated through a combination of immigration, trade, and land law. This assemblage of issues forms what I call "populist anti-imperialism."

Populist anti-imperialists rhetorically linked race, land tenure, and corporate monopoly as they fought to rein in overseas expansion. Senator Ben Tillman (D-South Carolina), another populist anti-imperialist, expressed his concerns about race and expansionism during the Spanish American War of 1898. Attributing the war directly to monopoly corporations and "land grabbers" hungry for land, Tillman worried that their actions would bring many people of color under the protection of the Constitution. Such people, he argued, were racially incapable of resisting capitalist exploitation or developing democratic political institutions. They were "slaves in thought and feeling, with an inherited slavery of centuries, Malay, Chinese, Japanese." Tillman repeated these concerns during the debate on the Philippines in 1899, when he said, "Some contract laborers may be imported from China who will work . . . who will be driven by the whip, as the slaves were in the South before the war, and as they are now driven in Hawaii, to develop the rich lands of which we have heard." He worried, further, that "there may be teeming imports coming to our country from such labor thus employed and protected by our bayonets, and the few will reap the benefits. . . . We must compete with 'pauper labor' held down by bayonets." Land monopoly and degraded labor were the logical outcomes when "capitalists or corporations" were allowed to "go out there and invest their capital" with military support.[9]

Newlands's and Tillman's concerns about land, labor, and monopoly are visible in the Joint Resolution annexing Hawaii, passed in the midst of the Spanish American War. Newlands had actually sponsored this resolution, believing that Hawaii could be whitened if it was subject to "wise exclusion laws" to prevent further Asian labor migration. Governed by white men since their coup against Queen Lili'uokalani in 1893, Newlands believed that the islands were a crucial outpost of military defense against Japan's imperial designs. Though the Joint Resolution annexed the Hawaiian Islands "as a part of the territory of the United States . . . subject to the sovereign dominion thereof," it also set the stage for Congress to enact unique policies tailored to the circumstances on the ground. Rights in all public property, including former crown lands, were transferred to the United States, though the Resolution exempted the islands from existing U.S. public land law. Populist anti-imperialists hoped to eventually enact public land laws that would level the playing field between Hawaiian plantations and beet farmers on the continent. New Chinese labor migration into Hawaii was prohibited, and the Chinese residing there were barred from migrating to the mainland United States. With these protections, mainland farmers would not have to compete against sugar produced by Asian workers, which would be inevitable if "land monopolists" had their way.[10] By enacting land and labor provisions, the Resolution anticipated that the customs laws of the United States would extend to Hawaii, though that would require a separate act of Congress.

Led by populist anti-imperialists, Congress debated the Organic Acts that created governments for Hawaii and Puerto Rico in 1900.[11] Hawaii's Organic Act provided that the U.S. Constitution applied to Hawaii in most, but not all, respects. It extended the customs and revenue laws of the United States to Hawaii and designated the territory as a customs district of the United States. As an "organized incorporated territory," Hawaii was thus within the domestic realm for trade purposes, and any tariffs legislated for the continental United States automatically applied there. Newlands was concerned, however, that even with Chinese immigration exclusion, Hawaii was still vulnerable to "the selfishness of monopolies and trusts." Because a handful of sugar corporations controlled most of the land and water, Newlands worried that U.S. policy risked perpetuating "an extensive system of land monopoly, the concentration of large areas of land in the hands of individuals and corporations employing laborers as mere machines for the cultivation of the soil." Railroads, waterworks, and even sugar mills ought to be publically regulated, he argued. Pointing out that public distribution of land and water had been used in the U.S. West, Newlands proposed a redistribution of sugar lands and water rights from existing corporate owners to white settlers. His plan was rejected, and the existing system remained intact. Congress did approve, however, a much milder limit on future corporate landholdings.[12]

Congress debated Puerto Rico's Organic Act at the same time as Hawaii's. Framers of the Puerto Rican bill were preoccupied with how to finance the island's government, and thus the debate centered on whether tariffs or property taxes should be the main source of revenue. Puerto Rican elites, many of whom initially welcomed U.S. administration, strongly advocated free trade and full integration with the United States. The U.S. consul, Philip C. Hanna, suggested that free trade was "the missing link in the moral education and religious training of this people."[13] Unlike Hawaii, however, Congress did not immediately include Puerto Rico within U.S. customs laws. Newlands argued against free trade for the islands. He pointed out that free trade—or even a reduced tariff—would result in a "drift into largeholdings," with a commensurate degradation in labor. Repeating language he had used in other contexts, he argued that "the best security for stable and intelligent government there will be small holdings, and a bill providing for the government of Porto Rico which does not take hold vigorously of the land and labor questions utterly fails in all the purposes of scientific government." Under the Organic Act (also known as the Foraker Act), Puerto Rico paid only 15 percent of the full tariff rate, with plans for eventual free trade. Free trade was implemented in 1901. These were significant tariff concessions benefiting Puerto Rico.[14]

To Newlands's chagrin, the Foraker Act offered Puerto Rico preferential tariffs but did not limit landholdings or immigration. Newlands immediately joined his southern colleagues to demand an amendment addressing these concerns. William A. Jones (D-Virginia), who would later take a prominent role in territorial legislation, agreed that a land law was essential, given the tariff reductions. Without a land law, he argued, the sugar industry would drive Puerto Ricans "to cultivate these lands for these corporations at whatever daily wage they choose to pay them." Newlands and Jones shepherded the so-called 500-Acre Law through Congress at the same time as the final version of the Hawaiian Organic Act, with its land laws, was approved.[15] These restrictions on landholdings were not, as some scholars have assumed, the outcome of lobbying on the part of sugar beet interests.[16] Instead, they were part of a coherent populist anti-imperialist approach linking land, labor, and sugar through a racialized economic theory.

Newlands had cemented his commitment to sugar as a vehicle through which to express his populist anti-imperialism by 1902, when Congress debated a proposed reciprocity treaty with Cuba. The treaty would give the newly independent Cuba a 25 percent reduction on the sugar tariff in exchange for tariff concessions on U.S. products. Newlands again argued for immigration restrictions as a necessary complement to sugar tariff concessions. A reciprocity treaty would give Cuba access to protected U.S. sugar markets without any legal means for insisting that producers there adhere to U.S. labor and immigration standards. "The effect," he said, "would be to rapidly stimulate the production of sugar in Cuba by every device known in the way of cheap labor." Hinting that the United States would eventually annex Cuba anyway, Newlands urged Congress to preemptively control Cuba's racial demography to ensure that white creoles remained the dominant group. If the Cuban sugar industry were included in the United States' tariff wall, its population would eventually be "much less desirable for annexation than it is now, composed as it will be of Chinese and other imported cheap laborers." As another congressman put it, the aim was to "Americanize a Spanish colony" by offering trade concessions and "keeping the coolies out."[17]

Newlands also saw an ethical problem, though. The United States could not insist that Cuba, soon to be an ostensibly independent nation, restrict contract labor and Chinese immigration. Newlands viewed as imperialistic any attempt to force another sovereign nation to implement particular laws, no matter how laudable they were. Thus the only fair way to extend Chinese exclusion to Cuba, Newlands explained, was to invite that country to join the United States as a territory destined for statehood through a voluntary "political union." I suggest that Newlands made this proposal for rhetorical purposes, since a political union with Cuba was not a realistic prospect at the time. For one thing, the 1898 Teller Amendment had declared that the intent of the United States was to secure Cuba's independence rather than annex it. Newlands knew this, and he shrewdly offered his proposal at the same time that Congress was renewing the Chinese exclusion laws and extending them to the territories. His proposal, then, aimed not to annex Cuba, but rather to force administrators to restrict Chinese immigration there.

The newly independent Cuba did implement Chinese exclusion. Under the Platt Amendment, the U.S. treaty instrument that limited Cuban sovereignty for the next thirty years, Cuba agreed to abide by all military orders in effect when U.S. troops withdrew. Shortly before withdrawing in 1902, the U.S. command in Cuba issued a military order prohibiting Chinese labor migration. With immigration restrictions in place, Congress finally passed a reciprocity treaty that granted Cuba a 20 percent reduction in the sugar tariff beginning in 1903. Newlands still voted against the treaty. Three years later, the Cuban legislature formalized Chinese exclusion, though that law did little to prevent other international labor migrations into the cane fields.[18]

Newlands correctly assumed that proponents of expansion saw the island territories as sites for new capital investment in the sugar industry. Based on early assessments of the soils, plants, and existing infrastructure, administrators in both the Philippines and Puerto Rico identified sugar as one of the key industries suited to the islands, employing essentialized ideas about the tropical environment as they imagined the islands' economies. When he served as governor general of the Philippines between 1901 and 1903, William Howard Taft forthrightly promoted the sugar industry as a civilizing influence. As Taft put it, "The investment of American capital in the islands is necessary to their proper development, and is necessary to the material, and therefore the spiritual, uplifting of the Filipino people."[19] Colonial administrators like Taft defended sugar's civilizing mission by using the same rhetoric of Anglo-Saxon racial superiority as Newlands. Territorial sugar production would be profitable, they argued, not because of the low-wage labor, but because of the technological efficiency and inborn ingenuity white capitalists would bring to fertile tropical landscapes. Government officials represented this logic visually by printing images that used the same idiom as opponents of expansion used to argue for restriction. For example, colonial administrators circulated images showing sugar production technology that highlighted and juxtaposed the categories of primitive and civilized. Images showed Filipinos using animal-powered mills to grind cane to produce a low-grade *muscovado* sugar. By contrast, U.S. investors were shown building modern mills that efficiently ground cane to produce high-quality centrifugal sugar. The modern process, as shown in schematic drawings with clean lines, was efficient, productive, and modern. The Filipino process was dirty, inefficient, and wasteful. The visual juxtaposition of "native" sugar technologies with U.S. investors' efficient machinery and management justified colonial developments.

Taft's interest in the industry was also practical. The war and its aftermath had created budget deficits which left U.S. colonial administrators wondering how to fund their own fledgling bureaucracies. Rather than impose property taxes, which were cumbersome to levy in a large, poorly mapped archipelago with scant infrastructure, Taft advocated import and export tariffs, which could be easily collected at the ports. At the same time, he knew that import and export duties must be carefully balanced if they were to achieve his goals. Tariffs had to be high enough to fund the colonial administration but low enough to stimulate capital investment. To strike this balance, Taft wanted the discretion to determine import and export duties.

Though colonial administrators like Taft wanted flexibility to enact diverse revenue and trade policies to meet different goals in each of the territories, there was no precedent in U.S. law for some territories to be administered outside of the constitutional requirement for fiscal uniformity. As a federal tax, import and export duties normally fell under the requirement that "all Duties, Imposts and Excises shall be uniform throughout the United States."[20] If the territory was deemed to be a part of the United States, then the tariffs could not be different from those levied on the states. Since Congress had not definitively said whether Puerto Rico and the Philippines were part of the United States, the Supreme Court had to decide whether the uniformity clause applied. The Court decided the issue as part of the series of decisions collectively known as the Insular Cases. In *Downes v. Bidwell* (1901), the Court argued that Puerto Rico, "though not foreign, [is] outside of the restrictions applicable to interstate commerce" because Congress had created a separate territorial administration through the Organic Act. The same held for the Philippines. The islands were "foreign in a domestic sense," much as Native Americans had been categorized as "domestic dependencies" seventy years earlier. Congress could set individual tariff policies for Puerto Rico and the Philippines since they were "unincorporated territories" and thus not fully part of the United States. The Supreme Court thus gave Taft what he hoped for—the freedom to administer the territories as exceptional spaces, outside the uniform framework of U.S. law.[21]

Congress could now make separate rules to govern trade between the territories and the mainland and between the territories and the rest of the world. Indeed, Congress authorized different trade policies for Puerto Rico and the Philippines. In the Philippines, the Treaty of Paris complicated matters because Spain had reserved preferential trade relations with the Philippines for ten years. This meant that if Congress offered tariff concessions to the Philippines it would be obligated to offer the same favors to Spain. Nonetheless, in 1902, Congress granted the Philippines a 25 percent reduction over the full tariff on sugar. It coupled tariff concessions with export duties, which slowed investment in the sugar industry but provided additional revenue to the insular government. Puerto Rico, on the other hand, was not subject to the same treaty provisions. The island received a much larger tariff concession than did the Philippines, coupled with land and other taxes for revenue. Administrators intended that the island would eventually have free trade in sugar, but they nonetheless levied property taxes since there was already a system in place to do so. Ironically, taxes in Puerto Rico accomplished much of what populist anti-imperialists feared tariffs would accomplish. Land taxes forced many smallholders off their land and gave larger sugar plantations opportunities to acquire good cane lands. Displaced smallholders had few options but to seek wage work on those same plantations. The combination of a land tax, lower sugar tariffs, and lax enforcement of the 500-acre law encouraged new investments by U.S. Americans in the Puerto Rican sugar industry.[22]

Despite populist anti-imperialists' efforts, Congress created policies that encouraged the sugar industries in Puerto Rico, the Philippines, Hawaii, and Cuba. Newlands and his peers had advocated for policies to slow overseas capital investment, and they had achieved a few limited successes, mostly in terms of immigration restrictions. Overall, early twentieth-century debates over trade and empire resulted in better terms of trade for the island territories. When all was said and done, the United States levied a high tariff on imported sugar, but each of the new island territories and Cuba received the benefits of at least some of this tariff. Beet sugar producers got their high tariff, but they had to share it with Hawaii, Puerto Rico, the Philippines, and Cuba. Encouraged by tariff protection, investors put vast sums of money into sugar production in each of these places. Faced with rapid growth in cane sugar production in the islands, Newlands increasingly turned to another strategy to assert racial sovereignty. He set about to build an inland empire in the arid West.

The Greatest Colonial Movement of the Age Is Now Being Crystalized: Irrigation Imperialism, Populist Anti-imperialists, and the Promise of Sugar

According to some observers, the "greatest colonial movement of the age" was taking place not in Hawaii, Puerto Rico, or the Philippines, but rather in the states and territories of the U.S. West. While Newlands lobbied to limit U.S. overseas expansion, he was aggressively expanding a different empire. Newlands's was an empire of western public lands reclaimed by massive public irrigation works from aridity, land speculators, and what he saw as Native American neglect. Newlands and other advocates of public irrigation complained that policymakers wasted time and resources on overseas expansion while neglecting continental opportunities. The National Reclamation Act, which he sponsored in 1902, sought to "break up existing land monopoly" in the West for the benefit of white settlers. As one editorialist lamented, "It is not to be expected that the United States Congress will suddenly turn from its pleasures of tariff play and Cuban war and Hawaiian annexation . . . and give its earnest attention and serious consideration to this matter of irrigation." Several years later, the same writer asked, "Did Mr. McKinley realize that the reclamation of the arid West carries with it the creation of a great and populous empire within our own territory?" Sugar beets were one of the newest answers to the question of how to develop this "great and populous empire within our own territory" in order to counter the monopoly of the Sugar Trust.[23]

Newlands used similar reasoning when he rejected overseas imperialism and embraced what historian Donald Worster calls "irrigation imperialism." Newlands built on an ideology well articulated in the 1890s by irrigation boosters like William Smythe, a prominent "irrigation imperialist" who wrote books and articles promoting irrigated agriculture as a "natural antidote" to monopoly capital. Smythe argued that irrigation would give farmers access to credit, facilitate land markets, attract investments in rural areas, and promote modern, scientific agricultural techniques. According to Smythe, the new inland empire would be based on "the water supply and irrigable land, its topmost arch a nobler civilization than the world has yet seen, based upon social equality, democratic liberty, and the greatest average prosperity." While a third of the land in the public domain remained open for homesteaders, scarcity of water made it impossible to settle. In the late 1890s and early 1900s, however, few private investors were willing to foot the bill for expensive new irrigation projects open to small-scale farmers. Corporations and absentee investors monopolized what little irrigated land there was, and cash-strapped farmers and new settlers had scant access. The 1900 census showed that the arid West actually lost population in the preceding decade. Reformers like Newlands responded to this revelation by redoubling their efforts to make public lands accessible and productive for white farmers.[24]

Like his proposals for limiting overseas expansion, Newlands's Reclamation Act of 1902 built on the racial logic of populist anti-imperialism. With limited opposition and President Roosevelt's support, the Reclamation Act passed by an overwhelming margin. It authorized massive new public works projects to bring dry lands under irrigation, creating the Reclamation Bureau to coordinate these efforts. Homesteaders could claim land in one of the new reclamation districts, along with enough water to irrigate a 160-acre homestead. Settlers agreed to pay back the costs of the irrigation project, but their payments would enter a revolving fund for new reclamation projects. The law prohibited the employment of "Mongolian" laborers in project construction, and Asian farmers were excluded from its benefits since immigrants racially ineligible for citizenship had never been eligible to claim homesteads. The Reclamation Act thus explicitly aimed to extend white smallholders' control over the land in order to limit large-scale corporate agriculture, in which Asian or Mexican workers might be employed.[25]

The menaces of corporate land monopoly and Asian labor migration were twinned in debates over the Reclamation Act because Congress was simultaneously hashing out the details of the Organic Act for the Philippines. The U.S. military had been fighting an insurrection in the Philippines for four years, and many people questioned whether the United States should govern the islands at all. As with earlier Organic Acts, opponents of the Philippine bill, including Newlands, worried that there were inadequate limits on corporate land ownership. The Organic Act for the Philippines also included provisions related to public lands which extended U.S. authority to distribute those lands as these authorities saw fit. Landholdings for individuals were limited to 16 hectares; corporations were limited to 1,024 hectares. Other provisions authorized land titling, gave preference to prior inhabitants for sales and leases, and required that the insular government conduct surveys to classify soils according to their best use. The Organic Act specified that water rights ought to be allocated using the precise method the Newlands Act required on the mainland. Provisions for the control and allocation of land and water were the outcome of pressure from populist members of Congress like Newlands and reflected the same agenda he pursued for the arid West. Yet these policies also gained the support of those, like Taft, who hoped to integrate the Philippines into modern systems of market exchange. Given the complexity of the social and political landscape in the Philippines, these measures in many cases had consequences very different from what their framers had envisioned.[26]

Irrigation imperialists' plans for reclaiming the arid West for white farmers intersected with reformers' "civilizing mission" among Native Americans. Just as in the island territories, the policymakers aimed to uplift and civilize subordinate races on Indian reservations by promoting commercial agriculture and wage work. Indian policy, like that for offshore territories, aimed to commodify land and water as a way to leverage workers into labor markets. A Supreme Court decision in 1903, *Lone Wolf v. Hitchcock*, strengthened Congress's right to forcibly parcel tribal lands out among individual tribe members. Supporters argued that individual landholding was superior to communal land tenure because individual initiative and efficient use of limited resources were crucial to the civilizing process. The *Lone Wolf* ruling extended the process initiated by the Dawes Allotment Act (1887) and resulted in more Native Americans entering the labor market after losing land to white settlers. At the same time, Congress passed a number of bills enabling non-Indians to lease reservation lands, which gave white settlers access to water previously controlled by Indians. Between 1904 and 1909, federal Indian commissioner Francis Leupp went even farther, explicitly promoting sugar beet cultivation as a means to civilize Indians.[27] He imagined them not as farmers but as wage laborers on white farmers' sugar beet farms, located on leased, irrigated reservation land. Indians indeed participated in migratory sugar beet labor early in the industry's development.[28]

The Reclamation Service created under Newlands's Reclamation Act asserted white settlers' claims over those of supposedly less civilized races, first in the arid West and later in the island territories. Even as advocates of irrigation and land reclamation expanded overseas, their agenda remained anchored in Newlands's original vision of white smallholder democracy. Frederick H. Newell, chief of the Reclamation Service, visited Hawaii in 1908 to assess whether public lands could be redistributed to white settlers there in order to address political problems. White homesteaders would offset the disproportionate influence of native Hawaiian voters and the future influence of Chinese and Japanese children born on the island and thus U.S. citizens and future voters. He noted that Hawaii lacked what he called "the 'plain people'—citizens descended from generations of freemen—in whom thrift, energy, and civic virtues are inborn." Newell found that the major sugar companies already dominated the best land and were making efficient use of it. Though he favored small homesteads, Newell saw no point in altering the existing arrangements of land tenure. Instead, he proposed that white settlers use smaller plots of land to grow coffee and pineapples. With sufficient publicly funded irrigation, white smallholders could prosper without disrupting the existing sugar economy.[29]

The Reclamation Service also advised on irrigation and public land distribution in Puerto Rico and the Philippines.[30] Sugar planters on the dry southern coast of Puerto Rico wanted better irrigation, and they asked the Puerto Rican legislature to fund a hydraulic survey.[31] The U.S. Reclamation Service sent an engineer to do the survey in 1907. A year later, Puerto Rico's legislative assembly authorized the construction of an irrigation system under U.S. Reclamation Service supervision.[32] The law followed many of the precedents set in mainland reclamation projects. The first major project was completed six years later.[33] Irrigation projects in Puerto Rico were relatively successful in rationalizing the allocation of land and water, and they encouraged the expansion of sugar plantations. The irrigation infrastructure wrote the civilizing mission onto the Puerto Rican landscape and virtually assured that sugar would be the mainstay of the economy. Irrigation and land policies were less successful in the Philippines. Though the U.S. Reclamation Service also helped the Philippine Commission develop water-use laws and draw up plans for irrigation projects, to colonial administrators' dismay, the mere act of creating a legal infrastructure in the Philippines was insufficient to integrate markets for land, water, and the goods and labor that could be produced from them.[34] Administrators repeatedly attempted to stimulate such developments in the Philippines and repeatedly failed.

In the first decades of the twentieth century, Congress consistently expanded its territorial sovereignty over land speculators and earlier inhabitants by finding novel means to bring land that had previously been held in communal title into the public domain. Once these resources were in the public domain, federal administrators could then distribute them in accordance with their vision of suitable proprietors, individual property ownership, and principals of market exchange. The logic undergirding these political and legal efforts—that white men ought to be protected from monopolies over land, water, capital, and low wages—played out simultaneously in the arid West and the sugar lands of the new island territories. In Puerto Rico and the Philippines, colonial administrators surveyed land, helped to irrigate it, and imposed new taxes on it. Taxes, mortgage payments, and irrigation fees made it harder for independent farmers to survive, and many of them instead found work on large-scale sugar plantations. Likewise, by the 1910s, long-term legal conflicts between whites and Mexican Americans and Native Americans over land in Texas, New Mexico, California, Colorado, and elsewhere brought those groups into migratory wage labor in the sugar beet industry.[35] By commodifying land, federal policies remade the landscapes of the arid West, Puerto Rico, Hawaii, and the Philippines into places that efficiently produced both sugar and sugar workers. Increased sugar production and labor mobility, in turn, intensified debates over trade and immigration restriction as the continental beet industry called for ever more protection.

Tariffs and Monopolies between 1909 and 1914

The culmination of debates over how to integrate the new island territories into the U.S. economic and political system was that, after 1898, four groups vied for a share of the sugar bowl: beet and cane producers from the continental United States; sugar refiners—commonly called the Sugar Trust—primarily based on the eastern seaboard; Cuba, which, in collaboration with the eastern seaboard sugar refiners, preferred lower tariffs; and cane sugar producers in the U.S. territories of Hawaii, Puerto Rico, and the Philippines. Between 1909 and World War I, debates over the United States' territories continued to play out through sugar policy. In this period, observers decried not only U.S. rule in the island territories, but also the expansion of the Sugar Trust into the beet industry and the growth of immigrants' so-called monopolies of land and labor. Each group used professional lobbyists who, in the process of arguing about tariffs, created a racialized geography of sugar production that compared the labor, climate, and technology in the different places.

Those preferring a low sugar tariff included Cuba and mainland sugar refiners. Since Cuba benefited from a preferential tariff after 1903, it supplied more than half of the sugar consumed in the United States, displacing other foreign sources. By the second decade of the twentieth century, countries paying a full duty on their sugar supplied less than 1 percent of the U.S. market.[36] While Cuban sugar had a decided advantage over other foreign suppliers, it still paid some tariff, so a lower duty had the potential to increase producers' already scant profit margins. Refiners, who purchased their raw materials on the world market, wanted low prices and low tariffs. They hoped to couple the low tariff on raw sugar with a high tariff on the refined product. By keeping a large differential between the tariffs for raw and refined sugar, they hoped to prevent any of the sugar-producing islands from developing their own refining industries. Prominent Republicans, including President William Howard Taft and Senator Nelson Aldrich, supported the bid for low raw sugar tariffs.

Those advocating for high sugar tariffs included mainland cane producers from Louisiana, western sugar beet producers, and cane producers in the new island territories of Hawaii, Puerto Rico, and the Philippines. Territorial producers lacked voting representatives in Congress, but they hired professional lobbyists who worked alongside U.S. colonial administrators in the War Department and Bureau of Insular Affairs to advocate high tariffs. Policymakers who endorsed the United States' new role in the island territories believed that the islands should not only enjoy free trade with the mainland but also benefit from tariffs meant to protect domestic industries. Mainland cane and beet producers, however, asserted that the new island territories should be excluded from the tariff protections offered to domestic industries. Alliances between the island territories and mainland beet and cane growers were thus quite tenuous, as Congress continued to debate whether differences of race and geography ought to exclude the territories from within the U.S. "tariff wall."

The 1909 debate over tariff revision was the first attempt to reconcile the bewildering array of concessions Congress had granted to Cuba, the

Philippines, Puerto Rico, and Hawaii. Since 1900, sugar production had doubled in the territories. Since most of this sugar paid reduced or no tariffs, it added little tariff revenue to federal or territorial coffers. And revenue was a major issue for the framers of the 1909 tariff, who thus faced a difficult proposition. They needed to respond to popular demands for a lower tariff, address lobbyists' demands to protect the "infant" sugar industries, *and* increase government revenue.

Democrats opposed most other high tariffs, arguing that they benefited corporate trusts while raising the price of goods bought by consumers, including farmers and laborers. Francis Newlands's ideas about race and monopoly led him to break with the Democratic stance on sugar tariffs, since the tariff brought together his concerns over immigration, empire, and monopoly. A high sugar tariff would protect his ideological and practical investments in the sugar beet factories that had recently been built on federally reclaimed lands. Together with other members of Congress from sugar-producing states, Newlands protested concessions to the territories, including free-trade for the Philippines. His colleague, Louisiana Democratic senator and sugar planter Murphy J. Foster, argued that "by the importation of free sugar from our colonial dependencies a conflict has been precipitated between the Anglo-Saxon of this country on the one hand and the cooly labor of the Orient and the cheap labor of the Tropics on the other." Foster and Newlands both hoped that a high tariff would limit the Sugar Trust's power.[37]

Ultimately, Congress kept the sugar tariff at virtually the same rates it had been at in 1897 and added tariff concessions for each territory. Despite Newlands's and Foster's protests, Congress granted the Philippines a duty-free allotment of 300,000 sugar tons per year. As a concession to those who would exclude all sugar from the Philippines, language was included in the bill positioning the Philippines outside of the United States and authorizing administrators there to levy export duties on sugar.[38] For Newlands and Foster, these concessions were inadequate, since the American Sugar Refining Company (ASRC) not only profited from duty-free sugar from the islands, but was also making inroads into the beet industry. Over the previous decade, the ASRC began acquiring beet factories, so that it now controlled 54 percent of the beet sugar produced in the United States.[39]

The pressing need for revenue in 1909 had generated a variety of proposals, many of which articulated broad concerns over the nature of not only imperial but also corporate expansionism. Some nativists proposed that a head tax on immigrants could serve as a "tariff" levied on "imported labor" in lieu of higher tariffs on imported goods.[40] As one commentator put it, drawing an explicit analogy between goods and bodies, a higher head tax would "make the cost of producing laborers in other countries and importing them into the United States more nearly equal to what it now costs to rear children for the labor market in the United States."[41] Though unsuccessful, the proposal was broadly consistent with populist anti-imperialists' exclusionary rhetoric. The newly elected president, William Howard Taft, proposed another means for raising revenue, the corporate excise tax. Pointing to the Supreme Court ruling in *Spreckels Sugar Refining Company v. McClain* (1904), Taft argued that Congress had the constitutional authority to impose "an excise tax upon the privilege of doing business."[42] Indeed, the 1909 Tariff Act included a new tax on corporations' net profits.

In proposing the corporate excise tax, Taft aimed to change the terms of debate over whether the federal government could limit corporate monopolies, a debate that had long focused on the sugar industry. Ever since the Supreme Court had ruled, in *U.S. v. E.C. Knight* (1895), that manufacturers did not fall within federal jurisdiction over interstate commerce, most observers had assumed that the federal government had little authority to control monopolies. In that case, which dealt with sugar refiners, the Court asserted that only states had the right to bring legal action against corporations because it was state governments, not the federal government, that chartered corporations. In fact, the federal Sherman Antitrust Act (1890) had been designed to maintain the primacy of state rather than federal legal action against corporations. The problem that Taft and others identified was that corporate mergers and trusts increasingly crossed state lines. After 1894, the ASRC entered into agreements with "practically all of its competitors" across the country to limit production, divide territory, and fix prices. Most states were unable and unwilling to act against the wave of mergers and incorporations in the early 1900s, especially those crossing across state lines. As a result, the *Knight* case and, by extension, the unregulated Sugar Trust became emblems of private corporations usurping state and federal sovereignty for both the popular press and policymakers. In Taft's view, corporate expansion was an abdication of governmental sovereignty that diminished private citizens' property and contractual rights. Seeking to reclaim sovereignty, Taft even proposed that the federal government be authorized to charter interstate corporations, a proposal that met resistance on a number of fronts. The corporation tax in the 1909 tariff was thus a compromise intended to achieve limited control over corporate expansion. Under the Taft administration, the Justice Department pursued actions against the ASRC with renewed vigor, and Congress initiated its own investigation.[43]

The congressional committee investigating the ASRC in 1911 reached conclusions that resembled Newlands's earlier critiques of overseas territories. A corporate monopoly created a state of exception within an otherwise egalitarian body politic, much as the United States exercised sovereignty unevenly in the colonies. Private economic organizations, ones not endowed with the public trust, could discriminate among customers and create a business environment in which all participants were not guaranteed equal opportunity. As one member of Congress put it during the hearings, "Under the sanction of New Jersey," the Sugar Trust "became a sovereignty, almost, in the business world of America."[44] The congressional committee found that the ASRC set prices, restricted free entrance into the businesses of manufacture and distribution, allocated territory among potentially competitive firms, and otherwise limited competition in order to increase its capitalization and the profits for its corporate directors. Congress responded by passing the 1914 Clayton Act to limit corporate sovereignty, by outlawing price discrimination, restricting the right to hold stock in other corporations, and controlling some other of the worst corporate abuses.[45]

Besides sugar tariff concessions to the territories and advances made by the ASRC into the beet industry, Francis Newlands identified other incipient threats to white hegemony. Newlands called for new restrictions to limit what he called immigrants' "monopolies" over labor and land. He was especially concerned about Japanese migration and settlement in the western states. He compared Japanese immigrants and their children to the "land grabbers" and "monopolists" who profited from overseas expansion. Japanese migrants had first established what he called their "monopoly" over labor when they worked for low wages on Hawaiian sugar plantations, which recruited Japanese workers in the 1880s and 1890s. Some Japanese eventually moved from Hawaii to California seeking higher wages and opportunities for independent farming. Japanese workers had labored alongside Mexicans in California's sugar beet fields. They later became labor contractors, and some started their own small farms. Newlands and others believed that the gains made by white civilization needed protection against the zealous ambitions—and the potential land monopoly—of Japanese and other "Mongolian" farmers. This was the problem of overseas expansion in reverse, since Asian farmers and laborers were cutting off white civilization's prospects on its home soil.[46]

Newlands and a broad coalition of westerners lobbied for formal immigration restrictions against Japanese. Diplomats opposed official restrictions because they would damage U.S. credibility in trade and diplomatic relations with China and Japan. Indeed, both nations enacted boycotts in retaliation for immigration restrictions in the first decade of the twentieth century.[47] Though boycotts limited overseas markets for U.S. goods, many people, including Newlands, did not care. As one writer put it, "The 'open door' is a door shut to American labor."[48] In response to continuing pressure, President Theodore Roosevelt negotiated a deal with Japan in 1907, hoping to avoid the embarrassment of U.S.-imposed immigration restrictions. Under the so-called Gentleman's Agreement, Japan voluntarily restricted labor migration so that the United States would not pass immigration laws aimed explicitly at the Japanese.[49]

In California, Nevada, and elsewhere, policymakers reacted angrily to Roosevelt's compromise. In 1909, western legislators reacted by passing alien land laws that restricted land tenure among aliens ineligible for citizenship. As one California lawmaker claimed, the Japanese "literally own or control the majority of the land acreage, and in Fresno county they have an absolute monopoly" in some agricultural industries. Against the advice of President Roosevelt, Newlands publicly supported an alien land law in Nevada. "The United States," Newlands wrote in a widely circulated letter, "as a matter of self protection and self preservation, must declare by statutory enactment that it will not tolerate race complications." He argued, as he had in the case of Cuba earlier in the decade, that policies on immigration, land, and trade were unequivocally domestic matters, and thus integral to a nation's sovereignty. The United States, Newlands insisted, should use its power to aid "the white race in their struggle for race integrity and supremacy." By making a diplomatic agreement about migration, the United States was giving up its sovereignty. Short of federal efforts, he reasoned, states should enact their own laws to limit what they liked to call "race complications." Between 1909 and the 1920s, nine states did so. Much as it was the states' duty to pursue legal action against corporate monopolies, Newlands argued that the states should claim sovereignty in matters of so-called immigrant monopoly.[50]

Four years later, in 1913, Democrats gained control of the presidency and Congress, many of these elected on a low-tariff platform. President

Woodrow Wilson followed contemporary economic theorists by arguing that U.S. industries would achieve greater efficiency through a low-tariff system, which would increase competition.[51] Democrats argued that tariffs as a source of revenue were inherently biased against consumers. The sugar tariff was an especially insidious "consumption tax," since it was levied on what ought to be a cheap, nutritious food for working families.[52] Democrats argued that the government should instead raise revenue through progressive taxation that would simultaneously counter the power of monopolies. Tariffs added money to the coffers of the monopolies; progressive taxes might limit some of those profits. The debate was drawn along party lines, with most Republicans lobbying to retain tariffs and most Democrats advocating other means to raise revenue.

In 1913, the evocatively named but anonymous Junius Aryan intervened in the tariff debate with a pamphlet titled *The Aryans and Mongrelized America: The Remedy*, in which he argued that beet sugar ought to have a high tariff in order to protect the *digestion* of the Aryan race. Aryan wrote, "The beet sugar is better for the Aryan stomach and other digestive organs than the cane sugars of the tropics. . . . The getting and using of cane sugars from the tropics . . . is unnatural, as the acids of the tropical cane sugars are more detrimental to Aryan stomachs . . . than the acids of beet sugars indigenous to the Aryan country."[53] He argued that "the Aryan race would certainly be retarded in its civilization, if the climate and soil in its own North country" were unsuited to beet production. "Aryan statesmen" in Congress should waste no time in passing a high sugar tariff. As the screed suggests, the proposal to eliminate the sugar tariff raised alarms not only among lobbyists for the sugar industries, but also among populist anti-imperialists. As the beet sugar industry grew into a substantial force in U.S. American politics, they drew on racialized rhetoric to buttress their position in contentious tariff debates.

While Aryan's ideas may (or may not) have represented the fringe of popular discourse, his readers included at least one prominent politician: Francis Newlands, who preserved the pamphlet in his papers. Indeed, Newlands made headlines in the spring of 1913 when he broke ranks with Wilson and the Democrats to defend the high sugar tariff. Newlands framed his defense of sugar beet producers as a matter of sectional fairness, since western beet producers paid higher freight rates than did eastern seaboard sellers. The newly emerging western beet industry needed tariff protection as it overcame its geographic barriers to success. Newlands's logic was equally about maintaining racial sovereignty, as is made clear in constituents' supportive letters. For example, one writer penned a poem: "When Hawaii her old independence regains, The Great 'Yellow Peril' will hold the reins. . . . More costly than earthquake, more costly than flood, We shall pay for free sugar—[with] our countryman's blood!"[54] In this view, whites could only defend against alien hordes if there was a sugar tariff.

Newlands also feared for the effect of free sugar on Nevada's single struggling sugar beet factory, which had opened in 1911. The beet factory was in Fallon, Nevada, within the newly completed Truckee Carson irrigation district, the first project completed by the U.S. Reclamation Service. Beginning in 1909, local farmers and businessmen had raised subscriptions and courted capital investors from the Michigan sugar industry to build the factory. The Fallon sugar plant was emblematic of the kind of progress Newlands had long envisioned for the Nevada desert, "the hope of the arid and semi-arid west," as he phrased it. The sugar plant signaled his desire for white settlers to coax productive, modern small farms out of the desert landscape, displacing Native American land and water claims in the process. Indeed, Paiute and Shoshone Indians performed much of the wage labor in the Fallon irrigation district, allowing beet growers to avoid the vilified Mexican, Japanese, and Filipino laborers who worked the crop elsewhere.[55] Despite his protests, Newlands eventually voted for the Underwood-Simmons Tariff bill in 1913 out of loyalty to President Wilson. The bill gradually eliminated the sugar tariff over a period of three years. Worse, it lifted the cap on duty-free sugar imports from the Philippines.[56]

For three years, sugar tariffs were lower, but the war in Europe changed both the Wilson administration's fiscal priorities and the economics of the sugar tariff. As the Wilson administration and Congress debated how best to prepare fiscally for the war, they formed an advisory Tariff Commission. Republican reformers had long hoped to convene a nonpartisan commission to compile statistical information to aid in tariff policymaking, but Democrats had resisted.[57] Finalized just days before the United States entered the war, the Tariff Commission immediately began a study to determine whether the United States should use tariffs or taxes to fund the war-preparedness effort. The Wilson administration advocated a revenue-generating strategy based on progressive taxation, since, it argued, tariffs disproportionately taxed working consumers. The Tariff Commission agreed that taxes were a better choice. But, it noted, the sugar tariff was different. As the date for

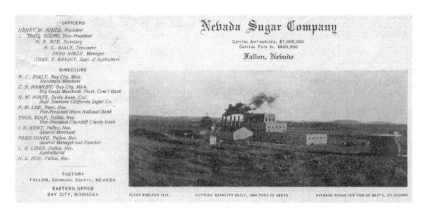

Nevada Sugar Company letterhead, ca. 1913. Newlands Papers,
Manuscripts and Archives, Yale University Library.

enacting the free sugar provisions of the 1913 tariff approached, policy-makers argued that "sugar [is] one of the best of all revenue-producing articles" and could not be sacrificed at this crucial moment. The sugar duty generated approximately $40 million per year in government revenue at the time. Together with prodding from Newlands and other advocates of the sugar tariff, Congress reinstated it.[58] As one commentator later wrote, "The war killed once and for all the old debate on whether sugar should be protected, and free trade in sugar, as planned for by President Wilson, was given a military burial."[59] Indeed, Congress did not again seriously consider eliminating the sugar tariff.

Conclusion

Between 1898 and the 1910s, policymakers across the political spectrum believed that sugar could play a crucial role in the civilizing mission, both on the continent and overseas. The parallel development of the sugar industries on the mainland and the islands was more than a coincidence. Cane and beet production were both understood to be civilized, modern, and efficient uses for irrigated land. Whether they advocated sugar beets or sugarcane, proponents of expansion believed that control over land, water, and labor was the necessary ingredient for civilized economic development. Though the conditions on the ground were different, expansionists on the continent and the islands hoped to make landscapes that privileged white over nonwhite and cash over subsistence economies.

Congress and the courts legally separated the islands and Indian reservations from the mainland by positing them as constitutionally neither foreign nor domestic. They created places that—by definition—could be administered in isolation from one another. Differences in how each place was treated under the law were the outcome of U.S. policymakers' disagreements over the project of empire. But the differences were also exactly what made this an imperial project. Within the U.S. American political context, codifying an economically differentiated geography was inherently imperial.

The outcome of U.S. expansionism in the early twentieth century was a cultural politics of sugar inextricably tied to notions of race and nation. The United States ultimately offered its territories reductions on the sugar tariff that, together with land, irrigation, and immigration policies, created landscapes uniquely suited to producing sugar. In a direct way, U.S. imperial policy created a chronic condition of sugar surplus because tariff protection encouraged intensive sugar production across the U.S. sugar empire. Thus began a cycle of increased production, declining prices, and greater sugar consumption. Eaters in the United States would have a big job to do if they were to make their way through the ever-growing quantities of sugar on the market.

CHAPTER TWO

SPECTACLES OF SWEETNESS

Race, Civics, and the Material Culture of Eating
Sugar after the Turn of the Century

"When sugar is first crystallized it is brown," wrote the then-renowned U.S. racial theorist Ellsworth Huntington in his geography textbook. He continued, "In this form it is sent to American coast cities, Boston, New York, Philadelphia, Baltimore, New Orleans, San Francisco, where it is refined not only to tickle our palates, but to please our eyes by its white-ness."[1] On the surface, Huntington was describing the color of sugar crystals, but his point hinted at the political and racial conflicts that resulted from overseas expansion. As the twentieth century progressed, many people in the United States understood that while sugar might appear pleasingly white in seaboard cities, it linked them to global racial impurities that were best excluded, segregated, or cleansed. In the years after Hawaii, Puerto Rico, Cuba, and the Philippines received tariff preferences, sugar consumption increased steadily, and the meanings attached to sweets shifted to accommodate these new geographies of supply. People did not just naturally eat more sugar; consumption increased in ways that required them to grapple with the political status of residents of the island territories, immigrants, and African Americans. The same civilizing mission that motivated policymakers to promote sugar production in the arid West and in the island territories was simultaneously articulated by reformers, journalists, artists, and others who weighed in on what it meant to eat sugar. Observers calculated whether people were civilized and capable of the responsibilities of citizenship in part by describing their racially coded practices of eating sugar. In turn, people contested their subordinate positions within the gender and racial hierarchies of empire through their choices about sugar.

For middle-class people in the United States after 1898, to eat refined white sugar was also to internalize a colonial and racial division of labor. New investments in the island territories reorganized the industry, which shifted to the centrifugal process for converting cane to raw sugar. High-quality raw sugar was then shipped in sacks to the United

55

"Native Sugar Mill," Detroit Photographic Co., ca. 1900. Courtesy of the Beinecke Rare Book and Manuscript Library, Yale University.

States, where it was refined for consumers there. Sugar refiners enjoyed high tariffs on refined sugar, so that there would be little risk that the territories would develop their own refining industries. Tariffs on refined sugar protected capital investments but also maintained the racial hierarchy encoded through the contrast between civilized and uncivilized, technology and nature, refined and raw, white and brown. People of color produced raw cane sugar in the tropics, closer to nature. White men refined sugar on the mainland where they could expunge the hidden risks of the tropics. Powerful U.S. corporations literally whitened sugar through an industrial process controlled by white technologists. Gleaming white crystals would eventually be served in sugar bowls, complete with silver tongs and spoons as part of refined table settings. The ensemble of material goods—white sugar, sugar bowls, silver spoons, and tongs—together with rules for proper use of those items, signified that the eater was fully civilized.

By contrast, African Americans and residents of the island territories were commonly associated with less-refined forms of sweetness. Middle-class eaters imagined that all but the most barbaric races liked the taste of sweetness, but they assumed that their preferred forms of sugar reflected their place in the hierarchy of civilizations. Rather than using sugar tongs, less-refined people chewed directly on sugarcane or ate unrefined molasses. Images showing African American and Afro-Caribbean children chewing sugarcane circulated widely in U.S. popular culture from the turn of the century forward.[2] Publishers reproduced these images commercially as postcards, stereoscopic views, book and magazine illustrations, and advertisements. The visual trope of black children eating sugarcane was so common that tourists to the tropics re-created such scenes in their snapshots. Typical captions—such as "native cane grinders" or "pickaninnies candy shop"—mocked the primitive scene while assuring observers that the desire for sweetness was universal and natural.[3] In his junior high geography text, Ellsworth Huntington evoked the image, writing, "Happy are the boys and girls who live on a sugarcane plantation! Nature's stick of candy, a piece of sugarcane, can be had at any time for the cutting. . . . Boys and girls who would enjoy this happy experience must betake themselves to warm regions." Huntington simultaneously extolled the pleasures of the tropics while also commanding that children who preferred such treats—implicitly black and brown children—"must betake themselves to warm regions." Known for his racial determinism, Huntington argued that the natural

"Sugar Cane," ca. 1904. Ulrich B. Phillips Collection, Manuscripts
and Archives, Yale University Library.

fecundity of the tropical landscape was closely linked with the racial characteristics of people who lived there. Tropical people were lazy, he reasoned, because they did not have to work hard to get their "stick of candy."
Nature provided it for them. By contrast, Huntington assured his young
readers that they could get more-civilized pleasures closer to home. Such
images placed black consumption in distant landscapes, remote from the
purity of white, granulated sugar, refined civilization, and table manners.
Huntington's logic suggested that the limits of nationhood and civilization were negotiated through goods which passed across U.S. borders,
and the firmness of these boundaries could be measured by the types of
sweets children preferred. Primitive people ate primitive forms of sweetness. Civilized people ate refined sugar and candy. Sugar consumption
thus naturalized the racial hierarchies of civilization that underwrote
both overseas empire and Jim Crow segregation.[4]

Images of children chewing on cane hint at another, liberal impulse
within U.S. expansionist rhetoric that blunted Huntington's crude
racial determinism. Progressive reformers and colonial administrators
assumed that if uncivilized people enjoyed eating cane, their preferences could evolve toward more civilized, refined sweets. They could be

tutored to eat candy. Perhaps, they reasoned, it was not an intrinsic characteristic of the tropical landscape but rather that the so-called barbaric races had not been taught the manners and material culture of refined consumption. Sugar could facilitate the integration of diverse consumers into an emerging regime of imperial capitalism. Images of young people chewing on cane thus held Huntington's determinism and colonial administrators' expansionist liberalism in tension.

Tasting sweetness was one way that people in the United States internalized the "civilizing mission" of overseas empire after 1898, but in doing so they also asserted their own claims to civic participation. Women claimed political virtue through their control of the sugar bowl. Building on their expertise in the dining room, they claimed a role in the civilizing mission by inculcating refined sugar habits through Americanization aimed at immigrants. Social reformers used ideas about sugar and sweetness to delineate who was worthy of political rights. Soldiers who served in the Spanish American and Philippines American Wars expressed intense cravings for sugar, cravings that brought new debates about the gendered meanings of imperial sugar consumption. Turn-of-the-century racial theorists, many of them building on their military experiences in 1898, argued that sugar was crucial to the advance of white civilization. Finally, African American and Asian American writers responded to widely circulated images of black children eating sugarcane in imaginative ways that expressed their desires not just for sweetness but also for the full rights of citizenship.

Refining Sugar Eaters: Sweetening to Taste and Embodied Civic Uplift

In a short story in *Harper's New Monthly Magazine* in 1899, Brander Matthews portrayed a widow entertaining a Navy officer in her parlor.[5] The Navy officer, working up the courage to propose marriage, tells his hostess about his confusion at reentering civilian life. The hostess is attentive to her guest's desires and is thoroughly in control of herself and her servant. The widow demonstrates her refined manners through the ritual of pouring and serving the tea, and by competently managing her maid, Jemima (whose name codes her as black). Though she is reconciled to marrying him, the widow muses that "she would bitterly regret having to give up her liberty, having to surrender the control of herself. 'You don't take sugar, I remember,' she said, as she poured out his cup of tea." It is no accident that her ruminations on the bonds of marriage are immediately followed by her memory of his sugar preferences. For one thing, her accurate recollection of this detail demonstrates her suitability as a wife. As well, the juxtaposition suggests that she understands marriage as a surrender of control to a polite form of social bondage, much like eating at a middle-class table required submission to rules and rituals. One could choose whether and how much to sweeten one's tea, but only within tightly prescribed limits (one lump or two?). As the widow well understands, the choice of how much sugar to take was one small moment in which civilized people could briefly taste liberty. As segregation, overseas expansion, and immigration seemed to undermine the democratic politics of individualism, authors of popular literature codified etiquette for serving and eating sugar. Because it hinged on a coordinated performance that could be learned, eating sugar highlighted the egalitarian promise of democratic consumer culture for middle-class Americans. Such literature placed the expression of contrasting political virtues—self-control and individualism—in the domestic sphere.[6] For women who were fighting for rights in public at the voting booth, the opportunity to exercise these virtues at the dining table was crucial.

By the end of the nineteenth century, many formerly exotic and expensive foods, including refined white sugar, were widely available to middle-class households.[7] Sugar consumption had already begun to increase after the 1876 Hawaiian Reciprocity Treaty and the expansion of the continental beet sugar industry in the 1890s, so by the time of the Spanish American War many of the meanings associated with sugar consumption were in place. These practices intensified after 1900. Families created new occasions to eat sweets and bought new household goods with which to serve them. Food, china, and tableware were centerpieces of social entertainment among the growing middle class, which could now afford to dine in a style that emulated that of elites. Elaborate, refined china and silverware were the stuff of wedding gifts and inheritances, goods that marked one's genealogy and social connections. To have the family silver was to have material evidence of one's pedigree. Yet with innovations in mass production, high-quality silver and china were also readily available for the newly affluent to purchase new at reasonable cost. Silverware had been a luxury for elites a century earlier, but by the late nineteenth century manufacturers were mass-producing visually intricate china and silver in a variety of patterns. For new middle-class consumers, decorative tableware could amplify the sweet taste of refined sugar, which had less of the distinctive molasses flavor of brown sugars.

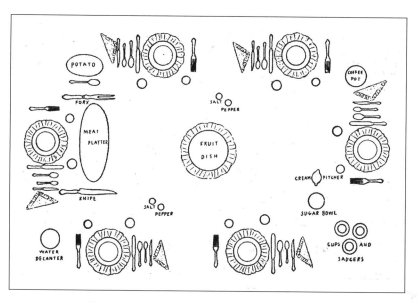

"Correct Arrangement of Table for a Family Breakfast,"
Good Housekeeping 35, no. 6 (1902).

A precisely laid table was built on a shared set of standards and codes for behavior, in which middle-class families trained their servants and children. They sought a balance between modesty and self-display in their material possessions and manners, and they idealized the display of "refinement" at the table. People with refinement were attentive to the details of social interactions, showed self-restraint, and were knowledgeable about how to use the proliferation of new material goods placed on the table.[8] In order to stage their elaborate rituals of refinement, housewives around the turn of the century sought instruction from a burgeoning genre of household advice and etiquette manuals, which counseled them on topics such as where to place the sugar bowl and tongs, how to serve brown sugar to accompany the breakfast oatmeal, and how to decorate with sugar. The dining table was a nexus at which experiences of tasting, possessing, and behaving fused into an embodied experience of class status.

In contrast to the middle classes, working-class and rural people ate less-refined sweets from less-refined tableware. Nannie Pharis, a white woman who worked in a rural North Carolina cotton mill beginning in 1901 at age nine, recalled that her family's "plates would be kind of heavy, made out of earthen ware."[9] Her family bought sugar mainly at fruit-preserving time and otherwise ate homemade sorghum molasses. Pharis rarely ate refined sweets, except when her parents allowed her to keep a few cents of her biweekly earnings to buy peppermint sticks. Pharis's experiences of sweetness and their disconnection from the material culture and manners of the refined table marked her subordinate position in the South's class hierarchy. After she married, though, Pharis continued to work in the mill and, with two incomes, could afford to hire a black woman for $3 per week to cook and clean. Having the wherewithal to hire domestic help distinguished Pharis from her peers. Her family could advance its class status by hiring help because black women were rarely hired for higher-paying mill jobs, which were racially segregated.[10] In a social hierarchy and labor regime in which Pharis was at an overall disadvantage, her racial superiority gave her a few advantages. Pharis recalled that the cook often prepared special pies and cakes, presumably with refined sugar. In this way, sweets prepared by an African American cook can be read as part of the wages of Pharis's whiteness.[11]

Nannie Pharis was not alone in hiring other women to prepare and serve food in her home. Domestic help was especially desirable for urban middle-class families struggling to showcase their refined habits.[12] Middle-class women hoped to remain experts in cooking and presentation but wanted other women to take care of the minutiae of day-to-day preparation and serving. In the South, white and black middle-class women could hire black cooks for relatively low pay. In other parts of the country where better employment opportunities were available, working-class women were less willing to work in other women's kitchens. As a result, urban middle-class women increasingly lamented the scarcity of servants who had internalized the rules of food preparation, etiquette, and table service.

Publishers responded to middle-class women's concerns with a proliferation of advice manuals aimed at both hostesses and their apparently underqualified servants. Though they cannot be read as evidence of how people actually behaved, etiquette manuals' codification of behavioral standards show how people defined a social hierarchy and placed themselves within it. As historian John Kasson argues, "If each individual was to be masterless, it was all the more essential that he be master of himself."[13] Etiquette books taught people to be masterless at the sugar bowl. Refined people simultaneously exercised restraint and choice in their sugar consumption. In short, the control over the self at table—refined sugar eaten with refined manners—demonstrated that an individual was capable of fulfilling the obligations of a free citizen in a democracy. At the same time, etiquette manuals presumed that hostesses and servers were new to the rules of decorum, since they had to rely on a book for advice. That such virtues could be learned from a book highlighted the democracy of class in the United States. For women seeking the right to vote, or men and women hoping to overcome racial prejudice, refinement at table could thus be one way to perform civic virtue in quotidian social encounters.

Typical of these manuals was Anne Frances Springsteed's manual for waitresses, whose charts enumerated objects and their arrangement for each stage of a meal. Table service was carefully orchestrated, with the silver, china, and sugar serving as essential props. Advice manuals implored that the procedures for each stage of a meal and each type of social occasion become rote for guests, hosts, and waiters. The stage directions were precise and left no doubt that if the performance was lacking, the sensory experience would be as well. For example, Springsteed instructed waiters and waitresses that "when the coffee is poured, place a cup at the right of each person. Offer sugar and cream at the left." The sugar bowl should always be put in front of the mistress of the house.

Etiquette manuals from the turn of the century consistently suggested that, while much about a meal was out of individual guests' control, when sugar was offered their preferences were of utmost concern. Tea and coffee ought to be sweetened "according to the preference of the person served," "to suit the taste of the guest," or "as the tea drinkers prefer." In addition, etiquette manuals instructed hostesses to pass the sugar so that guests could adjust to taste. After giving a guest her tea, "a teaspoon is placed upon the saucer beside the cup of tea. Two or three silver trays should be upon the table, each containing sugar, sugar-tongs, cream, and a dish with silver inset containing slices of lemon." "These little matters are necessary," wrote one author, "because upon them depends the perfection of his cup of tea or coffee." The same logic held at other times when sugar was offered. For example, one guide instructed that when serving hot cereals, many people preferred brown sugar, which should be offered by the waitress or passed among guests. Fresh fruit should be served with sugar. Toast or hot cakes ought to be served with both syrup and a dish of pulverized sugar mixed with cinnamon. But etiquette manuals also cautioned against oversweetening. While guests were often encouraged to sweeten to taste, people who took too many lumps or scooped too much sugar on their oats appeared as unrestrained and low class. Nonetheless, within the confines of prescribed etiquette, sugar allowed people, especially women, to enact the roles of both an individuated self and a socially attentive host.[14]

Middle-class African American women writers, like white ones, claimed respectability through civilized habits at the tea table. African American missionaries in Africa, for example, celebrated their success by pointing out that the "negroes of German east Africa . . . now use plates, cups, glasses and saucers. . . . In their market places they are seen drinking tea with sugar at table."[15] The adoption of proper material culture, manners, and taste preferences converged in such routines. For middle-class African American authors, refined manners signified their aspirations for social and political inclusion at a time when segregation and discrimination systematically limited such opportunities. In her novel *Contending Forces: A Romance Illustrative of Negro Life North and South* (1900), African American author Pauline E. Hopkins showed multiple generations of women navigating the painful legacies of slavery, emancipation, and the Jim Crow era. The novel opens in Bermuda as Charles Montfort considers how to emancipate the slaves who work his sugar plantation. He moves his family to North Carolina in the hope of retaining control over his slaves temporarily, but he discovers that his new neighbors disapprove of his intention to eventually free them. The neighbors murder Montfort, pillage his house, and attempt to enslave his wife and children, whom they suspect of being mixed race. The children escape north where they live in the free black community. The remainder of the novel tracks the fortunes of Montfort's descendants, ending with a portrayal of respectable, upwardly mobile African Americans in turn-of-the-century Boston.

For the African American women in *Contending Forces*, racial uplift depended on the careful production of civility in dress, comportment, material culture, and eating habits. Hopkins details her characters' elaborate rituals of domesticity and propriety in their boardinghouse, where people gather to discuss global social reform politics. The upwardly mobile young people in turn-of-the-century Boston set impeccable tea tables over which they debate political and social reforms. A young man courting his sweetheart brings her a box of bonbons, which she eats despite worrying they will make her fat. Ice cream and cakes are key attractions at fund-raising fairs hosted by churchwomen. As she prepares ice cream for a special guest, the boardinghouse keeper Mrs. Smith announces, "Good things to eat make a man respect himself and look up in the world. You can't feel that you are nobody all the time if once in a while you eat the same quality of food that a millionaire does."[16] For Hopkins, sweet treats are emblems of aspiration and a source of genuine pleasure and sociality. Yet the novel ultimately questions whether ice cream, bonbons, cakes, and white sugar bring durable civic uplift. Hopkins concludes the novel in Bermuda, where Montfort's descendants have rediscovered the family's long-lost history of racial violence and race mixing. They find the last surviving witness to the crimes against their family, a former slave who had returned from North Carolina after the Civil War. She made her living by "selling sugar-cane in small sticks—the same as our candy-shops sell sticks of candy to the children."[17] In Hopkins's rendition, this business is "humble" yet dignified and "the same as" civilized sweets. Her diction contrasts with Ellsworth Huntington's implicit ranking of candy above cane. In this way, Hopkins gently questions the racial hierarchy of sweetness.

As people in the United States debated segregation and overseas expansion in 1898 and after, they hoped that inhabitants of the newly acquired islands would learn to love refined sweets along with other American goods. For U.S. observers in the islands, the taste for refined sweets and candy indexed whether a group was civilizable. Did people desire civilized sweets? And if so, could they show the kind of self-restraint that was required for civilized citizens? Many observers believed that refined manners could be learned and material goods could be purchased, thus making it possible to civilize the uncivilized. In this sense, the sugar bowl held tremendous democratic promise as a means to incorporate diverse consumers within the U.S. body politic. Not only could the territories produce white sugar for the benefit of the home sugar bowls, but colonial subjects could also internalize a modern, market-oriented, and democratic ideology as they learned to eat sugar properly. Soldiers occupying Puerto Rico, Cuba, and the Philippines made this logic explicit when they offered candy to local children. But they also expressed confusion or suspicion when the children disliked the candy or preferred to earn money by selling it.[18] Ethnologist Albert Ernest Jenks reported that the Bontoc Igorots in the Philippines did not like the taste of sweetness, noting that "the Igorot cares very little for sweets; even the children frequently throw away candy after tasting it."[19] Though they did produce low-grade cane sugar, Jenks assumed that most of it would be fermented into *basi*, an alcoholic drink. Building on such observations, U.S. colonial administrators agreed that the Bontoc Igorots were likely uncivilizable. When they could not inculcate civilized desires for candy, U.S. administrators hoped at least to tame barbaric ones, such as those for basi.

Since women were in charge of the sugar bowl and mistresses of the etiquette surrounding it, they were in a unique position to assess the racial hierarchies of empire. They carried this sensibility with them into the social and political reform work they undertook during the Progressive era, including suffrage, food safety, labor reform, and especially Americanization of immigrants. As one strategy in the Americanization process, reformers and educators often encouraged immigrants to adopt U.S. foodways, including greater consumption of refined sugar.[20] English language primers and nutritional guides written by Progressive reformers for the growing population of immigrant schoolchildren all included sugar and candy in their lessons. Assuming that children would naturally be motivated by sweets, for example, one author proposed that teachers present sugar in their lessons. By tasting sugar first, he suggested, children would develop a "new and lasting interest" in geography if they then traced sugar's path from the place it was produced to their own "childish palate."[21] Likewise, in *A First Book for Non-English-Speaking People* (1904), Walter Leo Harrington included a lesson that began, "Do you like candy? Candy is sweet. Sugar is sweet." The lesson advanced to phrases like "He likes his coffee sweet" and "Which is the sweetest, bread, cake, or sugar?"[22] The book thus offered tutelage not only in English language literacy, but also in the desires of middle-class life. Likewise, Edward Lear's "Nonsense Alphabet" was a staple in elementary readers for both native-born and immigrant children during this period.

> S was the sugar-tongs,
> Nippity-nee,
> To take up the sugar
> To put in our tea.

That Lear's verse was so widely reprinted indicates that educators assumed that immigrant and working-class children should be familiar with sugar and the tongs used to serve it. Reading lessons for recent immigrants thus offered sugar and candy as some of the most elementary building blocks of Americanization, uniquely suited to children.

Middle-class social reformers in the Progressive era nonetheless found myriad faults with working-class immigrant children's candy habits even as they expected them to have a taste for sweetness. As historian Wendy Woloson has demonstrated, reformers worried about unsafe additives in cheap candies, and they did not approve of children spending too much money on sweets.[23] As well, they worried that candy was a gateway to cigarette smoking since it was often sold in the same shops as tobacco. But overall, the key issue for reformers was self-restraint. Reformers assumed children would spend pennies on candy because "the urge of the stick of candy is so much more powerful than the abstract moral urge" to save money.[24] Overcoming the urge for candy was one way for children and adults to internalize respectable morality and self-control, to be masters of themselves. One primer on language and citizenship for adult immigrants reminded readers that "some people go without candy, ice cream, and other good things to save money."[25] Their hope was that natural childish urges would be replaced in mature consumers by a more refined calculation about future rewards. The desire to eat candy marked a person as civilizable, while the ability to defer that gratification indexed that person's Americanization and social improvement.

Assumptions like these resonated with child psychologist G. Stanley Hall's theories of child development and race, then current. Hall argued that white children recapitulated the development of the entire race in the course of their growth, eventually evolving from little brutes into civilized, self-controlled adults. According to Hall, a brief early period of savagery was critical (especially for boys) if children were to develop healthy adult identities. Craving candy was not only natural for children at this stage, Hall said, but crucial, as they would only mature if they had given themselves over to base, pleasure-seeking urges as youngsters. He reported that children frequently mentioned candy, ice cream, cake, and sugar when describing their inner fantasy lives, and these items also appeared regularly in their play.[26] According to Hall, less-civilized races had halted in their development at the adolescent stage. It was commonly believed that white youth were at the same developmental stage of supposedly less-civilized groups. Thus the same moral lessons about self-control that were appropriate for white children could civilize the appetites of immigrants and residents of the tropics.

Eating refined white sugar at the right time and place and with the correct utensils was an embodied aspect of a particular Progressive-era political subjectivity, one that valued both individualism and cohesive social organization. Middle-class people in the United States were quick to compare their own civilized sugar consumption habits with the less-refined practices of the supposedly primitive races in the newly acquired territories and immigrants in the nation's growing cities. Americanization projects were simultaneously moral and material processes of inculcating manners, tastes, and political will through new consumption habits.

At the same time that middle-class women in the United States were civilizing their tea tables with sugar, soldiers overseas were on a militarizing mission that in the long run guaranteed that those bowls would be full of cheap sugar. Soldiers who were implementing the project of empire were also sugar consumers—voracious ones, it would seem—and they were increasingly dependent on sugar as a source of sustenance and pleasure. As one military surgeon put it, "When soldiers are exhausted they crave sugar in the same way as underfed women."[27] Beginning with the Spanish American and Philippines American Wars, commanders repeatedly requested that the sugar ration for soldiers be increased.[28] As an officer in the Commissary Department wrote in an 1899 letter, the sugar ration ought to be increased "because of the craving for sweets, to which it appears all persons living in a tropical climate are subject."[29] By claiming sugar as a necessity in the tropics, demands like these focused attention on men's bodies as a site for internalizing empire. The tropical climate justified soldiers' increased consumption of sweets, a taste otherwise deemed overly feminine or evidence of a primitive lack of self-control. Just as was the case for women at the tea table, soldiers balanced their submission to a hierarchically organized collectivity partly through the pleasure of sweetness. Yet soldiers dispensed with refined table etiquette, instead subsisting on rations outside the control of women and their domesticating rituals. While officers observed the rules of decorum when not in the field, a fact that marked their class status as above that of the crew, soldiers moderated their consumption not according to ideals of propriety but instead through the chain of command and the rigors of hunger.

When the United States first sent troops to Cuba, Puerto Rico, and the Philippines in 1898, medical officers debated the proper diet for white men in the tropics. To permanently station white men in the tropics seemed a breach of the laws of nature. Initially, some doctors advised that soldiers should "live on a diet closely approximating that of the natives of the tropics," which they assumed would be suited to the climate.[30] This idea was quickly rejected as unpalatable and overly starchy, but the debate over diet continued as the U.S. military fought a protracted battle to subdue anticolonial guerrillas in the Philippines from 1899 to 1902. Despite other differences, all observers agreed that soldiers needed more sugar, based largely on their bottomless desire for it.[31] The British in Burma and

USS *Massachusetts*, Junior Officers' Mess, ca. 1898. Detroit Photographic Co., Library of Congress, Prints and Photographs Division.

South Africa, the French in Algeria, and the Americans in the Philippines had each reached the same conclusion: the sugar ration for troops serving in the tropics must be increased.[32] Standard rations were categorized by location, activity, and soldier's race. North American soldiers serving in the tropics were allotted 3.5 ounces per day of sugar, while Filipino Scouts were given only 1 ounce per day. These rations were increased in the early 1900s, and soldiers got a variety of other sweets. The Chief Commissary in Manila reported that troops consumed 4.6 million pounds of sugar in 1902, a figure which does not include candy or other sweetened products. While troops were garrisoned, much of this sugar was handled by the cook. But when in the field, soldiers received granulated or cubed sugar "chiefly to be used with the coffee (or tea), although the man may eat it at pleasure."[33] Some soldiers placed a sugar cube "between the teeth and [allowed it] to dissolve."[34] Consuming sugar could simultaneously remind soldiers of the comforts of home and mark their civilized status on the battleground of the Philippines. As one observer pointed out, "The state deprives the soldier of his liberty, prescribes his exercises, equipment, dress, and diet," making the consumption of sweetness in various forms—condensed milk, jam, sugar, candy, or molasses—one of the few privileges and pleasures of soldiering in the tropics.[35]

Army surgeon Charles Edward Woodruff was among those who asserted that sugar was essential for the armies deployed to colonize the

USS *Massachusetts*, crew at mess, ca. 1898. Detroit Photographic Co.,
Library of Congress, Prints and Photographs Division.

tropics. He had served as a surgeon in the U.S. Army during the war, an experience that convinced him whites were prone to neurasthenia and degeneration in the tropics. He himself had to return from the Philippines after suffering from nervous exhaustion. After his return, he elaborated his theories in a pseudoscientific treatise on racial difference, diet, and empire. Woodruff's assessment of refined sugar habits in *Expansion of Races* (1909) lined up closely with the theories of refinement articulated in domestic advice manuals and in public debates over sugar policy. Woodruff described the evolution of white men's digestion from the supposed ancestral capacity to digest cellulose to the dependence on cooked starches, which are easier to digest. Natural selection, he wrote, had favored "the men who resorted to cooking exclusively, and there was through involution a still further reduction of our powers of digestion, and we are now weaklings dependent upon cooked starches." While the barbaric natives might be able to subsist on the cellulose in raw sugarcane, white men were unable to digest such foods. Woodruff reassured readers that "he who eats a little sugar is at a decided advantage, for he lessens the burden of digestion and can survive with less food and weaker digestion." According to Woodruff, then, sugar justified empire because of "the increasing dependence of Northern races upon the foods

" Science justifies
action not racists impulse?

produced by tropical peoples." Since tropical people were incapable of self-government, Woodruff reasoned that U.S. control was urgent, otherwise they might "relapse, as Hayti did, and we will suffer for this necessity [of sugar]. Anti-imperialism is, therefore, race suicide." Sugar was both the means to and the justification for the white man's burden. Though the white race was constitutionally unsuited to living in the tropics, whites needed to rule tropical regions in order to guarantee an adequate supply of sugar for their (over)civilized digestions.[36]

For theorists like Woodruff, sugar held out the hope that white men could dominate, rather than degenerate in, the tropics. It is worth noting, though, that opponents of imperial expansion made assessments about the digestibility of sugar that directly contradicted Woodruff's claims. Just a few years after Woodruff wrote, Junius Aryan argued that cane sugar was "unnatural as the acids of the tropical cane sugars are more detrimental to Aryan stomachs . . . than the acids of beet sugars indigenous to the Aryan country."[37] Aryan proposed tariffs to exclude all tropical sugar from the U.S. market in order to maintain white racial hegemony and digestive integrity. What is significant here is that both men articulated their discomfort with the racial complications of empire by considering the internal, cloacal reception of sugar. Racial impurities could not be safely kept outside the body but instead infiltrated the most intimate realms. Imperial bodies were thus constituted through the process of digesting sugar.

Men and women who visited the Philippines regularly reported that they saw locals chewing on sugarcane, and a few even tried it themselves. Women who visited the Philippines as military wives, missionaries, tourists, or teachers reported that they themselves had chewed sugarcane far more often than did men. For them, eating sugarcane was part of the exotic landscape, a new visual and taste experience. In her memoir of her experiences teaching in the Philippines, for example, Mary Helen Fee described an occasion when she was invited to a wedding in a distant rural area. On the way there, she and her companions bought a supply of sugarcane "and chewed affably all the rest of the way." For Fee, chewing cane was an emblem of having temporarily set aside her inhibitions during her "weird and incongruous" adventure. Her adventure was safely contained but nonetheless critical to how she explained the freedom she experienced as a single woman living in the Philippines. For her, the cost of living was low, the opportunity for adventure was high, and thus "provincial life here is a boon."[38] Such adventures were far better than the boring lives of married women, restrained by propriety. Emily Bronson Conger, a widow who toured the islands out of missionary curiosity, similarly described chewing cane, but for a different reason. She wrote that the sugar in the markets "seemed reasonably clean to look at," but after she saw where it was produced, she decided that it "was anything but clean." She would thus "buy the cane in the markets, peel off the outside and chew the pith to get the sweet juice."[39] She chewed cane because she worried that her body was vulnerable to impurities and hidden filth. Both women experienced freedom and independence by traveling in the Philippines, and in each case eating cane was a safely contained experience of "going native" that left their standards of civilization intact.

Raw Sugar Has More Protection To-day Than All the Negroes in the Country

In his autobiography, *Fact Stranger Than Fiction* (1920), African American politician John P. Green recalled an incident from his high school days in the late 1860s in which an employer denied him the privilege of eating white sugar. Green worked for room and board waiting tables in the train depot, and he reasoned that "since I received my board only for all this work, I ought to be allowed to sweeten my cup of coffee with white, granulated sugar." Instead, he recalled, the head waiter "forbade me to use it, restricting me to some very dark-brown sugar."[40] That Green would recall the insult of being denied white, granulated sugar after nearly fifty years speaks to the signifying power of sugar in the late nineteenth and early twentieth centuries. The color and texture of the sugar they ate was one way that people of diverse backgrounds declared their status and their aspirations, as well as their difference from those seen as less refined. But the episode also speaks to how African American politicians and writers drew on the metaphors of sugar and sweetness to challenge the increasingly rigid racial hierarchy at the turn of the century. Sugar was much more than sweetness for Green and many of his contemporaries. Sugar and sweetness were contested markers of the color line, enacted every day at the sugar bowl.

Green may have remembered the incident because other events had reminded him how closely African Americans' political status was tied to the politics of sugar. Nearly twenty years before writing his autobiography, Green had railed against the Republican Party's tendency to bow to sugar interests rather than support African American rights in the

South. Through the last decades of the nineteenth century, Republican obeisance to businesses and southerners had become increasingly clear. An incident in 1902 heightened African Americans' perceptions that their political fates were tied to sugar. As discussed in Chapter 1, during the spring of 1902 Congress debated a reciprocal trade treaty with Cuba. At the very same time, it was also considering whether to address voting discrimination against African Americans in the constitutions passed over the previous several years in North and South Carolina, Louisiana, Alabama, and Mississippi. Given the resulting large-scale disenfranchisement, some Republicans in Congress argued that southern Democrats were overrepresented: their allocation of seats in the House was based on white and black population even though blacks were legally disenfranchised. In 1901, Republicans proposed to reapportion congressional seats in line with the new, white-only voting laws. Representative Edgar Crumpacker (R-Indiana) and a few others argued in 1902 that southern states' representation in the House ought to be reduced "proportionate to the abridgement of the franchise" in the new state constitutions.[41] Democrats protested any attempts to address "the race problem," and ultimately few on either side of the aisle were willing to challenge the South on the issue. Though some African American editorialists questioned whether the resolution went far enough, many were glad that Republicans had even raised the issue. Most observers agreed that the proposal was unlikely to pass.

In late April 1902, newspapers reported that the resolution had been killed behind the scenes. Apparently Republicans had offered to squelch the Crumpacker resolution if southern Democrats would follow their lead in the Cuban reciprocity bill's sugar provisions.[42] Given the strident partisan divergences over sugar tariffs, this would have been a major concession. Southern Democrats did indeed vote with the Republican leadership on a few procedural matters, but decidedly not on the substantive questions about sugar tariffs. To the contrary: southern Democrats voted en masse against House Republicans on a controversial amendment related to the refined sugar tariff. Republican leadership killed the Crumpacker amendment in exchange for a relatively minor procedural vote, knowing well that they would never get southern Democratic support for their sugar proposals. In doing so, they showed how few members of Congress were willing to press the issue of African American rights in 1902. Indeed, Republicans would likely have found a way to sidestep the issue one way or another.

The African American press immediately decried white man's sugar triumphing over black men's rights. Republicans had demonstrated to African Americans that, like residents of the island territories, their rights were subject to a different, and subordinate, legal regime. As John P. Green described the failure of the Crumpacker amendment, "Once more the Negro had been auctioned off, and though the lyncher and disfranchiser plied their deadly trade, not a Republican voice in Congress was lifted up in defense of human rights."[43] Another commentator in the *Colored American* quipped, "Raw sugar has more protection to-day than all the Negroes in the country."[44] An anonymous editorialist wrote a tongue-in-cheek article claiming that members of Congress had foregone all political principals in obeisance to King Sugar, whose "Saccharine Majesty must prevail. . . . O! Sugar, what crimes are committed in thy name!"[45] Some commentators went so far as to question whether white sugar was indeed superior. A correspondent for the *Washington Bee* noted, for example, that "in England brown sugar is considered the only respectable sugar to serve with coffee. Cut loaf sugar is used with tea, while the American granulated is found only in the cheaper eating houses."[46] While African American activists generally accepted the ideals of respectability articulated at the tea table, they nonetheless recognized that the meanings of sugar consumption could be contested.

Pickaninnies' Candy Store

Sugar was a key emblem in negotiations over citizenship in the context of Jim Crow segregation, overseas expansion, and immigration exclusion. The significance of sweetness often hinged on racialized depictions of children, who were widely understood to be miniature encapsulations of civilization. White children were imagined to be the natural and voracious consumers of candy, while less-civilized children gravitated toward the less-refined sweets available to them in the fields. African American children were not only depicted chewing raw sugarcane; they were sometimes shown as objects of edible consumption such as chocolate or molasses candies.[47] Much as black editorialists had lambasted congressional sugar politics, African American writers and musicians responded to these popular stereotypes through their literary and musical productions. African Americans produced a counterhegemonic discourse that challenged the relationships among childhood, sweetness, and racial hierarchy.

Paul Laurence Dunbar's poem "Little Brown Baby," first published in 1899, describes an exchange between a father and his molasses-covered child.[48] The father playfully addresses his molasses-covered child in dialect, warning, "Bees gwine to ketch you an' eat you up yit, Bein' so sticky an' sweet." Later, the father jokingly invites the Boogeyman to come and eat the child. Violence against black bodies is cast specifically as the threat of being eaten and is linked to the child's own consumption of molasses. The child's skin, brown from the sweet, sticky molasses, implicitly teases and tempts the boogey of white desire and danger. Yet, in the next stanza, the father demands that the Boogeyman leave, denying him the right to eat the child. Dunbar rejects the notion that black children could be either eaten or made to work, because in the end the child safely consumes molasses at home with his family. Likewise, Daniel Webster Davis's 1897 dialect poem "Aunt Chloe's Lullaby" compares the child to molasses candy: "Mammy's baby, black an sweet / Jes like candy dat you eat / Mammy lay you in dis bed, while she mek de whi' folks' bread."[49] Yet, protected by the mother's watchful eye and her labor in the white folks' kitchen, the child is not eaten. In both poems, then, African American poets resisted the visual culture of sweetness and paternalist race relations by protecting children so they could consume sweets without themselves being consumed.[50]

Dunbar's "Little Brown Baby" was among the poems James Weldon Johnson selected for inclusion in his anthology of African American poetry published in 1922. Johnson also chose another poem that treated similar themes, "Two an' Six," by Claude McKay. Originally published in 1912 in his native Jamaica, McKay's poem, like Dunbar's, was written in dialect from the perspective of a father trying to protect his family. The semiautobiographical poem narrates a father's experience taking his sugarcane to market, only to find that the market price—"two an' six"—is so low that he will not have enough left to meet his expenses or, significantly, to buy candy for his "picknies." The poem emphasizes the father's sadness at having to disappoint his children's desire, a desire that is not for sweetness per se, since the family lives on a sugarcane farm and could thus at any time have "Nature's stick of candy, a piece of sugarcane," as white racial theorist Ellsworth Huntington put it. Instead, the purchased candy represents the margin of comfort created by paternal economic success. McKay's poem finally reconciles the father's economic failure by rejecting the market valuation of "two an' six." The poem concludes with the reassurance that the family itself—father, mother, and six children—was the "princely two an' six" profit. Together, the family—guided by the reassuring mother—creates a loving sweetness that protects it from the emotional vagaries of capitalist markets.

In "Little Brown Baby" and "Two an' Six," Dunbar and McKay used the themes of rural life—in particular, the associations between black children and sweetness—and the conventions of dialect poetry to challenge stereotypes about black families. Johnson selected these poems for his anthology in the early 1920s despite the fact that contemporary African American writers were abandoning dialect and rural themes. As a musician, poet, novelist, U.S. diplomat, and political activist, Johnson hoped that his anthology would demonstrate "intellectual parity" between whites and African Americans. Johnson argued that to demonstrate parity African American writers needed to reclaim the originality of their own music and folklore and "to find a form that will express the racial spirit by symbols from within rather than by symbols from without."[51] Johnson wrote, "Negro dialect is naturally and by long association the exact instrument for voicing [the rural] phase of Negro life; and by that very exactness it is an instrument with but two full stops, humor and pathos."[52] He selected these dialect poems because they resonated beyond the humor and pathos anticipated by their white audiences. Both created a pause in which readers could hear faith in loving, capable African American fathers and mothers. These poems used symbols from without—candy and rural pickaninnies—to express symbols from within—cohesive, self-reliant African American families.

Other authors contested the meanings of eating sugarcane through the emblem of the cane-chewing pickaninny. Edith Maude Eaton was among them. The daughter of a Chinese mother and a British father, she published short stories in U.S. women's magazines under the pseudonym "Sui Sin Far" in the 1910s.[53] Eaton grew up in Canada. She worked as a stenographer and journalist in Jamaica, later moving to the United States. Her fiction portrayed Asian Americans sympathetically at a time when legal discrimination against them was intensifying. Because she could pass as white, much of her work drew on the experience of being in-between and negotiating painful questions of inclusion. In her 1910 short story "The Sugar Cane Baby," published in *Good Housekeeping* magazine, Eaton suggested that eating sugarcane was not a sign of being racially inferior but instead was a logical choice for families working in cane fields. On an unnamed Caribbean island, nuns discover an infant "Hindu child" left on the ground amid the "miles of green meadows and fruitful plantations." They find the baby "sucking a piece of green sugar cane" while a snake lurks nearby. Believing that the baby has been abandoned and is in danger from the snake, they take it to live in the orphanage among the "pure pickaninnies" and those who "bore the mark of the white man in complexion and feature." To the nuns' surprise, the baby fails to thrive under their civilized care, growing listless and refusing to eat, refusing even a piece of sugarcane they offer him. An American woman reporter saves the day when she visits the orphanage and realizes that "the baby is breaking its heart for its mother." When she convinces the nuns to reunite the baby with its mother, he revives, taking the cane his mother offers. The mother explains that the snake had been trained to protect the baby. The story thus concludes by refiguring the snake and the cane as signs not of neglect but of parental protection.

Depictions of people chewing on sugarcane in the early twentieth century can be read as part of a contested migration narrative through which the intertwined stories of goods and people were told. White women, administrators, soldiers, and journalists developed dualistic conceptions of sugar during their travels throughout the Caribbean and Pacific. Their stories often cast those places as backward, unrefined, racially other, and in need of modernization. But middle-class African American and Asian American authors traveled within the same Pacific and Caribbean spaces and found a different set of meanings in them. Pauline Hopkins, Paul Laurence Dunbar, Claude McKay, and Edith Maude Eaton/Sui Sin Far each placed sugar and cane within a global frame in order to complicate the racial hierarchies articulated by white U.S. consumers and racial theorists. For these authors, the Caribbean in particular was a regenerative space in which binaries of race and refinement were unstable and more easily rewritten.

Concerns over sweetness and race found their way not only into fiction but also into musical productions. At least sixteen ragtime or jazz songs featuring themes of sweetness and black children were published between 1902 and 1920.[54] James Weldon Johnson would have been familiar with musical associations between African Americans and sweetness, since he had participated with his brother J. Rosamond Johnson and others in the formation of this musical culture in the early 1900s. These songs—authored by African American and white artists—played with the same images Dunbar laid out in his 1899 poem: the appetites of black children for sweetness; the dirtiness caused by consuming sweets; molasses or chocolate as the source of skin color; the sweetness of the child; the fond family setting; and the use of nicknames by family members. In

"Bon Bon Buddy the Chocolate Drop," sheet music, words by
Alex Rogers and music by Will Marion Cook (1906). Courtesy of the
John Hay Library, Brown University Library.

Bob Cole and J. Rosamond Johnson's 1906 "Sugar Babe," a male suitor
uses the metaphors of pie, fruit, sugar, and honey along with both dialect
and classical literary references to proclaim his love. Will Marion Cook
and Alex Rogers's "Bon Bon Buddy—the Chocolate Drop" was another
influential song among African American musicians.[55] Bon Bon Buddy
is a sophisticated young man who describes how his grandparents gave
him his nickname. Both numbers were performed for white audiences
on Broadway during the heyday of African American musicals before 1911
and were circulated more widely as sheet music.

White performers reworked these African American productions, though in their versions candy was generally a means of mocking black aspirations. Through the 1910s, white Tin Pan Alley composers used the same images and narratives embedded in earlier songs authored by African Americans. White performer Eddie Leonard's "Molasses Candy Song," published in 1910, riffed on the theme of sweet nicknames and mocked Bon Bon Buddy and his "sweet family tree."[56] "Bon Bon Buddy the Chocolate Drop that's my daddy; Honey Baby Sugar Lady she was my mammy; Molasses candy, 'lasses candy, 'lasses candy that's me," went the chorus. Leonard enacted the fiction of being "molasses candy"—a child whose skin was brown from the sticky sweet molasses he had just eaten—by performing in blackface. His blackface inverted African American musicians' efforts to remake consumption of candy and sweets into a "symbol from within," as Johnson had put it. Unlike those by African Americans, songs written by white musicians more often placed African Americans in rural settings and in the South. They alluded to watermelons, sugarcane, and cotton fields. Sam Coslow's "Pickaninny Dreams" described children and their mammies living in a rural land of plenty where "chocolate and molasses are a growing on the trees."[57] The song counseled young African Americans to stay put in the countryside and to dream of "jam and lots of candy." White lyricists imagined that African Americans dreamed not for rights and respect but rather for sweet treats.

During World War I, African American musicians revisited earlier musical comedy and ragtime forms in order to lament the disrespect they experienced as soldiers. Soldiers knew that neither chocolate nor molasses grew on trees, instead using them as metaphors to express experiences of displacement. "Mammy's Lit'l Choc'late Cullud Chile," written by Noble Sissle, a veteran of World War I, and orchestrated by Eubie Blake, for example, repeated the story and images of Dunbar's poem. But in his updated version, mammy replaces the father, who is absent, presumably in an army uniform or an urban job.[58] The mammy sings, "Boogie man'll get you sho' Why goodness lands, ain't you a dandy! Look at dose hands, all stuck wif candy!" The mother invokes the boogeyman, but, unlike the earlier poem, she never refuses it the right to eat the son. The son replaces the absent father as the mother sings, "Goodness lands, he's like his pappy. Never cares 'bout strife." Who will protect the child if he is carefree? Sissle's 1919 version of the story does not contain the child within the family. The song concludes, "I wish dat he could always be right at my knee, a tiny baby. His kinky head could rest each night on ma breast. He's mammy's little choc'late cullud chile." The song thus articulated African American mothers' and fathers' concerns as they grappled with the consequences for their families of migration out of the rural South.

Conclusion

Sugar eating in the early twentieth century revealed a Progressive-era tension between the demands of membership in a collectivity and the expression of individual will. This tension had profound implications for the political projects of empire and citizenship. In the context of overseas expansionism and rigid segregation within the United States, concerns over racial heterogeneity could be encapsulated in the contrast between sugar tongs and sugarcane. Civic ideals of uplift were animated in part through the quotidian, normative routines of sweetening to taste. Through sugar, individuals claimed opportunities to experience the democracy of desires offered in the United States, even as they limited their pleasures by adhering to social, political, racial, and military hierarchies. By eating the right kinds of sugar, diverse consumers claimed civic virtue in the face of expansion and segregation.

The process of commodification regularized and encoded categories of taste in ways that strongly correlated with the social practices and cultural distinctions that legitimated overseas expansion. This correlation did not mean that everyone experienced taste in the same way, or that the way taste functioned for one group—even the dominant group—was generalizable to others. Indeed, some people used the trope of sweetness to contest the normative hierarchies of civilization and citizenship. As we shall see, the same processes of commodification that codified the tastes for civilized refined sugar created gaps and loopholes through which people could articulate alternative interpretations of modernity and civilization.

CHAPTER THREE

THIS PECULIARLY INDISPENSABLE COMMODITY

Commodity Integration and Exception during World War I

Beginning in 1917, the United States Food Administration (USFA), a new wartime agency under the directorship of Herbert Hoover, counseled people, especially women and children, to restrict their consumption of sweets to support the war effort. The European conflict had wrought havoc on world sugar supplies. Since formal rationing was expensive and politically unappealing, Hoover and the USFA hoped consumers would voluntarily eat less. Administrators designed ads, articles, posters, and events in order to draw "imaginative support" for conserving sugar and other foods. These materials explained that sugar was "an essential food" and that voluntary self-restraint was the key to winning the war. As they encouraged greater civilian discipline, administrators relied on commonplace assumptions about what it meant for various consumer groups to eat sugar. Administrators contrasted U.S. civilian consumers with heroic soldiers and starving waifs in wartorn Europe, who needed sugar as a "fuel-food." If people in the United States were morally disciplined, more sugar would be available on the front lines.[1]

Despite calls for moderation, American consumers actually ate significantly *more* sugar during the war, and they did so with the USFA's tacit approval.[2] Observers attributed the increased consumption in part to Prohibition, enacted as a wartime measure in 1917. Sugar-sweetened sodas had supposedly replaced alcohol as the centerpiece of home-front entertainment. Others pointed out that high wartime wages and low unemployment meant that people had money to buy sweets. Policymakers also saw sugar as a strategic weapon in democracy's arsenal, and they recognized that a steady supply of cheap sugar could be used to their own advantage both at home and abroad. Administrators ranked some consumers as a greater risk to national security because they were more likely to be disorderly if they did not get enough sugar. In early 1917, urban immigrant women, for example, demonstrated that they would

"An Heroic Sacrifice," U.S. Food Administration, ca. 1918.

not tolerate a higher cost of living by overturning peddlers' carts.[3] Hoover interpreted such protests as evidence that urban immigrant consumers lacked moral restraint. He told the Senate Agriculture Committee that "if we do not look out and take measures we are going to be forced to reduce our consumption," which he feared would fuel public protest.[4] Thus, despite their repeated calls for restraint, food administrators' goal was to manage the sugar economy so that consumers would never actually need to show self-control.

Hoover's approach involved greater government intervention in the sugar trade than his public calls for voluntarism suggested. Using various tools, ranging from the local to the transnational, food administrators

In Who's Cup?

"In Who's Cup?" U.S. Food Administration, ca. 1918.

managed sugar supply and demand in an unprecedented experiment in public administration of private markets. The wartime sugar program was one of the first examples of coherent economic planning through which federal officials aimed to balance demands from industrialists, farmers, merchants, urban eaters, and workers, in the United States and abroad.[5] In wartime, Hoover and the USFA reasoned, the normal operations of supply and demand were inadequate for maintaining order in domestic and international markets. Though the USFA did not implement formal rationing for individuals, it did control domestic prices by rationing sugar among wholesalers, retailers, restaurants, and manufacturers. In cities across the country, small businessmen encountered new bureaucracies, rules, and scrutiny as they sold sugar during the war. Just as rebellious sugar consumers and grocer-profiteers made price controls necessary, the threat of profiteering on the global market similarly legitimated international market interventions. Legislators set high sugar tariffs to protect civilized producers on the mainland from "cheap tropical labor," and the USFA likewise ensured continental producers a higher price for their sugar than what foreign producers in Cuba could earn. Meanwhile, the Philippines were virtually excluded from the wartime sugar market because it produced sugar of a lower grade than what U.S. refiners demanded. Colonial administrators responded with new efforts to modernize and civilize the antiquated industry. At the heart of USFA sugar market controls, then, were administrators' judgments about where diverse sugar producers, consumers, and merchants fit in a global hierarchy.

They Were So Hungry for Sugar at That Time: Eastern European Jewish Immigrants and the Sugar Famine of 1917

After the United States formally entered the war, in April 1917, the president and Congress quickly strengthened government control over the economy. Herbert Hoover began unofficially serving as the U.S. food administrator in May, and his position was formalized three months later when Congress passed the Lever Food and Fuel Control Act and Wilson created the USFA by Executive Order.[6] The USFA was charged with controlling prices and distribution of "key commodities," including wheat, meat, fats, and sugar.[7] A special division within the USFA handled sugar. The Sugar Division was headed by George Rolph, on leave from his position as the general manager of the California and Hawaii Refining Company. The Sugar Division coordinated sugar supply, distribution, and prices for the entire Western Hemisphere. Since Great Britain had purchased virtually the entire Cuban crop in early 1917, Rolph initially scrambled to find enough sugar for U.S. consumers. To curb price fluctuations from speculation, the Sugar Division halted sugar futures trading on the New York Sugar and Coffee Exchange.[8] It centralized sugar distribution and created a system of state and local administrators who would license and monitor wholesale and retail grocers' sales.[9]

During the summer of 1917, the Sugar Division debated how to control prices. It generally agreed that if "left to natural economic forces," sugar prices would rise beyond the means of most workers. The war had caused "violent changes in the relations of supply and demand," and so natural economic laws could not be counted on to achieve equitable distribution of sugar.[10] Poor people would eat less sugar, but only because they could not afford it. This was hardly the ideal way to conserve sugar. The Sugar Division reasoned that this would be "a conservation of classes whereby the rich continue their purchases without restriction, while the poor are unable to buy at all."[11] By controlling prices and distribution themselves, administrators aimed to achieve a "more equitable distribution" between poor and wealthy consumers.[12] They intervened "so that the psychology of high prices and the exploitation by profiteers might have no chance to breed discontent."[13] Their concerns were again about urban ethnic consumers' lack of restraint.

"I suppose the great sugar eaters," Hoover had written to President Wilson, "are those of the least moral resistance in the community."[14] According to Hoover's thinly veiled racial logic, those people most likely to express their discontent through street protests were also the ones least able to curb their sugar consumption. He and Rolph hoped to maintain public order and avoid demonstrations such as those made earlier in 1917 by Jewish housewives in New York, sugar refinery workers in Philadelphia, and dockworkers in Cuba. With the Russian Revolution fresh in leaders' minds, the threat of urban radicalism seemed real. By keeping sugar affordable, administrators hoped to prevent leftist agitators from getting working families' attention.[15] The Sugar Division thus campaigned to control urban ethnic consumers' unruly appetites.

Early efforts by the USFA to address these concerns focused on Jewish consumers, especially in New York City. Hoover appointed a Commission on Food Conservation among the Jewish People, which coordinated with the New York Food Board (NYFB), the local arm of the USFA. With the participation of Jewish religious and social service agencies, the commission distributed posters and pamphlets in a dozen languages, including Yiddish, which asked immigrants to conserve food. Rabbis emphasized that frugality was a Jewish virtue and explicitly linked piety with patriotism. Jewish leaders in the United States asked their constituencies to heed "the call from our starving brethren, the call of humanity" by showing "constant restraint" so that food could be sent to Europe. During Chanukah, Jewish teachers instructed children to forsake candy "so that they can help their little brothers and sisters on the other side, who are crying daily for food." Some leaders went so far as to assert that "we are not Jews at a time like this; we are Americans." Indeed, many Jews contributed to Red Cross campaigns, bought liberty bonds, applied for citizenship, and assiduously followed USFA rules.[16]

Despite calls to eat less, administrators confronted what seemed to be insatiable sugar habits and un-American business practices among immigrant New Yorkers. The tenement groceries of the Lower East Side became administrators' frontline defense against urban discontent and profiteering. Like other Federal Food Boards under the USFA, the NYFB targeted businesses by setting maximum retail and wholesale prices for sugar, investigating violations, and prosecuting violators through quasi-judicial proceedings. During the "sugar famine" in the late fall of 1917, a network of neighborhood informants reported dozens of infractions by grocers, alleging that merchants were charging high prices, hording, and selling sugar illegally.[17]

By early 1918, the NYFB had gathered enough evidence to prosecute several high-profile cases. Their first case was against Max Markowitz, a Rumanian immigrant who ran a small grocery in the tenement basement where he lived with his wife and four children. In the fall of 1917, Markowitz applied for a USFA wholesale license and rented extra rooms to store sugar and flour.[18] Investigators discovered that Markowitz had bought sugar at prices above those authorized by the USFA. He bought directly from the refiners, through brokers, from other wholesale grocers, and in random door-to-door sales. Markowitz described one time buying "10 barrels of cube sugar from a driver of a milk wagon." Another time he bought five barrels from a woman "who came in an automobile to my place of business." His business doubled during the worst months of the sugar shortage, but his neighbors also began to notice irregularities. One reported that "in the early morning hours and the late evening, sugar and flour are taken away in large bags on push carts." Markowitz was so busy that police patrolled regularly. One witness described how "Markowitz received a big truck-load of sugar, and right after that there were big lines of people being kept in line by the police." Another woman wrote to the NYFB to complain that when she refused to buy other groceries besides the sugar, Markowitz "insulted me and told me to move on and immediately called an officer to chase me away." She, like other witnesses, was frustrated because the police did nothing about Markowitz's illegal sugar sales but punished them for trying to make their purchases. Working-class women insisted on the right to buy familiar foods at reasonable prices, and they were ready to defend this prerogative. But instead of protesting by overturning peddlers' carts, as they had done earlier in the year, women increasingly sought justice through the NYFB.

Markowitz and the small-time retailers who testified in the hearings explained their actions during the sugar famine in terms of loyalty and gender. They explained that their business decisions grew from their obligations to both their customers and their wives. Loyal customers, it turned out, were decidedly less devoted when their sugar bowls were empty. Markowitz claimed that "my women customers . . . depended on me to supply them. My customers would never believe me if I told them I had no sugar."[19] Another witness claimed that "Markowitz laughs at everybody—he has the sugar and all of our customers know he has it[,] and we are losing our trade for they are going to him[;] and in order to get one-half pound of sugar they buy all of their groceries from him."[20] During the worst shortages, grocers were willing to sell sugar at a loss in order to keep their customers and provide for their wives. Markowitz's neighbor explained that "this situation is terrible for I am losing my trade, my wife is sick and I am looking to the government for to help me." Like this witness, Markowitz also claimed to have broken USFA rules so that he could protect his sick wife. Annie Markowitz's doctor reported that she had worked in the shop until her recent "nervous breakdown."[21] Annie wrote that she could no longer withstand "the strain of working day and night together with my husband in the Grocery Store, and still be able to raise a family." In a fiercely competitive business that was vulnerable to shifting loyalties, merchants explained their commercial relationships in the gendered idioms of dependence and trust.

When Markowitz occasionally sold sugar to other grocers, he charged them double the USFA-authorized wholesale price. His competitors were savvy in their dealings with him, buying his overpriced sugar only after they had exhausted other sources, bargaining with him over the price, or sharing orders. Once, after Markowitz received a delivery, a group of grocers waited together to buy from him. When he eventually refused to sell, claiming that retail sales were more profitable, the group angrily confronted him. On this and other occasions, Markowitz lashed out rudely.[22] As a result of incidents like this, Markowitz was left with few friends in the neighborhood. One of his neighbors went to great lengths to implicate him, even allegedly instigating "a food riot" in front of Markowitz's shop.[23] Witnesses sometimes claimed to be reluctant to testify against him, but most had exhausted other resources for correcting his behavior. With their livelihoods at stake, they strategically invited the USFA—with its patriotic rhetoric and legalistic proceedings—directly into the Lower East Side's moral economy.

The NYFB investigated another more prominent merchant, Hyman Sklamberg, at about the same time. A Russian émigré who had lived in New York for more than thirty years, Sklamberg was a prosperous wholesale grocer serving the city's many tiny retailers.[24] Sklamberg's warehouse occupied an entire building and made $1 million per year in sales. He employed thirty people to sell, package, deliver, bill, and collect his accounts, belonged to prominent Jewish social organizations, was a benefactor of Jewish charities, and informally lent money to Jewish groups. Sklamberg's business boomed during the sugar famine. He employed two extra men just to weigh and package sugar, and police patrolled the street in front of his store to keep order.[25] Accused by the NYFB of overcharging for sugar, Sklamberg first defended himself by denigrating his customers, people like Markowitz. Sklamberg wrote, "The class of people that constitute my trade, are not responsible, and feel that they can say almost anything to retaliate for any inconvenience that they suffer from lack of sugar."[26] Though the NYFB may have agreed with Sklamberg's assessment of the grocers to whom he sold, they were unwilling to overlook his lapses. Their investigation continued, eventually leading to a full hearing before a judge, for which Sklamberg retained two lawyers.

Sklamberg's hearing reveals much about how grocers in lower Manhattan conducted their business, and also what sugar meant to their customers. The hearings show, for instance, that Jewish consumers largely rejected brown sugars, instead preferring packaged, white, granulated sugar. At least one grocer promoted such sugars as an emblem of piety within the context of kosher dietary law. Grocer Aaron Ashkanazy claimed that Rabbi Magolies, a major religious leader in New York in the 1910s, had granted him special permission to sell sugar labeled kosher for Passover.[27] According to Ashkanazy, the rabbi told him to purchase sugar in barrels and then to avoid the flour paste many factories used to seal the packages. Ashkanazy sold this sugar under a label that read, "Cube sugar for the Passover. Cleanliness and the weight guaranteed with the supervision of A. Ashkanazy." Sklamberg's lawyer later summoned Rabbi Magolies, who corrected Ashkanazy's account. He testified that between 1914 and 1916 he had granted a single factory the privilege of marking its sugar "kosher for Passover."[28] He asserted that his only concern was with factory hygiene, noting that "I was anxious ... that the factory should put in the clear clean sugar for the Passover holidays, and if that was done I was satisfied." But this was before the United States entered the war. Magolies discontinued his inspections in 1917—no doubt at the behest of the NYFB—because the practice seemed to raise sugar prices. He took out an advertisement in the Yiddish newspapers warning people that any sugar specially packaged for Passover was a scam. Nonetheless, the preference for white sugar persisted among Jewish customers who accepted claims like Ashkanazy's, especially during the holidays.

Food administrators were further frustrated because New York's tenement grocers did not use modern business practices. For many of these businessmen, USFA recordkeeping represented a fundamental shift in how they conceptualized their relationships with their customers and suppliers. Most grocers who testified against Markowitz and Sklamberg kept no books and only expected receipts when they were buying on credit. In most of their transactions, grocers relied on trust built through personal networks rather than on contractual invoices. In their view, a piece of paper gave no guarantee of honesty. Sklamberg gave his customers receipts, even when he was overcharging them. Markowitz had tried to hide his high prices by making his customers sign invoices showing a lower price than they actually paid.[29] In fact, some merchants explicitly rejected receipts and bookkeeping because they implied personal mistrust between buyer and seller. Though their approach contrasted sharply with Progressive-era ideas of business efficiency, grocers insisted that their practices made sense since they depended on daily face-to-face interactions and the exchange of informal credit.

The NYFB punished Sklamberg and Markowitz harshly. They revoked Markowitz's wholesale license for the duration of the war, ordered him to repay the money he had overcharged, and encouraged him to signal his patriotism by donating to the Red Cross. Markowitz moved his family to a new neighborhood where, over the next decade, he rebuilt a grocery business while his daughters sought office jobs. Sklamberg likewise received stiff penalties. Administrators considered allowing him to retain his license because his business, which moved several million dollars annually, "was a credit to the city." They worried that revoking his license "might interfere with the proper distribution of supplies on the East side of New York." But the judge finally decided that Sklamberg should serve as an example for "the many smaller dealers on the East Side." The USFA levied a high fine on Sklamberg, closed his business for one month, and prohibited him from trading in sugar for two months. They also encouraged him to make a large donation to the Red Cross.[30]

By January 1918, the new crop of cane sugar was on the market and prices were dropping. Administrators knew that this bounty would not last through the end of the year, and they began to make plans to avoid another "sugar famine." During the summer, the NYFB created a new license system for retailers, allocating quotas based on reported sales for the months of April, May, and June.[31] But since many of the grocers did not keep sales records, the system did not work smoothly. The NYFB mistrusted grocers' sales estimates, suspecting that they inflated their numbers to get higher quotas for the coming winter. Through the fall of 1918, the NYFB investigated more grocers, again confirming their belief that heavy-handed administration was needed to control urban ethnic buyers and sellers.[32]

Reflecting on the USFA's experiences over the previous year, Hoover wrote in 1918, "Sugar is the one commodity that voluntary conservation does not seriously reach. . . . Therefore we must put into effect some form of sugar rationing and a drastic control of distribution. Otherwise we shall have territorial and industrial injustices all over the country."[33] After witnessing New York's "sugar famine," administrators concluded that, as they had suspected, the mechanisms of supply and demand might reduce overall sugar consumption, but not without a lapse in public order. Without government controls, they ran the risk of profiteering and disorderly marketing, not just in New York, but in other parts of the country as well.[34] Indeed, New York was not the only place administrators sought to bring order to sugar sales.

These Inferior Grades of Sugar: Mexican and Chinese Merchants and Exceptional Sugars

In the dark of night on January 25, 1918, troops guarding the U.S.-Mexico border near El Paso, Texas, encountered a group making an unauthorized crossing into Mexico. The troops demanded that the group stop, and when they did not, the soldiers fired on them. Immediately, "a considerable number of men on the Mexican side of the river" returned fire. Though border skirmishes like this were hardly unusual at the time, it is worth noting that the group was not crossing the border empty-handed. They were in the act of smuggling sugar out of the United States into Mexico. Sugar was particularly scarce in rural northern Mexico, where ongoing fighting following the Mexican Revolution (1910–17) had cut into sugar production. In 1917, the governor of Nuevo Leon, a state in northern Mexico, prohibited all exports of corn, beans, and *piloncillo*—an unrefined, cone-shaped brown sugar. Under USFA regulations, individuals could carry only five pounds of sugar out of the United States without licenses issued by both the U.S. War Trade Board and the Sugar Division. People stood to make tremendous profits if they could negotiate these conditions, and entrepreneurs maintained a brisk cross-border sugar trade—both illicit and legal—during the war. According to the USFA, "It was a matter of common knowledge in Brownsville, [Texas,] that . . . sugar was being smuggled across the river into Mexico." The Sugar Division thus began to monitor sales and punish violators in the region.[35]

At the same time that the Sugar Division learned of smuggling across the Rio Grande, Mexican and Chinese merchants began petitioning it for licenses to import and export lower-grade sugars. One of the first Mexican merchants to contact the Sugar Division for permission to export sugar was J. M. Marroquin. Marroquin and his family operated a cross-border wholesale grocery business. Because there were few direct rail lines in Mexico, even shipments not destined for the United States passed across the border and through U.S. Customs. During the war, the Marroquins brokered a substantial quantity of piloncillo, purchasing it in Mexico and shipping it to other parts of Mexico under bond through Texas. They insisted that their transshipments were legitimate, even under the tightened wartime restrictions, because the goods were produced and consumed in Mexico. But Rolph was suspicious and initially reluctant to approve their licenses. Rolph grew alarmed when Marroquin petitioned to import low-grade raw sugar from Central America and then immediately asked for an export license to ship "low grade piloncillo made from imported raw sugar" back to Mexico.[36] Unable to buy piloncillo in Mexico, Marroquin and other merchants were buying raw sugar from Central and South America, melting it in Texas, and remolding it into conical loaves to be sold as piloncillo in Mexico.[37] Unfortunately for Marroquin, the timing could not have been worse since Rolph was in the middle of the New York "sugar famine." Rolph reasoned that "the exportation of sugar of any kind should be discouraged at this time . . . in view of the scarcity of refined sugar."[38]

Rolph believed—incorrectly, it turned out—that Marroquin was melting raw sugar that refiners instead could be using. Marroquin quickly corrected Rolph, pointing out that the sugar he used was "of such a grade to be difficult[,] expensive[,] and wasteful for the refiners to use."[39] Nonetheless, Rolph insisted that "it is simply a question of policy as to whether our ships, ports, dock facilities, rail facilities, motive power, etc., should be used for the transportation of these inferior grades of sugar coming in from foreign countries, for Mexico, when the transportation facilities of the country are at the greatest premium ever known." The Sugar Division and the War Trade Board, he argued, ought to limit all cross-border sugar sales. Noting that he had previously been "a bit too liberal," Rolph issued new rules governing raw sugars in early 1918. As he summarized

Sugar Business was mostly ruled by people's subjective thoughts as to what would be most effective the situation, "The system that was in vogue along the border could only be controlled by drastic action." The Sugar Division sent a message by revoking the sugar licenses of two Texas merchants, charging that they encouraged smuggling by selling large quantities of sugar. The War Trade Board tightened requirements for transshipments, which resulted in a backlog on the U.S. side of the border while they issued new export licenses.[40]

Ultimately, the Sugar Division adopted a policy of approving only export licenses that served U.S. strategic goals. Companies that were producing necessary war matériel, for example, were allowed to export sugar for their workers. One Los Angeles merchant got a license to import 100,000 pounds of brown sugar from Nicaragua, with the understanding that it was to be shipped directly under bond to mining companies in northern Mexico.[41] Such a shipment would not normally have been allowed. But Mexicans mining copper, drilling for petroleum, or growing sisal, along with Liberians and Congolese tapping rubber, were allowed sugar from the U.S. supplies since their work was deemed crucial for the war effort.[42] Likewise, Rolph considered intervening when he learned that 25,000 tons of sugar was en route from Peru to Mexico. He dropped his objections when the State Department intervened, claiming strategic necessity.[43] In this and other situations, administrators interpreted sugar as a reward for fulfilling the obligations of wartime. They hoped that sugar would forestall radicalism abroad just as they imagined it would at home.

The Sugar Division eventually coupled its rigid enforcement of import and export rules with selective lenience, however. It soon realized that some of the trade in unrefined sugar—such as that carried on by Marroquin—could serve its own ends. Though he had struck out with export licenses, Marroquin settled on a profitable, legal niche when he began to sell piloncillo to Mexican Americans and Mexican nationals working in the United States. During the sugar shortage, piloncillo was a popular, inexpensive choice for workers in Texas, California, and elsewhere.[44] In his campaign for a legitimate angle on the sugar trade, Marroquin explained that his "principal object in manufacturing Piloncillo is to offer to the Mexican consumer something similar to what is used in Mexico."[45] One California wholesaler reported to the Sugar Division that he typically bought 900 pounds of piloncillo per month from Marroquin and resold it to small groceries catering to Mexican clientele.[46] Marroquin insisted that "these Mexicans are laborers in the various fields of the UNITED STATES and actually consuming WHITE

Sugar policy was an easy vehicle to do what needed to be done here.

GRANULATED SUGAR in view of the fact that they cannot get this PANELA [low-grade solid sugar] for their consumption."[47] Administrators realized that when some people ate what they called "ethnic sugars," there would be less pressure on refined sugar supplies. If urban Jewish consumers demanded refined white sugar, they reasoned, all the better if other working-class ethnic consumers ate an unrefined product. Based on this logic, the Sugar Division allowed Marroquin to import raw sugar to process into piloncillo for domestic sale.

Marroquin indefatigably sought low-grade sugar to process into piloncillo, soliciting help from various brokers and from Rolph himself.[48] Because he used much lower-grade sugar than what refiners would process, Marroquin bought sugar that others had rejected. In May 1918, for example, 370,000 pounds of Venezuelan raw sugar languished in a New Orleans warehouse because the Sugar Division took so long to process the permits that the original buyers no longer wanted it. As the New Orleans broker reported to Rolph, the sugars "are beginning to sour, and the appearance of same with the molasses oozing out from the bags makes it quite apparent that the sugars are absolutely unfit for direct consumption."[49] In case it was not clear enough, the writer reiterated that "the odor from same would prove the sugar to be absolutely unfit for direct consumption." Marroquin was undeterred, promising to use it only for piloncillo for domestic sales. The food administrator in New Orleans urged Rolph to approve the deal so that the sugar would not go to waste. Though the Texas food administrator objected, pointing out that Marroquin had already exceeded his annual wholesale quota by 63,000 pounds, Rolph allowed the sale because it meant that food administrators could then reduce the refined sugar quotas for Mexicans in Texas, California, and elsewhere.[50] Exceptions such as these benefited the USFA as much as Marroquin.

At the same time, Chinese merchants were also seeking licenses to import unrefined brown and white rock sugar destined for Chinese American consumers. In February 1918, several New York wholesalers received an overland railroad shipment of Chinese sugar shipped through Vancouver, B.C., Canada. Ordinarily, all raw sugar imports went through the International Sugar Committee (ISC), a group within the Sugar Division that allocated raw sugar among the nation's refiners. One Chinese wholesaler, however, sought to skip the ISC and sell 5,600 pounds of Chinese sugar directly to its own customers, sending an English-speaking Chinese American merchant to Rolph's office with a sample of the sugar. The sample was enough to persuade him that this was "not a commercial grade of sugar as known in the New York market."[51] Other wholesalers soon requested similar exemptions, generally repeating the idea that "this class of merchandise is suitable for use by [no one] other than Chinese, as it is a brown sugar pressed into small cakes."[52] In all, Rolph exempted six Chinese firms in New York City from normal import rules and then applied this precedent in other cities, including San Francisco, Boston, Seattle, Portland, Chicago, and Oakland.[53] Rolph explained that "we do not want to inflict any hardship on any of the peoples living in the United States who are used to special food products." That the sugar was intended for "peculiar" palates guaranteed that it would not be diverted "into the regular channels of commerce," and thus would not earn Chinese merchants illicit profits.[54] Chinese merchants over the next year received shipments ranging from 100 pounds to 154,000 pounds (most were around 1,000 pounds), classified as either rock or brown sugar and designated for Chinese consumers in the United States.[55] Administrators insisted that Chinese sugar was to be deducted from Chinese wholesalers' normal allotments of refined sugar, and that it should replace customers' normal monthly rations.[56] Lesser sugars thus offered a loophole for Chinese merchants to expand their trade, just as they had for Mexican merchants in the Southwest.

Wartime sugar policies affected Eastern European Jewish, Chinese, and Mexican communities differently as each group grappled with an increasingly integrated network of standardized commodity production. Merchants from each group used the wartime sugar trade to make more money and bolster their own class status. Chinese merchants already occupied a privileged position above other Chinese in the United States because they were exempt from the race- and class-based immigration exclusion that prohibited Chinese workers from entering the country. Given the anti-Asian sentiment that limited their business opportunities in the United States, Chinese merchants sought to improve their financial and social positions by acting as labor brokers and selling to Chinese clientele.[57] Mexican merchants were likewise eager to distinguish themselves from the working-class Mexicans who were their main clientele. And Eastern European grocers in New York profited from the sudden wartime profitability of sugar sales. These merchants profited from the distinctiveness of their clientele, who were assumed to have unique appetites. In this way, control over commodities during the war created a limited condition of possibility for middle-class ethnic businessmen in the United States.[58]

The war brought major changes in the geography of sugar supply. Cane producers in the Caribbean and Pacific expanded their share of the world market as European beet production dwindled. Before the war, beet sugar accounted for 46 percent of the world sugar supply, but by 1918 that figure had dropped by half.[59] England and France scrambled to buy Cuban sugar to replace what they would have previously purchased from Germany. British ships were losing as much as 23,000 tons of sugar per week from German submarines hits.[60] Submarines had greatly reduced the Allied merchant fleet, and U.S. shipbuilding did not keep pace with these losses. Scarce shipping capacity limited how much sugar could be brought from Hawaii, the Philippines, Java, and Mauritius. Though Cuba was closer, labor strikes threatened to slow production there, and tight U.S. labor markets exacerbated beet growers' difficulties in increasing their production.[61] Administrators in the USFA coordinated prices using practices drawn from their prewar work as corporate managers. As they sought control over the sugar economy, businessmen-turned-administrators forged new relationships between corporate capitalism and the government.[62]

The USFA's decision to fix prices for producers and consumers represented a sea change from the governmental consensus only six years earlier, when a congressional committee reported on its investigation of the American Sugar Refining Company (ASRC). Its report asserted that the ASRC and its managers had created what would later be called an "administered market." By setting sugar prices based on managers' calculations of costs of production and their competitive strategies, the ASRC subverted the laws of supply and demand. Through administrative centralization and vertical integration, the ASRC maximized its own profit and efficiency at the expense of its competitors and customers. The ASRC had nearly complete sovereignty over the refined sugar trade. The report's authors believed there was nothing natural about "monopolistic combinations," and corporations only possessed the power they did because the government had failed to control them. The report concluded that "competition and individuality" were "the great remedies" for the nation's economic problems.

But while congressional investigators suggested that the government ought to regulate corporations, they also cautioned that the government should not try to do so by acting like a corporation itself. "To fix the price of commodities by law," they argued, "whether by commissions or by other method, would clothe the Government with dangerous power, rob the citizen of individuality, and embark the Nation into extreme paternalism."[63] A mere six years later—under a Democratic rather than Republican administration—the USFA exercised precisely this "extreme paternalism." Worried about how buyers and sellers would behave in an unfettered, wartime marketplace, the USFA argued that the natural forces of supply and demand had failed. Especially after the "sugar famine" of 1917, they sought to control the competitive actions of small-time grocers and consumers. People like George Rolph, who had been in the sugar industry for years, well knew that corporations had already perfected administrative techniques to limit competition. What had been a peacetime vice was a wartime virtue.

The USFA nonetheless faced criticism over price controls, so it asked the U.S. attorney general, T. W. Gregory, for an opinion on whether its efforts violated the Sherman Antitrust Act. Gregory gave the green light, arguing that "governmental action with respect to prices or methods of distribution is obviously not within the mischief at which the Sherman Law was aimed."[64] He continued, "When natural laws of trade can no longer be depended upon to regulate markets, the only choice is between artificial control imposed by private interests and artificial control imposed by public agencies." Even though the courts and Congress had restricted corporations' rights to "artificial control" over prices or distribution, food administrators found new legal authorization to embrace the corporate order.

Hoover testified to Congress that, based on his experience with food relief in Europe, setting prices had "proved a failure in all cases, except where the government controlled enough of the commodity."[65] Congress had earlier rejected Hoover's request for USFA authorization to buy and sell sugar, although it had allowed such control over wheat. Food administrators instead designed a system of price controls based on voluntary contracts between sugar producers and the USFA. They hoped to negotiate a price for producers that would be high enough to stimulate production across diverse production regions while also keeping consumer prices low. For the 1917–18 sugar crop, the USFA's Sugar Division and its committees negotiated separately with beet and cane producers. First, representatives of domestic beet sugar companies met in Washington, D.C., to work out the voluntary contract price for beet sugar. Administrators heard testimony and gathered data about costs of production in the beet sugar industry and considered these in relation to prices and freight rates for Cuban sugar.[66] By the end of September, all beet growers and processors had agreed to a price and signed contracts for the year.

Meanwhile, Cuban cane sugar producers began price negotiations with the ISC for the entire 1917–18 crop. The ISC, headed by representatives of the three largest sugar refineries, worked closely with England, France, and Italy to determine a purchase price for the world market and share supplies. By doing so, they hoped to avoid the kind of competition among buyers that had increased prices and exacerbated shortages the previous year. Since refiners' profits depended on the difference between the raw and refined prices, they were determined to negotiate a low price. On the other hand, Cuban negotiators, facing their own domestic political pressure, pushed for a higher price, eventually asking the State Department to intercede in the hope of getting a better offer from the ISC. Negotiators finally settled on a price that was significantly lower than the Cuban delegation's original proposal but higher than the refiners' offer. Despite their apparent success, the ISC's negotiations brought a variety of criticisms from abroad. The U.S. consul in Cuba admitted that he felt "apprehension about political and economic effects in Cuba of our fixing the price of raw sugar," because, as he noted, small cane farmers were "bitterly condemning the United States" and were "censuring the mill owners and the Cuban government" for accepting a low price.[67] Indeed, high food prices in Cuba had already brought protesters into the streets. British policymakers likewise quipped that "they were extremely uneasy at the apparent tendency of Mr. Hoover's International Sugar Committee to secure for America an undue share of the easily accessible supplies."[68]

Food administrators in the United States believed that they would need an even more aggressive approach for 1918–19. For one thing, they already had evidence that production costs were increasing rapidly everywhere. Staff statisticians and accountants used data from individual sugar factories to build cost curves, which they studied to determine the most efficient level of production for a company. While corporations used cost curves to identify and eliminate their least efficient subsidiaries, the Sugar Division used them for the opposite purpose. Food administrators' goal was to maximize sugar output, so they used cost curves to determine a price that would cover production costs and profits for most sugar factories in each region—including the least efficient ones. After assembling cost curves for mainland cane and beets, Puerto Rico, Hawaii, and Cuba, the Sugar Division faced a quandary. In order to stimulate sugar production in those places, it had to offer a price that was well above what it believed was needed to maintain Cuban production. Hoover ventured that this could cost U.S. consumers anywhere from $20 to $40 million.[69]

How could food administrators pay producers in Cuba less than they paid to mainland and territorial producers? They briefly considered a plan to equalize the price between domestic, territorial, and foreign sugar by imposing an emergency sugar tariff. After rejecting this idea, Hoover proposed that the government form a corporation through which food administrators would gain the power to set prices. Capitalized with $5 million from President Wilson's special coffers, the Sugar Equalization Board (SEB) was an independent corporation modeled on the Grain Corporation formed the previous year to control the wheat market. One of six corporations created by the federal government during the war in an unprecedented attempt to address "novel emergency problems of production and supply and finance," the SEB controlled world sugar prices through direct purchases and sales.[70] The corporation brought a number of advantages, both financial and bureaucratic. Food administrators in the United States, Britain, and France all supported the SEB because they did not see any other way to prevent Cuban producers from getting excessively high prices.

During the war, Hoover and Rolph embraced the corporate form precisely because they wanted to discriminate among their business partners—they wanted to pay Cuban producers significantly less for their sugar than they paid domestic producers. In creating the SEB, food administrators revealed a sophisticated understanding of corporations. They recognized that one of the most widely criticized tactics of corporations—that they set different prices for different customers and suppliers—could serve government purposes.[71] Corporate monopolies created different classes of buyers and sellers and systematically restricted independent producers' and consumers' options to freely buy and sell goods. As an earlier reformer complained, monopolies "discriminate at will, in order that they might be free to find the maximum function of their two variables, the variable of price and the variable of sales."[72] Chartered under Delaware state law in July 1918, the SEB functioned like any private corporation, aiming to maximize profit and strategically shape the market according to its own priorities.[73] The SEB's charter authorized it to buy sugar on the international market at whatever price it could negotiate. It could then sell raw sugar to refiners at a profit to the government. The Board of Directors for the SEB included Herbert Hoover, George Rolph, and four other industry representatives. Over the course of 1918, it replaced many of the ISC's functions, including price negotiations and distribution. In September 1918, the SEB reached an agreement with Cuban government representatives on a price for the Cuban crop, estimated at 4 million tons.[74] The SEB purchased from Cuba "on as cheap a basis as we could."[75] Cuba had little leverage to negotiate since the SEB represented all of its potential customers in Britain, Europe, and the United States. The SEB paid a higher price to mainland and territorial producers. The SEB then sold all of this raw sugar to refiners at a profit.[76] It thus "equalized" prices across a broad geography and effectively decoupled the Cuban price from the domestic price. This functioned as a de facto tariff on Cuban sugar, with the profit accruing to the U.S. government.[77] In fact, the SEB was quite profitable, depositing $30 million into the U.S. Treasury in 1920 alone.[78]

Food administrators effectively used the corporation to reinforce an international hierarchy in the sugar market and to assure the United States' place at the top of that order. Along these lines, some commentators noted a parallel between government-owned corporations and U.S. island territories. On the eve of the SEB's creation, W. F. Willoughby offered a frequently cited defense of government-financed corporations. Willoughby suggested that corporations and colonies had much in common. Territorial control, he argued, set a practical and legal precedent for the new government-owned corporations. Willoughby had been treasurer, secretary, and president of Puerto Rico's Executive Council between 1901 and 1909. Based on that experience, he argued that each territory ought to be treated as a separate legal and fiscal entity, though still under congressional oversight. A colony was akin to "a subsidiary corporation, with its own property, revenues, expenditures, accounting and reporting system, its own board of directors, administrative staff and personnel distinct from those of the general government." The same theory could work on the continent. Government corporations would "be given a legal, administrative and financial autonomy. Each will have its organic act, or charter, providing for its creation and defining its jurisdiction, powers and duties; its board of directors; its directing staff and subordinate personnel." Willoughby proposed that Congress act essentially as "the board of directors" for a national holding company.[79] Unbound by the restrictions of politics or bureaucracy, corporate governance could be an efficient way to manage hierarchical social relations and achieve sovereign states of exception.

The decision to form the SEB grew out of a racialized interpretation of labor and political conditions in Cuba. In early 1917, the U.S. Marines had landed in Cuba in response to widespread labor organizing over wages and prices, and expeditionary forces remained on the island—at least in small numbers—through 1922.[80] The SEB offered a price based on knowledge of explicit U.S. military control of the island and on reports from the U.S. consul, who repeated stereotyped descriptions of laborers and their motivations. He argued against a higher sugar price because he doubted it would increase wages in Cuba. Even if wages did increase, he speculated that this might *reduce* productivity. "In the past season," he wrote, wages in Cuba were high "not so much because of [labor] scarcity but because it was inefficient and unreliable." When a cane cutter earned more, he claimed, he "may work a few days a week and then . . . rest a few days, living on his high wages of his few working days." Given assumptions like this, the SEB agreed that "too high a price would defeat the object of the committee."[81] In fact, the U.S. military presence belied negotiators' claims that conditions in Cuba did not merit higher sugar prices. The Marines occupied the island precisely because workers in Cuba were vocally asserting that their wages were inadequate. The extraterritorial state of exception on the island, maintained through a show of military force, helped to suppress the cost of production in the face of laborers' demands. Policymakers in the United States thus asserted both Cuba's subordinate position in trade negotiations and its obligation to produce sugar and to produce it cheaply. The SEB achieved this because of its extraordinary powers as an independent corporation.

In their efforts to maintain a supply of cheap sugar for U.S. consumers, the SEB and its predecessor, the ISC, impinged on Cuban sovereignty in myriad ways. Because much of the productive infrastructure was dedicated to sugar, Cuba relied on U.S. imports of wheat, meat, lard, beans, and butter. Since these products were under wartime control in the United States, in order to provision their workers, Cuban sugar plantations submitted applications to the U.S. Consul General, the U.S. War Trade Board, and the USFA. Food sales were at U.S. food administrators' discretion, and they explicitly used food restrictions to manipulate the Cuban political situation. Consul General Henry Morgan counseled the USFA that "the only way to make the [Cuban] people realize the seriousness of the situation is to reduce their [food] supply."[82] Morgan recommended that Cuba be allowed an extra 10,000 barrels of flour during the harvest season. Once the harvest was complete, the amount should be reduced again.

The USFA also participated in expanding Cuba's foreign debt during the war. Because shipping was scarce, the ISC could not take possession of the 1917–18 crop all at once. It asked Cuban mills and farmers to advance the cost of warehousing in Cuba and to ship on a monthly basis. This would leave them unable to pay their labor. The ISC thus coordinated a massive loan by U.S. banks so that Cuban producers could pay their workers up front rather than waiting until all sugar was sold. Though U.S. banks had been loaning money to Cuban- and American-owned sugar companies since the turn of the century, the wartime loans were part of a broader move toward "dollar diplomacy," or the exchange of loans for increased financial oversight in the foreign economies. World War I proved to be a turning point, after which the pace of investments by U.S. banks in the Cuban economy accelerated.[83]

forcefully bankrupt them

Plantation Whites: Commodity Standards and Colonial Complications

According to the Bureau of Standards, more than forty varieties of sugar were regularly entering the U.S. market in the late 1910s.[84] Wartime scarcities raised new questions about how to classify these different grades of sugar and assign them value. The industry had evaluated sugar using the polariscope—an instrument for measuring sugar content—and the Dutch Color Standard for decades. Increasingly, those tools seemed inadequate, especially as centrifugal mills produced very high grade unrefined sugar. Sugar could be very white, but the polariscope would reveal a comparatively low sugar content. Likewise, sugar could be yellow, off-white, or even brown, but the polariscope test would reveal it as nearly pure. For this reason, Congress had, several years earlier, officially abandoned the Dutch Color Standard as a way to measure value in the sugar market. Nonetheless, consumers still counted on color to tell them something about their sugar. Sugar manufacturers exploited this ambiguity in their attempt to sell at the highest price allowable under wartime restrictions. By selling a perfectly white sugar at the legally allowed price for refined—even if it was not in fact refined—manufacturers tried to charge more than was officially allowed. Most buyers could not tell the difference. During the war, the Bureau of Standards received hundreds of sugar samples along with requests to "prepare specifications and definitions of these sugars which would make possible their accurate identification." They began the slow process of developing "a systematic

constantly trying to update industry

classification" of sugar. In the meantime, USFA officials had discretion in how to classify and price sugar, and they identified consumers whom they expected would eat sugars that fell outside of the normal range. Their decisions had consequences for producers and consumers across the U.S. sugar empire.

Statistics on mainland cane sugar production show that in the five years after 1914 there was a substantial shift toward producing white unrefined sugar, sometimes called "plantation refined" or "plantation whites." There was a commensurate decrease in both raw and refined production on the mainland.[85] The Sugar Division recognized that higher grades of unrefined sugars, especially what it called "plantation whites" from Louisiana, would appeal to many consumers. Administrators and sellers did not immediately agree about how to price such sugars, however. In one controversy, the Federal Sugar Refining Company in Philadelphia sold what it called "conservation sugar," claiming it was refined, though not quite white. After analyzing a sample, George Rolph called the company's bluff and asserted that it had never in fact been refined. Rolph, who had spent nearly his entire career in the sugar industry, used chemical analysis, taste, and comparison with the Dutch Color Standard to insist that it was, in fact, a nearly white raw sugar. As such, he argued, it needed to be sold at the price specified for raw sugars, which was much lower than the price the Federal Sugar Refining Company was charging.[86]

Personal animosity may have accounted for Rolph's ruling in the Federal Sugar Refining Company's case—he and its head, Claus Spreckles, were old rivals. But after further lobbying by producers in the U.S. South, Rolph eventually relented and agreed that unrefined white sugars could be sold at a slightly higher price everywhere.[87] One writer cited a U.S. Department of Agriculture (USDA) report, pointing out that "bleaching cane sugar to a *pure white* adds nothing to its food value, but is done to satisfy the consumers' fancy or whim." Rolph agreed, recognizing that they ought to encourage sales of this grade of sugar to alleviate demand for refined. Although the Dutch Color Standard had been officially abandoned a decade earlier, Rolph required that sugar sold at the higher price as "plantation whites" meet the Dutch Color Standard for white sugar.[88]

Administrators realized that many consumers would willingly eat lower grades of sugar since it was cheaper, more readily available, and in fact virtually indistinguishable from the refined product. Consumers in Puerto Rico, for example, were encouraged to replace refined sugar, imported from the mainland, with higher grades of raw sugar, which was produced on the island. In fact, there was a backlog of raw sugar on the island that could not be sold in New York for lack of shipping. For consumers in Puerto Rico, the white color of the sugar was more important than any abstract measures of polariscopic value advocated by refiners and customs inspectors. The Puerto Rico Food Commission decided to adjust prices so that they were based "more on color and on the demands of retailers and consumers." It authorized retailers to charge the same price for these sugars as for refined.[89] Several of the larger sugar centrals in Puerto Rico converted to produce more of this sugar for local consumption, and they promoted the product among elite consumers who would otherwise opt for refined. Though Rolph discouraged exports of those sugars, some of it did arrive in New York. During another shortage, the SEB offered washed Puerto Rican sugars to New York hotel, boardinghouse, and restaurant operators. Rolph described it as "sufficiently good for ordinary commercial use, though not as white as refined sugar."[90] Given the severe sugar shortages, buyers gladly bought this sugar at prices higher than those paid for refined sugar before the war.

The Philippines

The sugar industry in the Philippines did not receive the same stimulus from the war as other regions did. Wartime prices and tariff concessions granted by Congress in 1916 had seemed promising, but a boom never materialized. Congress had offered the Philippines free trade in sugar in 1916, which might have attracted investors had Democrats not pushed the Jones bill, which promised to grant independence to the Philippines as soon as a stable government was established. Since independence would eventually bring an end to sugar tariff concessions, Congress simultaneously discouraged U.S. investments in Filipino centrifugal sugar production.[91] What one hand offered, the other took away. Much of the raw sugar made in the Philippines was of a significantly lower grade than that from Hawaii, Puerto Rico, and Cuba. Most mills employed the older muscovado method for processing cane into raw sugar. Modern centrifugal mills produced a much higher grade of raw sugar, with a higher polarization, which refiners could more efficiently process. By the 1910s, most mainland refineries, including *all* the refineries in California, could refine muscovado only at a loss. The few mainland refineries equipped to efficiently handle muscovado sugar were in New York. Without ships to carry muscovado to New York, producers in the Philippines resorted to selling at a loss to ethnic Chinese merchants, who exported the sugar to China and elsewhere in East Asia.[92]

In the fall of 1918, realizing that Filipino farmers and mills were facing dire losses because of low prices and limited markets in the United States, the Sugar Division decided to purchase muscovado sugar for shipment to New York.[93] To coordinate purchases and shipping, the Sugar Division appointed George Fairchild, a U.S. sugar merchant in Manila. Fairchild reported that farmers and mills had been unable to hold out for higher prices because exporters controlled the only warehouse storage in the islands. Since exporters had already bought most of the crop—and they kept no records of where any of their sugar originated—the profit would not return to farmers even if the Sugar Division managed to buy the sugar. The USFA did not ultimately buy any sugar in the Philippines in the fall of 1918. Nonetheless, their actions helped stabilize sugar prices in Manila in the short term.[94]

Ultimately, the war revealed how poorly the Philippine sugar industry was integrated into U.S. systems of standardized sugar grades, coordinated prices, contracts, and shipping. Investors and administrators hoped to integrate the Philippine industry into the U.S. market to shift its focus away from the Chinese market. This would involve new equipment, warehouses, and business practices. As Fairchild explained to Rolph, "The real solution of the Philippine Muscovado Sugar problem is the erection of factories producing centrifugal sugars." Previously millers had not been interested in converting to centrifugal milling, but during the war, farmers, millers, merchants, and colonial administrators had new motivation to update the industry. The Philippine legislature and the colonial administration authorized various banks and boards to finance mill construction. Though progress was slow, over the next decade the Philippine National Bank financed six new centrifugal sugar mills in the islands.[95]

While he lobbied to expand centrifugal milling capacity, Fairchild also tried to find buyers for the muscovado produced by thousands of small farmers and millers in 1918–19. Shipping remained scarce, and there was insufficient warehouse space for the surplus. New York refiners were reluctant to pay prevailing freight rates, and Fairchild and Rolph struggled to secure cargo space at any price through the War Trade Board. Nonetheless, they did manage to schedule a shipment for New York for the fall of 1919. To their frustration, Filipino shippers and exporters repeatedly circumvented their arrangements, and muscovados arrived in New York in piecemeal rather than coordinated fashion.[96] When this happened, the Sugar Division could not guarantee prices or buyers. Thus, despite their best efforts to secure markets for muscovados, the Sugar Division ultimately advised shippers in the Philippines "to dispose of them in the Orient."

Ironically, despite the difficulties faced by food administrators and sugar merchants in bringing low-grade sugar from the Philippines during the war, some Philippine muscovado likely arrived in New York through a far more circuitous route. Most of the sugar sold from Manila was brokered by ethnic Chinese merchants, who sold it to trading partners in Hong Kong, Shanghai, and Canton, China. Merchants in China then exported small quantities of the sugar—at the full tariff rate—to Chinese merchants in the United States for sale to Chinese American customers. Philippine sugar could not be sold duty-free in New York because of its low grade and was thus shipped from Manila to Hong Kong, from Hong Kong to Vancouver, B.C., and finally overland to New York at the full tariff. Unsalable through the regular channels of the U.S. sugar empire, the sugar commanded a premium price through global ethnic kin networks.

Demobilization

The war ended in November 1918, before the Caribbean cane harvest started. For the first few months after the armistice, the sugar economy continued under government control.[97] The SEB had entered into binding contracts with Cuban and domestic producers, and these arrangements proceeded. In early 1919, statisticians again predicted a seasonal shortage so the SEB purchased and warehoused surplus sugar. Food administrators debated whether to continue export restrictions. Herbert Hoover, writing from Europe, noted that European purchasing power was likely to remain weak, but sugar was one product that U.S. exporters could likely sell there.[98] Since he anticipated that there would be few other opportunities for the United States to export to cash-strapped Europe, Hoover argued that the SEB should allow sugar exports even if this meant that it needed to restrict domestic consumption. By the end of 1919, global sugar demand far outpaced supply and the SEB tried to ration sugar for candy makers and soda bottlers.[99] But without its network of volunteers and local boards, the USFA was ineffective. Without its policing, wholesalers and retailers ignored SEB rules and charged exorbitant prices.[100] Congress authorized the SEB for another year, but President Wilson chose not to use the corporation to buy the 1919–20 Cuban crop.

To handle the hoarders and profiteers, Wilson transferred many of the USFA's enforcement functions to the Justice Department's new, short-lived High Cost of Living Bureau. In a fitting conclusion to Hoover's wartime campaign, for a short time profiteers and hoarders were investigated by the same agents, under Attorney General A. Mitchell Palmer, who were busily rounding up and deporting suspected leftists.

Conclusion

For a short time, the USFA's Sugar Division coordinated complex geographies of supply and distribution in order to balance the desires of diverse producers and consumers. It coordinated limited shipping in order to maximize transportation efficiency and level the costs of distributing goods across the country. It set purchase and consumer prices and allocated sugar on the world market. And it created one of the earliest examples of a government-owned and financed corporation, the Sugar Equalization Board, which briefly bought and sold all the sugar for the United States and the Allies. Food administrators during the war also worked with small-scale ethnic grocers to meet the needs of diverse consumers, even as they used new legal mechanisms to discipline and reform merchants' business practices. Administrators had achieved some of the key economic goals articulated by Democrats and Progressive Republicans over the previous decade. They sought stable, low prices for domestic consumers while also compensating producers for the costs of regional and international competition. Conservative business leaders also found confirmation of some of their core economic beliefs. Wartime economic planning showed the utility of corporate administration. Ultimately, the wartime sugar programs gave U.S. policymakers a new role in controlling the global sugar market while reinforcing the move toward corporate management in both public administration and private markets.

In his statement before the U.S. Senate in 1918, Herbert Hoover defended the government's unprecedented involvement in the sugar economy by arguing that sugar was "a sort of binding material on which our cuisine so largely revolves." Hoover's statement ignored the role government policies played in positioning the commodity as the fulcrum of U.S. diets. Though during the war urban dwellers surely had to work harder to buy sugar, the cumulative effect of wartime policies was to guarantee not only a steady supply of cheap sugar, but also that many people counted cheap sugar among the rights and pleasures of citizenship.[101]

CHAPTER FOUR

COMMODITY CULTURES AND CROSS-BORDER DESIRES

Piloncillo between Mexico and the United States
in the 1910s through the 1930s

In the spring of 1918, a year after the United States entered the war, Mexican American newspapers in the Southwest urged families to make their own sugar beet syrup to supplement scarce refined sugar.[1] "Make your own sugar [Haga usted su azúcar]" counseled one article, which called on Mexican American frugality and self-sufficiency. The articles urged families to write to the USDA for instructions on growing, slicing, and boiling sugar beets at home. The syrup could then be condensed into a brown loaf sugar.[2] This may have appealed to some families, since sugar was scarce and prices were high. And the results might have looked familiar, since it resembled piloncillo, the unrefined cane sugar common in rural Mexico. But for many Mexican and Mexican Americans, the advice to make beet sugar probably seemed ironic, since they were simultaneously being recruited as low-wage agricultural workers in the U.S. sugar beet industry. Homemade and industrially made beet sugars were flip sides of the same coin for many Mexicans and Mexican Americans during the war.

Mexicans had already been traveling north to work in the beet fields for several years. Some came to the United States seeking refuge from instability and violence during and after the Mexican Revolution (1910–17). Some had been recruited by sugar companies, which actively sought field laborers from Mexico on behalf of the farmers from whom they bought their beets. Wartime labor shortages and restrictions on European and Asian immigration drew more Mexican workers to the Midwest and the Rocky Mountain states. The Immigration Act of 1917 went farther than previous legislation by creating an "Asiatic Barred Zone," a geographically and racially defined region from which laborers could not legally enter the United States. Unlike many groups, Mexicans were not excluded on either geographic or racial grounds. Though they faced heightened restrictions at the border, the U.S. Labor Department collaborated with the Mexican government to create a temporary guest worker program during the war at the insistence of sugar beet and cotton growers. After the war, Mexicans continued to work beets and by the early 1920s did most of the hand labor in the industry. Indeed, sugar beets played a key role in shaping the geography of Mexican settlement in the United States.[3]

Beet sugar was not a product that most Mexicans had encountered in Mexico. Especially in rural areas, people typically ate piloncillo, or, depending on location and income, they might have eaten refined sugar. As Mexicans sought work in the United States, they increasingly ate refined beet sugar, which was cheap and widely available. But Mexican merchants in the United States also seized the opportunity to supply the familiar flavors of home by importing piloncillo. As we saw in the previous chapters, consumers in the United States contested their positions within a hierarchically organized sugar market in multiple ways. While some people claimed the privilege of eating refined sugar in order to assert their status, beginning during World War I, Mexican merchants and consumers valorized less-refined brown sugars because they strengthened workers' claims to being Mexican, even when they were in the United States. Simultaneously nostalgic and nationalist, piloncillo's social and cultural significance changed in the United States. In Mexico piloncillo had been poor people's food, but workers in the United States were eventually willing to pay more for piloncillo than they paid for refined sugar. While they could do so only for special occasions, piloncillo gave elite and working-class Mexicans a means to negotiate their place in U.S. race and class hierarchies.

Merchants expanded their cross-border trade in piloncillo in response to the same wartime sugar scarcities that brought Mexican workers into the sugar beet fields of the United States. Traders had shipped piloncillo from Mexico into South Texas for at least a century, as part of a system of regional commodity trade that linked the borderlands' cattle economies.[4] Before the construction of railroads that joined Mexico's expanding commercial networks with the United States in the 1880s, ox-carts and ferry boats carried piloncillo and other supplies across the Rio Grande. Norteños—Mexicans from the northern states—increasingly directed their market activity north, toward the United States, and south, toward Mexico's urban centers. San Antonio, Laredo, and Monterrey formed an axis through which an elite class of businessmen in Monterrey profited

Classic U.S. - exportable
on needs / wants
of money

from cotton and textile production, steel works, and breweries. In the 1910s, a few began shipping more piloncillo. This new era of trade differed from earlier ones in several ways. First, the trade was not conducted within the already existing ranching communities, but instead was the work of Monterrey merchants who arrived in Texas as refugees from the Mexican Revolution. Second, railroad cars carried larger quantities of piloncillo than previously, moving primarily through the border crossings at Laredo, Brownsville, and El Paso. Finally, merchants marketed piloncillo to a wider base of consumers outside of the Texas-Mexico border region. The simultaneous movement of Mexican merchants and laborers, along with sugar scarcities during and after the Mexican Revolution and World War I, had created a new market for piloncillo.

The movements of workers and piloncillo into U.S. sugar beet fields were closely interrelated facets of the U.S. sugar empire. While the relationship between Mexico and the United States was not imperial in a formal sense, the double movement of beet workers and piloncillo can nonetheless be interpreted as imperial. The beet industry capitalized on a history of land dispossession dating to the Mexican American War and the Treaty of Guadalupe Hidalgo (1848). These legacies shaped the legal position of Mexican-descent people in the United States, who found themselves increasingly unable to defend their land rights in a court system biased against them. By the 1910s, U.S. citizens of Mexican descent in the Southwest had lost much of the land to which they formerly held title and increasingly turned to migratory agricultural labor. New migrants from Mexico joined the same labor circuits.[5]

If territorial conquest had contributed to Mexican Americans' participation in wage labor markets, then the legacy of the Treaty of Guadalupe Hidalgo also meant that they occupied an exceptional niche in the U.S. racial hierarchy. The treaty, ratified at a time when only whites could legally naturalize as U.S. citizens, implicitly classified Mexicans as legally white by collectively naturalizing anyone living in territory ceded by Mexico. Court rulings upheld this principle in the era of race-based immigration and citizenship restrictions aimed at Asians. However, in social practice, Mexicans and Mexican Americans were rarely treated as white. Increasingly, through the 1920s, nativists cast Mexicans as racially reviled peons and sought to extend race-based exclusion laws to them. In the context of charged public debates over their status, middle-class and elite Mexicans and Mexican Americans distanced themselves from the laboring masses in the hope of claiming legal and social whiteness. The piloncillo trade was thus one route by which a few Mexicans strengthened their claims to a tenuous social status.[6]

This chapter is divided into three sections that elaborate the argument that Mexican piloncillo and U.S. beet sugar were parallel commodity systems. The first section describes the political significance of sugar in Mexico during the revolutionary and postrevolutionary periods. Next, the chapter describes some of the merchants who imported piloncillo from Mexico to the United States between the 1910s and the late 1930s. The final section describes food systems, consumer cultures, and formations of race and class among Mexican workers in the United States in the 1920s and 1930s, using piloncillo as a lens.

Sweetness, Mestizaje, and Modernity in Revolutionary and Postrevolutionary Mexico

The businessmen who produced, imported, and sold piloncillo in the United States were generally middle- or upper-class Mexicans from Nuevo León who came to the United States as refugees during the Mexican Revolution. Monterrey elites had been relatively insulated from fighting until 1913. But new conflicts after that brought the region fully into the Revolution. Troops took over key industries in Monterrey, and many elites relocated their money and families to Texas.[7] J. M. Marroquin, the merchant who convinced the U.S. Food Administration (USFA) to allow him to expand his piloncillo trade during World War I, arrived in the United States from Monterrey in 1914. He and his brother had already traveled to the United States a few times in 1913. Feliciano Marroquin Sr., the head of the family, arrived in late March 1914 as Mexican troops approached Monterrey. In October, he brought his family to live in San Antonio. A third son, Gregorio, lived in Laredo. The family stayed exclusively in the United States for the next three years.

The circumstances of the Marroquins' arrival remind us that their enterprise was profitable not just because of the world war, but also because of the state of affairs in Mexico. Mexican instability meant there were hefty profits to be made for those who could produce and transport sugar and other scarce foods. Merchant families like the Marroquins owned haciendas that, in good times, supplied their piloncillo trade. But at the time they fled their home in 1914, rebel soldiers were destroying railroads and haciendas, and conditions were risky for merchants who ventured into the countryside. This was especially the case between 1914

Molina de Caña (Cane Mill), San Pedro, Villa de Santiago,
Nuevo Leon, Mexico, postcard, n.d.

and 1917, when skirmishes were widespread in the borderlands. Some importers were forced to cancel their USFA import licenses because of "revolutionary conditions" in Mexico.[8] A Mexican federal hydrologic survey team witnessed the destruction firsthand when they found that soldiers had recently attacked an area they intended to survey. Though nearby haciendas had been burned and crops destroyed, the engineers found peasants using a small water-powered cane mill to produce piloncillo. Neither the cane nor their sugar-making equipment had been destroyed, and the inspectors' photographs reveal that this had been a fruitful harvest. What the peasants intended to do with the piloncillo is open to speculation.

The backdrop for both labor migration and the burgeoning piloncillo business was thus the Mexican Revolution and its extended aftermath, during which multiple groups vied for control over resources, national identity, and paths to modernization. Some participants in the Revolution saw the sugar industry as central to their calls for reform because of its links to ousted president Porfirio Díaz (1876–1910). During his tenure, Díaz had promoted national development and modernization through foreign investment. With Díaz's support, Europeans, U.S. Americans, and Mexicans introduced modern sugar-manufacturing equipment, irrigation, and rail transportation into the Mexican countryside.[9] The state of Morelos, south of Mexico City, was the heart of the Porfirian sugar industry, supplanting the former centers of sugar production along the coasts. By expropriating peasant landholdings, hacienda owners gained land, water, transportation, and labor in Morelos. They replaced antiquated equipment with new central mills that processed cane from an ever-widening area. Mexico's modernizers hoped that the resulting centrifugal sugar would replace piloncillo on most people's tables. Mexican policymakers saw mass-produced sugar as an efficient, inexpensive food that would free more people for urban industrial labor. When in 1911 peasants joined together to contest the dispossession and exploitation they had experienced during Díaz's regime, they targeted the sugar industry in Morelos, burning cane fields and destroying mills. When plantation owners fled, they used the land for subsistence production of corn, beans, and piloncillo. For them, piloncillo was a better use of sugarcane, one that stood for self-sufficiency and an alternative path to modernity.

By the conclusion of fighting in 1917, leaders were eager to rebuild Mexico's decimated sugar industry. In doing so, they tested the limits of their new political ideals and institutions. The 1917 Constitution restricted foreign land ownership, offered labor protections, and authorized land redistribution, thus holding out the promise that peasants might gain permanent access to former hacienda lands. Land reform proved politically useful for Mexico's new leaders, as in 1920, when northern leader General Alvaro Obregón gained national power, in part by making concessions to peasants in Morelos. He redistributed former sugar haciendas and divided them into *ejidos*—communally held lands. Obregón did not see ejidos as the main source for the nation's sugar, however. During his subsequent presidency (1920–24), he enacted policies to prevent the industry from following Morelos's example. Obregón decreed that sugar plantations outside of Morelos were exempt from agrarian reform. He also increased sugar tariffs in 1920 in order to stimulate new capital investments and, ideally, to achieve self-sufficiency in sugar.[10] Obregón couched his reforms in terms of national self-sufficiency and independence from the United States. But in truth, Obregón's land and trade policies opened opportunities for a new generation of investors, especially in the northern region, from which he and other leaders hailed.

Obregón's successor, Plutarco Elías Calles (1924–28), another norteño who had served as a general in the Mexican Revolution, was one such investor. Calles secured favorable loans, irrigation subsidies, and land rights for his sugar refinery at El Mante, in the northern state of Tamaulipas. In 1931 and 1932 he helped create a finance bank for sugar producers and Azúcar, S.A., a quasi-governmental cooperative marketing agency modeled on the U.S. Sugar Equalization Board. Together, Obregón, Calles, and others redirected sugar investments northward, and toward their own coffers. Because of their efforts, refined sugar consumption in Mexico increased threefold between 1921 and 1936 among industrial, transportation, and professional workers, particularly in the central and northern states.[11]

As refined sugar became more common, people increasingly deemed piloncillo to be suitable only for the poorest workers and peasants. Nonetheless, people continued to buy and sell piloncillo as a local and regional commodity. Mexican and U.S. researchers documented the persistence of piloncillo as a dietary staple and component of religious rituals. Small-scale piloncillo producers functioned as petty capitalists within regional trade networks, working at the fringes of other economic activities. Piloncillo sales provided income for the mill owners and sugar makers and the farmers who grew cane on the edges of their corn fields. Producers extracted cane juice using small mills, mostly animal- or water-powered until the 1930s, when some producers invested in small motor-driven mills. They then boiled the syrup, typically in a large copper pot, and skimmed off the impurities. Experienced sugar makers judged by the color, consistency, and smell of the boiling syrup when it was ready to be poured into wood or clay molds to cool. After cooling, the cones of sugar were wrapped in cane leaves or paper and boxed for shipment. Producers sold their piloncillo at weekly regional markets, and mestizo wholesalers resold the product more widely.[12] Small-scale piloncillo production of this sort was common across Mexico, and the sector maintained a relatively steady level of production, regardless of the vicissitudes of the national and international sugar markets.

Elites did not approve. One source of their resistance to piloncillo was its association with intoxication. Some people linked piloncillo with marijuana, a drug they vilified as a source of madness and social decay.[13] As well, government officials estimated that as much as half of all piloncillo was used to produce *aguardiente*, an alcoholic beverage. The image of drunken peasants was anathema to elite mestizos, who hoped that modernization would bring sobriety. They believed that taxes on aguardiente enriched local power brokers and detracted from efforts to centralize a national economy and culture. Elite Mexicans also associated aguardiente with indigenous people, whom they viewed as a barrier to Mexican modernization. Such views were summarized by sociologist Edmundo

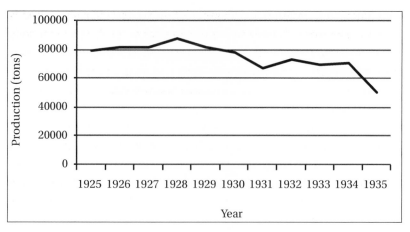

FIGURE 1. Piloncillo Production in Mexico (Tons), 1925–1935. Compiled from the Secretaria de Hacienda de México, *Revista de Hacienda* (June 1938), 19.

Mendieta Huerta in his investigation of indigenous *Huastecos* in San Luis Potosí. He found that the Huastecos consumed piloncillo daily. They produced it on a small industrial scale using animal power, and they traded it regionally. Despite evidence of both remunerative economic activity and the consumption of piloncillo as food rather than alcoholic drink, Mendieta Huerta concluded that these *"indios"*—the derisive term for indigenous people—were apathetic and drunk and led a vegetative life. He insisted—in all capital letters—that Huastecos could be part of Mexican civilization only when they adopted modern production and consumption practices, which included refined sugar and sobriety.[14]

Mexican American newspapers in the United States reflected Mexican ambivalence over the meanings of piloncillo through articles and serialized fiction. Perhaps the most explicit example was a 1935 short story, "Sangre en el Haurapo," published in San Antonio's *La Prensa* by Mexican author Rodolfo García Bravo y Olivera.[15] The story opens as workers cut cane and prepare for piloncillo and aguardiente production. The worker who operates the cane-crushing mill insists, against the boss's advice, on wearing his loose, peasant-style shirt. The man's sleeve is caught by the mill's rollers and his arm is pulled in and crushed. In gory detail, the story describes how his blood runs into the cane juice and the limb appears as a mass of meat. They succeed in amputating the damaged limb, thus saving the worker's life through swift action and bravery. The tale, written as part of a series depicting Mexican regional curiosities, suggests that older modes of rural production and material culture—small-scale mills, piloncillo, aguardiente, peasant clothing—result in a loss of bodily integrity. The worker's body serves as a metaphor for the national body politic, which is literally crushed by antiquated technology. In response to such destruction, Mexico's modernizing reformers promoted modern styles of clothing and food, monolingual Spanish education, and scientific agriculture.

One prominent advocate of Mexican modernization, José Vasconcelos, commissioned a series of murals to express this vision.[16] Between 1923 and 1928, artist Diego Rivera painted two large mural panels showing piloncillo production in the Secretaría de Educación Pública building in Mexico City. Rivera painted brightly colored, larger-than-life figures that embodied both masculinized, mestizo strength and the feminized fertility of the land. Rivera divided the agricultural and industrial production of piloncillo into two separate frescos that show the process chronologically from top to bottom and left to right, as one would read a book. In the foreground of Rivera's image of the farm, a man—barefoot and dressed in the clothes of a rural worker—holds a bundle of cut cane. Two barefoot women also stand in the foreground, one holding a baby. The figures' gaze draws the viewers' attention to the industrial process in the next panel, which shows rows of equipment. Unlike in "Sangre en el Huarapo," the mill poses no danger to the workers' bodily integrity. To the contrary, their bodies appear to be in harmony with the gears of the cane crusher, the vats, and the sugar syrup pouring into the molds. In other murals, Rivera depicted the past harsh conditions of colonial sugar production, which showed the Spanish introducing sugarcane to Mexico and slaves laboring in the fields. By contrast, Rivera's murals in the Secretaría de Educación Pública do not show this brutal history, instead presenting piloncillo as an alternative to the subservience of plantation peonage. By visually representing the mutual dependence and integrity of agrarian and industrial processes, Rivera's murals highlighted independent production and consumption of uniquely Mexican goods as crucial for modernization. His images named piloncillo as an emblem of national integrity.

Piloncillo, in Rivera's rendition, seemed to offer peasants and workers the dignity of independent labor in the postrevolutionary idiom of mestizaje. Along with other postrevolutionary intellectuals, Vasconcelos and Rivera imagined that Mexican modernity was a product of indigenous and Spanish heritage merging in mestizo bodies like those he showed producing piloncillo. Much as corn symbolized both Mexican indigeneity and independence, Rivera depicted piloncillo as an emblematic culinary contribution to Mexico's racial synthesis.[17] By lauding Mexicans as a unique, mixed race, Rivera, Vasconcelos, and others countered eugenic and biological racists who stereotyped indigenous Mexicans as idle, inefficient, drunken, and backward. Instead, Rivera and his contemporaries asserted that Mexicans could forge a uniquely modern, mestizo material culture.

Despite Rivera's attempts to valorize piloncillo, many of Mexico's modernizers remained ambivalent about both a modern Mexican racial synthesis and piloncillo. For them, industrially produced, refined sugar seemed a better icon of Mexican modernity than piloncillo. Class relations and racial divides cut through the postrevolutionary Mexican nation, and the cultural politics of sugar sharpened these distinctions in the 1920s and 1930s. Refined sugar fed a growing urban working class at low cost and facilitated capital accumulation for a few elites. While refined sugar offered a narrative of modernity for some Mexicans, others challenged this story by choosing less-refined sugar. When piloncillo crossed the border into the United States, its associations with Mexican nationalism and modernity changed in yet other ways.

Piloncillo Mexicano Blanco: Merchants, Race, and Class across the Border

Given the association between refined sugar and modernity in Mexico, it is ironic that piloncillo, the antiquated peasant sugar, proved so useful for Mexican merchants seeking elite status in the United States. Mexican merchants typically did not see themselves as mestizo, instead identifying as Spanish-descent whites. They would have signaled this by eating refined white sugar and wheat bread, not piloncillo and corn.[18] Contemporary commentators pointed to the resulting contradiction of elite Mexicans selling piloncillo in the United States. Folklorist Américo Paredes, for example, recorded a song dating to the 1914 elite exodus from Monterrey:

Como estamos en Texas [Since we are in Texas]
el inglés hay que aprender [we must learn the English language]
para que con nuestros primos [so that our cousins]
nos podamos entender [can understand us].
Y venderles charamuscas [And so we can sell them charamuscas]

en la lengua del Tío Sam [in the language of Uncle Sam]:
—Mucho bueno palanquetas, [—Very good palanquetas,]
piloncillo *very fine.* [piloncillo very fine.][19]

Paredes points out that the song may have been performed to raise money for refugees. This *zarzuela*, or musical comedy, parodies Mexicans' attempts to fit into U.S. society by speaking English and putting on airs even as they sell typically lower-class Mexican street foods—candies and piloncillo. The song highlights the dissonance between the manners and language of middle-class merchants and other working-class Mexicans in the area. The song persisted in the repertoire of South Texas musicians, likely because a visible class of Mexicans continued to sell themselves as refined merchants by offering lower-class Mexican goods such as piloncillo.

For many middle-class Mexicans, the Revolution resulted in downward mobility as they lost assets and wound up performing manual labor, sometimes in the United States. Those middle-class and elite Mexicans, like the Marroquins, who emerged relatively unscathed from the Revolution often did so by juggling resources from both the United States and Mexico. The Marroquins in particular made strategic use of the wartime crisis in both places. As we saw, Marroquin was adept at navigating the U.S. Food Administration regulations during the war. He reestablished his regular trade with relative ease as the war wound down, eventually returning to Monterrey in 1920. His brothers remained in Texas, while other family members lived in Mexico City. Over the next twenty-five years, the Marroquins crossed the border dozens of times. By the late 1930s, the Marroquins had expanded to Veracruz and San Luis Potosí. They had their own freight and customs agents, and in addition to wholesale offices they operated two retail shops in San Antonio.[20] Merchants who sold piloncillo in Los Angeles, and those who eventually expanded into the Midwest, had similarly diverse strategies and connections to the borderlands. They used familial connections and cultural affinity with both Mexico and the United States to negotiate cross-border trading.

Some merchants who sold piloncillo in the United States owned haciendas and farms on which laborers produced significant quantities of piloncillo.[21] A review of the petitions submitted to the Mexican secretary of agriculture and development requesting rights to use federal water in the state of Nuevo León, for example, suggests that many of those who made such requests for the purpose of fabricating piloncillo were also merchants conducting cross-border commerce. J. M. Rodriguez, for example, returned annually to his family's hacienda in Nuevo León to oversee the sugarcane harvest and piloncillo production. Merchants thus accumulated capital by exploiting productive resources like water and labor in Mexico to produce low-cost goods that sold at higher prices in the United States.[22]

As piloncillo crossed the border, it was commodified in new ways, and its meanings in the United States changed to reflect its buyers' and sellers' social experiences. In rural Mexico, there were great variations in piloncillo's color, texture, shape, size, and sugar content. Customs inspectors at the border quantified piloncillo by weighing it and measuring its sugar content. Beginning in the 1920s, U.S. plant quarantine inspectors banned the importation of sugarcane leaves, the traditional packaging for piloncillo. Instead, merchants began using paper or cardboard boxes, sometimes labeled with their brand name. As merchants expanded their wholesale distribution in the United States, they found new reasons to offer standardized sizes. Besides negotiating with customs, standard sizes and prices made mail-order purchases more attractive. For the same reason, merchants began to brand their piloncillo and to use printed labels and advertisements. Ads typically noted what region the piloncillo originated from and made claims about the product's authenticity and purity.[23] Ads and packaging also pointed out other, ephemeral characteristics of the product. The Marroquins named their brand of piloncillo "El Rubio," "the blond one." In Mexico, as in the United States, the language used to describe sugar often paralleled that used to describe skin color: *trigueño* (wheat-colored), *rubio* (blond), *blanco* (white), *claro* (clear), *oscuro* (dark). The lighter the sugar, the higher the market price, because lighter sugars were presumed to be sweeter, purer, and more modern. The Marroquins' brand name signaled not only the color of the sugar, but also that it was the product of modern production methods, which apparently produced whiter piloncillo. El Rubio was, in fact, a popular brand that was widely distributed throughout California, Texas, Colorado, New Mexico, Arizona, and Kansas. Their brand name was thus one way that the Marroquins negotiated the contradiction of claiming whiteness by selling brown sugar.[24]

Merchants imported and distributed products that appealed to lower-class consumers, even though those goods may not have reflected their own ideas about what it meant to be Mexican. They bolstered their own identities as modern business elites by facilitating working-class material and consumer cultures. They participated in the formation of a borderlands business culture that extended far into the United States and Mexico and was aligned with U.S.-style business practices even as it was framed in terms of Mexican nationalism. Meeting the diverse needs of Mexican workers provided the Marroquin family with a lucrative niche and a way to maintain its status despite anti-Mexican sentiment in the United States. But what piloncillo meant to merchants was different from what it meant to the workers who purchased it.

Betabeleros and Piloncillo: Geographies of Mexican Settlement in the United States

As much as Mexican merchants used piloncillo to assert their white, middle-class status, beet sugar tells another story about Mexican and Mexican American working-class struggles. Advertisements for mail-order piloncillo ran side by side with ads recruiting *betabeleros*—beet workers—in *La Prensa*. The paper also carried ads for J. M. Marroquin's other business. Not only did he sell piloncillo; Marroquin also transmitted remittances from migrant laborers in the United States to their family members in Mexico.[25] This was probably the most lucrative branch of the business. Marroquin provided workers a practical link to the homeland by transferring some of their wages to family in Mexico, and he offered them a symbolic connection by selling them the familiar flavors of home. As one advertisement reminded readers, "When you are far from your beloved land, you want to taste something that brings back the memory of the fatherland."[26] But as they moved farther from the border, workers increasingly turned not to merchants like Marroquin but instead to U.S. markets for their provisions. They would have purchased much of their food from hostile white grocers in segregated towns or on credit from employers. In this context, piloncillo became a food for special occasions and nostalgic celebration rather than everyday fare.

As we have seen, the growth of the sugar beet industry in the United States was the product of efforts by white U.S. modernizers to remake arid western landscapes into wonderlands of agricultural and industrial productivity. Westerners boasted that their achievements in beet sugar production placed them at the forefront of modern civilization. The beet sugar industry emerged from an imperial moment, and it should come as no surprise that it produced a landscape polarized around differences of race and class. Sugar beet agriculture entrenched stark differences in

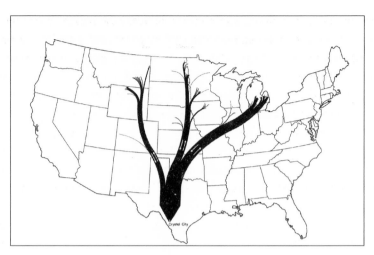

"Destinations of Mexican Sugar Beet Workers."
Works Progress Administration (1938).

access to resources among industrialists, bankers, farmers, and laborers. Some farmers owned their own land, but even they sometimes found themselves in dependent and disadvantaged relationships with the sugar companies and, increasingly, the banks that financed their crops. Sugar companies and bankers were at the top of the hierarchy, with control over cash and capital, and they leveraged their influence to shape trade and immigration policies that benefited the industry. Farmers, who were mostly (though not exclusively) native-born whites, occupied a marginal position beneath the sugar companies and bankers. But seasonal field laborers were at an unequivocal disadvantage. Though their labor was crucial to the enterprise, their rewards were scant.[27]

Sugar beet companies sometimes employed their own labor recruiters and sometimes hired independent contractors to coordinate the movement of Mexican workers from Mexico and Texas to Colorado, Wyoming, Nebraska, Michigan, Minnesota, and other states where beets were grown. During the war, the sugar beet and cotton industries had lobbied the U.S. Immigration Service to allow Mexican agricultural workers to enter the United States without fulfilling literacy requirements. Sugar companies actively recruited Mexican men to the beet fields during this period. A few beet workers returned to Mexico in 1921, during the brief recession. Mexicans began traveling again to the beet fields after 1923, as the sugar economy recovered and companies again recruited workers. This time, whole families, rather than single men, migrated together, since the labor of women and children allowed the family to eke out a reasonable season's wage. Sometimes families stayed only for the beet season, returning to Texas or Mexico during the winter. In response to laws in Texas prohibiting labor recruiting, sugar companies increasingly encouraged families to stay through the winter by building houses, usually in segregated colonies far from white towns. Others spent the winter in nearby cities, where they might find year-round industrial jobs.

The modernizing impulse that led boosters to promote sugar beets came with an equally forceful xenophobia toward the workers they recruited to do the brutal, seasonal stoop labor. These workers typically were not welcome to live in the towns and cities around which the beet industry was organized. In Greeley, Colorado, for example, only a handful of Mexicans lived within the city limits, all in crowded housing at the edge of town near the sugar factory. In Colorado during the 1920s, Mexicans encountered a revived Ku Klux Klan, whose members were vocally anti-Mexican and anti-Catholic but also prominent community leaders. Beet workers filed complaints with both Mexican and U.S. authorities about the worst examples of segregation and discrimination, including "White Trade Only" signs in businesses and restaurants. But such complaints did little to alter Mexican beet workers' limited mobility. Social reformers noted that Mexicans' exclusion from white businesses resulted in poorer nutrition, since workers could not easily buy fresh fruits, vegetables, meat, or milk. Outside of the Southwest, few Mexicans owned grocery stores, wholesale grocery businesses, or restaurants. Rather than patronize bigoted local stores, a few Mexicans purchased groceries from Mexican mail-order merchants in Chicago, San Antonio, or Los Angeles.

Segregation limited Mexicans' choices about where to live and shop, and low wages limited their choices of foods. They generally depended on provisions sold by their employers, and many families relied on credit from sugar companies or farmers to purchase groceries before they were paid at the end of each season. When they bought on credit, Mexicans could only buy from a designated list of approved provisions. The sugar companies provided local merchants with lists of what they regarded as "necessities." A typical list included "flour, Mexican beans, potatoes, salt pork, sugar, coffee, tobacco, canned tomatoes, chile peppers, vermicelli, spaghetti, white corn meal, matches, salt, pepper, lard, soap, and baking powder." Despite their dependence on white grocers, Mexicans could usually maintain familiar diets of beans, corn, tortillas, and chilies. In Colorado, for example, Mexicans could buy locally grown and canned pinto beans.[28]

Women took an important role in mitigating the effects of segregation and limited food choices by adapting available ingredients using Mexican cooking techniques. In his study of Mexican immigration in the late 1920s, Mexican anthropologist Manuel Gamio and his research team asked their informants to describe their eating habits and found that many immigrants ate in "the Mexican style."[29] Attachment to Mexican flavors and preparation techniques emerged in Gamio's interviews as a gendered narrative of sentimental patriotism. A person's ability to maintain familiar foodways was almost always linked to the skills of a wife or mother who prepared the family meals. Nivardo del Rio's was a typical response. He told the interviewer, "I haven't changed from what I was in Mexico. I eat according to Mexican style, for my wife makes my food." Like many of the other male respondents, del Rio took for granted that mothers, sisters, and wives could reproduce familiar flavors in the United States. Women told a different story. Nivardo's wife—Concha Gutierrez del Rio—told the interviewer that "the food stuffs, besides costing a lot, are no good for making good Mexican food. One can't get the things that one needs, so that it might be said that the food is half-Mexican and half-American, being neither the one nor the other." Women relied heavily on chilies as a seasoning, which they bought by mail order from San Antonio merchants, or through informal trade networks linking them to the hispano farmers of northern New Mexico and southern Colorado.[30]

Outside observers made special note of children's diets, pointing out that in Mexican families children ate a paltry diet of beans and wheat flour tortillas, supplemented with sweetened coffee. Reformers did not think coffee was a suitable beverage for children, and they discouraged the habit. Gamio noted several instances where families had stopped giving children coffee because a nurse or teacher had told them it was dangerous. Describing a middle-class family that had otherwise retained Mexican eating habits, Gamio wrote, "They don't give coffee to the children because the 'nurse' from the school has told them that it is very bad for the children to take things which irritate them." About another family he wrote, "The influence of the American environment keeps them from giving coffee to the boys, and much less chile and tortillas." Yet the consumption of sweetened coffee was probably an important source of calories for working children. Just as African American children ate cheap candies as they picked cotton in the South, Mexican American children working sugar beets drank sweetened coffee within their families' protected space.

Gamio, an advocate of postrevolutionary Mexican modernizing efforts, approvingly noted how quickly Mexican immigrants adapted to U.S. material and food cultures. Of course, they often had little choice, since there were limits to what they could find and afford. Unlike in Mexico, where piloncillo was inexpensive, refined sugar was the much cheaper choice in the United States.[31] In 1929, for example, piloncillo sold for about 18 cents per pound outside of Texas. Refined sugar, on the other hand, sold for a little less than 6 cents per pound. At these prices, refined sugar became a daily dietary staple for many poor workers—urban and rural—in the United States. It was this dependence on mass-produced foods that endowed Mexican goods with meaning for many migrants. Given the substantial changes in Mexicans' diets in the United States, the occasional consumption of piloncillo was one way they expressed what it meant to be *mexicanos de afuera*—Mexicans outside of Mexico. Eating piloncillo was a form of nostalgia for noncommercial modes of production and the imagined self-sufficiency of Mexican rural life. As one beet worker, heavily indebted for groceries, reportedly put it, "To hell with the U.S. We don't have to be slaves in Mexico."[32] Short of returning to Mexico, workers purchased Mexican foods to remind them of home. Piloncillo tended to be traded along with Mexican grocery items, like beans and cheese, medicinal herbs, chocolate, nixtamal mills (for grinding corn), and sometimes hats, pottery, or other regional specialties from across Mexico. Most of these items had links to specific cities or regions, thus summoning memories of familiar places. If one could feel like a Mexican by buying and eating goods imported from Mexico, then it did not matter where in the United States one was. In this sense, the grocery trade helped workers to create a sense of autonomy as they navigated hostile consumer cultures in the United States.

At nearly three times the price of refined sugar, piloncillo was a pleasure linked closely with family ritual, religious celebration, and nostalgia for a way of life not dominated by wage labor. Migration changed the contexts in which people ate the product, intensifying its use for rituals, holidays, and celebrations. During the war, advertisements presented piloncillo as an item for everyday consumption. By the early 1920s, however, merchants advertised it as either a candy treat or a special holiday product, usually for Lent or Christmas. Recipes in the women's section of newspapers called for piloncillo as an ingredient in seasonal foods at the same time. For example, a 1924 recipe printed in *La Prensa* described how to use piloncillo to make *capirotada*, a special bread pudding served during Lent.[33] Given its great expense in the United States, piloncillo could also demonstrate material success through the conspicuous consumption of what had become a luxury good. As class distinctions sharpened within Mexican immigrant communities, the purchase of piloncillo signified both nationalism and financial stability.

Conclusion

The story of piloncillo illustrates how elite and working-class Mexicans negotiated their racial and national identities in the United States. While piloncillo was bought and sold on a much smaller scale than refined sugar, this seemingly insignificant product sheds light on a significant, transnational cultural economy. Piloncillo brought both merchants and workers into new regimes of labor and consumer culture. In the context of transnational labor migration, the significance of consuming piloncillo was turned on its head: instead of connoting rural poverty, outside Mexico the product registered working-class nostalgia for home and elite business acumen. Customs enforcement, tariffs, immigration, and agricultural inspection were all tools the U.S. government used to control the border. Mexican merchants successfully negotiated these barriers in order to strengthen their own privileges of class and race. They created markets through which workers' desires could be named, advertised, bought, and sold. The coercive imperatives of capitalist labor migration were remade into consumer desires for products "de México para los Mexicanos."[34] These desires were fleeting, but they took concrete form on freight cars, store shelves, and dinner plates. For Mexican workers, piloncillo articulated the vast distance between exploitative beet sugar labor and independent cane production. Commodities and the practices that surround them created spaces of resistance to global capitalism even as they naturalized inequalities of power. If, when they ate piloncillo, Mexican workers tasted an idealized Mexican landscape, that flavor could only have been fleeting.

CHAPTER FIVE

FROM CANE TO CANDY

The Racial Geography of New Mass Markets
for Candy in the 1920s

Beginning in 1922, a song called "The Sugar Blues," first published as sheet music during the sugar shortages of 1919, caught the attention of working-class African American women singers who recorded versions of the song through the 1920s.[1] "The Sugar Blues" contained elements of earlier ragtime music but also offered a new perspective based on women's experiences as urban consumers and workers. African American women used the song to claim the pleasures and pains of sweetness and to articulate a sense of camaraderie among urban consumers. "The Sugar Blues" linked the themes of love and loss, migration and movement through double entendres and playful laments. Its lyrics lamented the scarcity of sweetness, implicitly understood as both sugar and male companionship: "My loving man just as sweet as he can be, but the dog-gone fool turned sour on me." Sweetness offered a metaphor for women to critique the limits of gendered norms of domesticity, especially in the context of an unprecedented migration by single people and whole families leaving the rural South for southern and northern cities. The song's lyrics omitted the productive landscape, and the singers were not old-fashioned mammies comforting pickaninnies with their dreams of candy. For the female subjects of "The Sugar Blues," sugar mapped an emerging economy of desires—for economic independence, companionship, and refined consumer goods.

New forms of labor and consumer culture, such as those alluded to in "The Sugar Blues," contributed to a dramatic increase in sugar production and consumption during the 1920s. As well, heavy investments in sugar production and the reorganization of the industries in Cuba, Puerto Rico, Hawaii, and the Philippines during and after the war stimulated sugar production to an unprecedented degree. Between 1920 and 1930, the quantity of refined sugar available in the United States increased from 85 to 110 pounds per capita.[2] Soldiers had received candy as part of their rations during World War I, and they came back from Europe "with a greater taste for sweets" than ever before.[3] Consumers in the United States found a multitude of new ways to enjoy the bounty, including an explosion of manufactured, canned, packaged, and mass-produced products that filled storekeepers' shelves.

The U.S. government played a role in this market expansion. While the 1920s has typically been viewed as a period in which the U.S. government took a back seat in the economy and in overseas expansion, a slightly different picture emerges when one considers the role played by government agencies in the processes of commodification at work in this period. Federal agencies played a crucial role in regularizing and standardizing the national routes of trade and the categories through which goods were exchanged. The Interstate Commerce Commission (ICC), the Bureau of Foreign and Domestic Commerce (BFDC), the Food and Drug Administration (FDA), and the Women's Bureau, for example, all had a say in how goods would be marketed. While the federal government had limited control over trade conducted within the borders of a single state, once goods crossed state lines reformers realized that the government might claim greater authority to ensure better working and eating conditions. The ICC, the FDA, and the Women's Bureau all sought such changes, with varying degrees of success. The Commerce Department was more successful in its collaboration with businessmen, who eagerly accepted government assistance in market expansion and business data collection.

This chapter describes how businessmen and federal officials fostered a mass market for inexpensive sweets during the 1920s, mostly intended for working- and middle-class consumers. Government agencies, candy producers' trade organizations, and urban and rural workers each played a role in shaping candy sales. Through national marketing, confectioners and advertisers cultivated white middle-class and working-class African American and Asian American consumers. In creating and differentiating markets for various grades of candy, the industry relied on older racial stereotypes about working-class consumers' preferences for less-refined sweets. As African Americans moved into cities, they encountered the brutality lurking below the surface of confectioners' seemingly innocent renditions of edible black bodies. Cheap candy signaled workers' embeddedness in coercive systems of labor control as much as it marked the innocent pleasures to which confectioners alluded. In this context, African Americans sometimes preferred less-refined, homemade sweeteners because they emblematized autonomy in otherwise exploitative labor regimes, much like Mexicans' choice to eat piloncillo.

The final sections of the chapter describe labor and market structure in the southern confectionery industry, which was tailored to what I call the Jim Crow candy hierarchy. Not only were the final products differentiated according to the race of the intended consumers, but work in southern candy factories was segregated to reflect the same hierarchy. At the same time, candy manufacturers on the west coast in the 1920s moved to integrate Asian American businessmen from Hawaii and California into their associations. They did so as they sought to develop new overseas markets. Seeking to balance the uneven annual cycles in their businesses, confectioners looked for markets abroad, again relying on the familiar contrasts between civilized and uncivilized consumers. Taken together, the successes achieved by confectioners in the 1920s represented the realization of earlier reformers' hopes to tutor immigrants, African Americans, and colonial residents in civilized sugar consumption.

Producing Sweetness, Producing Little Laborers

Through the 1920s, small-scale local and regional candy production thrived alongside a growing number of nationally distributed brands such as Hershey, Mars Milky Way, Mary Jane, Oh Henry, and Honey Scotch. Sugar and candy were cheap, ubiquitous, and a source of calories most experts at the time believed was healthful. The birth of a national market would not have happened without the abundance of cheap sugar or the efforts of a few manufacturers who spearheaded a national trade movement to standardize products, equipment, and advertising. Their advertising strategies often echoed old associations between African American children and sweetness but also revealed the changing demographics of their markets as more people left rural areas for cities. Many working-class African Americans sought jobs and fled violence, poverty, and disrespect, and they traveled the same rail routes that increasingly carried sugar and candy into the South. The availability of mass-produced, inexpensive foods like sugar and candy in the countryside and in the city was integral to workers' experiences as they made their way in an urban industrial order. Advertising, music, and the candy itself created shared desires among consumers as they moved between different regions of the United States. The result was the gradual formation of a market for candy, with national tastes, distribution, and supply chains.

Candy makers in the 1920s struggled to build brands with national recognition and to create new occasions for consumption. They used advertising, radio, traveling salesmen, and especially their industry-wide cooperative organizations. They used national cooperative advertising campaigns to saturate cities with images of men, women, and children as entitled candy consumers. Rather than focusing on particular products, cooperative advertising encouraged consumption of candy in general. If everyone ate more candy, confectioners' reasoned, then there would be a bigger market for all to share. Confectioners portrayed the taste for sweetness as a natural human desire by circulating images, particularly of children eating sweets. Confectioners' advertising strategies emphasized the wholesomeness and inevitability of the middle-class white child's sweet tooth. Such publicity was bolstered by nutrition science, which named simple carbohydrates as an intrinsic component of many foods.[4] According to contemporary theories, children acquired a taste for sweetness in infancy after feeding on mothers' breast milk. The *Western Confectioner* built on this logic, advising that a child was "a customer who has a natural craving for sweets. This customer will spend for candy first, as the desire for confectionery is not only mental, but physical."[5] Ideally, parents would give their children candy every day, and children would have coins of their own with which to buy candy. The confectionery trade press was filled with images of white children at birthday parties and soda fountains, ecstatically enjoying candies and ice creams.[6] For confectioners, this form of eating signified financial independence for the family and a particularization of childhood as a privileged, "sweet" time of innocent pleasure.

Confectioners actively constructed sweetness as natural and corporal, and they did so in part by depicting African American children as natural consumers. Advertisers drew on musical and visual cultures of the preceding decades, repurposing them as racist marketing strategies aimed at white middle-class consumers of candy. Advertisements, packaging, store displays, and postcards showed African American children as consumers of molasses or watermelon fresh in the field, as in the nationally distributed Pickaninny Freeze, a watermelon-shaped ice cream bar patented in 1922.[7] The children often served as a visual metaphor for the candy itself, as when confections were named to create an allusion to African American children's bodies. For example, the egregious confection invented in Portland, Oregon, in 1923 called "nigger's toes" invited consumers to perform an imaginative act of cannibalism.[8] The image in the advertisement showed a gun-toting, cowboy hat–wearing blackface character whose feet were oversized Brazil nuts, dipped in chocolate.

This was "Bon-Bon Buddy" or "Little Brown Baby," who did not have families to protect them from white appetites. In such advertisements, black bodies served as proxies that normalized and naturalized white consumers' candy consumption.

While working-class African Americans and immigrants were key consumers of candy in both rural and urban areas, they rarely appeared in advertisements or articles as confectioners' targeted customers. There was one important exception. Confectioners gladly showcased African American and immigrant children eating their products during free community giveaways.[9] Confectioners believed that children—perhaps especially African American and immigrant children—were not yet fully civilized, and thus did not have control over their impulses. They would thus give themselves over to their appetites in public, where adults would modulate their own. To prove this theory, candy companies created opportunities for public displays of indulgence. Events with free candy or ice cream cultivated their reputations as wholesome community members and brought new customers. Photographs of an event in 1927 in Denver, Colorado, showed Italian and Mexican American children in work pants in line along with neatly dressed white children. At another event, held in San Francisco in 1928, the candy company posed an African American boy, a Chinese boy, and an Irish boy together in what, at first glance, was the familiar pose of eating sugarcane. But the boys, mouths open, were actually pretending to eat a giant peppermint-striped candy cane.[10] By changing the setting from rural to urban, these children were transformed from consumers of cane to consumers of candy cane. This image offered an updated urban location for labor and pleasure, but in doing so it persisted in naturalizing a taste for sweets by associating them with racialized bodies. Images of children chewing sugarcane might have adequately represented their subordinate social status twenty years earlier. But marginal consumption at the fringes of market production was not enough in the 1920s. Instead, children needed to eat *candy* in order to perform their critical new roles as both producers and consumers.

Advertising was not the only strategy confectioners used to expand their markets. Through the 1920s, large-scale confectioners aggressively marketed to an ever-wider territory, focusing especially on the South. As a 1930 report by the BFDC counseled, "The extensive colored population in the Southern States suggests that emphasis in that territory should be placed on moderately priced items." Northern and midwestern confectioners were especially successful at reaching new southern markets.

"No Race, Creed or Color in Candy's Appeal. Irish, Chinese, and Negro
Lads Snapped as One of San Francisco's Candy Day Stunts,"
Western Confectioner 15, no. 2 (November 1928).

New York, Chicago, St. Louis, Minneapolis, Philadelphia, Boston, Atlanta,
San Francisco, and Los Angeles far out-ranked other western and southern states in candy production. The J. N. Collins Company, for example,
began in 1920 with one factory in Minneapolis. By 1924, it had expanded
to a second factory in Philadelphia and opened a network of warehouses
in Norfolk, Atlanta, Memphis, Los Angeles, and San Francisco, to which
it shipped carloads of Walnettos and Honey Scotch. In 1929, the company
merged with Peter Paul, Inc., to form one of the largest national candy
companies in the United States.[11]

One important strategy wholesalers and industry associations used
as they sought new sales territory was to challenge railroad freight rates
before the ICC.[12] Freight rates, like sugar tariffs, were a tool in policymakers' repertoire for maintaining a hierarchically organized productive
geography. In theory, the ICC was charged with assessing fair rates to
level competition among producers regardless of region. However, rates
out of the South were historically higher than those moving goods *into*
the South. Likewise, rates for long hauls of merchandise were typically
lower than for shorter distances. This differential, though technically illegal, was often overlooked by regulators and amplified the economies of
scale big producers already enjoyed. In 1926, for example, the Strasser

	Corporate Location	Pounds Shipped Annually
F.W. Woolworth Company	Unspecified	8,000,000
New England Confectionery Company	Cambridge, Mass.	2,000,000
D. Pender Grocery Company	Norfolk, Va.	1,500,000
Harry L. Schlessinger, Inc.	Atlanta, Ga.	1,500,000
Bennett Hubbard Candy Company	Chattanooga, Tenn.	4,015,000
National Candy Company	St. Louis, Mo.	2,010,000

FIGURE 2. Annual Candy Shipments into and within the South by Major Shippers, 1928–1930. Compiled from the Interstate Commerce Commission, Investigation and Suspension Docket No. 3361, Classification Rating on Candy and Confectionery in Southern Territory, *Interstate Commerce Commission Reports*, vol. 161 (January–March 1930), 588.

Candy Company of Denver, Colorado, took advantage of low freight rates and expanded its warehouse by 10,000 square feet in order to sell in the South.[13] Southern manufacturers found little relief through the ICC, which often decided in favor of large candy producers in Denver, Chicago, and New York. Even though they advocated for better freight rates, southern confectioners faced increasing competition from national firms. The result of this heightened interregional competition among candy manufacturers was ever lower candy prices for consumers of moderate means.

Bound by the realities of freight rates, southern confectioners struggled to maintain a share of the candy business despite the dominance of northern and western manufacturers. Southern manufacturers excelled in providing cheap candies to the region's rural hinterland. Meridian, Mississippi, provides a case study of the dynamics that linked southern urban manufacturers with their rural consumers. A large town in east-central Mississippi near the Alabama border, Meridian was at the center of a regional commercial network. With train lines connecting it to all major manufacturing and farming districts across the South, people from Mississippi and Alabama sold their lumber and cotton harvests in Meridian. In exchange, they bought fertilizer, ice, and furniture as well as wholesale dry goods and groceries. Indeed, one of Meridian's most lucrative businesses in the 1920s was wholesale grocery distribution. Plantation shopkeepers in the Mississippi delta bought food wholesale, which they resold to sharecroppers and tenants, usually at a steep markup.

Local Meridian confectioners produced a sizable quantity of candy for distribution through this wholesale network. As many as six wholesale candy manufacturers were in business at any given point through the 1920s and 1930s.[14] Two firms, Rogers Candy Company and Meridian Candy Company, dominated the business. Owned by well-established local families, these businesses complemented other family enterprises, including grocery distribution. Since rail freight rates were high, the increasing availability of cars and trucks in the 1920s offered southern confectioners a better means to expand sales. They employed young white men as traveling salesmen to distribute their products to small rural stores. At least six men in Meridian worked as traveling candy salesmen in 1930. One candy salesman, for example, had begun his career at age twelve, working as a grocery salesman in his parents' general store. Located in an unincorporated farming community near Meridian, the store sold groceries and staples to nearby tenant farmers. After the family moved to town, this man took a job as a traveling candy salesman, no doubt plying the same rural routes he had known as a youth. Traveling salesmen sold to general stores, plantation commissaries, and filling stations.

Small-scale entrepreneurs, especially in Georgia, Mississippi, and Alabama, also produced inexpensive cane syrup, which was a staple for southern rural families. These states were the heart of the cotton belt, and no one produced sugar on an industrial scale there. Instead, cane syrup was an adjunct to cotton production and other industries, intended as a way to provision low-wage workers cheaply.[15] In Meridian, for example, white entrepreneurs like Henry Green and his two sons manufactured cane syrup as the W. P. Green Company through the early 1930s. The FDA heavily regulated such syrups, exercising a decisive role in making it a salable commodity in interstate commerce.[16] Its rulings on what could be labeled as syrup—and its seizures of stocks it deemed to be improperly marketed—regularized the regional cane syrup and molasses trades, ultimately bringing more mass-produced goods to rural and urban families.

Whether and when candy and store-bought syrup would entirely displace homemade forms of sweetness was a contentious issue for many people in the rural South. By shifting a key source of calories from family production to a commercial market, manufacturers, salesmen, and plantation owners asserted their priorities for the best uses of land and labor. But rural African Americans expressed a different view as they produced homemade cane or sorghum syrup, fruit, and honey on the margins of their cotton fields. By providing themselves with a modicum of independent family subsistence, they tried to resist debt to white grocers and landlords. W. E. B. Du Bois had explicitly linked store-bought sugar to the cycle of debt and dependency in sharecropping. Cotton sharecroppers, he pointed out, would often be "encouraged to buy more" extravagant goods, like sugar, by the merchant who supplied and financed him. Likewise, Booker T. Washington taught home-scale cane syrup production at Tuskegee as a crucial skill for self-sufficient black farmers. As cotton prices declined with the deepening agricultural depression in the 1920s and 1930s, sharecroppers and tenants faced pressure to use every available piece of land to grow that crop. By restricting sharecroppers' subsistence production and requiring them to purchase food on credit, landlords increased workers' immobility. They were fully aware that the same freight trains that brought goods south could carry their workers north. Landlords and merchants thus policed tenant and sharecropper compliance by regulating consumption and through extralegal violence, particularly in response to suspicions of labor organizing. Radical organizers in the Sharecroppers' Union, which met violent repression, had in fact complained about restrictions on subsistence production when they formulated their demands in 1931. They stated that "because the landowners have made us plant cotton on almost all the land, we have not enough vegetables, molasses cane and fruit for our own use."[17] In one sense, commercially produced candy and syrup can be read as sweetened coercion.

In his oral autobiography, *All God's Dangers*, African American sharecropper and Sharecroppers' Union activist Ned Cobb recalled the special place of homemade sweeteners in his family's struggles for autonomy. Cobb experienced the oppressive plantation system firsthand, having served twelve years in prison after a violent encounter between the Sharecroppers' Union and the Alabama sheriff in 1932. Cobb understood that commercial consumer cultures tied African Americans to a violent labor regime in the South. He fondly remembered chewing sugarcane, saying, "There aint ten people out of a hundred but what dearly loves to chew that old-fashioned sugar cane." Cobb described how he and the other farmers grew cane and sorghum to produce syrup for home consumption. "I'd cut down the cane, strip it, haul it to the man's mill out there close by the furnace," he said. Cobb remembered that his father also "made barrels of syrup, that old native sugar cane syrup, pure syrup; I was born and raised up eatin syrup. My daddy raised sugar cane every year he farmed—white man never did take his syrup. He didn't make no overproduction of syrup, he just made it for home use, and sometimes he'd make fifty and sixty gallons."[18] This mention of sugarcane and syrup is one of the few places in the autobiography where Cobb notes his father resisting white domination. Otherwise Cobb depicted his father as a product of slavery, questioning his authority and accusing him of failing to provide for his children or protect them from white employers.

Cobb's ability to provide for and protect his children was crucial to his own narrative of resistance to southern racial oppression. In Cobb's view, children needed to work because they needed to *learn* to work, as he had when he was a child. Even more, without their labor, families could hardly meet the demands of a prejudiced economic system or have a chance to eke out a modicum of independence. But Cobb insisted that children's work needed to be insulated from white control. Parents ought to personally direct children in their labor and also provide them adequate food and treats. Cobb believed his own father had failed to provide enough food and to manage his children's labor with attention to their ages and skills. It was in the context of such negotiations over the significance of children's rural work that merchants sold increasing quantities of commercially produced sweets in the countryside. Children got more candy during the times of year when their labor was most in demand. Indeed, factory surveys made by U.S. Women's Bureau inspectors in Meridian candy factories noted that cotton-picking season was the busiest time for producing cheap candy. Parents also increasingly chose to protect their children from the brutalities of Jim Crow capitalism by sending them to live with family in cities.

In his coming-of-age novel *Not without Laughter* (1930), Langston Hughes recognized the significant relationship between children and candy for African American families. In the novel, a young boy, Sandy, learns a difficult lesson in honesty by stealing money to buy candy and then lying about it to his grandmother. Rather than endure Sunday school, he regularly takes the nickel he was to put in the collection plate and buys candy with his friends. He is finally caught when he forgets a piece of candy in his shirt pocket and "it melted, stuck, and stained the whole front of his clean clothes." In his grandmother's parlor, a place of propriety and upward mobility, Sandy guiltily lies about where he got the money to buy the candy. When his father, Jimboy, returns home, Sandy is unable to continue the lie. Jimboy reprimands him, "White folks gets rich lyin' and stealin'—and some niggers gets rich that way, too—but I don't need money if I got to get it dishonest." Sandy's theft was not motivated by deprivation, for, as his father later says, "Don't I give you nickels for candy whenever you want 'em? . . . And don't I go with you to the store and buy you ice-cream and soda-pop any time you ask me?"[19] Sandy's punishment is not violent, but it is a temporary, symbolic separation from his family. His father "went out on the porch, slamming the screen door behind him," and his grandmother "returned to the kitchen and left him standing disgraced in the parlor." The child learns through this exchange that family is more important than the fleeting taste of sweetness.

Though African American families increasingly tried to protect their children by sending them north, children were not necessarily safer from racism there. Lucius Harris, age nine, learned this lesson when he was stabbed and beaten by shopkeepers in a Buffalo, New York, candy store in 1931.[20] Harris left rural Capron, Virginia, to live with relatives in a crowded working-class neighborhood in which immigrant whites lived side-by-side with black industrial workers. His mother, Annie Harris, remained in Virginia. She may have sent her son north in the hope that he would get a better education or perhaps earn wages in one of the steel mills that attracted black southerners in the 1920s. Either way, the movement of children like Harris into urban areas introduced them to a new world of consumer culture and brought them into contact with candy on a daily basis. For many children coming of age in these years, their first encounter with the brutalities of consumer capitalism was in the candy store. The rudiments of exchange, value, and desire were learned in front of the glass candy cases and trading penny candy with mates outside in the alley. Children, especially boys, had the run of bustling street corners, where soda fountains, candy stores, and cigar shops beckoned. As one social survey noted, small boys "compare their cash; they count their change; they boast how much ice cream, candy, peanuts and soda they consume."[21] In this sense, children, particularly migrant children, were critical agents in the commercial reorganization of national markets.

In the rural South, Lucius Harris would have had fewer opportunities to buy candy, and the candy he did get would have had different meanings. He grew up in a small farming community where African American and white farmers grew cotton, peanuts, and hay. The area was a base for seasonal labor migration to Atlantic coast cities. Trains connected Capron to the Norfolk seaport to the east and Emporia to the west, and the Atlantic Coast Railroad took migrants to industrial cities in the Northeast. Men could supplement meager farm incomes by finding work on the railroads and state highways or riding those railroads to cities. The Harris family conducted their day-to-day lives in a landscape contoured by rural roads, fields, and forests. Their lives were shaped by the seasonal routines of agricultural work, though the children went to school for at least a few months in the winter. In the town of Capron, located several miles away from the Harris home, the general store or the filling station would have sold candy. A small rural grocery served the needs of farmers in the outlying areas. Stores such as this were often owned by landlords and generally sold groceries and supplies to tenant farmers and sharecroppers on credit. This debt was secured as a crop lien, and it often carried high rates of interest. Through the 1920s, rural grocers increasingly stocked inexpensive candies, intended for children like Lucius Harris. Annie Harris might have sometimes bought her children candy in exchange for their agricultural labor. But since margins from year to year were so slim, sharecroppers and tenants limited their store purchases to the bare minimum. Low prices for cotton, tobacco, and peanuts could easily turn candy into a luxury. On the other hand, as cheap, mass-produced candies spread across the South through the 1920s, low commodity prices might equally have created a situation in which candy was the cheapest source of calories for working children. Families using every square inch of soil for cash crops had to rely on the provisions sold on credit by plantation merchants. Coercion and desire were two ends of the same stick.

Besides the candy in nearby plantation groceries, Harris might have seen candy if he went to a nearby town at harvest time. Franklin, Virginia, for example, was home to the peanut processing plant, the cotton gin, saw mills, an ice factory, numerous restaurants, groceries, drugstores, bakeries, a movie theater, and other retail shops. Candy would surely have been sold at any of these places, but Harris would have been unwelcome in many of these segregated establishments. Merchants displayed candy in glass cases, so a child would have had to interact with the store clerk to get any of it. Such displays highlighted the distance between Harris's desires for sweetness and the realities of his impoverished, segregated existence.

Meanwhile, in cities like Buffalo, candy stores were a flash point for social tensions in neighborhoods being reconfigured by migration. As children scrambled for the cheap pleasures they could scavenge or earn, they regularly faced both helpfulness and hostility from shopkeepers. Lucius Harris was stabbed by candy shopkeepers Israel and Millie Weiss, Polish

Jewish immigrants who had lived in Buffalo for twenty years.[22] They struggled to improve their social standing and to distance themselves from their working-class neighbors, and they were prepared to violently defend their status as the neighborhood changed around them. Harris's conflict in the Weiss candy store was hardly unique. According to local labor organizers, the Weiss family had attacked other African American children before Harris. Scenes like this were enacted in candy stores across the country and helped forge violent links between candy and children. The irony, of course, is that Harris would have first encountered candy's violence not in an urban but rather in an agrarian capitalist landscape where candy increasingly circulated as a strategy for incorporating African American children into prejudiced and violent systems of labor control. In this way, regionally produced goods facilitated the emergence of a national market for both labor and goods in the United States.

Working at Candy's Color Line

Confectioners did much to strengthen the association between African American children and sweets, but they also used other images and rhetoric in their campaigns. Confectioners linked candy with the bodies of attractive young white women in order to emphasize the healthfulness and naturalness of sweets. They depicted young white women as avid consumers of candy and as eager to work in candy factories, at least until they married. Confectioners' pairing of African American children and white women reveals a color line in the world of candy. Candy's color line was marked by the price point: expensive hand-dipped chocolate bonbons represented the desires of and for marriageable young white women, while cheap stick candies were icons of childhood desire, especially for poor African American children. This color line extended into segregated candy factories, where white women were hired to produce fancy hand-dipped chocolates. By contrast, African American women worked in departments specializing in cheap candies intended for black customers. African American women's candy work enacted yet another desire—for economic independence in a changing southern landscape.[23]

Confectioners frequently highlighted their female labor force, repeating a common stereotype that young women were drawn to work in the candy industry because they craved sweets. They staged photographs of young, neatly clad white women workers to highlight the sanitary, homelike production and sales of their goods. Advertisements frequently

"Chocolate Dippers' School," *Western Confectioner* 7, no. 1 (October 1920).

showed line drawings of women dipping chocolates or packing candy. The crisp lines of this illustration style emphasized the uniformity and tidiness of candy production. Young white women's purity, "sweetness," and appetites were idealized qualities that sold candy, but confectioners also implied that the women themselves were available for marriage.[24] They portrayed work in a candy factory as a dream-come-true for white women, since it promised the sweetness of both candy and domestic love. Soda fountains and candy shops offered an acceptable public space in which women could socialize with men and suitors could woo future mates with gifts of candy. Such gifts promised luxury and material support in the marriage to come. In order to show that attractive and marriageable young women ate candy, confectioners hired film and stage actresses as spokespeople during the dieting craze of the 1920s.[25]

Candy factory work was far less ideal than confectioners suggested. As one factory inspector put it, "The picture so often imagined of a worker in a spotless white apron and cap was not often seen."[26] Government and private sector labor reformers publicized women's poor working conditions and advocated better sanitation, hours, and wages to benefit both workers and consumers. Interviews conducted by state labor commissions, the Federal Women's Bureau, and the Consumers' League in the late 1910s and early 1920s found that conditions were generally unhealthy, employment was unsteady, and the industry as a whole was disorganized.[27] Machine operators, wrappers, packers, and general workers were usually women in their teens or twenties. In the North and West they tended to be from immigrant European backgrounds. In Denver and Boston, for example, many women were second-generation

Italian Americans. In New York and Chicago, they were as likely to be Southern or Eastern European. In the South, native-born white and African American women wrapped and packed candies and worked as general helpers and cleaners, though usually in separate factories. Men held more stable, skilled jobs as candy cooks. Reformers found that women's employment in the candy industry was among the lowest-paid industrial work available to women. In larger cities, young women could not live independently on the miniscule wages. Their wages would have been a contribution to a meager combined family livelihood. Despite the low wages and seasonal unpredictability of the candy industry, women's employment was usually critical to family survival.[28]

As candy production increased through the 1920s, African American wageworkers made candy in Meridian, Mississippi, as well as in other centers of southern candy production like Birmingham, Atlanta, Norfolk, and Richmond. They were generally only hired to produce cheap candies intended to be sold to children and poor workers. Most candy factories had strict divisions of labor by gender, race, and age. African American women and men worked in factories that produced hard stick candies, penny candies, peanut candies, and machine-coated chocolates. African American men worked as candy cooks, truck drivers, and general laborers. Their work required both physical strength and skill and tended to be a more stable type of employment than the work performed by women. The average age of African American men who worked in candy production in Meridian, Mississippi, in 1930 was thirty-six and most were married. Many of them had worked in candy production for more than ten years. African American women were younger than their male counterparts and tended to be unmarried. All of the African American women who worked in candy factories in Meridian worked as wrappers and laborers—unskilled jobs—for a company that produced only inexpensive stick candies.

White women, by contrast, worked for companies that produced a wider range of products and were hired not just as wrappers and packers but also as stenographers, bookkeepers, salesladies, and chocolate bon-bon dippers. Hand dipping fancy chocolates was a special job, deemed suitable only for white women, who were also the intended consumers of the product. African American women were never hired to make soft candies or fudge or to dip chocolates, all jobs requiring training and paying hirer wages.[29] Social reformers loathed hand dipping because dippers spent hours with their hands immersed in warm chocolate. To

	African American	White
Average age	23	20
Percent living independently	86%	14%
Percent living with family	14%	86%
Percent widowed	21%	0%
Percent with skilled jobs	0%	27%

FIGURE 3. Women Working in the Candy Industry in Meridian, Mississippi, 1930. Compiled from 1930 United States Federal Census and City Directories of the United States, Meridian, Mississippi.

reformers' consternation, the job often resulted in dermatitis, which they saw as risky for both consumers and workers. But hygienic concerns over dermatitis were magnified by candy's color line: Reformers saw chocolate dipping as an act of both contagion and intimacy. There is, of course, some irony in the fact that white women enacted a symbolic violation of the color line when their skin was darkened with chocolate. Their bodies became chocolate-coated delicacies, the object of sexual desire and figures of sexual transgression. In the vein of blackface performers, white women candy workers temporarily crossed the color line with their chocolate-coated skin. By guarding this job as a racial prerogative, white women implicitly claimed the right to be the objects of sexualized consumption. They could both produce the sweets and be the sweets.

Candy work meant something quite different for African American and white women. For white women, a job in the candy industry was a youthful endeavor and a stepping-stone to other types of employment, like sales or clerical work, or to marriage. Of the white women who worked in the candy industry in Meridian, 86 percent lived with their families, and they were on average twenty years old. By contrast, African American women gained freedom from menial domestic service by working in candy factories since their employment opportunities were otherwise restricted to cooking, cleaning, and washing. Candy factory jobs paid higher wages than much of the work available to southern African American women. The average age of African American women in Meridian's candy industry was twenty-three, and none of these women were married. Unlike their white counterparts, African American women did not live with their families, though a few of were widowed with small children. Candy work allowed these women to live alone or with room-mates. The work was not isolated, as domestic service could be, since women worked together to complete specified tasks and took breaks and traveled to work together. More so than that of the white women in Meridian, African American women's employment in candy factories inscribed desires for self-sufficiency and mobility in the context of urban growth and rural transformation. These candy workers' desires were not easily contained within the visual tropes of marriageable white women and insatiable children. Their labor charted new territory for African American women, even as it marked candy's color line.

The "Oriental" Sweet Tooth

In 1931, the *Western Confectioner* reported that Richard C. Ching, a con-fectioner from Honolulu, had traveled to the mainland United States to learn about the latest production practices and equipment.[30] Mainland confectioners were impressed with Ching and lauded his Americanized business practices. As they put it, "Mr. Ching is a fine example of the modern American of Chinese descent to be found in the Islands and in our own West Coast." But confectioners found people like Ching fasci-nating for other reasons. Asian merchants and consumers seemed to be a key to new overseas markets. Just as they had expanded into the rural South, confectioners eagerly sought new foreign and territorial markets, which might even out fluctuations in their nearly saturated U.S. markets. The territories were especially appealing for confectioners since there were no customs duties. As they sought markets outside of the conti-nental United States, Asian American producers and consumers offered confectioners an ethnographic window into what they hoped was a vast, untapped market across the Pacific.[31]

Confectioners' evaluations of potential customers and business part-ners revealed a more flexible notion of race when it came to Asians and Asian Americans than when they described African American consum-ers. White confectioners offered positive valuations of Asian American merchants in the context of restrictive laws limiting labor migration. Chi-nese people had been subject to immigration restriction since the 1880s, with the exception of merchants or members of one of a few other exempt categories. The small number of Chinese who had arrived and remained in the nineteenth century had built relatively prosperous lives. Richard

Ching was typical. His parents arrived in Hawaii to work on a sugar plantation in the 1890s, where he was born in 1896. The family soon moved off the sugar plantation and found other ways to earn a living. Ching was like other members of the Chinese American middle class who sought social and economic status in the face of limited opportunities. In Hawaii and the Chinatowns of the west coast, Chinese business owners had greater opportunities to advance their own social positions. In the 1920s, many embraced U.S.-style business practices and engaged with white trade associations, like the western confectioners. White confectioners welcomed people like Ching as exceptional and unique and as exemplars of immigrant assimilation. White businessmen understood that ethnic merchants were crucial middlemen who could help them navigate new markets, including those reinforced by race- and class-based immigration exclusion.[32]

Confectioners hoped that people like Ching could be native informants on the potentially lucrative candy markets in Hawaii, the Philippines, and Puerto Rico. Confectioners marveled at the supposed sweet tooth of "the oriental races," citing regular shipments of U.S.-made candy, premade ice cream, and manufacturing equipment to Hawaii as evidence of their assimilability. One researcher estimated that Japanese and Filipino children living on sugar plantations ate nearly a quarter pound of candy per month, which they purchased from plantation stores.[33] Children in the bigger Hawaiian cities had much greater access to candy and apparently favored lollypops. As one writer noted, "The Oriental sweet tooth continues to develop along Occidental lines and to look to the Occident for machinery and methods to cater to that sweet tooth."[34] The *Western Confectioner* reported that a large number of soda fountains had been sold on the islands, all imported from the mainland. Over two-thirds of them were operated by Japanese or Chinese proprietors, like Richard Ching. While the trade press sometimes reported on the "weird concoctions" that Asian American confectioners sold, these reports ultimately lauded proprietors' training in U.S. techniques and their use of U.S. machinery.[35] The creation of clean, mass-marketable, low-cost candies suited to local tastes—no matter how foreign—was evidence of Asian American confectioners' having mastered lessons from their mainland tutors.

As they had for decades, merchants often described territorial markets using the language of tutelage and education. Hawaiian children "go to American schools and receive an education along American lines. They spend their nickels for candy just as American children do." The taste for sweetness indicated that these children could be educated and civilized, but they still needed to be coached in what to buy. The Honolulu Dairymen's Association made this theory explicit in its 1927 campaign to "teach Hawaiians to eat ice cream." Frozen sweets were especially emblematic of U.S. control over the tropics, since the technology for freezing and transporting frozen foods was a relatively new innovation. The Dairymen collaborated on the campaign with mainland confectioners and the BFDC.[36] They noted that "ice cream consumption in Honolulu is far below the average of that on the mainland, although the cost is not any more." The root of the problem, the Dairymen argued, was racial, since "80 per cent of the population is made up of other races than white," who apparently rejected dairy products out of hand. The Dairymen focused on educating schoolchildren, believing they were contributing to the political education of the future citizenry. Like mainland confectioners, they hosted ice cream giveaways and offered school children tours of their production facilities. They advertised heavily in Japanese and Chinese newspapers, hoping to lure young customers from competing street vendors who sold flavored, shaved ices.[37]

Mainland confectioners believed they had discovered untapped appetites for sweets among people in Hawaii, and they wondered whether they might exploit the same desires even farther from home. The largest U.S. candy manufacturers were the only ones to successfully expand overseas in the 1920s, and they did so with cooperation from the BFDC's Sugar and Confectionery Division. Henry Heide, Life Savers, the Imperial Candy Company, and the New England Confectionery Company all sold their products in Latin America, Asia, and Europe. Under the direction of Secretary of Commerce Herbert Hoover, the BFDC conducted research on foreign tariffs, trade treaties, and foreign market conditions for candy. These activities contrasted sharply with the activist role desired by the U.S. Women's Bureau, which hoped that its research and factory inspections would support federal labor laws and consumer protections. The BFDC sought only to provide up-to-date information and technical assistance to companies seeking to expand.[38]

Confectioners and the BFDC remained fascinated with less-civilized forms of sugar consumption, consistently contrasting civilized-versus-unrefined production practices, retail outlets, and products. Unrefined habits promised new markets. As one editorialist put it, "Sugar is a product of civilization," and thus "as the hundreds of millions of people in Asia, Europe and Africa secure more of the advantages of civilization,"

THE ICE CREAM MAN OF JAVA

The contrivance carried by the Javanese ice cream vendor looks like the marmites or soup-cans used to convey food to the trenches during the war. In his picturesque costume of skirt peplum and short sleeves, the ice cream man does a thriving business.

"The Ice Cream Man of Java," *Western Confectioner* 7, no. 10 (July 1921).

they would also use more sugar.[39] Confectioners regularly showcased the uncivilized but quaint ways that people in Asia and Latin America consumed sweets. In 1926, the Sugar and Confectionery expert at the BFDC, Rupert Purdon, wrote to the commercial attachés of Cuba, Panama, and China for photographs "illustrating peculiar and exotic features of the confectionery industry." Purdon made the request on behalf of the major U.S. confectionery trade journals, which wished to publish "pictures illustrating novel means of transporting and packing confectionery, unusual retail store arrangements, street venders." He received a number of suitable pictures from China, but the images he received from Cuba were not sufficiently "exotic." Confectioners wanted images that emphasized the contrasts between modern, civilized candies and less refined sweets. They published, for example, an image of an ice cream vendor in Java, barely clad and with buckets balanced across his back. Other articles described Mexicans strolling happily along, munching on stalks of sugarcane, or boxes of strange candies exhibited on the edges of rough roads. Such images suggested that the world was crowded with potential consumers of exported sweets.[40]

Confectioners' depictions of overseas and Asian American candy consumers resonated with their images of African American consumers but also offered a vision of worldwide economic integration, with U.S. manufacturers at the helm. Overseas markets promised stability for the major confectioners, who needed new markets to keep their assets in constant production. Such markets also revealed the success of earlier civilizing missions, since children in Hawaii were now eagerly consuming U.S.-style sweets. While confectioners showcased less-civilized forms of candy consumption, they did so to reiterate that people could be educated to consume their products. They needed new customers, and new markets overseas, in the territories, and in the rural and urban mainland all promised to produce them.

Conclusion

In the process of accommodating themselves to new rituals and geographies of work in the 1920s, people in the United States internalized empire as they ate their way through huge quantities of sugar. The formation and re-formation of nationhood in the 1920s was built around both integration and exclusion. People and goods were excluded at the borders, but these borders were not enough to assure integration for those within them, especially those outside mainstream white culture. In cities and in the countryside, people forged cultures of work and consumption that linked them with others in the United States and that bound them—often invisibly—to workers abroad. Candy manufacturers played a crucial role in integrating new consumers into a national— and international—marketplace as they expanded their businesses in the 1920s. They did so by pursuing new regional markets, conducting national advertising campaigns, and developing name-brand products. In these efforts, confectioners emphasized that cravings for sweetness were natural and normative, using long-standing contrasts between civilized and unrefined consumption. Their efforts to naturalize, normalize, and nationalize candy consumption drew from the work of diverse cultural producers, including advertisers, journalists, and reformers. While images of children eating candy and less-refined forms of sweets had circulated for decades, such images authorized a new gendered and racialized regime of labor and consumption in the 1920s.

Cheap candy—the bulk of confectioners' production—was intended for poor workers. Manufacturers, grocers, and plantation owners intended cheap candies to displace homemade sweets as a source of calories and pleasure for families who were only tenuously bound to labor on the land. Unlike homemade sweets, through which families protected a part of their lives from the pressures of the marketplace, purchased sweets brought them more fully into the cash nexus. Mass markets could remake coercion into desire. While confectioners and merchants took an active role in making a place for sweetness in modern social life, consumers did not eat sugar passively as they negotiated their transitions from rural to urban consumerism. Migrants altered the social geography of American cities—Buffalo, San Francisco, Chicago, Atlanta, Denver, and Honolulu, to name a few—and as they did so, they renegotiated the meanings of their exchanges. Workers sought greater access to the fruits of consumer culture as they migrated to cities, but they also continued, as best as they could, to preserve sweetness as a realm of independence.

CHAPTER SIX

SWEET INNOCENCE

Child Labor, Immigration Restriction, and Sugar Tariffs in the 1920s

Nineteen twenty-nine was a bitter year for sugar. Advocates for the U.S. beet and cane industries called for more tariff protection as they faced steadily declining sugar prices. But they faced opposition from Cuba and mainland refiners whose profits depended on lower tariffs. As policy-makers, farmers, and reformers debated the sugar tariff, they embraced a narrative of women and children as deserving consumers. Represent-ative Fiorella La Guardia (D-New York), for example, criticized the high tariff, arguing that "the American Congress is too big to take a stick of candy from the American children."[1] At the height of the 1929 tariff debates, candy manufacturers waged a battle with tobacco companies in the advertising pages of newspapers and magazines.[2] Advertisers described sugar consumption as either a feminine, childlike weakness or a sound nutritional practice and source of innocent joy. Lucky Strike cigarettes ads recommended that women stay slim by replacing sweets with smokes. Candy and sugar manufacturers replied with a volley of ads defending their goods as healthful. Eventually, sweets and tobacco sellers came to a truce, agreeing to show cigarettes and candy together as goods for the new, modern woman. *Good Housekeeping* and other women's magazines pondered how permissive mothers ought to be with children's requests for candy. Lobbyists built on such media coverage, making direct links among the tariff, women, and children consumers, who were the very people threatened by proposed tariff changes.

By the end of the 1920s, politicians, reformers, and the media depicted children not just as consumers, but also as workers. As was by now usual, race and labor played a major role in debates over how to shape U.S. sugar policy in the 1920s. This time the image of the Mexican child stooping for long hours in Colorado's beet fields figured large in the tariff's racial calculus. Policymakers interpreted the growing crisis in the sugar indus-try through the interwoven stories of child labor reform, tariffs, colonial administration in the Philippines, and Mexican immigration restriction.

The chapter begins by describing reformers' interest in agricultural child labor in the 1910s, the decade before the issue gained national attention. As sugar prices declined, beginning in the early 1920s, beet growers and territorial cane producers renewed their demands for higher tariffs. Beet sugar companies came under pressure when they asked for higher tariffs, in large measure because immigration opponents publicized the industry's reliance on Mexican workers. Child labor reformers seized this chance to bring greater attention to their concerns. During those same years, a growing chorus called for independence for the Philippines in the hope of excluding both Filipino workers and Filipino sugar from the United States. Debates over the Philippines revealed the limits of U.S. administration of those islands. The chapter concludes by describing the consequences of the 1930 tariff, which enacted rates much higher than the already high duties of the early 1920s. The territories received the protection of the high 1930 tariff on sugar, which exacerbated an already-grave crisis in the global sugar economy. Production in the territories increased, and prices everywhere fell. A new generation of policymakers proposed radical changes in how the United States protected mainland farmers.

I Hooked Me Knee with the Beet-Knife: Child Labor Reform and Sugar Beets

Between 1916 and 1933, dozens of formal and informal surveys by the National Child Labor Committee (NCLC), the U.S. Children's Bureau, the National Catholic Welfare Council, school superintendents, state labor officials, sugar company sociologists, and charity groups documented the extent of children's work in the beet fields. That they defined such work as a problem represented a significant change in prevailing views of sugar beet agriculture. Western school officials, farmers, factory workers, the U.S. Reclamation Service, business boosters, and government agents had all welcomed new sugar factories in the first decades of the twentieth century. They had not only accepted children's agricultural work in the early years but had often lauded it as a positive opportunity for youngsters. Urban child labor reformers likewise ignored agricultural work, focusing primarily on children in factories, sweatshops, and city streets. They imagined farmwork as an opportunity for children to get healthful fresh air, physical activity, and parental guidance. When reformers finally began to study children's work in agriculture in the 1910s, they found that farmers resisted intrusion on decisions about their families' work.

Reformers faced off with the beet industry, but in doing so they also found support among progressives who had begun to question whether the beet industry brought its promised benefits.[3]

Attention to child labor in the beet fields represented a major shift, in both perceptions about the beet industry's benefits and child labor reformers' strategies. The NCLC, founded in 1904, was a significant national organization whose efforts helped frame child labor as a reform problem.[4] These urban middle-class reformers worried that premature labor burdened children's bodies and deprived them of education, which they feared would cause Anglo-Saxon racial degeneration. Their journalistic reports and photographic exposés used racialized rhetoric and sentimental concepts of childhood to catalyze public opinion in favor of child labor laws at the state and national levels. Following the 1910 Federal Census, which showed a large number of children working in agriculture, the NCLC turned its attention to that sector, finding that conditions in agriculture often resembled those in industry.[5] The NCLC took a conservative approach to rural issues because it feared alienating the few allies it had in the South, where the mere suggestion of extending regulations to agriculture would have undermined tentative moves toward industrial child labor legislation. The NCLC privately resolved to investigate commercial agriculture but agreed not to publicize its findings.[6] Early forays into agricultural child labor focused almost exclusively on crops employing white children, and reformers protested primarily that work prevented school attendance.[7]

The NCLC publicized its first substantial study of children's work in the sugar beet fields in 1915. Conducted by NCLC field secretary Edward Clopper and reform photographer Lewis W. Hine, the study shifted away from the NCLC's earlier complacency about agriculture.[8] Clopper and Hine visited Colorado and Wisconsin, where they found Russian German, Mexican, and native-born white children working long hours at difficult field labor. They reported their findings in "Child Labor in the Sugar-Beet Fields of Colorado," published in the *Child Labor Bulletin*, as a NCLC pamphlet, and condensed in the *Survey* and other national magazines. Staffers presented the research in dozens of public lectures, especially among progressive reformers in Colorado and Nebraska. Together with the statistics and textual details, Hine's photographs aimed to excite viewers' sentiments. He focused on working children's white bodies, their dirty clothes, and their sweet faces. Hine only made close-up portraits of white children, shots whose intimacy invited white middle-class

Lewis Hine, "Seven-Year-Old Alex Reiber Topping. He said, 'I Hooked Me Knee
with the Beet-Knife, but I Jest Went on A-Workin.'" Sterling (vicinity), Colorado
(October 1915). Photographs from the records of the National Child Labor Committee,
Library of Congress, Prints and Photographs Division.

viewers to make comparisons with their own precious children. Hine
implied that working children deserved government protection because
their own families had failed them. He repeatedly photographed children holding large knives, used for cutting off the tops of beets. A typical caption read, "I hooked me knee with the beet-knife, but I jest went
on a-workin."[9] The knives, which evoked bloody fingers and knees, were
intended to alarm and outrage. Images of children with knives became
iconic as reformers re-created such scenes in new photographs and illustrations in the 1920s. Hine's visual record revealed only part of the story,
largely omitting Mexican children. He took photographs of only two
Mexican families, which he posed together in front of their house rather

than at work. These photographs, which were not widely reproduced, showed that Mexicans were in the beet fields but did not include Mexican children as deserving of reform. It would be another decade before Mexican children came into focus for child labor reformers.

Hine and Clopper found a tradition of progressive, labor, and women's activism in Colorado. The NCLC report, publicized in the *Rocky Mountain News*, was widely discussed among Colorado's progressives, who quickly took action. The Colorado Federation of Women's Clubs and the state Bureau of Labor supported an anti–child labor campaign, and both investigated conditions on their own. Mabel Costigan, a Colorado reformer active in the NCLC and other organizations, chaired the Colorado Federation of Women's Clubs investigation. In 1917, it submitted a bill to the state legislature that would have restricted child labor in the beet fields. Congressman Edward Keating (D-Colorado), who had sponsored an unsuccessful federal child labor law the previous year, endorsed the bill. "When my federal child labor law was being discussed in the House," he wrote, "our opponents called attention to the conditions in the beet fields of the West, and sneeringly suggested that we should begin our work of reform at home."[10] Keating promised an immediate investigation and appropriate legislation. Nonetheless, the Colorado legislature rejected the bill, revealing political divisions within the state that persisted as the issue made its way onto the national stage.

In contrast with progressive advocates for child labor reform in Colorado, many state residents and their advocates in the USDA promoted the beet industry as the best means of economic development in the arid West. A growing federal agricultural bureaucracy supported the industry through irrigation development, land reclamation, crop research, and economic analysis. For the USDA, beet farmers represented the best combination of new technologies and older agrarian democratic ideals of independence. Agricultural studies depicted beet farming as being as efficient and well-planned as any industry. Through technology and scientific management, a man and his family could live the life of a yeoman farmer without burdensome stoop labor. The USDA saw the industry not through the eyes of individual laborers, as child labor reformers did, but on a macroscale that emphasized farm efficiency, scientific management, crop improvement, and technological advancement. Child labor reformers' publicity focused in detail on each step done by hand in the process of growing beets: beets needed to be thinned, blocked, hoed, pulled, topped, and piled. Agricultural researchers rarely described these tasks in detail, lumping them together as "handwork" in contrast to mechanized tasks, on which they focused. Their reports included assessments of equipment, horsepower, acreage, and labor requirements in man-hours. They used the passive voice and omitted the age, gender, family composition, or ethnicity of the people doing the work. Indeed, they optimistically anticipated that technology would replace burdensome handwork, by far the biggest expense and the most loathsome for "American farmers."[11]

Child labor reformers found a receptive ear not in the USDA, but in the U.S. Children's Bureau, another federal agency. Founded in 1912 and staffed by progressive women, the Children's Bureau promoted maternal and child health through a variety of initiatives. Though it had no regulatory role, the Children's Bureau conducted numerous studies and advocated for policies to improve children's health and education.[12] It conducted a study of child labor in sugar beets in the early 1920s, which it published as *Child Labor and the Work of Mothers in the Beet Fields of Colorado and Michigan*. The Children's Bureau collaborated closely with the NCLC and with local reformers in Colorado and Michigan to publicize the study. While it shared the USDA's desire for efficient farm management, it also tactfully criticized the sugar beet industry's habit of employing children.[13]

Though they were increasingly interested in children's agricultural work, reformers strategically sidestepped these questions while they were campaigning for national child labor legislation. They needed rural support for these efforts, especially as they lobbied to pass a federal anti-child labor constitutional amendment in the early 1920s, which they hoped would overcome problems with other attempts at federal child labor laws. Southern cotton mill lobbyists, who opposed federal child labor laws, spread rumors that such an amendment would prohibit farm families from requiring chores and farm help from their children, thus interfering with states' and families' rights. This was an inaccurate characterization of the proposed law, but reformers nonetheless worried that they would lose crucial support if they focused on rural children. The NCLC and the Children's Bureau thus agreed not to report on sugar beets while Congress was conducting hearings on the amendment. When, in early 1923, Congress finally announced that it would defer its decision on the child labor amendment, the NCLC published the results of its new study of child labor in the beet fields.[14]

Sugar beet farmers and consumers alike felt the crunch of the post-war economic contractions as inflation was soon followed by collapsing prices and unstable employment. As Congress grappled with problems in the sugar economy, reformers developed new strategies in their efforts to regulate child labor in beet fields in the 1920s. The NCLC, the Children's Bureau, local clubwomen, and school and labor officials continued to investigate and publicize their findings. Increasingly, they saw the structure of the international sugar economy as a crucial component of the issue. As one reformer put it, child labor in the beet fields was "a problem of big industry which is trying to maintain itself against competition with a more firmly established industry by the use of cheap agricultural labor and a tenant system of farming." Sugar beet farmers relied on children workers, she reasoned, because it was the only way they could compete against the lower costs of tropical cane producers. As reformers embraced such insights, they found new allies among policymakers who were debating the merits of the sugar tariff.[15]

A Sort of Fetish among the Protectionists: Comparative Cost of Production as Racial Practice

Before the 1920s, policymakers who advocated high sugar tariffs—people like Francis Newlands—had been able to make their case by reminding their audiences of the dual effects of immigration and unprotected trade on U.S. American living standards. Foreign competition came in the form of goods and workers. But in the 1920s, Newlands's successors increasingly found their positions on immigration and tariffs diverging. Rather than erecting barriers to both trade and immigration, some trade protectionists defended open immigration. And advocates of strong race-based immigration restrictions increasingly rejected sugar tariffs. William S. Culbertson exemplified these contradictions and new alignments. Culbertson, appointed to the newly formed Tariff Commission by President Wilson, was a Pennsylvania Republican who generally supported moderate tariffs. Culbertson attracted public attention for his support of race-based immigration restriction as Congress debated the National Origins Act in 1923 and 1924. "The white race," he said, "is exhausting its vitality and risking onslaught by Asiatics." He made the case, as Newlands had more than a decade earlier, that humanity was composed of distinct and incompatible races that should live separately. Unlike Newlands, who had advocated strict limits on both immigration and sugar imports,

Culbertson now argued for tougher immigration restrictions coupled with *lower* sugar tariffs. Culbertson thought that immigration was the result of a "rising specter of overpopulation and underproduction," especially in Asia. His experience during World War I had convinced him that the only way to address this crisis was to stimulate food production in the rest of the world. Until people had access to food and livelihoods closer to home, they would never stop migrating to the United States. Culbertson argued that lower tariffs would encourage trade, which would slow immigration to civilized, temperate climates. Though his strategy differed from the earlier generation of nativists, Culbertson's goal was the same: to protect white civilization from foreign degradation. Low tariffs did not triumph in the 1920s, but Culbertson's approach signaled the dawn of a new approach to protectionism.[16]

Culbertson made headlines not only for advocating immigration restrictions but also for his work on the Tariff Commission. The Tariff Commission gained new authority through the 1922 Tariff Act, which institutionalized the wartime statistical and cost-accounting methods used by the Sugar Division and the Sugar Equalization Board. The 1922 act codified comparative cost of production into trade law by authorizing a "flexible tariff" under which the president could change the legislated rate in order to equalize the cost of production between the United States and its chief foreign competitors.[17]

The Tariff Commission did not have the power to actually set tariffs, but it could demand access to private business records, subpoena witnesses, and otherwise compel compliance with its investigations. Obtaining production data from firms within the United States was a significant undertaking, though the widespread adoption of cost-accounting methods in the 1920s simplified the task somewhat. The Tariff Commission faced still-greater challenges in gathering comparable statistics from territorial and foreign producers. Accountants had to travel extensively, work with producers who often did not speak English, and make sense of idiosyncratic bookkeeping systems. During the 1923 sugar investigation, for example, five Tariff Commission employees and eight accountants—some Spanish-speaking—traveled to Cuba for three months.[18] Upon returning to Washington, a team of statisticians tabulated the results under the directorship of Joshua Bernhardt, the chief of the Tariff Commission's Sugar Division. Bernhardt had been the Sugar Statistician for the U.S. Food Administration and the Sugar Equalization Board. The team gave their preliminary calculations to sugar industry representatives, who could then respond by filing formal briefs and testifying at hearings. Finally, Tariff Commission members debated among themselves about how to interpret the data before making a final report.

Consensus on the sugar report was elusive for the tariff commissioners. Between 1923 and 1925, they were nearly deadlocked over whether to recommend a sugar tariff increase or not. The supposedly impartial commission was charged with making "scientific" and apolitical investigations based on statistical calculations and cost-accounting data. But such methods could not resolve differences of opinion about how to define domestic and foreign production in the context of empire and racial heterogeneity. After more than a year of study and debate, the commission sent two separate reports on sugar to Coolidge. Using the same data but different statistical methods, one report recommended lower sugar duties, while the other recommended maintaining or increasing existing rates.[19]

Joshua Bernhardt authored the majority report, which Culbertson and Commissioners Edward P. Costigan (married to Colorado progressive Mabel Costigan) and David J. Lewis signed. They recommended that the sugar tariff ought to be lowered, thus reducing protection for territorial and mainland producers. Their recommendation was based on how they interpreted the categories of "foreign" and "domestic" producers, whose production costs the 1922 tariff law called on them to compare. They were concerned that the tariff rate needed to accurately reflect conditions in all of the places that would receive tariff protection. If they did not take account of lower costs in some producing regions—namely Hawaii and Puerto Rico—they risked overstimulating sugar production in these places. The best method for estimating domestic costs of production, they argued, was to calculate a weighted average of the costs of Louisiana, beet growing states, Puerto Rico, and Hawaii. How they averaged production costs might seem like an abstract technical detail, but the method reflected tariff commissioners' desire to prevent territorial producers from earning excess profits from the sugar tariff. This concern is ironic since Congress had explicitly excluded the Philippines from the Tariff Commission's authorization to make cost-of-production studies. The commission did not do any studies in the Philippines, and, in fact, none of its estimates on the sugar tariff during the 1920s took account of conditions there.[20] Despite this omission—or perhaps because commissioners were worried about its consequences—the Tariff Commission majority report insisted that a weighted average was the most accurate way to set the tariff rate.

Authors of the dissenting report demanded that the sugar tariff remain the same, insisting that Bernhardt's results were biased against mainland farmers, who were the intended beneficiaries of the tariff. The authors of the minority report did not like the weighted average since lower production costs in Hawaii and Puerto Rico counterbalanced the high costs of Louisiana cane and western sugar beet growers. The second report thus argued it would be more equitable to compare Cuba's production costs to the single most representative region among U.S. producers. They argued that the cost of beet sugar production ought to be the basis of comparison with Cuban costs, omitting high-cost Louisiana and lost-cost Hawaii and Puerto Rico from the calculations. This, they argued, was a better representation of domestic costs. Based on this comparison, the sugar tariff ought to be left alone.[21]

Coolidge held the two reports for more than a year before announcing that he would not change the sugar tariff. Costigan, a progressive lawyer and politician from Colorado who would later play a prominent role in New Deal sugar policy, was particularly disgusted by the proceedings. According to Costigan, Senator Reed Smoot—widely known for supporting high sugar tariffs—organized a meeting with sugar beet representatives during which they pressured Culbertson to reject the majority report. When this failed, Coolidge appointed Culbertson as ambassador to Romania. Coolidge and Smoot thus derailed attempts to adjust the sugar tariff, to Costigan's dismay. In 1928, Costigan resigned from the Tariff Commission in protest.[22]

The tariff remained an open topic for both public deliberation and the work of well-funded lobbyists in Washington through the rest of the decade. The language of comparative costs of production, promoted as a neutral concept by the Tariff Commission, had always been racialized. In the hands of politicians, lobbyists, and the popular press, comparative production costs were reduced to simplified notions of climate, labor, and race. As we shall see, lobbyists for the Cuban sugar industry sent investigators to observe Mexican children in the sugar beet fields, decrying at once their brutal conditions and racial inferiority. At the same time, beet lobbyists hastened to point out the racial heterogeneity of the Cuban labor force. Longtime sugar beet industry lobbyist Truman G. Palmer wrote to President Coolidge in 1924 complaining that Cuban sugar plantations relied on "labor brought in from Jamaica, Haiti, Santo Domingo, Barbados and the Canary Islands."[23] And beet industry supporters intensified their efforts to exclude the territories from the realm of the domestic, at least when it came to sugar. As would become increasingly clear, none of the Tariff Commission's research had adequately considered the effect of tariff protection on sugar production, since it had not discussed the Philippines at all. It was in this context that child labor reformers, with the support of Edward P. Costigan, successfully brought the plight of Mexican children beet workers into the national spotlight.

Sugar, Child Labor, and Mexican Migration

In May 1923, after months of precipitously rising sugar prices, 25,000 women and children filled the streets of New York in protest. At the same time that New Yorkers were protesting sugar prices, the NCLC was putting the results of its Michigan beet sugar study to press. It was also working closely with the Colorado Federation of Women's Clubs to pass state legislation covering children's work in the beet fields, with staffers addressing women's clubs and religious groups and testifying before the legislature on the proposed child labor bill. Children consuming sweets— or refusing to do so out of principle—contrasted sharply with children forced to produce the sugar elsewhere in the United States. The Colorado child labor reform campaigns and the sugar boycott were connected in multiple ways. They used the same grassroots methods, were conducted at the local level by chapters of the same organizations, and appealed to a shared notion of innocent childhood exploited by greedy, profit-hungry corporations. Though the organizers of the sugar boycott did not directly suggest a connection between child consumers and child laborers, the link between sugar and children caught on in wider reform circles. Citing the NCLC study, for example, a 1923 editorial in the leftist *Nation* argued that "the demand for an inquiry into speculation in sugar prices should include a demand for legislation to prevent the exploitation of children in the beet-fields." High sugar prices that robbed innocent children of their candy were all the more treacherous if they were built on the backs of working children.[24]

Before these events, child labor had scarcely been mentioned in the tariff debates. Senator Reed Smoot (R-Utah) dismissed concerns about child labor in the beet fields during earlier debates, arguing that a little field labor was good for young people. But in 1923, following the energetic boycotts, Owen Lovejoy, the head of the NCLC campaign, realized that sugar politics offered a way to gain broader public attention for their efforts. He wrote the secretary of labor to inquire about conditions in cane sugar production. Grace Abbott, head of the U.S. Children's Bureau, replied that investigations revealed no major child labor problem in domestic or territorial cane fields. Abbott's reply reassured Lovejoy that a campaign against beet sugar would not benefit yet another child-employing industry. So the NCLC proceeded to become "steeped in beets—almost to the exclusion of everything else."[25] This decision brought the NCLC into a wider range of policy deliberations, including the tariff and immigration debates.

Beginning in 1923, the NCLC made explicit links in its campaign literature between the children who ate candy and those who worked in sugar production. In the June 1923 issue of its magazine, *American Child*, NCLC staffer Frances B. Williams published a poem that portrayed sugar consumption as akin to cannibalism. "Youth pulled and topped, and granulated," she wrote, "and weighed—weighed out in bags for us to buy, and please our tooth for sweets." Williams authored another story, "Wlad of the Beets," about children exploited in sugar beet production that was published a few months later in the *New Republic*.[26] Michael Doran, a lobbyist representing Atlantic seaboard refiners and Cuban sugar financiers, reprinted the story as a flier with the provocative caption, "Was It to Protect the Beet Sugar Industry of Michigan, Responsible for the Labor Conditions Which Brought About Such Demoralization, That the Highest Tariff Rate on Sugar in 32 Years Was Imposed by the Last Congress?" Doran distributed copies of this flier to congressional representatives, which enraged the beet industry. The Michigan state legislature ordered an investigation, intended to vindicate the industry, and called on the NCLC to defend its actions. Lovejoy wrote, "We have been accused of being in the pay of Cuban cane sugar growers." The NCLC denied connections with the Cuban industry, claiming that "our interest in the sugar industry is brought about only by our interest in child labor."[27]

The "Wlad of the Beets" fracas brought the NCLC and the Children's Bureau new allies. A. E. Carlton, president of the Holly Sugar Company, sent a reprint of "Wlad of the Beets" to the Children's Bureau with a beseeching note, in which he described the story as "vicious propaganda of destruction against the American beet sugar industry by the Cuban sugar people."[28] Carlton wrote regularly to the Children's Bureau, reporting, for example, that the company had spent $30,000 to improve worker housing. Even though beet field workers were technically employed by farmers, not sugar companies, the companies took an active role in recruiting and housing workers, efforts coordinated by their social welfare departments. Sugar beet companies, agricultural professionals, farmers,

American Child 8, no. 6 (June 1926). Reprinted courtesy of the National
Child Labor Committee.

educators, and child welfare reformers cooperated in unprecedented
ways during this period. A milestone in the cooperative work between
the sugar industry and reformers came when the Colorado Agricultural
College invited the NCLC to conduct a joint study of child labor in the
beet fields. They did four separate studies, focusing on education, family
composition, nationality, land tenure, and management on beet farms.
Published between 1925 and 1928, the studies added authority to reformers' campaigns since they originated from an agricultural college.[29]

Besides reporting on the Holly Sugar Company's improvements for workers, Carlton complained to the Children's Bureau about the "uncertainty of the activities of the Tariff Commission," hoping it could influence a favorable recommendation. Despite Carlton's lobbying, the Children's Bureau and the NCLC refused to take a public stand on the sugar tariff. But other influential supporters of the child labor campaign publicly called for a lower tariff, much to the beet companies' displeasure. Tariff Commissioner Edward Costigan was one such advocate. He kept the NCLC and the Children's Bureau updated on the Tariff Commission's work on sugar. He added questions about workers' ages to their cost-of-production studies and he insisted on a mention of child labor in the Tariff Commission's report to Coolidge.[30]

The sugar beet industry faced another challenge to its labor practices from Texas congressman John C. Box, who campaigned to extend immigration restrictions to Mexicans. The 1924 National Origins Act did not directly limit immigration from the Western Hemisphere, though it did impose literacy tests and a head tax. Insisting that these measures were inadequate, Box called on Congress to fully exclude Mexican "peons." He pushed Congress to debate numerical restrictions on Mexican migration through the late 1920s at the same time it was discussing the sugar tariff. Representatives of the sugar beet industry were some of the most vocal spokesmen against Box's proposals, testifying regularly before congressional committees, where they faced difficult questions on the ethnic composition of their labor force.[31] They could hardly deny that Mexican and Mexican American families performed most hand labor in the beet fields, so they presented it as unavoidable, benign, and temporary. They complained, "If we can not get Mexicans, we will have to quit growing beets, unless some substitute for Mexican labor is found." Beet growers and refiners repeatedly pointed out that labor in the beet fields was work "that the white laborer will not perform," thus making it obligatory to employ Mexicans. They also made a direct link between their labor practices and tariffs. In his testimony before the House Committee on Immigration and Naturalization, J. C. Bailey, the vice president of the Holly Sugar Company, testified that his company was "suffering tremendously right now from cheap sugar produced by Jamaican negroes in Cuba and by Filipinos." The only cure was a higher tariff, but "meanwhile our burden should not be increased by cutting off our only available labor supply."[32]

Sugar company officials and farmers also praised Mexicans in their testimony. While most historians have emphasized the racial and eugenics discourse in the 1920s debates over immigration, the testimonies and cross-examinations about education and child labor in the beet fields of the Rocky Mountain region reveal a different way of discussing Mexican migration.[33] Drawing on their work with social reformers, some witnesses at congressional immigration hearings valorized Mexican American workers, emphasizing that many were actually U.S. citizens. Thomas F. Mahoney, a Colorado businessman, officer of the Knights of Columbus, and labor reformer, was especially influential in shaping how industry representatives described Mexican and Mexican American workers. Prompted by his Catholic faith, Mahoney worked closely with the sugar beet industry to demand social justice on behalf of the Mexican Catholics. He collaborated within regional as well as national reform circles and emphasized that Colorado was home to an established community of "Spanish Americans," people of Mexican descent who had lived in southern Colorado and northern New Mexico since the Treaty of Guadalupe Hidalgo. By making the distinction between Mexican nationals and U.S.-born people of Mexican descent, he and sugar company officials shifted the discussion about labor away from "peons" and racial degeneration.

Child labor reformers embraced a pluralist view of Mexican and Mexican American workers that was much like Mahoney's. Though earlier child labor reformers had placed fears of racial degeneracy at the root of their campaigns, in the 1920s reformers revised those concerns. They instead used a more-inclusive discourse of citizenship that portrayed people of Mexican descent as honest, hardworking, and fully American. Reformers broadened their appeals to highlight not only the plight of children, but also the profound economic difficulties their families faced. An article titled "America's Stepchildren," for example, argued that "the first step in improving the conditions in [Colorado beet fields] is the acceptance by this country of the children for what they are—Americans, an American privilege and an American responsibility." The child labor problem would never be solved, they argued, until nativism and racial antagonism were addressed. As one NCLC investigator wrote in 1926, "So long as the Mexican is held to be 'beyond the pale' there is no hope of attacking the child labor evil or any of the other social or economic evils reported here." Such sentiments countered the virulent racism of lawmakers and nativists lobbying for restrictive immigration legislation.[34]

Beet growers and sugar manufacturers found themselves embattled on multiple fronts by the late 1920s. Farmers endured low beet prices,

As your Christmas gift to the children of America will you not work for the observance of Child Labor Day in your community?

The material listed above will be sent free of charge. Estimate how many copies you can use, enter it on the above list and return to:

NATIONAL CHILD LABOR COMMITTEE
215 Fourth Avenue
New York City

National Child Labor Committee pledge card, *American Child* 8, no. 12 (December 1926). Reprinted courtesy of the National Child Labor Committee. Note that the hooked knife mirrors the shape of the candy cane.

increasing debt, and farm foreclosures. Their survival seemed tied up in a knot of proposed tariff and immigration legislation, by the challenge from child labor reformers, and by the vicissitudes of the international sugar market. As lawmakers and lobbyists prepared for the 1929 tariff hearings, it was clear that the political stakes would be high. Child labor reformers could hardly have guessed how thoroughly their work would come to inform the sugar tariff debate.

The Great Western Sugar Boa Constrictor: Child Labor in the Smoot-Hawley Tariff Debates

The 1929 sugar tariff debates, which lasted more than a year, rehashed many of the debates that had taken place about labor, immigration, and empire over the previous years. As the debates progressed, defenders and opponents of the beet industry dragged out nearly every piece of testimony, government report, news item, or hearsay on Mexican immigration and child labor from the previous decade. The *Congressional Record* for the 1929 sugar tariff debate reads like a bibliography on child labor in the beet fields. Sugar was the only commodity for which child labor was a dominant theme throughout the nearly fifteen months of debates. Representative James Frear (R-Wisconsin), who had not been a major figure before 1929, introduced extensive evidence about the conditions of child labor in the beet fields into congressional debate. "Some of the descriptions regarding children of the mothers in these pages," Frear intoned, "are so heart-rending that they condemn the entire sugar-beet business as conducted in this country." He argued that the sugar beet industry was not worth protecting because the "sugar profiteers" who controlled it reaped their profits in part by exploiting "an army of children." Decrying the "Great Western sugar boa constrictor" as a "Colorado crusher of 6-year old infants in beet fields," Frear introduced letters, reports, and photographs showing the depraved condition of beet workers.[35]

According to later testimony during a Senate investigation, James Frear had decided to speak about child labor and the sugar tariff without input from lobbyists. But lobbyist Gladys Moon Jones contacted Frear immediately after his first speech, providing him with additional information, letters, and testimonials about labor conditions in the beet fields.[36] Jones gathered extensive documentation, wrote articles, issued press releases, and sent circulars about child labor to members of Congress, as her colleague Michael Doran had been doing for years. Jones even went to Colorado and Michigan herself to observe labor conditions. Jones brought many more politicians into the discussion of child labor in the beet fields, including American Federation of Labor (AFL) president William Green. Jones persuaded Green to sign a letter she had drafted, arguing against a higher sugar tariff as "an unfair tax upon the millions of workers." Why, the letter wondered, should workers be taxed to protect an industry that "employs women, children, and Mexican labor at indecent wages and under intolerable conditions"? New York Republican representative Ruth Baker Pratt presented the letter to Congress and, at Jones's behest, made a second speech about the tariff and child labor in which she concluded that "sugar belongs to the tropics." She and Jones printed 80,000 copies of the speech, which they distributed to members of the American Federation of Women's Clubs. Together, a small group of representatives and aggressive lobbyists for Cuban exporters and U.S. sugar refiners kept the discussion of child labor going throughout the entire tariff debate.[37]

Representatives from Colorado, Michigan, Utah, and other beet growing states reacted strongly to James Frear's speeches, rebutting his characterizations of the beet industry. Colorado representative Charles Timberlake joined several representatives who spent as much time criticizing Frear's accusations as Frear had spent presenting them. Timberlake claimed that beet workers enjoyed an American standard of living, went to school, drove cars, and were in most respects better off than the "cheap black labor" employed in Cuba. Claiming personal knowledge and using language remarkably similar to that used by the NCLC, Timberlake argued that "the Mexican at work in our beet-sugar industry is not altogether an alien or foreigner. For the most part he is a Spanish-speaking American-born citizen." When pressed later on how beet farmers had previously advocated for unrestricted immigration from Mexico, Timberlake reiterated that the "production of beets is labor that is not enticing to American manhood." John C. Box next stood up to read aloud from the 1926 and 1928 hearings on Mexican immigration, quoting beet industry witnesses on their desperate need for tractable Mexican workers.[38]

Sugar beet lobbyists retaliated with close scrutiny of Cuban labor practices, arguing that horrible conditions in Cuba justified a high protective tariff. Cuba's detractors frequently mentioned Haitian and Jamaican workers in Cuba's cane fields. In publicizing this issue, sugar beet lobbyists drew on work by Cuban nationalists, who were increasingly alarmed at political repression and economic stagnation in Cuba. Many observers there were alarmed by the sugar industry's dominance and by the fact that Wall Street investors seemed to be profiting from it. Nationalists drew on Cuban historian Ramiro Guerra y Sánchez's influential critique of the sugar plantation system, *Azúcar y Poblacion en los Antilles* (1927), in which he argued that Cuba was troubled equally by both "foreign capital and imported cheap labor." Cuba's independence rested on its white farmers, who were under assault by U.S. corporations, which imported black workers to produce cane at very low wages. Guerra argued that Cuba ought to restrict immigration and levy higher tariffs to protect white Cuban workers and farmers, just as the United States had done. He lauded the Chinese exclusion laws in Cuba and called for further immigration restrictions to whiten the island. Sugar beet lobbyists used Guerra's nationalist critique, arguing that the tariff only benefited corporations, which were busily undermining Cuban sovereignty.[39]

At the end of the 1930 tariff debates, Oklahoma representative Milton Garber compared the sugar beet industry to "the weakling among a family of healthy children." He continued, "It has been pampered and coddled and fed upon delicacies denied to the others, treatment which has proven about as effective in promoting its sturdy growth as the overindulgence of a sick child in its taste for sweets." That Garber compared the beet industry to a spoiled child should come as no surprise, given how effectively Cuban sugar lobbyists publicized the child labor issue. But

Garber's interpretation was not as persuasive as beet lobbyists' descriptions of black workers in Cuba's cane fields. Neither child labor reformers nor Cuban lobbyists achieved their goals in 1929 or 1930, though they clearly set the stage for later successes.[40] In June 1930, after a year and a half of debates and over 20,000 pages of testimony from witnesses, lobbyists, and experts, the Republican-controlled Congress finally passed the Smoot-Hawley Tariff, the highest in U.S. history. As had been the case for more than two decades, the sugar tariff protected mainland beet and cane producers as well as cane producers in Hawaii, Puerto Rico, and the Philippines. The results were disastrous, and many blamed the tariff for the crumbling world economy and the collapse of the Cuban political system in the early 1930s.[41]

The Philippine Sugar Industry in the 1920s and the Origins of Independence

Besides child labor and Mexican migration, the political status of the Philippines was a significant issue for policymakers as they debated the sugar tariff in the late 1920s. In the Philippines, the sugar industry had not been especially successful, though investors and colonial administrators had tried to encourage its growth. Rather, sugar had revealed the limits of U.S. control in the Philippines and had helped push many young men off of the islands, in search of work in Hawaii or on the mainland. Filipino author Carlos Bulosan's semifictional, semiautobiographical memoir, *America Is in the Heart* (1943), highlights these themes. Bulosan frames his early life as a story of U.S. colonialism, which brought "a radical social change" that was "slowly but inevitably plunging the nation into a great economic catastrophe that tore the islands from their roots." He opens by describing his childhood home, where his family had long produced corn, rice, and beans. Under U.S. colonial rule, Bulosan argues, elites gained political power by holding corrupt elections fueled by *basi*, an alcoholic drink made from fermented sugarcane juice. Powerful elites created "a new class of dispossessed peasants who were working in the factories or in the vast haciendas." "We the peasants," Bulosan wrote, "were the victims of large corporations and absentee landlords." Indeed, his family soon loses their land through usurious mortgages and political corruption, after which they combine small-scale peddling with migratory wage labor. The Bulosan sons leave for military service, to seek education, and to find work on sugar plantations.[42]

Bulosan's narrative reveals some of the ways that sugar and migration intersected in the colonial Philippines, intersections that were also critical for U.S. policymakers as they debated sugar policy in the 1920s. On the heels of the new tariff concessions from the United States earlier in the century, investors had built new sugar mills across the Philippines. Investors had in fact tried to revive an old sugar mill near Bulosan's home village. They updated its equipment and reorganized the business several times but never succeeded in providing consistent markets for cane growers or workers in neighboring villages. Rather than finding steady work near home, Bulosan's brothers left to work on sugar plantations in distant provinces. One brother found work in a modern sugar mill, built in the mid-1920s by a U.S. American businessman long resident in the Philippines. Another brother worked as a labor recruiter for a sugar company in the Philippines. In those years, prospects for the sugar industry looked good since U.S. tariffs were high and sugar from the Philippines enjoyed unrestricted access to this market. Investors put money into sugar machinery manufacturing, and producers organized the Philippine Sugar Association to lobby for better trade policies and financing.[43]

Despite these new investments, the sugar industry in the Philippines was ultimately unstable and poorly developed, which meant that young men like Bulosan and his brothers found they "could no longer tolerate existing conditions." The sugar industry in the Philippines foreclosed other possible uses of land and resources but could not offer steady or remunerative work. As a result, development of the Philippine sugar industry ran parallel with labor recruitment for Hawaiian sugar plantations. Ultimately, more Filipino men left the island to work in the Hawaiian industry than were able to find work in sugar production closer to home. Many Filipinos who traveled to Hawaii came from places where newly erected sugar mills disrupted systems of labor and land tenure. For example, among a group of 212 Filipinos recruited by the Hawaiian Sugar Planters' Association in 1928, a third came from the provinces clustered around one of the Philippines' seven modern sugar mills.[44] Sugar work in Hawaii was decidedly more lucrative than in the Philippines. Officials estimated that workers sent remittances from Hawaii totaling $3 million per year in the early 1930s. Returning migrants brought another $600,000 back annually.[45]

Colonial administrators found it less than ideal that Filipino workers left the islands to work in Hawaii or on the mainland, in part because they had intervened more aggressively to promote the sugar industry in the

Philippines than had administrators in the other territories. Their earlier interventions left colonial administrators keenly interested in the progress of the sugar industry. Until World War I, Filipinos and Chinese-Filipino mestizos owned much of the sugar industry, primarily selling lower-grade muscovado in China. During the war, colonial administrators sought to change this structure. They worked to attract new U.S. investors to modernize and expand the industry, in part by creating the Philippine National Bank (PNB) to finance modern mill construction.[46] By 1918, the PNB had financed six centrifugal mills but had exceeded the capital it had been authorized to loan. The colonial administration thus had made investments that depended on high sugar prices. When the world sugar market collapsed in the early 1920s, the central mills could not make their loan payments, which brought the government-financed PNB near to collapse. The six struggling mills—called the "Bank Centrals"—presented a major problem for administrators through the 1920s. Colonial administrators believed they had been mistaken to finance the Bank Centrals, but they had too much money invested to abandon them.

During the 1920s, the governor general, Leonard Wood, and the chief of the Bureau of Insular Affairs, Frank McIntyre, considered various proposals to sell the Bank Centrals to private investors, arguing that only private capital could make the mills profitable.[47] But the original articles of incorporation limited their options. As a vestige of the anti-imperial populism that had guided earlier policies in the Philippines, the Bank Centrals were originally incorporated as cooperatives between the PNB and the farmers who grew the cane. Their contracts specified that the PNB could not sell or refinance the mills without authorization from the farmer cooperatives, which would own the mills after they repaid the loans. To colonial administrators' chagrin, the Filipino farmers refused every refinancing offer because they all entailed intensified management by U.S. investors. As Leonard Wood summarized the situation, "The native planters are suspicious of the Americans, and the Americans know from observation and experience that unless they have final control, the management will possibly not be sufficiently efficient to justify so large an investment."[48] Colonial administrators repeatedly described Filipino farmers as degenerate, inefficient, and dangerously dependent. Cane planters had become "careless and improvident," as well as "debauched and demoralized," after taking out loans from the U.S. administration.[49]

It was not just farmers but also Filipino elites who resisted management by U.S. investors. Frank McIntyre wrote that "the owners of the land are generally easy-going people, free spenders, and careless of their own interests. They have led contented, happy lives and have worried little about their constant debts."[50] Ben F. Wright, a special auditor for the PNB, wrote to the Bureau of Insular Affairs in Washington, D.C., that the "pride of the politicians" was crushing the sugar industry, since "American *management* and *control* are absolutely essential" but are refused by the Filipino elites. Wright worried that without American auditors and engineers, the Bank Centrals would fail. Building on Wright's insights, Frank McIntyre argued that under Filipino control, "the management will rapidly deteriorate." Colonial officials noted that several prominent Filipino politicians had built mills, using their political influence to limit U.S. American control of the industry. Administrators thus worried that the "great investments the Government has made" through the PNB had only benefited a few elite families, who prioritized their own profits above the common good.[51]

Since their chances to extract the territorial government from the sugar business were slim, colonial administrators also lobbied aggressively for tariff protection in the 1920s. Colonial administrators in the Philippines needed tariff protection to cover mistakes they believed they had made and to compensate for the inefficiency and stubbornness of Filipino farmers and politicians. In this regard, they faced substantial obstacles on the mainland, especially from beet sugar lobbyists. In the spring of 1928, Senator Charles Timberlake (R-Colorado) proposed a cap on how much sugar the Philippines could import without paying the tariff. Timberlake opposed the "unlimited duty-free importation of sugar from a tropical region with cheap labor," instead proposing that the Philippines be allowed to import a maximum of 500,000 tons of duty-free sugar. Timberlake's assertion that beet farmers needed protection from the cheaply produced sugar of the Philippine Islands was somewhat disingenuous since no one had systematically collected data on the costs of sugar production there.

Officials from the Bureau of Insular Affairs rallied to block Timberlake's resolution, arguing that the colonial government itself had substantial investments and would be "seriously prejudiced by the proposed restriction." Frank McIntyre quipped that Hawaiian sugar interests were behind such moves; they felt that "if the Filipino desires to produce more sugar he must come to Hawaii and work in the cane fields of Hawaii."[52] McIntyre's comment addressed Timberlake's other major constituency— nativists who demanded an end to Filipino labor migration to Hawaii and the mainland, much as they had rejected Chinese and Japanese laborers in earlier decades. As one cartoon from 1929 put it, "Not the tariff, not Philippine sugar, but the steady flood of Filipino laborers into the United States—that is the real menace."[53] Colonial administrators hastened to point out that the sugar tariff could stimulate economic development in the islands, which was the only sure way to keep potential labor migrants home. Colonial trade preferences, they argued, could prevent Filipino migration to the mainland.[54]

Timberlake's proposal failed, and he was unsuccessful in his efforts to restrict sugar from the Philippines through the 1930 Tariff Act. These failures galvanized representatives of sugar beet growing areas in their campaign for Philippine independence and had other unintended consequences. A new coalition of sugar lobbyists, nativists hoping to restrict labor migration, and Filipino nationalists worked together over the next six years to achieve independence for the Philippines. Beet industry representatives allied with Hawaiian, Puerto Rican, and Cuban producers, all of whom stood to benefit if Filipino sugar was excluded from the U.S. market.

Ironically, agitation for independence contributed in unexpected ways to increased sugar production in the islands, especially after the 1930 Tariff went into effect. Timberlake's proposal and various other plans for independence included some form of quotas that would limit how much sugar the Philippines could sell in the U.S. market. The quotas, producers assumed, would be divided among mills and farmers based on their average production over the preceding years. Anticipating future quotas, Filipino sugar producers scrambled to improve productivity and efficiency by investing in new equipment and crop research. Sugar production in the Philippines skyrocketed after 1930, and policymakers responded by devising new approaches to the U.S. sugar market.[55]

Reassessing Domestic and Foreign Trade after the 1930 Tariff Act

Colorado lawyer, progressive politician, child labor reformer, and former tariff commissioner Edward P. Costigan campaigned for the U.S. Senate in 1930 on an unusual platform for a sugar beet state. He called for a lower sugar tariff. His Republican opponent hoped to win the sugar beet vote by campaigning for a high sugar duty, as Colorado politicians had done for decades. But Costigan had advocated a lower sugar tariff ever since the mid-1920s when he criticized labor conditions and problems with the cost-of-production approach. In the early 1930s, the crux of Costigan's opposition to the sugar tariff was different. His main concern was the "disproportionate returns" tariffs gave to the island territories.[56] Politicians had complained for years about the islands' tariff advantages, but after the 1930 Tariff, sugar production in the Philippines increased dramatically. The tariff was as high as lobbyists had demanded, but farmers were still going bankrupt. The islands' sudden boom in sugar production brought new debates about whether to classify them as foreign or domestic. Costigan intervened in this debate by proposing to reduce the sugar tariff, thereby eliminating the artificial stimulation to the territories. The tariff reduction would be offset with a 1.5 cent per pound bounty paid to continental farmers. To many people's surprise, Costigan won the election in 1930. His win on the heels of the Smoot-Hawley Tariff marked a shift in how voters understood the tariff. As one Costigan constituent wrote, "The popular delusion commonly shared is that higher and higher tariffs will cure many if not all the ills. This delusion has become a fetish in most beet sugar localities."[57] Over the next several years, many constituents came to agree with Costigan that the high tariff was part of the problem.

Costigan began working on his new plan for the sugar economy as soon as he took office, relying on advice from experts he had met on the Tariff Commission. The Tariff Commission had enjoyed limited influence during the 1920s when it had been unable to alter the trend toward higher tariffs. Nonetheless, it built professional expertise, trained a cadre of bookkeepers and economists, standardized statistical practices, and laid the groundwork for a new era of sugar policy. Costigan's advisors included Joshua Bernhardt, Kemper Simpson, and Lynn Ramsay Edminster, who embodied progressive ideals of efficient government bureaucracy. Edminster had worked for the Tariff Commission, the Bureau of Agricultural Economics, and other government agencies. Simpson worked for the Tariff Commission and as an independent sugar statistician for progressive politicians. Bernhardt drew directly on his experience setting prices and negotiating contracts under the U.S. Food Administration's Sugar Division during World War I, as well as his work for the Tariff Commission.

Costigan and his advisors aimed to end the practice of "colonial equality," whereby the territories were treated the same under the tariff law as continental sugar producers. If they were all protected by the same tariff, then lower-cost Filipino and Puerto Rican sugar earned what was in essence a bounty as compared with higher-cost mainland sugar. Costigan's goal, drawing on his constituents' concerns, was to supplement mainland farmers' income and protect them against territorial competitors and monopolistic sugar refiners.[58] Costigan's approach reflected a growing consensus in policymaking circles that the tariff had exacerbated an already-oversupplied market by stimulating production in Puerto Rico and the Philippines.[59] As the 1931 and 1932 crops entered the market, it seemed patently obvious that the tariff had done just that. Newspapers in the United States reported record sugar crops in the Philippines in 1932.[60] After conducting a cost-of-production study for the sugar industry in 1932, the Tariff Commission agreed that the high sugar tariff was a disaster, and it advocated import quotas, especially for the Philippines.[61] Costigan sought guidance from Bernhardt, Simpson, and Edminster as he considered how to limit imports for territorial producers. They agreed that mainland farmers could not be adequately protected with tariffs but instead should be compensated for differences in production cost with bounties and import quotas for the islands.[62]

The high sugar tariffs in the 1920s had been premised on assumptions that Costigan and the Tariff Commission now believed were faulty. They had assumed that the tariff itself did not affect the cost of production, refusing to recognize that the tariff might stimulate production or alter producers' choices about how to produce the commodity. In 1932, the chairman of the Tariff Commission reversed this view, stating that "it is the tariff that makes the cost of production rather than the reverse." To support this stance, he cited conditions in Cuba, which had taken a decidedly dangerous turn since 1930. High tariffs not only reduced the profits Cubans could earn on their sugar, but the increased production coming from the U.S. territories had also displaced a share of the market that Cubans had formerly dominated. Cubans had substantial investments in the sugar industry and were ill equipped to produce anything else. As a result, the high tariff had forced Cuban production costs to extremely low levels, and investigators reporting from Cuba noted that "labor is the only thing left to squeeze."[63] Cubans could only "take the tariff hurdle" to enter the U.S. market by suppressing their labor costs, which presented a dangerous situation of widespread unemployment and escalating political tensions. In their new analysis, U.S. policymakers realized that Cubans' production costs and standards of living were inseparable from the price of sugar in the United States. Cost of production and standards of living had previously been equated with immutable factors like the subservient labor force's lifestyle and inherent efficiency. Policymakers' emerging theory held that differences in the cost of production were not natural, environmental, or racial, but instead were artifacts of international trade policy. The new recommendation was for a lower tariff coupled with import quotas, which together aimed to raise U.S. prices. Cubans, who had been squeezed out of the U.S. sugar market, needed to be let back in. If they could sell more sugar they would be able to buy more wheat, pork, corn, and canned milk from U.S. farmers. This approach, which anticipated the core assumptions of New Deal planning, offered a broad view of economic recovery rather than one narrowly focused on the interests of one commodity sector.

While Costigan proposed that the United States ought to stop offering preferential terms of trade to its territories, others took a more extreme approach to the question of how to stop the influx of sugar from the Philippines and Puerto Rico. Secretary of State Henry L. Stimson, who had served as governor general in the Philippines in the late 1920s, saw independence as the best way to exclude both Filipino workers and Philippine sugar. Stimson described a private conversation with President Herbert Hoover in which Hoover worried about "what a bad breed we were breeding up in Puerto Rico." Hoover worried that "we were letting in these undersized Latins from Puerto Rico," a thought that logically led him to "the Philippine question."[64] Later Stimson argued that the United States "ceased to be an annexing power when we . . . adopted the policy of our immigration laws and were against mingling in our population any more divergent elements."[65] For Hoover and Stimson, independence for the territories was the logical sequel to immigration restriction, but also the only good way to deal with mainland sugar problems.

Conclusion

During the 1920s, policymakers sought to overcome the sugar industry's crisis of overproduction. As had been the case for decades, they turned to the sugar tariff to bolster farmers' returns and counter foreign competition. Even as Congress increased protection, some people began to realize that the tariff was not solving all economic problems in the U.S. sugar empire. Reformers, lobbyists, and policymakers pointed out a number of ways the tariff had failed to fulfill its promises of racial homogeneity and profits for white farmers. For one thing, evidence of Mexican children laboring in the beet fields provided new indications of the tariff's shortcomings. People had, of course, long debated sugar policy by focusing on labor conditions in the cane fields. Attention to the conditions in the beet fields was new and the result of child labor reformers, who had not originally intended to add to the tariff debates. The sugar beet industry defended itself, insisting that its labor practices were more efficient and humane than those in the Caribbean cane industry. Sugar beet defenders instead called for revisions in U.S. policy toward the Philippines, pointing out that the sugar tariff would never work as long as the territories benefited from its protection.

As the nation entered a deepening economic depression in the early 1930s, child labor reformers and advocates for Philippine independence continued their calls for change. They drew on the Tariff Commission's work and a growing reform literature on labor problems in the beet fields. Evidence of new political and economic instability in Cuba, together with higher sugar production in the territories, finally convinced leaders to revise their approach to empire and sugar policy. In the 1930s, reformers began to look for new ways to redefine who benefited from U.S. protective policies and to exclude territorial sugar producers from the realm of the domestic.

CHAPTER SEVEN

DROWNED IN SWEETNESS

Integration and Exception
in the New Deal Sugar Programs

In the popular 1932 film *White Zombie*, Bela Lugosi plays a diabolical plantation owner who produces sugar with a docile zombie workforce. "The living dead," warns one character, are "taken from their graves and made to work in the sugar mill." They are ideal workers, Lugosi says, because they "are not worried about long hours." For contemporary viewers, Lugosi's power to make sugar by making slaves was a horrifying vision of U.S. entanglements in the Caribbean. Over the previous decades, people's daily experiences of sweetness had naturalized imperial capitalism, obscuring the brutality through which sugar was produced. But zombie sugar workers on the big screen disrupted this seamless narrative. White zombies carried cane to the mill; zombified black men pushed the groaning mill as it ground the cane. One white zombie, dressed in clothes typical of a Caribbean tenant farmer, was crushed in the mill's machete-like blades, a scene that encapsulated anxieties over empire and authority in the early years of the Great Depression. Zombies emblematized widespread concerns over political developments across the U.S. sugar empire, changes that many observers attributed to the 1930 Tariff. Policymakers were just beginning to understand that the excessively high sugar tariff had not only failed to protect the industry, but had in fact brought Cuba, the Philippines, Puerto Rico, and the continental United States to the brink of disaster. Mainland farmers were going bankrupt, Cuba was embroiled in a crisis aggravated by the tariff-induced loss of its market for sugar, the Philippines was expanding its sugar output, and investors were threatening Atlantic seaboard refiners' monopoly by building new sugar refineries in the territories.[1]

People at the time wondered whether a leader with a more authoritative hand could bring this economic and political chaos under control—a dictator, though perhaps one less evil than Bela Lugosi. In 1932, leftist intellectual Oswald Garrison Villard wrote in the *Nation*, for example, "If I were a dictator . . . I should first of all abolish the sugar

Zombie sugar mill workers in *White Zombie* (directed by Victor Halperin, 1932). Courtesy of Derek Merleaux and the Miami–Dade County Public Library.

tariff against Cuba." The sugar tariff, Villard argued, had reduced "the working masses in that country to misery and despair." Cubans had been rendered "helpless and hapless victims of a ruthless dictator" in order to assure profits to Wall Street investors. But was the dictator Cuba's authoritarian president Gerardo Machado y Morales? Was Wall Street the dictator? Or was the sugar tariff itself the dictator, an invisible hand with cruel power? Nationalists in the U.S. territories pondered similar questions, also calling for tariff reforms. In 1932, Puerto Rican leader Luis Muñoz Marín argued that the U.S. tariffs could "incidentally annihilate Puerto Rico, in an almost thoughtless step, with the same brutal innocence as an elephant that stamps on an ant colony." He knew that if Puerto Rico lost tariff protection, mass starvation would follow. Muñoz Marín nonetheless argued that Puerto Rico's dependent economy ought to be gradually weaned from sugar tariff protection. The sugar industry lived on catastrophe and destruction, "like ravens, feasting on bloody massacres." This, he pointed out, was a recipe for political uprising. All across the U.S. sugar empire, political leaders feared that the economic crises brought on by the high sugar tariff would bring popular political discontent and further instability.[2]

After Franklin D. Roosevelt took office in 1933, policymakers began to implement new methods to control the sugar economy. The New Deal approach to the sugar economy built on Edward P. Costigan's earlier proposals—drafted between 1931 and 1933—to end "colonial equality" by lowering tariffs, paying mainland farmers bounties, and imposing import quotas on the territories. Since policy reforms aimed to exclude territorial sugar from mainland markets, the economic crisis at first seemed to call into question U.S. commitment to its sugar empire. Indeed, contemporary and subsequent observers sometimes label the New Deal as anti-imperialist and isolationist, noting that Roosevelt's administration disavowed some direct overseas intervention. Between 1933 and 1935, for example, U.S. troops withdrew from Nicaragua and Haiti, the Platt Amendment—which had, since 1902, authorized U.S. control over Cuban political and economic affairs—was abrogated, and the Philippines took definite steps toward independence. Despite some efforts to move away from direct control of foreign territories, when viewed through the lens of sugar policy the New Deal appears neither anti-imperialist nor particularly isolationist. Foreign trade was crucial to policymakers' strategies for overcoming economic stagnation during the 1930s, and so they found new ways to project U.S. economic power abroad.

The first section of the chapter describes the political and labor activism across the U.S. sugar empire, activism that alarmed policymakers and pushed them toward reform. Especially in 1933, policymakers grew alarmed as they saw workers across the U.S. sugar empire demand better conditions. Beet workers in Costigan's home state staged a series of protests, and Cubans ousted their president in August 1933. Recognizing the dire political consequences of cutting off Cuba's sugar market, policymakers sought to forestall such problems elsewhere, including the mainland and the Philippines. Leaders in the Agricultural Adjustment Administration (AAA), the New Deal agency charged with reorganizing agricultural commodity markets, at first tried to work with sugar industry representatives to develop a new marketing system for sugar. This effort failed, largely because the industry offered too few concessions to Cuba, the territories, and laborers. Administrators in the AAA insisted on a fairer allocation of the sugar market, and they placed new emphasis on workers as consumers whose purchases were critical to economic stability. Nonetheless, the notion that the island territories could and should be treated differently than mainland sugar producers was at the heart of the new approach.

The chapter goes on to describe the movement to grant the Philippine Islands independence, showing that policymakers saw independence as part of a broader readjustment in the sugar economy. Administrators developed a new approach to the political status of all of the island territories, articulating a pluralist approach to colonial administration that aimed to address the failures of colonial policies developed over the preceding decades. Even as they excluded the Philippines, by the late 1930s some policymakers began to tentatively include Hawaii and Puerto Rico more fully in the realm of the "domestic." These changes represented some of the first substantial alterations in colonial policy since 1898. Nonetheless, thanks to congressional pressure from sugar industries in the continental United States, key limitations on territorial sugar production persisted. Restricted sugar quotas signified the islands' ongoing colonial status and, together with decades of dependence on a few extractive industries, contributed to their uneven economic recovery during the 1930s.

Radicalism and Reform: Sugar Politics from Colorado to Cuba

Leo Rodriguez caused quite a stir when he entered the AAA hearings in August 1933 wearing overalls and a work shirt. "Leo's appearance was dramatic," wrote the general secretary of the National Child Labor Committee (NCLC), Courtenay Dinwiddie, who added, "His overalls and sun and wind beaten face told a story before he opened his mouth." The appearance of an actual sugar worker in a meeting, called so that sugar industry representatives could draft an agreement to stabilize the price of sugar, was unprecedented. "I am appearing in this manner," Rodriguez stated, "for the reason that I am not able to buy other clothes on account of my pay." His testimony that day had been organized by the NCLC, the Catholic Conference on Industrial Problems, and the U.S. Children's Bureau. Those same activists who paid Rodriguez's travel expenses of course could also have bought him a suit, but his work clothes identified him as a farmer, and farmers were at the forefront of political debate in 1933. The AAA hearings at which Rodriguez testified were but one step in a longer process through which New Deal policymakers aimed to reduce sugar production in order to raise prices for farmers and wages for workers. By increasing workers' and farmers' purchasing power, New Deal planners believed they could stimulate overall recovery.[3]

In this family, a fine type of Latin-American, the father, Phillip, 14, Jennie, 13, Ben, 11, Consuello, 9, Bert, 8, all work on beets. The mother and the three youngest children, ranging from 2 to 6 years, do not work. They were supposed to receive $15 a month from May to October on a 30-acre contract, with the balance (about $270) at harvest time; but up to July 1, they had actually received only $17 and did not know when they would get more. They owed $100 on groceries. Last winter they were on relief for four months, at $15 a month. The father said, "I consider my children well dressed if I have one pair of overalls for each of them." They live on beans and bread *(tortilla)* with fresh meat once or twice a month.

"The Price of Beet Sugar," *American Child* 15, no. 6 (September 1933). Reprinted courtesy of the National Child Labor Committee. The names in the caption are likely pseudonyms for Leo Rodriguez and family.

Rodriguez, of course, stood out not only because of his farmers' clothes but also because he was Mexican American. He was a Colorado-born U.S. citizen, English-speaking, who stood in sharp contrast to the reviled Mexican peon who had been the focus of immigration restriction debates during the 1920s. More important, he was not associated with the radical beet workers who had staged a 14,000-worker strike the previous year in Colorado. Given anti-Mexican sentiment and the Mexican repatriation campaigns of the early 1930s, the appearance of a Mexican American father who put his own children to work represented a shift from earlier strategies used by child labor reformers. Rodriguez's formal testimony signaled not only a change among reformers; it also marked greater public activism by poor workers across the U.S. sugar empire. In fact, at the very same moment that Leo Rodriguez was testifying in Washington, Cubans were in the streets of Havana, demanding political and economic change following years of stagnation and corruption. Social welfare reformers chose

Rodriguez precisely because he was politically moderate at a time when sugar workers everywhere were becoming more radical.

Though Rodriguez had been unemployed and on relief at least since 1930, he had worked sugar beets every year since 1903. He now supported a family of ten, and his five oldest children worked beets with him. In its article about the AAA sugar hearings in the *American Child,* the NCLC reproduced a photograph of a poor but clean and neatly dressed Mexican family, which the caption identified as "a fine type of Latin-American." The caption quotes the father—who likely was Rodriguez—as saying, "I consider my children well dressed if I have one pair of overalls for each of them."[4] The image proposed that Mexican American families were just like other U.S. American families: although they lacked purchasing power, they did not lack respectability. By portraying beet workers as consumers, reformers made a move that was broadly consistent with New Deal reforms. Twenty years earlier, the NCLC had centered their appeals on the figure of the dirty, suffering, and exploited white child oppressed by selfish parents. But reformers carefully orchestrated Rodriguez's appearance in 1933 to show that agricultural child labor was inextricably linked with problems of rural purchasing power, adult wages, and, ultimately, the threat of mass rebellion on the part of poor, marginalized workers.[5]

Reformers and New Deal policymakers seized on working-class consumers in part because of intense protests by unemployed and underpaid workers, which they hoped to diffuse by improving living conditions. Until the early 1930s, most national labor unions did not organize agricultural workers, and sugar beet companies pitted Mexicans and Mexican Americans against one another as an antilabor tactic. Repatriations in the early 1930s created a climate of fear, but beet workers nonetheless sought help from both moderate reformers and radical labor activists. With the help of Thomas F. Mahoney of the Knights of Columbus, for example, workers in Colorado had formed an independent union, known as the Beet Workers' Association. Mahoney was involved because he hoped to offset more radical influences, including the International Workers of the World (IWW) and the Communist Party (CPUSA), both of which sent organizers to the beet fields.[6]

In the early 1930s, the CPUSA sent Alberto E. Sanchez to organize workers in the Colorado beet fields. A Puerto Rican organizer who had been living in New York, Sanchez was deeply committed to anti-imperial struggles. He maintained contacts among anti-imperialists in New York, Mexico, and Puerto Rico and published articles linking the exploitation of Mexicans in the beet fields to sugar workers elsewhere.[7] The New York-based newspaper *La Vida Obrera* and the Mexico City *El Machete* carried Sanchez's articles alongside extensive coverage of politics in Cuba, and Sanchez circulated leaflets among beet workers about nationalist struggles in Mexico and Cuba.[8] His articles and fliers called for workers to identify with a broad-based Latin American working class. Thomas Mahoney was alarmed that Communist organizers like Sanchez were making progress among beet workers, and he wrote of his concerns to national politicians, including Senator Edward Costigan. Mahoney argued that revolution might be on the horizon if dramatic improvements in living and working conditions did not materialize quickly. Of course, the CPUSA vehemently denounced both Mahoney and Costigan.[9]

Tensions between Communist organizers and reformist Mexican American unions had troubled previous strike attempts, but these factions bridged their differences and jointly planned a strike in 1932. At the beginning of each season, farmers set a price per acre of beets, which they agreed to pay workers after the work was complete. But cash-strapped farmers faced pressure to keep wages low from the bankers to whom they were indebted. Beet workers organized the 1932 strike after hearing a rumor that farmers planned to drop wages for beet work to a record low. Eventually, 14,000 workers went on strike, though they only stayed out for a few weeks because beet growers found strikebreakers and organized vigilante groups. Farmers, police, sugar company officials, and a few members of the Ku Klux Klan terrorized striking beet workers. After the failed strike, Sanchez grew increasingly frustrated with the lack of support for agricultural unionism by the CPUSA, and he finally wrote to the national office requesting a transfer back to Puerto Rico. Though the strike did not change the overall conditions under which Mexican families worked, it sent a loud warning about workers' radical potential, which catalyzed federal policymakers in their work to reorganize the sugar industry.[10]

Policymakers faced serious challenges as they sought to incorporate diverse consumers into their vision of economic recovery, in large measure because their plans called on farmers to cut their sugar production. New Deal planners insisted that the supply of sugar in the U.S. market had to be reduced and that these cuts had to be shared by farmers and millers everywhere, whether they were on the mainland, in the territories, or in Cuba. The USDA hoped to use the Agricultural Adjustment Act of 1933 to implement marketing quotas and set prices. By reducing the sugar supply

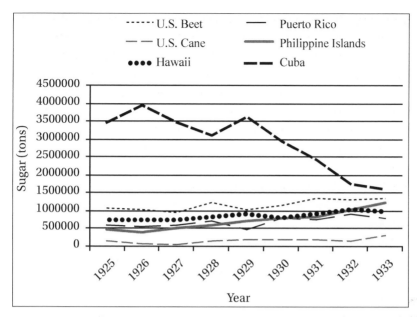

FIGURE 4. Sugar Consumption in the United States from All Areas, 1925–1933. Adapted from Joshua Bernhardt, *The Sugar Industry and the Federal Government*, 171–72.

through quotas, it believed it could raise prices and restore producers' purchasing power. To forestall criticism about government overreach, the AAA initially invited sugar industry representatives to negotiate their own plan for recovery. It was at these hearings in the summer of 1933 that Leo Rodriguez testified. But leaders in Washington were disappointed with the industry's proposal. Mainland farmers insisted that they should not have to reduce their production at all, instead arguing that Cuba and the Philippines should take the brunt of the cuts. The sugar industry's plan gave virtually none of the market to Cuba. Secretary of Agriculture Henry A. Wallace insisted that the plan for recovery would only work if everyone— in and out of the nation—accepted a fair share of production cuts. Wallace argued that the situation in Cuba directly affected U.S. producers, who had lost exports of sugar-manufacturing equipment, cars, pork, beans, and milk—all of which had ground to a halt when the 1930 Tariff curtailed U.S. purchases of Cuban sugar. According to the State Department, Cuban purchases of U.S. goods had dropped 89 percent since 1924, a significant loss for U.S. farmers in sectors that depended on exports.[11]

Wallace rejected the sugar industry's plan for stabilization, insisting that the USDA would redraft a new quota plan through the winter of

Free Press (Manila), October 21, 1933. Reprinted in McCoy, *Philippine Cartoons.*

1933–34. This was a politically volatile stance for Wallace, Costigan, and Roosevelt—they faced scathing criticism from farmers, who accused them of being "ruthless dictators" bent on destroying an American industry. Especially after 1933, when Hitler's anti-Semitism came to light, people worried that violence and repression might follow, as it had in Germany, if a dictator gained too much power. Eager to deflect such criticisms, policymakers emphasized the urgency of the economic crisis at home and abroad. They argued that the natural workings of the market had broken down, bringing forth "economic disasters" and "bitter peace-time crises." As Secretary of State Henry Stimson summarized it, "An emergency was presented in tariff making which justified . . . greater flexibility and initiative on the part of our Executive."[12]

As it turned out, violent political crisis in Cuba enabled policymakers to deflect some criticism of excess executive branch authority. There was an actual dictator in Cuba, Gerardo Machado y Morales, and an acute political crisis rooted in the collapse of the Cuban sugar economy under the weight of foreign debt and high tariffs. Machado had maintained tentative political stability between his election in 1925 and the early

1930s, despite problems in the sugar market. Among U.S. diplomats, the received wisdom was that Cuba was "a one-crop country" whose stability rested on the global sugar market. Sugar was the country's only significant export, occupying the majority of its productive and natural resources. State revenue derived from taxes and tariffs on the sugar industry, and the country purchased foreign foods, consumer goods, and industrial machinery using the export credit from sugar. Cuban nationalists attributed their dependence on sugar to the "diabetic octopus" of U.S. capitalism, embodied by Wall Street bankers, who sucked the life blood from the nation.[13] Under Machado's leadership, Cuba struggled to service its rising foreign debt, much of it held by Wall Street bankers, despite plummeting sugar prices. Machado's administration created special national agencies authorized to buy and sell sugar, taking its cues from corporatist programs elsewhere. Sometimes called "valorization" or "proration schemes," advocates of government economic management argued that the only way to stop communism and fascism was by controlling unfettered competition. Cuban efforts to play "sugar dictator" culminated in the so-called Chadbourne plan of 1930 and 1931, which would have created a global sugar cartel to limit production and raise prices. Like Machado's other attempts to control sugar, the Chadbourne plan failed when nonparticipating countries dumped their excess sugar on the world market at low prices. Indeed, sugar poured into the market at ever-lower prices. Cuban sugar revenue dropped, the country could not service its debts, and more Cubans went hungry.[14]

The collapse of sugar prices and Cuba's reduced access to the U.S. market had disastrous consequences. Machado altered the Cuban constitution so that he could serve a second term as president, despite growing protests against his dictatorship. After a failed coup in 1931, Machado retaliated by abrogating constitutional rights and intensifying repression. Dissidents fled to New York, where they planned another coup and publicized conditions in Cuba. In the United States, journalists depicted Machado's brutality by describing and picturing victims of violence and torture. Newspapers and magazines reported in detail on the "bullet-riddled bodies" of murdered and tortured Cubans. Commentators, especially on the Left, argued that the Wall Street bankers to whom Cuba was indebted were to blame for Machado's regime. By mid-1933, he could not contain the discontent of workers, students, and middle-class intellectuals. Violent mobilizations, mill seizures, and a general strike brought Cuba to a standstill.[15]

Machado's regime crumbled and the Cuban economy came to a halt in the summer of 1933 at the same time that the sugar industry was gathering to discuss marketing quotas under the Agricultural Adjustment Act. Under intense pressure, Machado resigned and fled Cuba. This happened just at the time that Secretary of Agriculture Henry A. Wallace was studying whether or not to accept the sugar industry's proposed quotas. The Tariff Commission and the State Department each wrote to Wallace, urging that Cuba needed access to the U.S. sugar market to regain its purchasing power and political stability. Costigan wrote to his constituents in Colorado that U.S. leaders were anxious "not to increase the revolutionary tendencies in Cuba, the roots of which are fed by near-starvation." Beet farmers cared little about Cuba, but policymakers in Washington saw Cuba's broader significance for U.S. recovery.[16]

Wallace rejected the industry's proposal in the fall of 1933, and the USDA went to work on a new plan that built on Costigan's earlier proposals. The USDA version of the quota plan allocated quotas among the domestic, territorial, and foreign producers. Beet growers were furious that they would be asked to cut production so that Cuba and the territories could continue to sell in the U.S. market. Colorado newspapers rumored that Joshua Bernhardt, the sugar statistician, had authored a plan to make Wallace the "absolute dictator of the beet sugar industry."[17] Accusing Bernhardt of favoring Cuba, beet growers blocked his appointment as head of the division charged with drafting the new sugar program. Planning went ahead, though, and in February 1934 Roosevelt presented the new proposal, which incorporated many of the ideas Bernhardt, Costigan, and others had developed. The sugar stabilization program was written as an amendment to the Agricultural Adjustment Act, and it included production quotas, a processing tax, and benefit payments for continental farmers. Costigan sponsored the bill—which was later known as the Jones Costigan Act or simply the Sugar Act of 1934—in the Senate.[18]

As Congress debated the proposed Sugar Act, Secretary of Labor Frances Perkins appointed a committee to recommend labor provisions for the bill. Colorado College sociologist and labor activist W. Lewis Abbott drafted recommendations, which included restrictions on child labor and minimum wage provisions.[19] Colorado and national women's and labor organizations rallied support for these labor protections.[20] Farmers who received benefit payments under the sugar program would be prohibited from employing children, and they would be required to offer beet workers minimum wages. Remarkably, the labor provisions did not stymy the bill's progress. Even Colorado representative Fred Cummings, who grew beets himself and had testified in defense of child labor five years before, spoke on behalf of the bill. The Senate watered down the language to read "limit or regulate" child labor rather than "eliminate" it, but most senators agreed not to fight the issue. The Senate rejected minimum wage provisions, though they added authorization for the secretary of agriculture to arbitrate wage claims. When the bill finally went to the president, agricultural sugar workers had a place, at least on paper, as beneficiaries of the New Deal.[21]

It is quite remarkable that Congress passed protections for sugar workers in a period when advocates for agricultural labor failed in so many other campaigns. Though reformers and policymakers strengthened labor laws for industrial workers during the New Deal, none of that legislation applied to agricultural workers, including later federal restrictions on industrial child labor. Sugar was different, in large measure thanks to the efforts of sugar lobbyists and child labor reformers over the previous decade. By the early 1930s, child labor in the sugar beet fields had become a stock element in sugar policy discourse. Reformers succeeded by linking family labor with foreign trade and by building new alliances among policymakers eager to head off radicalism and increase workers' purchasing power. While the labor provisions for sugar workers ended up being relatively ineffectual in the long run, agricultural workers' conditions were not otherwise addressed through federal law for several more decades.

Though child labor regulation had been extremely controversial in the 1920s, these provisions were the least controversial aspect of the 1934 Sugar Act. Production limits and quotas were far more controversial for most members of Congress, whose constituents insisted that no limits be placed on their own sugar production. Congress might not have passed the Sugar Act, with its child labor protections, domestic production quotas, and assertion that foreign producers had a right to participate in the U.S. market, except that it had just approved another controversial trade law. The Reciprocal Trade Agreement Act, passed the previous week, replaced the old tariff system in which Congress had set uniform tariff rates for all trading partners. The new program authorized the president to set tariffs and negotiate bilateral trade agreements directly with other countries.[22] Members of Congress from sugar-producing states voted for the Sugar Act because they knew that they were about to lose tariff protection. They repeatedly said they felt they were looking down the barrel of a gun.[23] Roosevelt planned to use this authority to immediately negotiate a lower sugar tariff with Cuba in the hope of reviving Cuban purchases of U.S. goods. As Roosevelt's economic advisor Mordecai Ezekiel put it, "If we wish to sell abroad, we must be prepared to buy." The combination of the Reciprocal Trade Agreement Act and the Sugar Act represented a new direction for U.S. sugar politics, one that acknowledged the failures of earlier trade and imperial policies. Policymakers hoped that lower tariffs coupled with marketing quotas would control the supply of sugar in the U.S. market in order to increase purchasing power and regain political stability at home and abroad.[24]

The Cycle of Colonial Policy Is to Be Completed: The Philippines Redefined

Shortly before President Roosevelt announced the plans that would become the Sugar Act, Philippine Governor General Frank Murphy cabled Washington to express concerns about the future of the islands' economy. Unlike his predecessors who had seen a bright future in sugar, Murphy wrote, "Until the rapid expansion of sugar production is checked I find it extremely difficult to attempt that correction of Philippine economic tendencies which is patently demanded."[25] Murphy was alarmed because the overproduction of sugar "now menaces the Philippine economic establishment in much the same way as it has for long menaced that of Cuba." He and other administrators worried that dependence on a single commodity would lead to political instability, as it had in Cuba. Still, as they worried about the consequences of a monocrop economy, administrators recognized that there *already* was a large sugar industry, and to abruptly curtail it would also bring disaster. The question was all the more urgent because Congress and the Philippine legislature were negotiating the terms of independence, which was sure to include limits on Filipino access to protected U.S. sugar markets. Just what these limits would be was still up for debate.

After years of lobbying on the part of both Filipino nationalists and U.S. nativists, the Tydings-McDuffie Act, passed in March 1934, created a definite plan for independence. Historians have correctly emphasized the nativist aspects of the bill, since its provisions authorized the exclusion of racially undesirable Filipino migrants. The Tydings-McDuffie Act declared that Filipinos were "aliens" and applied National Origins Act immigration

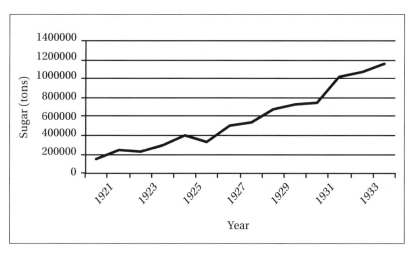

FIGURE 5. Philippine Sugar Exports to the United States, 1921–1934. Adapted from John A. Larkin, *Sugar and the Origins of Modern Philippine Society*, 150.

quotas to them.[26] Beyond immigration, independence and sugar were inextricably linked for the Philippines. The act was conceived as part of a broad program of readjustment in the sugar economy; it cannot be fully understood in isolation from the Sugar Act, debated and passed at the very same time. Reflecting several years later, administrator John Dalton wrote that the legislation "represented the first real change in our colonial policy in 35 years."[27] Policymakers believed that problems in the U.S. sugar economy were the result of treating the territories equally under the tariff law even though they were inherently not equally deserving of protection. By granting the Philippines independence and assigning it specified, limited sugar quotas, policymakers reasserted a colonial hierarchy.[28]

In 1933 and 1934, U.S. sugar refiners joined the coalition supporting independence as Philippine refined sugar entered the U.S. market for the first time. Before the early 1930s, the Philippines had previously exported only raw sugar. In the late 1920s, investors there had considered building refineries but had worried that the tariff situation was too precarious to justify such major investments. George Fairchild, a longtime investor in Philippine sugar, also held back because he did not wish to antagonize Atlantic seaboard refiners, who were his best customers for raw sugar. But the 1930 Tariff changed investors' calculations about building sugar refineries outside of the mainland. For decades, the tariff had maintained a colonial division of labor in which the territories produced raw materials, which were in turn refined on the mainland. Called the "differential," there had always been a lower tariff on raw sugar than on refined. Refiners' profits depended on this differential, and it prevented producers in the territories and foreign nations from investing in refineries outside of the mainland. The 1930 Tariff virtually eliminated the differential, opening a new market for sugar refined in the territories. Investors responded quickly by building new refineries; the Philippines increased its refined sugar output by 294 percent in 1932.[29] When the territories began to produce refined white sugar, they threatened not only mainland capital investments, but also the racial logic that authorized the U.S. sugar empire. Racialized categories of civilization and refinement were organized around sugar's colonial division of labor. Tropical goods were whitened on the mainland for U.S. American palates.

The American Sugar Refining Company (ASRC) aggressively lobbied to reinstate limits on territorial refining that had been dropped in 1930. In doing so, the ASRC built on the racialized rhetoric that linked sugar and whiteness to civilization's progress. For example, it published a map on which dark ink indicated that territorial sugar was blotting out the white spaces on the U.S. map. Territorial refined sugar was literally darkening the continent. The ASRC encouraged refinery workers and consumers to write letters to Congress and the Tariff Commission, decrying the loss of refinery jobs on the mainland. One constituent wrote, "Think of some poor devil who worked in a refinery, maybe he has not the price to even buy sugar for his wife and kids." "The more you buy of foreign white sugar," he reasoned, "the less sugar will be refined in the United States, and the more men will have to be laid off. It's War and you can not shirk your duty to your country." He concluded: "Foreign White Sugar is not as sweet as that refined in the United States."[30] The ASRC took the problem directly to influential members of Congress, including Senator Millard Tydings (D-Maryland), chair of the Senate Committee on Insular Affairs. The ASRC pointed out that its Baltimore factory—in his district—was laying off workers because of territorial imports. It convinced Tydings that "the great sugar refining business of the Atlantic Seaboard is seriously threatened," a point he repeated more widely.

Tydings, who sponsored the bill to grant the Philippines independence, had complicated views on sugar quotas for the islands.[31] He increasingly believed that it would be dangerous to cut off Philippine access to the U.S. sugar market too quickly, worrying that severe restrictions would lead to "economic revolution and mob violence." The earliest sugar stabilization plans had proposed an extremely low quota for the Philippines, far lower than its annual production. In response to mainland producers' complaints, these punitive quotas aimed to virtually eliminate the Philippines from the U.S. sugar market. In 1933 and 1934, colonial administrators advocated that the islands' quotas be slightly higher. The political chaos in Cuba was still ongoing, and U.S. policymakers wanted to prevent a similar situation in the Philippines. Governor General Frank Murphy drew a direct parallel to Cuba, warning that banks, railroads, and other elements of the Philippine economy were built around sugar, just as in Cuba. Even Costigan agreed. As he put it, "One of the difficulties about shutting out Philippine imports of sugar precipitately will be the tendency of such action to throw many Filipino workers in the sugar fields into the plight which has long made Cuban economic conditions volcanic." The comparison with Cuba softened policymakers' approach to the Philippines' quotas.[32]

After much debate, the Tydings-McDuffie Act and the Sugar Act each separately required that the Philippines reduce its overall sugar exports, but the sharpest reductions focused on refined sugar. The Tydings-McDuffie Act gave a quota of 800,000 tons of raw sugar that could be imported duty-free and a quota of 50,000 tons of refined sugar. The law required that the new Philippine government levy a gradually increasing export duty over five years. Under the Sugar Act, the secretary of agriculture also assigned the Philippines a market quota of 900,000 tons. The difference between the quotas under the two bills created another limit for the Philippines, since, in order to comply with both quotas, exporters would have to pay the full tariff on some sugar.[33]

Independence was the culmination of years of work by Filipino nationalists, nativists in the United States, and sugar lobbyists. The trajectory of the sugar industry in the Philippines, together with the labor migration of Filipinos to work sugar in Hawaii and on the mainland, strengthened the movement for independence. Philippine independence was both an emblem of the United States' sovereignty—what greater power than to abdicate power?—and the consequence of failed U.S. policies. Colonial administrators in the Philippines perceived independence as a culmination of their own failures. Production increases had been an artifact of U.S. policies. Administrators had helped to modernize sugar mills at great cost to the colonial coffers but had failed to attract the private economic development they had intended. As they represented the Philippines in debates over the Tydings-McDuffie Act and the Sugar Act in 1934, colonial officials realized that neither they nor private investors had succeeded in creating a smoothly functioning economy. Farming, milling, marketing, and shipping remained heterogeneous and disorganized. The failure of imperial capitalism—the inability to create an organized commodity network through which capital could be accumulated and racial differences rearticulated—was painfully clear to those working out what the quota system would mean in an independent Philippines. Had mainland investors developed stronger ties with the sugar industry, the Philippines might have had more forceful allies during the quota negotiations. In the end, the newly minted Commonwealth of the Philippines received better quotas only because Cuba's political and economic crisis scared policymakers.[34]

Even after the transition to a commonwealth status in 1935, U.S. administrators continued to play a major role in the administration of the Philippines' sugar quotas. In 1937, the U.S. Supreme Court ruled that "so far as the United States is concerned, the Philippine Islands are not yet foreign territory. By express provision of the Independence Act, we still retain powers with respect to our trade relations with the islands."[35] In this sense, even as the Tydings-McDuffie Act appeared as an outward expression of anti-imperialism, it simultaneously reinscribed U.S. imperial sovereignty. This would become clear as U.S. administrators on the ground in the Philippines—and Puerto Rico—implemented the sugar quotas over the coming years.

Administering the Sugar Acts in the Territories: Integration and Exception Revisited

New Deal administrators found themselves more deeply involved in colonial administration than ever before as they applied the Sugar Act in the island territories. The Sugar Act, administered through the USDA's AAA, extended agricultural policymakers' colonial reach. The Sugar Act greatly expanded executive branch authority over the economies of the territories, and its uneven application to continental-versus-territorial areas revealed its imperial underpinnings. Territories might or might not receive the same benefits from the Sugar Act as continental producers, and whether they did or not was subject to AAA discretion.[36] Ironically, as administrators worked more closely with territories, a few of them began to argue that the territories ought to be treated as integral to the U.S. political economic system. Indeed, one of the most remarkable changes resulting from the New Deal sugar program was that when it was revised through the 1937 Sugar Act, the president and officials in the Departments of Agriculture, Interior, and State advocated for Hawaii's and Puerto Rico's equality before the law. This position contrasted with the exclusionary impulses that had originally motivated the 1934 Sugar Act and the Tydings-McDuffie Act. This shift emerged from New Deal officials' on-the-ground experiences administering the sugar programs among workers and elites in the territories.

As we have seen, the original framers of the 1934 Sugar Act aimed to balance the needs of mainland constituents with threats to political and economic stability in the territories and Cuba. The Sugar Act asserted that production limitations needed to be shared by all producers—mainland, territorial, and foreign. The AAA reasoned that sugar prices were determined on an oversupplied world market, so all producers needed to do their share to reduce world supplies.[37] Despite this principal, the 1934 Sugar Act *did* maintain the distinctions among mainland, territorial, and foreign producers in several key respects. Foremost, the law guaranteed mainland cane and beet producers a substantial portion of the market. It redrew the line of what counted as "domestic" by establishing different administrative procedures for mainland-versus-territorial areas for determining production quotas, levying processing taxes, and paying benefits in exchange for production limits. This meant that producers outside the bounds of the continental United States disproportionately bore the burdens of the quota system.

The most obvious difference in the treatment of the territories was in how the secretary of agriculture determined their sugar quotas. The secretary of agriculture was charged with estimating the total annual sugar requirement for consumers in the United States. The economists and statisticians in the sugar division of the AAA used the consumption estimate to decide how much sugar could be sold while still maintaining an adequate price. Prices for producers had to remain above a guaranteed minimum, and prices for consumers could not be too high. Congress specified fixed quotas for beet and cane growers that stood *separate* from the consumption estimate, and these quotas were high enough that they did not need to curtail production.[38] After deducting mainland quotas, the USDA then used its discretion to divide the remainder of the consumption estimate among each of the other regions—Hawaii, Puerto Rico, the Philippines, and Cuba. If one area was unable to fill its quota, the secretary of agriculture could reassign its share to another area, usually on the mainland. The territories, Cuba, and the Philippines did not have fixed quotas, which meant they had no guarantees that they could market their crops. Their economies thus depended on administrative discretion and lobbying conducted behind closed doors.

The Sugar Act privileged continental producers over those in the territories in other ways too. The Sugar Act levied a processing tax, which was collected on all manufactured sugar and which funded benefit payments to compensate mainland farmers for voluntarily restricting their output. This was a revision of Costigan's earlier proposal for bounties as a counterbalance to lower sugar tariffs. The tax aimed to redistribute the industry's profits equitably between farmers and processors, which were mostly corporations that continued to earn dividends even in the depths of the Depression. Millers and refiners paid the tax on all sugar sold in the United States. Sugarcane and beet producers on the mainland could receive individual benefit payments in exchange for adhering to fair labor practices and voluntary production restrictions. The payments were the heart of the reform, because they aimed to equalize foreign and domestic competition, much as tariffs had previously been intended to do. As administrator John Dalton described it, the goal of the benefit payments was to separate "the returns to producers in the United States from [the price on] the world market" by making an adjustment payment that would bring farmers' receipts up to the "fair exchange value" for their cane or beets. Fair exchange value was calculated based on the average producer prices during "the pre-war period before a ruinous foreign trade policy and a planless national economic policy" brought chaos to the industry.[39]

The processing taxes funded individual payments for mainland farmers who agreed to production adjustment contracts, but in the territories the tax proceeds were segregated into separate funds over which the secretary of agriculture had discretion. The general idea was to use the special funds to encourage crop diversification and socioeconomic rehabilitation, eventually shifting the territories away from sugar production. According to John Dalton, the intentional result was that "contracts with producers in these areas do not in all cases assure fair exchange values." The special funds formalized a hierarchy of earnings between continental and territorial producers. Rehabilitation aimed not at individual economic improvement, as did the benefit payments for mainland farmers, but instead represented a paternalist assertion of neocolonial uplift through broad-based collective recovery. Production adjustment contracts for mainland farmers thus embodied a liberal form of citizenship premised on property rights in the inherent value of the crop, while the special tax funds in the territories established a lesser form of economic citizenship for farmers there.

Representatives of the Hawaiian sugar industry immediately recognized the inequalities embedded in the Sugar Act. Harold Ickes, chief of the Department of the Interior, had already asserted that Hawaii was different than Puerto Rico and the Philippines. Apparently Henry Wallace privately agreed that Hawaii ought to be treated alongside the continental industry but for political reasons was unwilling to press the issue publicly. Ickes grew more agitated about Hawaii's treatment when his department's representative was excluded from the committee appointed to allocate sugar quotas.[40] Probably at Ickes's urging, representatives of the Hawaiian industry challenged the sugar program's constitutionality, in *Ewa Plantation v. Henry A. Wallace* (1934). They contended that U.S. citizens living in Hawaii, which was an incorporated territory, had the same property rights as residents of the mainland. The secretary of agriculture's discretionary power over territorial quotas thus deprived them of their property rights without due process of law. The judge who heard the case in the Supreme Court of the District of Columbia ruled against the Hawaiian plaintiffs, arguing that the Insular Cases had authorized Congress to treat the territories as foreign for the purposes of commerce. He wrote that "differences in race of many of its inhabitants" constituted sufficient "grounds for legislation as to its commerce which would not apply to the continent." The Hawaiian plaintiffs reached a compromise with the AAA, agreeing not to appeal the ruling. In exchange, farmers in Hawaii began receiving individual benefit payments, much as continental farmers did. Benefit payments in this case represented a step toward political incorporation for planters in Hawaii.[41]

By contrast with Hawaii, many Puerto Rican leaders hoped that the quotas and processing taxes would bring a substantial economic reconstruction to the island, reducing its dependence on sugar. Most of the proceeds of the processing tax in Puerto Rico were allocated to a special reconstruction fund, with a small amount set aside to pay farmers for unused cane.[42] In the first season, only a few farmers received such payments. The next year, a few more growers signed contracts and received a small payment, which, as administrator James Dickey complained, "represented neither parity, nor a return of the total processing taxes collected on Puerto Rican sugar, nor full compensation for the income lost as a result of the reduction in quota."[43] Likewise, in the Philippines, funds were allocated to diversify agriculture, while only a very small amount was used for individual payments. Puerto Ricans and Filipinos thus received more restricted benefits from the sugar program than mainland farmers did.[44]

The Sugar Act required a great deal of on-the-ground coordination, which ultimately changed how administrators viewed the U.S. sugar empire. They needed to allocate quotas among mills and farmers, identify farmers to sign production contracts, and check to be sure they were adhering to the contract requirements. On the mainland, these tasks were delegated to local farmers' and processors' organizations in order to devolve as much control from the federal agencies as possible. But in the Philippines and Puerto Rico, federal control by U.S. Americans remained the norm. Filipino and Puerto Rican bureaucrats performed much of the day-to-day work, but under the direct supervision of resident U.S. Americans. Many of the administrators who went to the islands to set up the sugar program were not career colonial administrators. For example, Carl Rosenquist, who directed the early stages of the sugar program in the Philippines, was a South Dakota farm boy turned agricultural economist who taught at the University of Texas. Likewise, James A. Dickey, who coordinated the program in Puerto Rico, was raised on a North Carolina farm before becoming a college professor. Once on the islands, these men exercised wide discretion in administering the programs.

Administrators in the Philippines faced some unique difficulties since they had to coordinate the Sugar Act with the transition to independence. During the 1935 crop season, the Philippines was still a territory, so the governor general's office managed the sugar program. It audited mills and plantations, determined quotas, levied processing taxes, and made contracts with individual farmers.[45] Three U.S. American staffers oversaw the program with help from three AAA field workers and the insular collector of customs, who tracked quotas at the islands' sugar-shipping ports. After 1935, the Philippines became a commonwealth, but the United States maintained control over the sugar program with staff transferred from the former governor general to the new high commissioner's office. The program again changed hands in 1937, when it shifted to the Philippine Sugar Administration, a program within the office of the president of the Philippines. But even this ostensibly independent agency remained under AAA control, which had two offices in Manila housing a staff of thirteen U.S. Americans and thirteen Filipinos. Thus, even after the Philippines' status shifted toward independence, employees of the

U.S. government carried out key administrative work and farmers continued to sign legal contracts directly with the U.S. government.[46]

In the Philippines, U.S. administrators claimed authority over only two grades of sugar: centrifugal milled sugar and refined sugar. Before about 1930, a significant amount of cane was processed into either muscovado or molasses, which sold briskly in local markets. Following the 1930 Tariff, however, more cane was diverted to the newer centrifugal mills to take advantage of newly opened U.S. markets.[47] These sugars interested U.S. administrators since it was the U.S. market they hoped to control. But in focusing on centrifugal sugar, administrators threatened the stability of local markets for less-refined products. At the beginning of the program, administrators levied processing taxes on all milled cane regardless of what kind of sugar it would become. Farmers and local officials complained, requesting that administrators stop levying processing taxes on cane destined for unrefined sweeteners. They noted that the processing taxes made it difficult for small farmers to meet mortgage payments. Millers resisted the expense of polariscopes and weighing machines, which would have been necessary to accurately levy the taxes. Administrators eventually abdicated authority over lower-grade sugars when they realized that processing taxes threatened local outlets for cane. They removed the processing tax on muscovado sugar and a variety of locally consumed products made from this milling technique, such as *inuyat* (an unrefined liquid sugar) and *panocha* (similar to piloncillo).[48]

The situation in Puerto Rico was different from that in the Philippines in a number of ways. Unlike in the Philippines, Puerto Rico's sugar program was not premised on the island's eventual independence, though some nationalist factions in Puerto Rico would have preferred it. Administrators in the United States took a great interest in Puerto Rican recovery because they hoped that it could be a model for U.S.-influenced reform elsewhere in Latin America. Roosevelt assembled a committee in 1934 to develop plans for Puerto Rico. Their report, called the Chardón plan after its author, Puerto Rican agronomist Carlos Chardón, called for agricultural diversification on the island and labor migration off the island. The committee proposed that the federal government purchase large, absentee-owned sugar mills and operate them essentially as public utilities. The government would buy land, which it would then offer to workers and farmers to grow cash and food crops. Chárdon and his committee hoped that moderate land tenure and mill reforms, aimed at reducing foreign ownership of Puerto Rican infrastructure, would forestall the more radical redistribution and expropriation they observed elsewhere in Latin America. Undersecretary of Agriculture Rexford Tugwell was an early supporter of Chardón's vision for Puerto Rico and actively promoted it in the USDA.[49]

The USDA collaborated with the Department of the Interior and its newly minted Puerto Rico Reconstruction Administration (PRRA) in efforts to diversify the island's economy. The PRRA built on Chárdon's original plan, though administrative infighting delayed its implementation and changed some of its key features. In 1935, Roosevelt authorized $1.5 million for the purchase of a mill and land and another $7.5 million to fund its operations. In order to avoid the taint of expropriation, the PRRA considered only voluntary sales. It purchased its first mill, the Lafayette Central, from its French owners in 1936 and reorganized it as a farmer cooperative.[50] Administrators also organized landless workers into twelve land cooperatives, coordinated by a central administration to assure efficient use of what they called "good cane lands." By 1940, the land cooperatives had failed, and, though the mill cooperative survived, the model was clearly flawed. The cooperative members were saddled with substantial debt, and they had little hope of getting adequate sugar quotas to meet their obligations. Lafayette was ultimately only one of many plantations struggling with very low quotas, excess productive capacity, and frustrated, hungry workers. The PRRA, and later the Farm Service Administration, operated a handful of cooperative mills and plantations. It never controlled a majority of the island's sugar output and ultimately failed to redirect resources toward other industries.

The Sugar Act had been premised on the notion that economic reconstruction would be possible and that Puerto Rico would thus be able to cope with lower sugar quotas. But administrators were not especially successful at promoting other sectors, and low sugar quotas intensified Puerto Rican unemployment. As unemployment worsened, labor organizers gained ground on the island. The Sugar Act had given the secretary of agriculture very narrow authority to set minimum wages and adjudicate wage disputes for farmers who signed production adjustment contracts. But few such contracts were made in Puerto Rico, so the AAA had practically no influence over labor conditions there. The Puerto Rican legislature passed stronger labor laws designed to improve wages and working conditions, but even these protections were not enough to overcome low sugar quotas. Several major sugar strikes convinced administrators that they were facing a major social crisis, and they sought ways to prevent it. The PRRA and the Department of the Interior, with the support of the AAA Sugar Section, began a legal campaign to enforce the 500-acre law, on the books in Puerto Rico since 1900 when populist anti-imperialists insisted on landholding restrictions. In the late 1930s, administrators revived the law in the hope of giving workers and peasants access to good land on which they might make a living, or at least grow enough food that they would not starve. These and other efforts did not fundamentally alter the island's economic base or its relationship with the mainland.[51]

A Wrench in the Works: Revising the Sugar Act after U.S. v. Butler

In January 1936, the AAA received a major blow. In the middle of the 1935–36 sugarcane harvest season, the U.S. Supreme Court, in *U.S. v. Butler*, invalidated the processing tax feature of the Agricultural Adjustment Act. The sugar program relied not only on the processing tax, but also on the quota provisions, which the Court did not specifically address in its ruling.[52] The Sugar Division kept the quotas in operation for the remainder of 1936. But since they did not collect the processing tax they could not make new production adjustment contracts with farmers, nor pay benefit payments. The purpose of the processing tax had been to redistribute the profits among processors, farmers, and workers. The farmers were guaranteed a higher price for their beets than what the processors paid for them. The difference was made up for by the benefit payments funded through the processing tax. Without the processing tax, the processors still bought at a low price, but farmers did not receive the benefit payment to earn "fair exchange value" on their crops. As a result, during 1936, processors disproportionately benefited from the quotas. Administrators grew increasingly frustrated with this situation, since it undermined the law's goals. The Sugar Division responded by quietly adjusting the consumption estimate upward in order to raise everyone's quotas. Farmers were thus able to sell more beets and cane, which brought them slightly more income, if not higher prices. It was a temporary fix.[53]

Through 1936 and 1937, the Sugar Division developed proposals for a new sugar program that would meet the constitutional requirements laid out by the *Butler* decision. Joshua Bernhardt, now head of the Sugar Division, formed an interdepartmental committee with the State Department and the Division of Territories to work out a new plan. "Present sugar legislation," the committee argued, "provides for price enhancement through sugar quotas without public control of uneconomic expansion of production or division of returns between processors and growers."[54] Furthermore, without contracts with farmers, administrators were left "without means for coping with depressed agricultural labor conditions or increased employment of child labor." Under these circumstances, the brief continued, "there is a danger that the sugar quota system may become a form of concealed high tariff protection." The ideal solution, the brief argued, would be to maintain import and production quotas, impose a high excise tax, and offer conditional payments to farmers as a means to assure fair returns to them and enforce minimum labor and soil conservation practices. The trick would be to separate the excise tax and the conditional payments so that they did not violate the *Butler* ruling.

Building on the recommendations from the interdepartmental committee, the USDA Sugar Section drafted a bill, which Roosevelt submitted to Congress in early 1937. The bill aimed to redistribute industry profits among farmers, workers, and capital and, for the first time, to gain more favorable treatment for the territories. Bernhardt explained that "this Administration has always stood for greater freedom of trade with foreign countries," and it was "certainly not prepared to adopt a system of trade barriers within the United States." Bernhardt overlooked the fact that the administration had defended trade barriers within the United States just a few years earlier when it passed the 1934 Sugar Act. Indeed, administrators articulated a surprising new willingness to consider Hawaii and Puerto Rico as "domestic." As the head of the Division of Territories summarized the proposed legislation, it "recognizes only two categories—domestic and foreign." In practical terms this meant that for the first time the words "insular," "offshore," "territorial," and "dependencies" were eliminated from the bill, and only "domestic" and "foreign" remained. The bill included Hawaii and Puerto Rico in the "domestic" category and the Philippines and Cuba in the "foreign" category. Roosevelt, Gruening, Ickes, Wallace, and Bernhardt built a strong consensus on the new sugar plan, "standing pat on the Administration bill" with its provisions for territorial equality.[55] In this, the administration had support from former Sugar Division employees who had taken posts as lobbyists for, or employees of, the territorial sugar industries. Among them were James A. Dickey (Puerto Rico), Chauncey Wightman (Hawaii), John Dalton (Sugar Division head), and Rexford Tugwell, (undersecretary of agriculture). Among other frustrations, they had all balked at the unequal treatment of Puerto Rico and Hawaii as they facilitated economic recovery in the islands.

Efforts by Roosevelt, his cabinet, and lobbyists paid off when, in late 1937, Congress passed a new Sugar Act. Quotas would still be based on the USDA's calculation of consumption requirements, but the secretary of agriculture had less discretion to differentiate between the territories and the mainland, and they had a clear formula for dividing quotas among all production regions. Farmers in the continental United States, Puerto Rico, and Hawaii were all eligible for benefit payments when they signed production adjustment contracts, conditional on labor, soil conservation, and marketing practices. The benefit payments were set on a progressive scale so that the largest sugar corporations would receive the least benefits. Farmers could also get additional payments on crops damaged by natural disasters. The extension of benefit payments to the islands ended what Puerto Rican commissioner of agriculture Rafael Menéndez Ramos had called "taxation without compensation," a practice "as unfair as taxation without representation."[56] Unlike the Sugar Act of 1934, the new law offered farmers in the territories and the mainland the same rights to fair exchange value. While some inequalities persisted, the Sugar Act of 1937 embodied a new direction in colonial policy, one that would have been difficult to imagine in 1932 when the sugar program was first conceived.

Just as the new law took effect, with the 1937–38 crop, the economy entered a new recession and consumers' buying power plunged. The Sugar Division decided to revise the consumption estimate downward in mid-1938, believing that prices would continue to fall if it did not reduce the sugar supply. If prices fell too low, producers' incomes everywhere would suffer. If producers on the mainland and in the territories and abroad could not sell their sugar, they would not be able to buy goods produced by other sectors. The AAA reduced all marketing quotas, which caused farmers and processors on the mainland to complain bitterly.[57] Sugar producers remained unconvinced that conditions for U.S. corn, wheat, pork, and lard producers improved if Cuba and Puerto Rico had a share of the U.S. sugar market. And why should sugar beet growers take cuts that might benefit wheat or hog farmers in a distant state? But during this crisis, the Sugar Division adhered to Henry Wallace's explicitly international and egalitarian vision of agricultural recovery. Bernhardt, who drafted replies to most of the complaints about sugar quotas, wrote that Wallace had a "theory that any person asking for an excessive share of the national income should be put to shame in a courteous way."[58] The Sugar Division courteously shamed many supplicants, repeatedly refusing calls for quota changes by patiently explaining the rationale behind the law. In hindsight, one of the more radical features of USDA planning was the extent to which, despite the creation of narrowly defined commodity programs, administrators saw past those divisions to argue for globally integrated economic recovery.

Conclusion

When Secretary of Agriculture Henry Wallace signed the first production adjustment contracts for sugar beets in November 1934, he also enacted the first national labor provisions covering children working in commercial agriculture. As with other New Deal programs, the sugar program ultimately did little to alter prevailing relations of power in the beet fields. The labor provisions did not offer a comprehensive means of establishing better conditions for working families. Nonetheless, many people across the U.S. sugar empire took seriously the promise of improved working conditions, holding the federal government accountable for labor standards in the fields and living standards at home. Workers wrote letters to federal government agencies, organized meetings, and presented testimony at AAA hearings. They also continued to go on strike through the late 1930s, eventually with the support of national labor organizations like the Congress of Industrial Organizations (CIO). In these ways, sugar workers asserted that they were crucial to New Deal recovery.

Despite its anti-imperial trappings, the New Deal reconsolidated the U.S. sugar empire by reconciling issues that had first emerged after the Spanish American War. Policymakers hoped to protect mainland farmers by creating a system of marketing quotas to rebalance trade among the mainland, the islands, and Cuba. For some policymakers, the imposition of immigration restrictions in the 1920s had signaled that the United States would no longer tolerate encroachments from the tropics, in the form of either workers or sugar. They hoped to limit territorial sugar producers' market share in order to bolster the position of mainland cane and beet farmers. The movement to grant the Philippines independence encapsulated the impulse to exclude both workers and sugar. However, as policymakers implemented the sugar programs, their perspectives became increasingly inclusive. Policymakers renegotiated a domestic geography that tentatively included Hawaiian and Puerto Rican sugar producers, excluded the Philippine Islands, and offered renewed concessions to Cuba.

Some policymakers asserted an altruistic sense of fairness toward the territories, but their goodwill did not overcome the systemic inequalities of empire. Rather than affirming the sovereignty of each of its trading partners, quotas reproduced the United States' hegemonic position in the sugar economy it dominated. The United States continued to direct the flow of sugar by deciding which nations and possessions were included and which were excluded from its markets. The U.S. government opened new offices and required new forms, procedures, and inspections to control trade across the U.S. sugar empire. If, as I have argued, empire is defined as the uneven exercise of political sovereignty across space and between different social groups, then the New Deal sugar programs were, from their inception, imperial.

CHAPTER EIGHT

NEW DEAL, NEW EMPIRE

Neocolonial Divisions of Labor, Sugar Consumers, and the Limits of Reform

In the final days of congressional negotiations over the Sugar Act of 1937, President Roosevelt wrote an open letter to the chair of the Senate Finance Committee, Pat Harrison (D-Mississippi), criticizing the bill because it limited the amount of sugar the territories could refine. This discrimination against refining, Roosevelt wrote, "has no economic or social justification . . . and would constitute a dangerous precedent."[1] Despite Roosevelt's protest, Congress passed the Sugar Act, which explicitly limited imports of "direct-consumption" sugar—any sugar that could be eaten without further processing—from Puerto Rico, Hawaii, the Philippines, and Cuba. The bill as a whole was a triumph for Roosevelt's administration. But he and his advisors saw the direct-consumption provisions as a defeat because they meant that the territories remained unequal to the mainland. While continental producers could sell any grade or type of sugar, territorial and foreign producers could only fill their quotas with raw sugar requiring further processing on the mainland. Worrying that a veto would only harm the farmers it was supposed to aid, Roosevelt did not reject the bill. Instead, he issued a special message asserting the premise of territorial integrity.[2] He argued that the bill was "seriously impaired" because of the "provision intended to legalize a virtual monopoly in the hands of a small group of seaboard refiners" at the expense of territorial citizens.[3] He hoped that future sugar legislation would "recognize the fact that Hawaii and Puerto Rico and the Virgin Islands are integral parts of the United States and should not be discriminated against." That Roosevelt was ready to offer the islands full economic integration through refined sugar represented a sea change in both colonial policy and the meanings attributed to refined sugar.

Refined sugar had long been symbolically charged and racially coded, a literal example of the refinement of civilization. For that reason, debates about whether and how to protect the refined sugar industry had, for years, invariably hinged on a racial hierarchy that subordinated territorial producers and consumers. The powerful and highly monopolistic sugar refining industry maintained an aggressive, well-funded lobby to assert its prerogatives, actively using racialized language to bolster its case. Refiners relied on the emotional appeal of the historical colonial division of labor whereby raw goods were produced in the colonies and refined in the mainland. As we have seen, a colonial division of labor meshed with the restricted forms of citizenship typical during the U.S. imperial expansion in the early twentieth century. The stability of the refining industry, and their exceptional profits, depended on this colonial logic. As policymakers negotiated the economic crises in the sugar economy in the 1930s, though, they increasingly asserted that the older hierarchical distinctions among groups of citizens and territories were outdated. Likewise, the category of "refined" was outdated, replaced by the broader designation "direct consumption." That policymakers asserted that inequalities and hierarchies were a thing of the past did not, of course, make it so. Inequality persisted all around them, often as a result of their own actions.

Roosevelt's was a moderate position in the debate over colonial political status. There were proponents of statehood in both Hawaii and Puerto Rico, and there were advocates of independence for Puerto Rico on the island and the mainland. In fact, a commission headed by Millard Tydings had proposed Puerto Rican independence the previous year. The administration's experience with that proposal, along with subsequent events in the island, convinced them that neither statehood nor independence were viable political options until there was a thorough economic reconstruction.[4] Indeed, what Roosevelt advocated through the Sugar Act was neither full integration nor full exclusion for the territories. He avoided questions of territorial *political* equality by advocating *economic* equality without the legal foundations of either statehood or independence. His approach foregrounded the economic rights of citizens in the territories, who would be able to earn fair exchange value for their crops and labor. This was the linchpin of what policymakers believed was a better, more liberal approach to the territories that nonetheless maintained the existing colonial structure.[5]

This liberal approach to economic citizenship mirrored a liberalization in the sociolegal categories through which sugar was commodified and consumed. Among working people in the United States and in the island territories, less-refined sweeteners had consistently offered a means to articulate a sense of disjuncture. By the 1930s, a broader range of sugars, including those that had not been refined, were recognized by policymakers as legitimate trade goods. But, ironically, rural and urban workers increasingly found that the least expensive sweets were not unrefined homemade products, as had always been the case. Instead, the cheapest foods were those that had been mass-produced and distributed on an industrial, national scale, such as the inexpensive candies that confectioners sold in steadily increasing quantities. Refined sugar was cheap and plentiful, while less-refined products were more expensive because they did not enjoy the economies of scale commanded by mass producers. Reflecting both their new urban locations and changes in the sugar market, by the late 1930s poor people were more likely to buy mass-marketed candy canes than to eat sugarcane in the fields. New Deal policymakers asserted that workers had the right, even an obligation, to consume products of modern industry. But even as refined and processed sweets became viable food choices for colonial residents and immigrant working classes, nutrition researchers began to criticize these exact foods. Commenting on the teeth and girth of people with "typical western diets," a new generation of moralizing health reformers complained that refined and processed foods were weakening civilization. Sugar's place in the hierarchy of civilization was turned on its head, but poor people, including poor people of color, were still at the bottom.

Commodification, Political Status, and Neocolonial Divisions of Labor

Along with the other problems afflicting the sugar industry through the 1920s and into the early 1930s, a crisis was brewing in the standards and categories through which people understood sugar as a commodity. Recall that commodities are trade goods whose value depends on their interchangeability with goods of the same type or grade. The criteria by which people define those types and grades can and do change. People understood the value of sugar in terms that were simultaneously economic, cultural, social, and technical. Sugar refiners on the mainland had long depended for their profit margin on a commodity system that valued refined over raw. Observers had imagined a close parallel between the racial characteristics of the workers who produced sugar and the visual appearance of the final product. In popular imagination, brown workers produced low-grade brown sugar and white workers purified it into high-grade white sugar. Centrifugal mills and polariscope testing, first introduced in the nineteenth century but increasingly common after World War I, complicated these assumptions. Like the blood quantums of racial theory, the degrees of the polariscope supposedly revealed impurities that could not otherwise be seen. Using the newer centrifugal mills, though, cane sugar producers in the islands could wash sugar until it was nearly white. Such sugar had a high sugar content as measured by the polariscope but had never technically been through a refining process. People had once imagined that refining on the continent removed the "tropical impurities." Once these impurities were no longer visible to the naked eye or through the polariscope, it was not clear what purpose refining served. The centrifugal mill and the polariscope test thus together disrupted the associations among the color of sugar, its purity, and its commercial value.

The 1930 Tariff Act changed the situation for sugar refiners in several ways. The law virtually eliminated the differential that protected domestic refiners from foreign and territorial ones.[6] What was more, the 1930 Tariff made no distinction for sugars that had "gone through a process of refining," as earlier tariffs had. A sugar polarizing at 99 degrees (refined) would still pay a higher duty than 96 degree (raw) sugar, but it was not proportionately higher, as it had been before. But many centrifugal mills could now produce virtually white sugar that polarized at close to 99 degrees without ever putting it "through a process of refining." For the first time, refiners received no special protection for the part of the manufacturing process they controlled. As one member of Congress said at the time, "The tariff rate given to refined sugar is absolutely rotten."[7]

The consequences of changes in the refined sugar tariff in 1930 were far more dramatic than anyone predicted. After 1930, investors updated mills and built a few refineries in Puerto Rico, Hawaii, the Philippines, and Cuba. Mainland refiners worked hard through the 1930s to re-create the colonial division of labor that technology and the 1930 Tariff had disrupted. Refiners effectively made their case in 1934, marshaling support for Philippine independence by decrying the flood of imported refined sugar from the territories. Both the 1934 and the 1937 Sugar Acts addressed refiners' loss of their protected market by assigning import quotas for territorial and foreign "direct consumption sugar," a designation that acknowledged the changing nature of the sugar trade. Neither law used the word "refined," replacing it with "direct consumption sugar." The 1934 Sugar Act defined "direct-consumption sugar" as sugar "in any form whatsoever, for any purpose other than to be further refined or improved in quality, or further prepared for distribution or use."[8] This included refined sugar, but it also included any high-grade centrifugally milled raw sugar that had been washed to appear white, together with a range of less-refined sugars that consumers ate as is. On the one hand, the new classification reflected policymakers' realization that a wide range of sugars were bought and sold in the United States and its territories. But this classification also meant that refiners got greater protection, including protection from not only imported refined sugar but also sugar of any other color or polarization that would be sold without further processing.

Though refiners continued to use the old rhetoric about white sugar for white people through the 1930s, their political maneuvers and congressional lobbying were increasingly scrutinized by policymakers who rejected the old colonial division of labor. Calls to protect white purity by refining sugar on the mainland rang hollow for many in the Roosevelt administration. Administrators believed that since mainland producers' quotas did not restrict the kind of sugar they could sell, the territories also ought to be able to market any type of sugar. This approach reflected their new theory of liberal colonialism, which contrasted with the "Old World colonialism," focused on the "commercial interests in the mother country."[9] Administrators pointed out that the refiners sought protection for their monopolistic business practices, protection that looked like the brutal, feudalistic, fascist colonialism. As one lobbyist complained, "It is the exercise of might rather than right for Congress to say you cannot exercise your natural right to establish refineries for the manufacture of your own farm products."[10] Indeed, policymakers began to formulate an approach to colonial rule that emphasized rights rather than might. Writing about the sugar bill, Roosevelt deplored the "imperialistic classification of citizens and a tyrannical abuse of minority rights that is utterly contrary to the American concept of fairness and democracy."[11]

The Agricultural Adjustment Administration (AAA) Sugar Division under Henry Wallace and the Department of the Interior's Division of Territories under Secretary of the Interior Harold Ickes together drafted new sugar policies. They built on the principle that residents of Hawaii and Puerto Rico were "citizens of the United States in the fullest sense of the word."[12] In actuality, sugar policy offered economic equality—the rights to spend, earn, purchase, own, and profit—without full political rights and representation. Unequal political status among colonial citizens was, according to Ernest Gruening, head of the Division of Territories, a key "reason why their economic equality should be vigilantly protected."[13] Economic rights were particularly crucial because residents of the territories did not have full political rights on the mainland; they lacked "legal power to take countermeasures in self-defense," as Roosevelt later put it.[14]

With dire unemployment in the territories, the stability offered by a refinery could provide many poor people the opportunity to participate in society as consumers who enjoyed a decent, healthful standard of living. Puerto Rico's existing refineries provided year-round employment, whereas agricultural and milling operations were seasonal. Sugar refining was, as Carlos Chardón had put it in 1934, "a question of life or death" for Puerto Rico.[15] And, as Ickes pointed out, after Puerto Rico adopted wages and hours legislation, it was "no longer possible to cloud the issue by raising the cry of unfair competition because of cheap labor allegedly obtainable in the tropics."[16] For New Deal policymakers, nothing short of multiethnic economic citizenship promised global economic recovery.

Ickes and Wallace's approach to economic citizenship among territorial residents was consistent with their broader overall approach to the Depression, which focused on working consumers. But their interpretation also reflected a particular moment in debates over Puerto Rican status, which took place in 1936 and 1937. Millard Tydings, chair of the Senate Committee on Territories and Insular Possessions, who had sponsored the bill to grant independence for the Philippines in 1934, authored a hotly debated independence bill for Puerto Rico in 1936.[17] The bill, which many people perceived to be unnecessarily punitive, would have provided virtually no economic transition, scant tariff concessions, and little assistance for economic reconstruction. Opponents pointed out that the economic features of the bill made it seem like a disingenuous offer, intended to scare Puerto Ricans into opposing independence. Puerto Rican politician Luis Muñoz Marín, who up until this time had supported independence, characterized Tydings's proposal as "a gesture of political chicanery in extreme bad taste, and of economic terrorism." Though he rejected Tydings's proposal, Muñoz Marín and many others, both on the island and in Roosevelt's administration, believed that something needed to change.[18] Muñoz Marín argued that the only acceptable options were statehood or independence, both of which offered Puerto

Rico dignity and "juridical permanence."[19] Muñoz Marín rejected statehood because it would not improve the island's economy "but would rather tend to perpetuate the present unsound economic system based on the overwhelming preponderance of sugar." The only reason for the United States to "continue to own Puerto Rico" would be to protect "exploitation of the people of Puerto Rico by a few privileged interests over here."

Muñoz Marín proposed that independence, properly and gradually carried out, could end Puerto Rico's status as a "one crop country." Together with Roger Baldwin of the American Civil Liberties Union (ACLU), who was taking an interest in the civil rights of territorial residents, Muñoz Marín drafted an alternate independence bill with more favorable trade provisions. Baldwin and Muñoz Marín contacted Harold Ickes in early 1937 to discuss the proposal and hopefully find someone willing to introduce the bill in Congress.[20] Muñoz Marín was unable to garner sufficient support for a new independence bill, however. He and Baldwin offered their draft to radical member of Congress Vito Marcantonio (R-New York), who rejected it as "imperialistic." The bill, he wrote, failed to treat the island's "diabetic economic life."[21] Marcantonio pointed out that political independence had to include a plan to reclaim the smallholder economy from absentee sugar companies. He thus called for an "indemnity for the 38 years of American exploitation" and collectivization of land. Other, more moderate commentators also rejected Muñoz Marín's draft because it did not sufficiently address the problems in the sugar economy. Ralston Hayden, for example, drawing on his experience as acting governor general of the Philippines in 1935 during the first years of the AAA sugar program there, cautioned Baldwin that it would be difficult for the island to undergo economic and political reconstruction at the same time.[22] Ultimately, none of the independence proposals succeeded. The following year, even Muñoz Marín pulled back from his public advocacy of independence.

It was within the context of these debates over Puerto Rico's status that the Roosevelt administration renewed its interest in territorial sugar refining in 1937 and 1938. With neither independence nor statehood viable political options, economic change seemed all the more urgent. Reeling from the political fallout of Tydings's independence proposal and subsequent events in Puerto Rico, Ernest Gruening, in the Division of the Territories, took a novel approach to the problem. In the hope of testing the constitutionality of the direct-consumption provision, he turned to civil rights attorney Morris Ernst to draft a brief on the issue.[23] Gruening reasoned that a successful legal challenge in Hawaii, which was in a stronger legal position than Puerto Rico, would lay the groundwork for later overturning the law for Puerto Rico. Ernst laid out the legal precedent for Hawaii's status as an incorporated territory, based on the treaty of annexation and its Organic Act.[24] The Supreme Court had ruled that there was a distinction between incorporated and unincorporated territories in the Insular Case *Balzac v. Porto Rico* (1922). Incorporated territories were presumably moving toward statehood, at which time the constitutional uniformity and commerce clauses would apply. Ernst asserted that "the power to regulate commerce among the *incorporated territories and the States . . . must be grounded in the interstate commerce clause and not otherwise.*" The direct-consumption provision was thus, he reasoned, "repugnant to the requirement of equality in regulations of interstate commerce." Ernst also argued that the law violated due process under the Fifth Amendment, citing Supreme Court rulings in *Yick Wo v. Hopkins* (1886) and *Wong Wing v. U.S.* (1896), cases that extended equal protection regardless of race or citizenship. He found it "unthinkable" that "American citizens resident in Hawaii" would have fewer rights than "alien Chinese who happen to be resident in continental United States." Ernst's choice of these precedents highlighted the fact that it was white men's property rights in Hawaiian sugar refining that were at stake. Plaintiffs in *Ewa Plantation Company v. Henry A. Wallace* in 1934 had argued and lost their case on essentially the same grounds. Gruening approved Ernst's opinion and hoped to convince representatives of the Hawaiian industry to file suit, though he did not find anyone to do so.[25]

Meanwhile, mainland cane and beet growers intensified demands to roll back concessions for Cuba, the Philippines, and the territories. Led by Louisiana senator Allen Ellender in 1939, lobbyists and members of Congress proposed a revision to the Sugar Act that would have gutted it in favor of the continental producers. Ellender proposed to give quotas only to mainland farmers and to reinstate the distinction between mainland and territories. Behind the scenes, the president and the Departments of Interior, Agriculture, and State all opposed Ellender's bill.[26] Ernest Gruening, in an interdepartmental memo, criticized the theory of colonialism he believed it embodied. Writing immediately after Hitler invaded Poland, Gruening compared Ellender's proposal "with the attitude of old-world powers" and cruel dictatorships.[27] As opposed to the United States' democratic tradition, which held "that all American citizens were equal and entitled to the same rights and privileges everywhere under the flag, these old-world powers, these dictatorships, believe in two classes of people under one sovereignty—what Hitler calls the 'Herrenvolk,' or ruling people who desire to exploit and enjoy the efforts of the labor of the other and lesser category of people under their sway." According to Gruening, the narrow interests of the monopolistic sugar industry were analogous to Hitler's Herrenvolk. He condemned the "inexcusable and unjustifiable distinction between 'continental' and 'off-shore' Americans" as cruel. Though many people in the Roosevelt administration shared this interpretation, they believed they were not in a strong position to intervene publicly in the congressional debate. They hoped, instead, that the conflicting sugar interests in Congress would be unable to pass a new bill because of infighting.[28] Indeed, the congressional sugar bloc, as Bernhardt called it, did not pass new legislation in 1939. Senator Ellender's failure to undo the Sugar Act was not only the result of conflicts among diverse constituencies, but also a genuine, broad-based shift in how policymakers conceptualized the relationships among domestic, colonial, and global economies. By the end of the 1930s, administrators in the USDA and the Interior Department and the president himself were advocating more equitable quotas for Hawaii, Puerto Rico, and Cuba and were working to remove legal distinctions between the territories and the mainland.

The war in Europe cast a long shadow over debates on colonial status, racial difference, and sugar policy. As soon as the war began in Europe, consumers and merchants began hoarding sugar. Fearing speculation and high prices, the AAA recommended that Roosevelt temporarily suspend the quotas and excise taxes. The sudden suspension of the quotas upset the Cuban economy, which had come to rely on the price and market stability created by the program. This geopolitical threat was unacceptable to the State Department, given the looming world war, so, not long afterward, the Sugar Division recommended that the president reinstate the quotas.[29] As the United States debated whether and when to join the war, it did so with the sugar economy already firmly under government control. What remained was a neocolonial division of labor: mainland manufacturers still enjoyed protected markets for their direct-consumption sugars, but this protection was enshrined within a liberal colonial policy that policymakers hoped would compensate for the more invidious distinctions between mainland and territorial producers.

Eating through the New Deal:
A Neocolonial Division of Consumption

At the November 1937 sugar wage rate hearings before the AAA in San Juan, Rafael Alonso Torres, head of the Workers' Federation of Puerto Rico, testified that "the life of a laborer in Puerto Rico is a tragedy. He thrives on the bananas the owner of the farm allows him to take, and sometimes they are prosecuted for taking those bananas."[30] In contrast with this bleak picture, Ramón Ramos Casellas, representing nearly all Puerto Rican sugar millers, insisted that the typical working family's diet included rice, beans, codfish, vegetables, and sometimes even chicken. Despite widespread evidence to the contrary, Ramos testified that workers had ample diets. Almost as an afterthought, Ramos noted that on the sugar plantations workers "eat a lot of cane, too." Joshua Bernhardt, head of the AAA Sugar Division, who was chairing the proceedings, did not blink. Bernhardt was ready to accept the notion that cane-eating was a major source of calories for destitute workers and that the practice was so widespread as to constitute a substantial loss for plantations. So he asked, "What would you say was the estimated loss per year for cane eaten by laborers?" Ramos jokingly replied, "Well, it is quite an item." A few members of the audience laughed, though Bernhardt did not. The hearing quickly moved on, but this brief exchange reveals a critical shift in how policymakers conceptualized the role of consumers in the racial hierarchy of empire. Three decades earlier, most policymakers would have agreed with Ramos that eating cane was a legitimate form of provisioning for field workers, and they would have laughed at his joke. It would have been brushed off as a harmless stereotype. But in the late 1930s, New Deal administrators saw cane-eating as a sign of an economic system horribly off-kilter. For them, access to adequate food, including processed sugar rather than raw cane, was counted among the basic rights the New Deal sought to guarantee for rural and urban workers.

Policymakers' commitment to assuring adequate consumption did not necessarily bode well for poor people's nutritional status. Overall, during the Great Depression, sugar and candy consumption remained stable despite widespread poverty. The per capita consumption of sugar, as estimated by the USDA, was only slightly less during the 1930s than it had been during the sugar frenzy of the 1920s.[31] By reducing the excess stocks of sugar and limiting production, policymakers during the New Deal slowed the trend of ever-increasing per capita sugar *availability*. They did not, however, stop or reverse the trend of per capita *consumption*. Indeed, people during the 1930s consumed a wide variety of sweets. Candy makers developed new, inexpensive candy lines. Louisiana and Florida cane producers stepped up their production of the cheaper grades of sugar and syrup. Those too poor even to buy these goods might still have received some of the 26 million pounds of sugar, cane, and sorghum syrup distributed to poor families by the Federal Surplus Commodities Corporation between 1935 and 1939.[32]

Besides the Sugar Division, the AAA also operated a Consumer's Division, whose goal was to educate and advocate on behalf of consumers, especially those with moderate means. Together with the Bureau of Home Economics (BHE), these entities reinforced the connection between producers' and consumers' economic well-being. With adequate purchasing power for those at society's lowest rungs, both malnutrition and commodity surpluses would evaporate. The BHE argued that if people ate better diets they would be more productive workers, while also helping the farm economy. Researchers found that families made good food choices when they had the money to do so, but that it was difficult to eat a high-quality diet on a very low income. Based on data collected by the Bureau of Labor Statistics in the mid-1930s, the BHE analyzed poor families' food-purchasing habits, comparing the diets of African American wage earners in the South with those of whites in the Northeast, in the West, and in the central states.[33] Not surprisingly, they found dramatic differences in the amount of money families spent on food and the quality of the diets they could afford. Southern African Americans, for example, had significantly less money to spend on food. But researchers also noticed that, regardless of race or region, when their incomes increased, families augmented their diets predictably. Working families bought more fruits, vegetables, eggs, milk, and meat when they could. By contrast, their purchases of sweeteners for table use and cooking were relatively constant, regardless of improvements in their income.[34] Aggregate data on food spending revealed that poor families saw sugar and syrup as integral elements in their diet, but they gave priority to other dietary improvements when they had the money. Researchers concluded that income was the most crucial determinate

Still true today.

of diet, and policymakers ought not underestimate its importance in their efforts to improve the nation's nutritional status.[35] They no longer assumed that there was a close association between poor diets and intrinsic racial characteristics.

Poor families' food choices meshed remarkably well with the advice offered by home economists, who no longer promoted low-cost, high-calorie foods like sugar as a panacea for working consumers. In contrast with an earlier generation of nutrition reformers, home economists in the 1930s suggested that the chief problem with an inexpensive diet was that it lacked what they called "protective foods," including fruits, vegetables, dairy, and meat. These were, as we have seen, the very foods that people purchased when they had more money. Drawing on new research about micronutrients, home economists insisted that diets deficient in vitamins and minerals were as dangerous as those lacking adequate calories. Home economists did not classify sugar as a "protective food" and, unlike their predecessors, did not generally promote sugar consumption. While the market might be glutted, this was no reason for consumers to eat more sugar. Indeed, many of the "protective foods" were also ones with oversupplied markets—dairy, leafy vegetables, and fruits.

People did not treat candy as a luxury just because money was tight. Rather than eating less candy, they ate cheaper candy. As the Depression deepened, the average value in cents per pound of candy decreased, even as the total poundage of candy increased. In 1936, confectioners produced a record 2 billion pounds of candy, surpassing even the high candy consumption in the 1920s.[36] Candy manufacturing was the eighth-largest food industry in the United States, employing 52,000 workers and producing an average of 16 pounds of candy per capita.[37] Dentists complained that their patients were consuming mind-boggling and tooth-decaying quantities of inexpensive hard candies.[38] As the AAA's *Consumer's Guide* pointed out, "Consumers can buy it almost any way they want it," including very cheaply. The AAA estimated that 16 percent of the trade was aimed at "the grimy fisted little codger and urchin trade," who bought penny candies.[39] But customers also bought plain bulk candy, 5 and 10 cent packages at the movies, and molded chocolate bars. Fancy confections dropped to a mere 1 percent of sales. Besides buying inexpensive types of candy, people increasingly made their purchases at chain stores rather than independent candy stores. By buying at chain stores, people were able to purchase more candy at a lower cost since they benefited from economies of scale at the retail, freight, and manufacturing levels.

During the New Deal, policymakers in Washington began to think seriously about the sugar eaten by people in the territories. AAA officials envisioned that sugar farmers and processors could weather the sugar readjustment program in Puerto Rico, Hawaii, and the Philippines by drawing on the strength of their local markets. Local consumption in each place could take up the slack when production exceeded the U.S. marketing quotas. Because capacity for refined and raw was so much in excess of the allowed import quotas, there was much more of this type of sugar available than consumers in the territories could eat. Previous versions of the consumption estimate had not included territorial consumption. The 1937 Sugar Act required that the secretary of agriculture estimate Hawaiian and Puerto Rican local consumption. After 1937 the populations of Hawaii and Puerto Rico were recognized as consumer markets in need of price and marketing controls in their own right.

Consumers on the islands responded in different ways to the changing sugar supply under the AAA. In Puerto Rico and Hawaii, residents ate more of the higher grades of locally made sugar, which were widely available and cheaper, since the mainland markets for them were restricted. The preference for refined sugar imported from the mainland had a long history among elites in both places. In Hawaii, however, by the 1930s, most sugar consumed on the island was also processed there, through either refining or "washing."[40] Pineapple canners purchased refined sugar, in turn selling their canned goods to the mainland. Though some specialty cube sugar was still imported from California, for the most part even elite Hawaiians ate local sugar. Likewise, Puerto Ricans ate more locally processed sugar, which producers marketed more aggressively on the island as the quota restrictions limited their markets on the mainland. Less refined sugar was imported from the mainland to Puerto Rico in the 1930s. The overall result was that choices about sugar were no longer the obvious marker of class difference that they had been in the territories previously.

Puerto Rican workers increasingly understood themselves as sugar consumers and integral participants in the U.S. economy. Workers protested to the AAA about the processing tax on sugar because, as working consumers in the territories without the labor protections afforded their peers on the mainland, they bore a double burden from the tax. As they put it, "The factory and field laborers of the sugar industry of Puerto

Rico, who produce as well as consume said commodity, are the ones who must pay the special tax."[41] Workers insisted that the only way to equitably assess such a tax was to legalize collective bargaining so that workers would be guaranteed a living wage. Though the Sugar Act did contain labor provisions, they fell far short of a collective bargaining, only providing labor oversight through production adjustment contracts made with individual farmers. Nonetheless, labor unions repeatedly asserted that the living and eating standards among Puerto Rican workers were low and sought to achieve better conditions. In doing so, workers claimed the right to eat processed sugar.

In comparison with Puerto Rico and Hawaii, where higher-grade sugars had a ready market, Filipino consumers ate lower-grade sugars, even after centrifugally milled white sugar became cheaper and more widely available. Over the span of two decades, farmers had increasingly diverted their cane from the old-fashioned, lower-grade muscovado mills to modern centrifugal mills that could produce sugar for the U.S. market.[42] As centrifugal sugar production increased in the late 1920s and early 1930s, muscovado production decreased. The peak production of centrifugal sugar in the Philippines was in 1933, the year before quota controls went into effect. After 1934, when the AAA imposed strict limits on the amount of centrifugal that could be marketed in the United States, farmers began to make products that had a steady local market, rather than those for export. While muscovado and molasses production increased or decreased depending on the market for centrifugally milled sugar, other unrefined sugars had steadier markets in the Philippines. The production of *panocha* (unrefined brown loaf sugar similar to piloncillo) and *basi* (a fermented, alcoholic cane juice beverage) was *not* sensitive to the overall trend toward centrifugal milling. Neither product had a large export market, suggesting that Filipinos continued to eat them despite the availability of white sugar. As the high commissioner noted in his report to President Roosevelt in 1937, "Efforts to increase the domestic consumption of sugar [in the Philippines] have been only moderately successful." He continued, "It is doubtful if it can be increased very rapidly, even with low retail prices."[43]

Farmers in the Philippines petitioned the AAA to exempt unrefined sugar from excise taxes.[44] They argued that muscovado production was minor compared to centrifugal and "in good times barely covers the needs of the local market," suggesting that consumers readily bought this grade of sugar.[45] The AAA agreed to the exemption and ruled that farmers could process molasses into alcohol for local consumption without affecting their production adjustment contracts. The AAA also ruled that farmers could sell "sugarcane for the purpose of being chewed as and in the form of sugarcane" outside of the quota and without a tax.[46] This decision recognized that raw cane was a commodity with exchange value. Though it was outside of the bounds of the export market because people in the United States did not consume it this way, administrators no longer categorized chewing cane as a practice located beyond the realm of civilized market exchange.

When local and export markets in Puerto Rico, Hawaii, and the Philippines failed to provide enough cash for families to feed themselves, administrators saw subsistence production as an option. Where sugar markets had failed, they encouraged workers to withdraw from them. Rexford Tugwell at the USDA encouraged the Federal Experiment Station in Mayaguez, Puerto Rico, and the Agricultural Experiment Station at the University of Hawaii to study subsistence crops. The Puerto Rico Reconstruction Administration provided small subsistence plots on marginal land for rural workers, which labor leaders on the island criticized as a bucolic fantasy.[47] Nonetheless, leaders in Washington and San Juan hoped that by temporarily redirecting both land and labor toward subsistence rather than cash production, they could buy time to shore up the core institutions of the capitalist sugar industry.

Policymakers revised older, racialized, and hierarchical assumptions of consumption practices as they debated how best to rehabilitate and reconstruct the sugar industry. They no longer fixated on distinctions between civilized and uncivilized consumption habits. Instead, they considered consumers at home and overseas as equally critical to global economic recovery and aimed to maintain purchasing power among diverse consumer citizens. What had formerly seemed to be uncivilized consumption habits, such as chewing on raw cane, were now interpreted as evidence of poverty. Increasingly, the paucity of workers' food choices signaled not their racial inferiority but what policymakers saw as those workers' subordination within a flawed socioeconomic structure.

Please, Could I Get a Little Sugar for My Table: Mexicans and Piloncillo in the 1930s

In 1935, Colorado social reformer and lawyer Albert Dakan wrote a vignette describing a poor family that was unable to collect its wages for a season of beet work, despite the labor provisions in the Sugar Act. Dakan described how Catholic welfare reformer Thomas Mahoney helped the family get an order of groceries at the expense of the Great Western Sugar Company. At the end of the exchange, the worker turned to the company superintendent and asked, "Please, could I get a little sugar for my table."[48] This was the climax of Dakan's story, which for him revealed the empty promises of New Deal reforms. Beet workers' inability to purchase sugar for their families was emblematic of the endemic exploitation in beet production. Mexican and Mexican American workers had achieved important recognition under the AAA Sugar Acts and through their own activism. But they also faced unique challenges, in part because the Sugar Acts were managed at the local level by the same farmers, bankers, and millers who profited from suppressing beet worker wages. Wages remained inadequate, and families continued to depend on credit and charity from local agencies and sugar companies. When they sought relief or credit, their food purchases were limited to a list of "necessities," which typically included only flour and beans and not always sugar.[49] In negotiations over the 1936 beet contract, workers' demands included irrigated garden space and the right to trade at any store.[50] Workers' inability to make decisions about their own food thus revealed the limits of New Deal reforms.

This situation was one that AAA administrators had hoped to correct through the Sugar Acts, which aimed to raise Mexican American beet workers' purchasing power alongside that of white farmers.[51] Despite high hopes, the AAA wage and child labor provisions had proven difficult to enforce and had not done much to improve workers' standards of living. In order to counter concerns about excess federal authority, the USDA preferred to leave wage negotiations and enforcement to local growers' committees.[52] The wage increases that did happen were scarcely adequate to compensate for the families' loss of children's labor, a fact at which some working families balked.[53] When in 1935 the Children's Bureau conducted a follow-up study to determine whether the Sugar Act had improved conditions in the fields, it found that little had changed.[54] Published in 1939, the investigation concluded that while there had been a reduction in child labor in some areas, compliance with the law was erratic since local officials remained in charge of its enforcement.[55] The report argued that living and working conditions needed to be improved before children could gain "a position of respect in the communities in which they live."[56] The report included photographs taken by Farm Security Administration photographer Russell Lee, who depicted Mexican families at work, at home, and as consumers. Though working conditions may not have changed, Lee's photographs identified Mexican Americans as constituents of the New Deal and as consumers with potential purchasing power.

As Mexican Americans and Mexican nationals who remained in the beet fields struggled to survive on beans and wheat flour, piloncillo would increasingly have been a luxury for most. Indeed, few merchants advertised piloncillo in Mexican American newspapers during the 1930s. The few salesmen who did advertise the product did so almost exclusively as a seasonal specialty for urban residents. The Sugar Act of 1937 exempted sugar imported for religious or sacramental purposes from import quotas. This exemption encouraged merchants to market piloncillo as a religious article, which allowed them to sidestep exclusionary regulations. Mexicans would have reserved piloncillo for special occasions because it was not sold by the company grocers who offered them credit, and because it cost so much more than the cheap refined sugar. For working people in the United States, piloncillo was an expensive luxury.

At the same time as Mexicans in the United States found piloncillo prohibitively expensive, in Mexico piloncillo continued, as it had in the 1920s, to embody contradictions between modernity and nationalism. For example, at the very same time that President Lázaro Cárdenas (1934–40) took steps to nationalize the sugar refining industry, he made a point of publicly eating piloncillo. Cárdenas drank coffee sweetened with piloncillo as a kind of populist gesture as he sought to legitimate his reformist projects of capitalist modernization.[57] Between 1937 and 1939, his administration initiated the lengthy process of dividing large holdings of sugarcane lands into collectively managed *ejidos*, or small land grants for peasants.[58] But rather than producing piloncillo from these cane lands, Cárdenas's administration encouraged peasants to make refined sugar. They envisioned that small farms could "replace the traditional Mexican hacienda with modern machinery and full technical resources, and they will erase forever the semifeudal face of the country."[59] Mexican leaders idealized the small farmer, much as New Deal policymakers in the United States did. Cárdenas aimed to broaden the appeal and legitimacy of refined sugar among Mexican workers and peasants. Indeed, by the end of Cárdenas's presidency, refined sugar production was the most lucrative food production industry, and the fourth most important industry in the nation.[60] Cárdenas's policies resulted in cheaper refined sugar, ostensibly produced in an industry that allocated resources more equitably to rural Mexicans of all classes. With refined sugar more widely available, the negative view of piloncillo as a degenerate relic of the past only seemed to intensify.[61]

When the United States joined World War II, it negotiated a new agricultural guest worker program with Mexico, which brought a new generation of migratory guest workers, many of them single males. For these workers, called *braceros*, piloncillo offered an ambiguous alternative to the refined sugar they labored to produce. Mexican workers had long commented on their complicated positions in U.S. American society by composing *corridos*, Mexican-style ballads. A handful of corridos focused on the commodities, including sugar, that Mexicans produced. Mexican-born Bartolo Ortiz, who had done agricultural labor in Texas for years, composed a corrido in which he reflected on the politics of sugar rationing for beet workers.[62] In "La restrinción del azucár," Ortiz revealed that workers were acutely aware that the sweetness they produced was intended for others and was beyond their reach. He claims to be a "good Mexican, coming to bring joy," by producing sugar for U.S. Americans. By doing so, though, he makes himself a clown—*un payaso*—the laughing stock of his countrymen, since he earns but a pittance, "ganando algo de pastilla." The word *pastilla* here hints that he earned nothing but gum or candy for his labor, as much as it suggests the paucity of the coins he might have gotten (or the aspirin he needed to soothe his aching body).[63] By calling himself a clown, Ortiz suggests that the clowns'/beet workers' job was to hide personal suffering so as not to diminish others' pleasures. If the audience recognizes that the clown is working to be a clown, the clown has failed in his task, which is to entertain and divert. Similarly, the beet worker labors to entertain others, without the privilege of enjoying the same pleasures himself. In this sense, Ortiz offered a sophisticated theory of the relationship between labor and culture.

Ortiz draws attention to Mexican workers' ironic roles as producer and consumer in other ways, such as by repeatedly mentioning the displeasure of unsweetened coffee,

El azúcar se ha escondido [Sugar has become scarce].
Ya es artículo de lujo [It is now a luxury item].
Si el café es desabrido [If the coffee is unpleasant now],
que puedo hacer, nomás pujo [what can I do, I just grunt
    (complain)].

As Russell Lee's 1937 photograph of beet workers drinking coffee together shows, consuming the warm, sugar-laden beverage was a daily ritual demarcating a space and time of familial integrity for Mexican American beet workers. Ortiz further articulates Mexicans' contradictory roles as producers and consumers of sugar by describing the difficulty of registering for sugar rations during the war. He narrates the registration process, in which "la raza chicana" lined up at the school on May 5, a significant Mexican national holiday about which the white woman conducting the registration is ignorant. She asks probing questions of applicants, implying that they do not deserve full sugar rations. Ortiz notes that the rations were inadequate for large families anyway. Another applicant waiting in line tells him, "No me gusta el café amargo [I don't like bitter coffee] . . . son diez bocas en mi casa [there are ten mouths to feed in my house]." For beet laborers who drank sweetened coffee as a source of sociality and calories, the scarcity of sugar marked a difficult adjustment within an already harsh environment.

Ortiz refers explicitly to the Bracero program later in the corrido. Policymakers framed the Bracero program as a cooperative effort against fascism by the United States and Mexico, but Ortiz played with the notion of farmwork as political obligation. By working in the beet fields of the United States, Ortiz claims to be a good Mexican. But he also juxtaposes the wartime demands for cooperation with the actual difficulties of the work.

¡Hijo de la remolacha [Child of the beet fields],
pariente del betabel [kin to the beet]!
Que por su puntada gacha [Because this stooping pain]
nos está llevando al jel [is taking us to hell].

Musing on whether the pain is worth it, Ortiz briefly ponders piloncillo.

Si me voy para Laredo [If I go to Laredo],
el asunto es más sencillo [it will all be more simple],
ya veré allí si puedo [there I will see if I can]
pasar mucho piloncillo [bring in a lot of piloncillo].

The stanza locates the consumption of piloncillo in Laredo, a key port of entry for both Mexicans and Mexican goods. By placing piloncillo in Laredo, far from the beet fields, Ortiz suggests that the product was receding toward the border as Mexicans relied on U.S. sugar rationing. Merchants do not seem to have taken advantage of the sugar scarcities during World War II to sell piloncillo, as they had twenty years earlier. Indeed, Ortiz's tone in the stanza is tongue in check, because he implies that workers were unlikely to actually go to Laredo for piloncillo. Instead, it was understood, they would continue to be good Mexicans not by consuming the Mexican product, but by producing and eating rationed beet sugar.

At the Points of Contact with Modern Civilization
There Was the Same Dismal Story: Cavities, Obesity,
and the Decline of Civilized Sugar Eating

In his *Los Angeles Times* health column in 1939, William Brady wrote that "civilized man has lost the instinct for choosing" nutritious foods and instead eats only "highly refined modern food" that lacked "the vitamins and minerals, which are largely removed and discarded by refining, preserving, cooking, and the like."[64] Refined sugar was "delectable, inexpensive, [and] available to everybody everywhere."[65] Brady's theory was reminiscent of earlier associations among sugar, civilization, and racial purity, except that Brady turned this logic on its head by celebrating the "mongrel" and decrying the decay of civilization caused by refined foods.[66] He recommended freshly milled whole wheat flour and "crude, unrefined brown sugar or raw sugar and molasses," which retained the B vitamins and other nutrients lost through refining.[67] Beginning in the mid-1930s and continuing over the next several years, journalists, dentists, and medical practitioners began to sound the alarm: waistlines in the United States were expanding and teeth were rotting. Modern, civilized foods, including sugar, were to blame. Press services offered a steady stream of stories, picked up by newspapers across the country, about the deaths and illnesses of the extremely obese. For the first time in the twentieth century, nutritionists, scientists, dentists, and journalists began to seriously question the positive association between sugar and civilization.[68]

Criticism of civilized eating habits came, with renewed intensity, from dentists whose experiences in the last decades had convinced them that something was seriously amiss in civilized mouths. While modern diets might appear to be plentiful and healthful, dentists increasingly questioned how this could be the case when 96 percent of children exhibited tooth decay. Brady helped popularize the latest dental research, especially the works of Weston A. Price. Price was an Ohio dentist whose extensive study of the teeth of "primitive races" formed the basis of a recommended diet of natural foods.[69] In his 1939 book, *Nutrition and*

Physical Degeneration: A Comparison of Primitive and Modern Diets and Their Effects, Price describes his world travels in search of people without tooth decay. Price compared the teeth of people who ate "primitive diets" with members of the same sociocultural groups who lived in modern settings and ate "civilized diets." He described his method as a scientific one, in which primitive people with "natural" eating habits were the control group against which he could test the influence of refined wheat, sugar, and fats. The primitive man served as a scientific control in the "great experiment of civilization."[70] Based on his ostensibly scientific comparisons, Price concluded that different diets produced different outcomes in people with similar genetic profiles. In this way, Price inverted the theories of racial heredity put forth by eugenicists, even as he continued to use the racialized language through which they ranked racial groups. Malnutrition, not race-mixing, was the cause of white civilization's decline.

Price collected data on diet, analyzed food samples, examined the contents of people's knapsacks, and performed detailed exams of their teeth and facial bones. Wherever civilization had not yet reached, where there had been no effort to "conquer or modernize," he found sound teeth, healthy people, and simple diets rich in a variety of fats, meat, organs, and whole grains. Where people ate such diets he also noted an "absence of prisons and asylums," which he interpreted as a sign that moral and social problems did not beset people when they were properly fed.[71] Nature, he argued, produced a "superior quality" of "human stock."[72] To Price, rather than being degenerate by nature, "primitive races" were healthier and wiser because they lived closer to nature. But this was not merely a rank comparison between primitive-versus-civilized groups, because eating practices resulted in profound physical changes. As soon as so-called primitive people began to eat foods like white sugar and flour, they began suffering the diseases of "white civilization," including dental decay, malformed bodies, diabetes, and tuberculosis. As one reviewer summarized, "At the points of contact with modern civilization there was the same dismal story. Destruction was found everywhere."[73] Price highlighted international trade and migration as sources of these unwholesome dietary changes.[74]

Price was persuaded that improving the course of human history was as simple as changing what people ate. Primitive "nutritional wisdom" would be its salvation.[75] In particular Price argued that sugar, from which U.S. Americans got 25 percent of their calories, was a key factor in "thwarting Nature's orderly processes of life."[76] As one reviewer summarized Price's argument, primitive people held an advantage over civilized people because they were not burdened with "great milling concerns, drug companies, chain bakeries and candy stores selling consumers adulterated, processed, refined and thus devitalized foods."[77] Price tested his hypotheses by treating cases of severe dental decay and infection with his proposed diet, which was high in fats, fat-soluble vitamins, whole milk, meat, organ meat, and freshly ground grains. He concluded that such a diet, which eliminated white flour and sugar in all forms (including maple, cane syrup, and honey), could prevent or slow the progress of most health problems.

Price was but one of several dentists actively researching the broad social and physical problems associated with consuming refined sugar and wheat. Another researcher, Martha Jones, reached similar conclusions based on her studies of children of sugarcane workers living on the Ewa Plantation in Hawaii in the 1930s. Between 1928 and 1930, she conducted a dental survey of Filipino, Japanese, Hawaiian, and white children in working families on the island. Like Price, Jones compared the teeth of children fed traditional foods with those of children fed modern processed foods. And like Price, she found severe tooth decay and health problems among children eating processed food such as polished rice, candy, and soda pop. Japanese and Filipino migrants seemed especially vulnerable.[78] In fact, "grain-eating people of all nationalities" appeared to be at risk for dental problems.[79] By contrast, she found healthy teeth among native Hawaiians, who ate a traditional diet of poi (porridge made of fermented taro root), vegetables, and fish. Based on her findings of widespread malnutrition and dental disease on sugar plantations, she founded the Plantation Health Project.[80] Beginning in 1931, the Health Project was supported by the Ewa Plantation, a local hospital, and the Hawaiian Sugar Planters' Association. The Health Project operated a free clinic from which Jones ran a child-feeding program, provided nutrition education for workers, and conducted her own research. One of her key questions was, "Can the masses of rice-eating people in Hawaii today be taught to eat native foods, particularly taro and sweet potato?"[81] This question was of particular interest to New Deal administrators like Rexford Tugwell, who hoped that underemployed sugar plantation workers might produce subsistence crops like taro to compensate for the lack of work in the industry.[82]

Not surprisingly, given that she worked in a sugar plantation–sponsored clinic, Jones's conclusions about sugar conflicted with Price's. She argued that a diet high in sugar did not necessarily increase dental decay, given the right balance of other dietary elements and assuming that the sugar was not highly processed.[83] The stigma associated with sugar was "wholly unwarranted," she wrote. "Sugar-cane and sorghum and the syrups made from the juices," she wrote, "are associated with sound teeth and dental perfection" because they are rich in iron, potassium, calcium, phosphorous, and other nutrients. In her experimental feeding protocols at the Ewa Plantation, she provided children with poi, vegetables, milk, and small quantities of unrefined cane syrup. She found that this diet did not increase rates of tooth decay, and it improved the children's health. She reported other examples of healthful uses for sweeteners. She told of dining with a Samoan family in Hawaii free of dental caries who ate raw sugarcane with dinner. She was impressed with "the speed and skill with which these people can master 2½ feet of sugar-cane without the aid of any kind of implements other than their teeth."[84] Jones thus sought to salvage chewing raw sugarcane as a healthful primitive eating habit. She dwelt at length on the history in the Pacific world of chewing raw cane and using its syrup medicinally.

Jones, like Price, believed that migration brought dietary risks. She claimed, for example, that "plantation Negroes" in the rural South—she was originally from Tennessee—consumed many of their calories as molasses, supplemented with turnip greens, corn, and pork. "It is a matter of common knowledge," she wrote, "that tooth troubles are exceedingly rare" among "plantation Negroes."[85] By contrast, she pointed out that when African Americans moved to cities, they replaced the sorghum or cane molasses with purchased corn syrup, they substituted fresh-ground corn meal with packaged wheat flour, and they omitted turnip greens from their diets. By replacing traditional foods with their modern, processed equivalents, southern migrants had ruined their teeth and their health. Jones saw African American laborers, like Japanese and Filipino migrant laborers in Hawaii, as vulnerable because of migration. Building on these observations, she suggested moderate amounts of unrefined sweeteners as an adjunct to a healthful diet for people at the "contact points" between primitive and modern diets. She eventually left Hawaii and returned to her native Tennessee, where she patented an infant feeding supplement for poor children based on raw cane syrup and orange pulp.[86]

Weston Price and Martha Jones disagreed about sugar, but they had much in common. They each designed research to test the differences between civilized and primitive eating, and they each subtly (and sometimes overtly) rejected biological explanations of racial difference as they blamed modern diets for dental decay, obesity, and other health problems. Another researcher in an entirely different field, Hilde Bruch, reached similar conclusions as she rejected racial explanations for obesity and ill health. Bruch, a German Jewish psychoanalyst who studied overweight children in New York City in the 1930s and 1940s, argued that it was not race but rather psychological influences from childhood that shaped a person's vulnerability to obesity.[87] In her medical training in Europe in the 1920s, Bruch had been taught that Jews were racially predisposed to obesity because of their inherent compulsive eating habits and lack of self-control. These, apparently, were group characteristics capable of being transmitted between generations. A refugee from Nazi Germany, Bruch found it especially important to replace this racialized theory of group differences with one that accounted for individual variations, family patterns, and socioeconomic circumstances. She found that the children in her clinic ate too much and exercised too little. But, she argued, these habits were traceable to "'environmental' factors, including the emotional milieu" within their families, frequently rooted in poor relationships with their mothers. Her approach was radical because it upset the racial theories of disease proclivity that had previously dominated discussions of fatness and diabetes.

Bruch collected data on hereditary patterns of obesity, place of birth, and race of the children she was treating in her clinic. The obese children she saw were disproportionately second-generation Eastern European Jews from poor families. But where other researchers might have identified this as a biologically determined racial group characteristic, Bruch saw significant commonality among the children in other nonracial factors. To begin with, most of the parents were immigrants, "and the struggle to find a place for themselves in a new country exhausted their energies." Many parents had grown up in extreme poverty and experienced constant hunger before migrating to the United States. They recounted the many difficulties of transnational family migration—loneliness, separation, estrangement, financial obligation, homesickness. They resented their sacrifices, and "they all felt that they had been thrown upon their own resources and had been deprived of affection and security too early in life."

Many families had experienced some upward mobility but then, coinciding with the Great Depression, had suffered reversals of fortune and declining socioeconomic status. A family's financial difficulties exacerbated children's weight problems. As Bruch observed, "The marginal economic level of these families seemed to be a contributing factor in the overfeeding." Few of the fathers were good providers and thus did not seem "to be proud, secure, and self-reliant men." The mothers compensated for the fathers' failings by providing an "abundance of food" as the only luxury. Fathers were resentful and bitter; mothers were self-pitying and insincere. Mothers' "dissatisfaction and hostility," Bruch wrote, "manifested itself in endless complaints, exacting impatience, and aggressive irritability." In this sense, childhood obesity was a result of unbalanced gender roles and psychological problems in the family. Bruch also noticed that many of the children, particularly the girls, had been unwanted babies and were thus mistreated or, at minimum, secretly resented as a drain on time, money, and living space. But resentment combined with excessive attention. Lacking "emotional security," children sought solace in sweets. As Bruch put it, "Food is offered and received not alone for the appeasement of a bodily need but it is highly charged with emotional value." Mothers did not refuse their children's requests for sweets because they found satisfaction in satiating their children's hungers. Thus the twin effects of "maternal rejection and overprotection" fostered weight gain. Bruch believed that families spent a "disproportionately large" amount of their limited budgets on food, candy, and ice cream. Though food expenditures were high by her standards, families only complained about food costs when "dietary changes were recommended." Despite the clinic's efforts "to teach economic ways of shopping so that the new diet could be provided at the same or even lower price than the previous meals," families were reluctant to change their habits. In sum, Bruch saw obesity as a behavioral problem within immigrant families.[88]

The irony was that Bruch criticized unhealthy appetites and Price condemned refined foods at precisely the moment that New Deal policymakers redoubled their commitment to giving poor people access to those very foods. Policymakers, as we have seen, were insisting that poor and working people have full access to foods, including refined sugar, instead of the subsistence fare they gleaned from the fields, forests, and dirty tenement shops. As Bruch and Price asserted, it was impoverished immigrants and newly conquered primitives who suffered most from the ravages of civilization. Such people lived at the "points of contact" with civilization and were at the front lines of decay and degeneration, being but a generation removed from a more perfect diet and social life. Price's and Bruch's insights were prescient. Through the remainder of the century and beyond, the bodies of the urban poor increasingly have become signifiers of the dangers of processed foods and obesity. People, now more than ever, mark their privilege not by consuming refined white sugar, but rather by choosing more expensive, less-refined goods. They have the means to opt out of a food system built on cheap food. New Deal policymakers, in securing a piece of the pie for workers, were ironically assigning them to what was becoming a reviled place in the hierarchy of consumers.

Conclusion

President Roosevelt and his administration had correctly predicted that if the territorial limitations on refined and direct-consumption sugars were written into the 1937 Sugar Act such discrimination would be intractable.[89] Despite the efforts of New Deal administrators in the late 1930s and early 1940s, the direct-consumption provisions remained on the books and never provided a wedge through which to change the territories' political status. Congress repeatedly extended the Sugar Act, each time maintaining the limited direct-consumption sugar quotas for the territories.[90] Debates over direct-consumption sugar revealed that some administrators had embraced a new approach to empire, but the limitations signified the territories' ongoing subordinate status. For policymakers in Roosevelt's administration, refiners' political pressure to maintain the colonial division of labor in raw/refined sugar appeared anachronistic and baldly racist when juxtaposed with repressive political regimes in Europe. Nonetheless, the colonial contradiction remained. Roosevelt and his administration may have moved toward a new mode of colonial governance, but they did not fundamentally alter the power relationships between the United States and its territories. Indeed, the opportunity and political will to renegotiate colonial status through sugar policy passed as quickly as it had arrived.

New Deal policymakers hoped ethnic and territorial consumers would be able to do their economic duty as citizens by buying and eating more processed sugar. At the same time, though, a new generation of health reformers challenged those very appetites. Hilde Bruch, Weston A. Price, and Martha Jones all focused on control over individual food choices as an antidote to modernity. Their emphasis on personal choice paralleled the discourse of economic rights promoted by policymakers as they devised new sugar and colonial policies in the late 1930s. In each case, the emphasis on individual rights and choices was part of a move away from constructions of intrinsic racial difference and toward racial liberalism. Yet liberal interventions remained limited in their ability to address the systemic inequalities that shaped which choices were available to which individuals. New Deal planners and nutritionists offered a form of economic citizenship that was less meaningful, given the broad failure of economic reconstruction in the territories, the ongoing subordination of workers and people of color within the nation's economy, and the prevalence of low-cost sweeteners in the nation's food system. People still lacked the means to choose foods they perceived to be the healthiest or most toothsome. Rather than attributing these problems to inherent racial degeneracy, mainstream observers in the twentieth century increasingly described them as problems of individual will or poor mothering. By emphasizing personal factors, people placed the blame for obesity and dental caries onto poor people of color, foreshadowing how their food choices signify anxieties about globalized, industrialized food systems in the early twenty-first century.

EPILOGUE

Imperial Consumers at War

As the United States prepared to enter World War II in late 1941 and early 1942, Farm Security Administration/Office of War Information (FSA/OWI) photographer Jack Delano traveled to Puerto Rico to photograph social conditions and document the state of the sugar industry.[1] Started in 1937, the FSA photography project had employed Delano and other photographers to document rural poverty and federal interventions to improve it. Some of their photos were reproduced in government reports, posters, and promotional materials, while others remained largely unseen. During the war, the few remaining photographers employed by the project, now combined with the OWI, turned their cameras on the social consequences of the impending conflict, producing images intended as wartime propaganda. Their work showcased a vision of laborers' dignity in the face of deprivation and projected an inclusive image of U.S. American workers. The photographs revealed that U.S. American workers were not just white people. They were African American, Mexican American, and Filipino. They were Puerto Rican and Japanese American. The inclusion of these workers in the visual record of the war effort built on more than a decade of inclusive reform rhetoric that positioned workers as citizen consumers, albeit consumers who were sometimes unable to consume because of economic maladjustment. Such images made visible the economic theories of New Deal policymakers.[2]

The same New Deal policies that remade Puerto Rican workers into consumers had also created a neocolonial sugar system from the ruins of the old colonial tariffs. Building on a history of exclusion and territorial inequality, the New Deal sugar programs diminished territorial access to the protected U.S. sugar market. In their most liberal moments, New Dealers hoped that the decline of sugar would open the way for a more diverse and stable economy in the territories. But policymakers never committed substantial resources to reworking a productive landscape, which had been designed only to produce sugar. Delano's images interpreted the Puerto Rican agricultural economy through the contrast between the massive scale of industrial agriculture, shown through vast

Jack Delano, "Yabucoa Valley, Puerto Rico. This Sugar Cane Land Is Owned by the Sugar Mill in Yabucoa," December 1941. Farm Security Administration—Office of War Information Photograph Collection, Library of Congress.

panoramas of the alluvial cane fields, and close-up portraits of workers. Overall, Delano's images argued that, in the context of large-scale land-holding and centralized mill ownership, Puerto Ricans were struggling in an economy dominated by sugar.

Policymakers increasingly believed that sugar was not the route to modernization for Puerto Ricans. Wartime problems exacerbated the situation. Limited shipping during the war slowed the movement of goods to and from the island, which brought unemployment and hunger. Delano carefully documented workers' sometimes scanty meals, which typically centered on imported foods like rice and salt cod. Indeed, the "interruption of the normal flow of trade" with the United States had created a "food crisis" in Puerto Rico, which required federal action to prevent "famine, revolt, bloodshed."[3] As Dennis Chavez (D-New Mexico) and Millard Tydings (D-Maryland) wrote in a 1943 congressional report on Puerto Rico, "Not only does the cash crop make their economy dependent on our markets and our every determination, to the point where we can dictate terms without restrictions, but our tariff walls confine them to our markets." For Tydings and Chavez, as for colonial administrators in the Philippines ten years earlier, tariff protection and sugar quotas seemed to be illiberal instruments of subjugation, limiting the island economy's self-sufficiency and flexibility. Rather than encouraging sugar production, then, federal policy toward Puerto Rico during the war focused on increasing local food self-sufficiency. Tydings and Chavez went so far as to argue that Puerto Ricans could best contribute to the war effort by migrating to the mainland, where they might work in war industries and learn to speak English. The insular government, the War Department, the War Food Administration, and the Department of the Interior tried to find a way to transport workers to the mainland. Though they did not succeed at the time, the proposal represented a dramatic shift from earlier policies aimed at preventing migration and foreshadowed later efforts during Operation Bootstrap.[4]

A few months after Delano traveled to Puerto Rico in 1942, photographer Russell Lee traveled to the U.S. West to document sugar beet production. Lee found Japanese Americans living in FSA camps in Nyssa, Oregon, and Rupert, Idaho. They were employed at weeding and thinning sugar beets for nearby white farmers. While elsewhere in the West such work would soon be performed by Mexicans under a formal guest worker program, here the need for agricultural labor dovetailed conveniently with President Franklin Roosevelt's Executive Order 9066, the racially motivated removal of 120,000 Japanese Americans from the west coast.[5] The workers Lee photographed had been judged trustworthy enough to receive special permission to leave the camps to fill urgent agricultural labor shortages.[6] Lee's images and accompanying captions avoided the semicompulsory nature of the Japanese American presence in the FSA camps and beet fields, portraying the work as a positive example of wartime cooperation. One caption pointed out that "they are guaranteed standard wages. The U.S. Employment Service stands back of this guarantee and furnishes no labor to farmers who do not abide by all agreements." While this may well have been true, it elided the extent to which Japanese Americans had few other choices.

Though the incarceration of Japanese Americans was the brutal climax of decades of anti-Asian discrimination, the visual tropes through which Lee depicted them in July 1942 incorporated them as model U.S. consumer citizens. Like Delano and other FSA/OWI photographers, Lee shot long panoramas that dwarfed the human workers against the scale of beet production, as well as portraits of workers in the process of hoeing and thinning the beets. Lee dwelt at length on food preparation and

Russell Lee, "Nyssa, Oregon. Japanese-Americans Work in Sugar Beet Fields,"
July 1942. Farm Security Administration—Office of War Information
Photograph Collection, Library of Congress.

consumption in the camps. His photograph of "supper plates in the community mess hall of the Japanese-Americans" echoed Delano's image of
Puerto Rican cane workers' midday meal. By documenting meals, both
plentiful and simple, Delano and Lee claimed workers' rights to an adequate standard of living and a full lunch pail. More notable are Lee's
images of Japanese Americans consuming sweets, such as one photograph that shows a man and a young girl enjoying an ice cream soda at a
fountain in town on their day off, or another showing a delivery of Coca-
Cola. Japanese Americans in the camps may have been deprived of their
civil rights, but at least they received plenty of cold soda pop. Lee's and
Delano's photographs thus generated a narrative of labor and consumer
culture that offered a kind of proxy citizenship, however spurious.

As the FSA/OWI images suggest, the visual culture of sugar production had changed since the turn of the twentieth century, much as sugar
politics more broadly had. For years after the Spanish American War,
depictions of sugar consumption and production had hinged on the
contrast between civilized and primitive, contrasts that simultaneously
legitimated both expansion and race-based exclusion. Over the next
forty years, colonial administrators, reformers, policymakers, workers,
and consumers remade both public policy and visual culture to conform

Russell Lee, "Nyssa, Oregon. Japanese-American Farm Workers Have an Ice Cream Soda on Weekly Trip to Town," July 1942. Farm Security Administration—Office of War Information Photograph Collection, Library of Congress.

to their notions of national and ethnic belonging. In the early 1940s, the visual culture of sugar had shifted away from the idiom of civilizational hierarchy, instead registering a contrast between deprivation and plenty.[7] People no longer saw consumption and production as immutable racial attributes, but rather as the consequence of social and economic policies.

Deprivation was the result of poorly considered government policies rather than the consequence of racial failures. The idiom of scarcity and plenty shifted the terms of debate toward rights and gave workers a place at the table, at least in theory.

The contrast between scarcity and plenty—and policymakers' interest in ethnic consumers—can be traced to sugar policies crafted during World War I as administrators sought to fulfill working-class consumers' demands for full sugar bowls. Fearing public disorder and protest, administrators began to seriously pay attention to the preferences of ethnic consumers during the war. They sought balance between private enterprise and government intervention and, in doing so, set precedents that New Deal policymakers took up again as they addressed out-of-control prices and oversupplied markets in the 1930s. During World War I, government action had been premised on scarcity, as administrators aimed to keep producer prices high enough to stimulate production yet low enough to stave off cost-of-living protests. During the 1930s, on the other hand, the government premised its action on curbing excess. Administrators used similar methods to set prices high enough to guarantee farmers a return on their efforts, while also curtailing sugar production to match anticipated consumption. They did so in the hope of bolstering the purchasing power of farmers and workers, so that those who grew sugar would be able to enjoy the sweetness of their labor.

Between the Spanish American War and World War II, the meanings of sugar consumption kept pace with ongoing negotiations over political and economic status in the U.S. sugar empire. The grades and standards through which businesses and the state organized the sugar market shifted to reflect new technologies, consumption practices, and ideas about race and citizenship. Policymakers earlier in the century had dismissed workers' food needs by implying that they could get as much sustenance as they craved by chewing sugarcane, but in the 1930s workers' nutritional needs were seen as crucial. Policymakers recognized the significance of less-refined forms of sugar. They did so by exempting chewing cane and muscovados from quota regulations and by creating the category "direct-consumption sugar." Ethnic consumers, whose political citizenship remained constrained in many ways, could exercise their economic rights by participating in national mass markets for commodities whose producers suffered surpluses. Ultimately, New Deal purchasing power theorists hoped that workers would buy the cheap, mass-produced sugar whose markets needed rehabilitation.

Meanwhile, a few observers began to worry that refined sugar might not be the healthiest choice.

The legislation enabling New Deal control over the sugar economy demanded that the federal government estimate domestic sugar consumption as the basis for allocating production quotas to each region. The consumption estimate, though it might seem minor, was in fact the culmination of decades of imperial sugar politics through which U.S. consumers internalized their obligation to eat more sugar. This seemingly innocuous feature of the law institutionalized and naturalized the sugar consumer as the measure of the market in a way that reflected the complicated histories of race, labor, and empire in the United States' sugar economy. Embedded in the consumption estimate was the notion that the desire for sugar and sweetness was natural, and that government could legitimately curtail production—as long as it compensated farmers for their lost earnings—but it could not legitimately ask consumers to eat less sugar. New Deal politics enacted the desirability of sugar consumption and took steps to ensure that the right to consume was equally available to all social and ethnic groups. New Dealers saw laborers as consumers and sought ways to increase their purchasing power as part of an overall plan of economic revival.[8] Indeed, the new scheme of territorial sovereignty enacted through the New Deal sugar programs rearticulated the relations of empire as consumer politics, with increasing attention to the significance of Cubans, Hawaiians, Mexican Americans, African Americans, and Puerto Ricans as purchasers and eaters. Though Roosevelt and his cabinet sought to expand political rights for territorial residents, these were not forthcoming. Policymakers imagined consumer equality in ways that were still unattainable in other realms. For both Puerto Rican cane farmers and incarcerated Japanese American beet workers during World War II, sugar produced both states of exception and routes to incorporation through rehabilitated consumer cultures.

While workers and consumers may have welcomed new opportunities to participate in mass consumer cultures, they had also long contested the values and meanings of the goods they produced. Because commodities are by nature cultural productions, the commodity fetish is nowhere near as straightforward as Marx's seminal formulations would imply. Workers and sugar producers chose which sugars to make, sell, buy, and eat. Though U.S. administrators and investors could shape these decisions in profound ways, Mexican workers and rural southerners in the United

States and farmers in the Philippines continued to produce, sell, and eat less-refined sweets despite the overwhelming hegemony of industrially produced sugar. In the cases of piloncillo in the Southwest or homemade cane syrup in the rural South, the products were initially excluded from the category of commodity because they did not have exchange value according to mainstream businesses and policymakers. Such exclusions opened possibilities for small-scale trade among workers and merchants who were otherwise marginalized from civilized commodity cultures. Likewise, Philippine sugar mills produced low-grade muscovado sugars until after World War I, returning to them later in the 1930s when they lost full access to the U.S. market. Though U.S. administrators and colonial officials had prompted the modernization of the Philippines' industry, when modern, centrifugal sugar began to enter the U.S. market in larger quantities in the late 1920s and early 1930s, policymakers hastened to limit those imports. Farmers returned to older forms of unrefined sugar, which still enjoyed local markets unswayed by U.S. preferences. Goods outside the limits of regularized commodities gave workers and merchants a way to challenge the limits of integration and exclusion.

Sugar and Civilization has argued that the U.S. sugar tariff was a site for an emerging imperial racial formation as policymakers, workers, and consumers negotiated how U.S. sovereignty would be exercised in the movement of commodities and people across borders. When the sugar tariff failed as a means to regulate competition between the territories and the mainland, policymakers set about to devise a new approach to empire that could reallocate the sugar market to mainland producers. The diverse meanings attributed to sugar consumption were critical to these processes of change. What is more, there was much consistency between the economic thought of an earlier generation of policymakers and those who came to power during the New Deal. Policymakers had long shared the faith that export markets were crucial for U.S. American economic well-being. Their faith in exports had always been coupled with confidence in the ability of U.S. American goods to promote civilized values abroad. New Deal policymakers no longer assumed that exports would civilize consumers, but they nonetheless shared the belief that people outside the nation would be better off for trading with the United States. The sugar quotas developed in the 1930s, which continued to operate for many decades, aimed to manage prices and allocate shares of the market among different groups of producers, at home and abroad. Tariffs had aimed to do precisely these same things—manage prices and allocate markets among domestic and foreign producers. As administrator John Dalton put it, the tariff had been "an unintelligent, loose, uncritical and deceptive use of a foreign economic policy."[9] Protective tariffs were a blunt instrument that could not be calibrated to unique sociopolitical aspects of a complex productive geography. When the United States took a leading role in multilateral trade institutions after World War II, the policies it had made during the New Deal provided an important template.[10]

There is no better summation of the changes between 1898 and 1942 than Jack Delano's images of Puerto Rican children eating sugarcane, which contrast dramatically with earlier images of the same subject. In one photograph, Delano captured a group of boys sitting on the flatbed of a truck. The image alludes to turn-of-the-century pictures of children eating cane while sitting on cane carts, but Delano made no effort to reproduce the familiar trope. Though barefoot, the boys wear clean clothes and are well groomed. Only one boy looks into the lens, and he seems disinterested. One boy holds sugarcane but does not actually chew it, instead using it to poke the ground. That it is cane is signaled only by Delano's caption. Delano does not romanticize the relationship between children and cane. Another series of images shows two shabbily dressed young girls, sitting on bare dirt in a location Delano describes as a slum. They show no pleasure as they chew the cane. Delano's images suggest that these children eat sugarcane not because it is "nature's stick of candy," as Ellsworth Huntington had fantasized years before, but because their families could not afford to buy proper food. Chewing cane was not a sign of nature's bounty, nor was it a sign of workers' inherent racial inferiority. It was a sign of political failure and a call for renewed social and economic reforms.

Sweetness was always contested, and through it people negotiated their transitions from rural to urban consumerism and their statuses within shifting racial and economic hierarchies. At the turn of the twentieth century, policymakers and the general public fixated on distinctions between civilized and uncivilized consumption because those differences were crucial to the project of U.S. empire. By the 1930s, these assumptions were replaced as policymakers developed a new form of liberal expansionism. Their liberalism represented the success of an earlier U.S. civilizing mission, which had proposed that residents of the new territories could be tutored to eat refined sugar and candy. But the success of this mission and the ascendance of racial liberalism did not mean the end of

Jack Delano, "Farm Laborer's Children Eating Sugar Cane in the Hills near Yauco, Puerto Rico," January 1942. Farm Security Administration—Office of War Information Photograph Collection, Library of Congress.

inequalities in the U.S. sugar empire. Social differences were reframed in the language of economics, including economic rights and individual choice. Twenty-first-century eaters mark their privilege by choosing *not* to consume refined white sugar, instead selecting more expensive, less-refined sweeteners. Today's organic eaters have the means to buy out of a food system built on cheap food. All too often, though, embedded in such consumers' healthy food choices are judgments about the people who choose less expensive or allegedly less healthy foods. The story recounted in this book thus has its parallel, if not its direct heir, in our contemporary panic over obesity. It is—once again—the bodies of poor people that bear the burden of representing this crisis.

NOTES

ABBREVIATIONS

AAA	Agricultural Adjustment Administration
ACLU Archives	*The American Civil Liberties Union Archives*, microfilm edition, Princeton University
BFDC	Bureau of Foreign and Domestic Commerce, U.S. Department of Commerce
Cong. Rec.	*Congressional Record*
Files of the CPUSA	*Files of the Communist Party of the USA in the Comintern Archives*, microfilm edition, IDC Publishers, 1999–2000
Coolidge Papers	*Papers of Calvin Coolidge*, microfilm edition, Manuscript Division, Library of Congress, Washington, D.C.
EPC Papers	Edward P. Costigan Papers, Western Historical Collections, Norlin Library, University of Colorado, Boulder, Colo.
FGN Papers	Francis G. Newlands Papers, Manuscripts and Archives, Sterling Memorial Library, Yale University, New Haven, Conn.
FRUS	*Foreign Relations of the United States*
HLS Papers	Henry Lewis Stimson Papers, Manuscripts and Archives, Sterling Memorial Library, Yale University, New Haven, Conn.
NARA-NY	National Archives and Records Administration, New York, N.Y.
NARA-OPA	National Archives and Records Administration, Online Public Access Catalog
NARA-II	National Archives and Records Administration II, College Park, Md.
NCLC Papers	National Child Labor Committee Papers, Manuscript Division of the Library of Congress, Washington, D.C.
NYT	*New York Times*
PST Papers	Paul Schuster Taylor Papers, Bancroft Library, University of California, Berkeley, Calif.
RG	Record Group
SRE	Dirección General del Acervo Histórico Diplomático, Secretaría de Relaciones Exteriores, Mexico City, Mexico

Stat.	U.S. Statutes at Large
TFM Collection	Thomas F. Mahoney Collection, University of Notre Dame Archives, Notre Dame, Ind.
USDA	U.S. Department of Agriculture
USFA	U.S. Food Administration
USTC	U.S. Tariff Commission
WC	*Western Confectioner*

INTRODUCTION

1. Reports varied as to whether it was the battleship *Maine* or the *Colorado*. "State Banner for Colorado," *Colorado Springs Gazette*, August 23, 1898, 2; "Grand Patriotic Fete at Wolhurst Has Become History," *Colorado Springs Gazette*, August 28, 1898, 1; "The Wolhurst Festival," *Harper's Weekly*, September 17, 1898, 919–20; "The City in Brief," *Waterloo (Iowa) Daily Courier*, December 19, 1907, 10; "Metcalf Welcomed Home," *Oakland (California) Tribune*, May 3, 1908, 22; Stanley, *A Century of Glass Toys*; Eikelberner, *More American Glass Candy Containers*.

2. Major works on American sugar politics include Hollander, *Raising Cane*; Ayala, *American Sugar Kingdom*; Mapes, *Sweet Tyranny*; Okihiro, *Cane Fires*; Heitmann, *Modernization of the Louisiana Sugar Industry*; Larkin, *Sugar*; and Woloson, *Refined Tastes*. "Political devils" is from Leland Hamilton Jenks, *Our Cuban Colony*, 5.

3. On the idea of the tropics, see Okihiro, *Pineapple Culture*; Duany, *Puerto Rican Nation on the Move*; and Sutter, "Tropical Conquest."

4. My interpretation of U.S. empire builds on the excellent work in American Studies over the last two decades, most notably Jacobson, *Barbarian Virtues*; Kramer, *Blood of Government*; Kaplan and Pease, *Cultures of United States Imperialism*; Hoganson, *Consumers' Imperium*; Lowe, *Immigrant Acts*; Klein, *Cold War Orientalism*; McAlister, *Epic Encounters*; Stoler, *Carnal Knowledge*; Gómez, *Manifest Destinies*; Love, *Race over Empire*; Bederman, *Manliness and Civilization*; Greene, *Canal Builders*; and Wexler, *Tender Violence*.

5. Sparrow, *Insular Cases*; Duffy-Burnett and Marshall, *Foreign in a Domestic Sense*; Einhorn, *American Taxation*; McCoy and Scarano, *Colonial Crucible*. On "imperial repertoire," see Burbank and Cooper, *Empires in World History*.

6. Tomich, *Through the Prism of Slavery*; Mintz, *Sweetness and Power*; Eric Williams, *Capitalism and Slavery*; Heath, *Wine, Sugar, and the Making of Modern France*.

7. Mintz, *Sweetness and Power*, 184.

8. Frank, *Buy American*; Gabaccia, *Foreign Relations*.

9. McGillivray, *Blazing Cane*.

10. Fradera, "Reading Imperial Transitions," 45.

11. Mathias and Pollard, *Industrial Economies*, 119.

12. Tomich, *Through the Prism of Slavery*, 83.

13. Follett, *Sugar Masters*.

14. J. P. Benjamin's Address on Agriculture, *DeBow's Review* 5, no. 1 (January 1848): 48.

15. J. D. B. De Bow, "Sugar—Its Cultivation, Manufacture, and Commerce, No. 1," *DeBow's Review* 4, no. 2 (October 1847): 230.

16. Follett, *Sugar Masters*; Heitmann, *Modernization of the Louisiana Sugar Industry*; Look Lai, *Indentured Labor, Caribbean Sugar*; Gabaccia, *Foreign Relations*; Jung, *Coolies and Cane*.

17. Gabaccia, *Foreign Relations*.

18. Einhorn, *American Taxation, American Slavery*, 117.

19. Colby, *Business of Empire*; Pérez, *On Becoming Cuban*; Ayala, *American Sugar Kingdom*.

20. Atkins, *Sixty Years*, 51–52; "West Indian Sugar," *DeBow's Review* 2, no. 4 (October 1846): 321.

21. McGillivray, *Blazing Cane*, 22.

22. Atkins, *Sixty Years*, 66–69.

23. Ibid., 79.

24. Taussig, *Tariff History*; MacLennan, *Sovereign Sugar*.

25. Atkins, *Sixty Years*, 133.

26. Ibid., 143, 152.

27. Ibid., 345. See also McGillivray, *Blazing Cane*, 36.

28. Atkins, *Sixty Years*, 257.

29. Ibid., 323. See also Colby, "Race, Empire, and New England Capital."

30. Takaki, *Pau Hana*; Jung, *Coolies and Cane*; Hollander, *Raising Cane*; Heitmann, *Modernization of the Louisiana Sugar Industry*; MacLennan, *Sovereign Sugar*.

31. On this history, see Ayala, *American Sugar Kingdom*; and Chandler, *The Visible Hand*, 328–29. On the Supreme Court ruling in *United States v. E. C. Knight* (1895), see Sklar, *Corporate Reconstruction*, 124–27.

32. Griffin, *Who Set You Flowin'?*; Hahamovitch, *Fruits of Their Labor*; Hunter, *To 'Joy My Freedom*; Gregory, *Southern Diaspora*; Ngai, *Impossible Subjects*; Lee, *At America's Gates*; Jung, *Coolies and Cane*; Okihiro, *Cane Fires*; Ngai, *The Lucky Ones*; Stern, *Eugenic Nation*; Gutiérrez, *Walls and Mirrors*; Sánchez, *Becoming Mexican American*; Pegler-Gordon, *In Sight of America*.

33. Mintz, *Sweetness and Power*; Woloson, *Refined Tastes*. On consumer cultures more broadly, see Cohen, *Making a New Deal*; Cohen, *A Consumers' Republic*; Hoganson, *Consumers' Imperium*; Jacobs, *Pocketbook Politics*; McCrossen et al., *Land of Necessity*; Leach, *Land of Desire*; and Seigel, *Uneven Encounters*.

34. My definition of empire draws on Kramer, "Power and Connection," 1349, 1377; Burbank and Cooper, *Empires in World History*, 8; Agamben, *States of Exception*; and Colby, *Business of Empire*.

35. Mintz, *Sweetness and Power*, 148, 166.

36. "Sugar Tariffs and the Dutch Standard," Senate Doc. no. 151, August 4, 1909.

37. Marx, *Capital*, vol. 1, pts. 1 and 2, "Commodities and Money," especially "The Fetishism of Commodities and the Secret Thereof" (1867). See also Polyani, *The Great Transformation*.

38. Key literature on commodities and culture includes Appadurai, *Social Life of Things*; Stallybrass, "Marx's Coat"; Cronon, *Nature's Metropolis*; Taussig, *Devil*;

Okihiro, *Pineapple Culture*; Sackman, *Orange Empire*; Soluri, *Banana Cultures*; Domosh, *American Commodities*; Walsh, *Building the Borderlands*; Gootenberg, *Andean Cocaine*; Striffler, *Chicken*; Alvarez, *Mangos, Chiles, and Truckers*; Ortiz, *Cuban Counterpoint*; McClintock, *Imperial Leather*; Fischer and Benson, *Broccoli and Desire*; Cook, *Commodification of Childhood*; Guthman, *Agrarian Dreams*; Harvey, "Spatial Fix"; Tinsman, *Buying into the Regime*; Heath, *Wine, Sugar, and the Making of Modern France*; Benedict Anderson, *Imagined Communities*; Agnew, *Worlds Apart*; and Powers, *Gain*.

CHAPTER 1

1. Oliver, *Roughing It with the Regulars*, 207.

2. Love, *Race over Empire*; Jacobson, *Barbarian Virtues*; Streeby, *American Sensations*; Gómez, *Manifest Destinies*; Horsman, *Race and Manifest Destiny*; Worster, *Rivers of Empire*.

3. On tariff politics, see Gabaccia, *Foreign Relations*; Frank, *Buy American*; Sanders, *Roots of Reform*; and Skocpol, *Protecting Soldiers and Mothers*.

4. See Omi and Winant, *Racial Formation in the United States*, 55–56.

5. Rowley, *Reclaiming the Arid West*; "Race Issue Plank for the Democrats," *NYT*, June 17, 1912. Newlands argued that African Americans should emigrate to Africa. See Newlands Speech, April 2, 1912, folder 709, box 69, group 371, series II, FGN Papers. For earlier attempts to insert a "white supremacy" plank into the Democratic platform, see "Platform Makers Ride over Bryan," *NYT*, July 7, 1904.

6. 33 *Cong. Rec.*, Appendix, 200, 3863.

7. On southern populists with whom Newlands aligned, see, for example, Kantrowitz, *Ben Tillman*; and Sanders, *Roots of Reform*.

8. On Newlands's motivations, see Worster, *Rivers of Empire*, 362.

9. Coman, *History of Contract Labor*, 46; 31 *Cong. Rec.*, 5830; *Extension of Immigration and Contract Labor Laws to the Hawaiian Islands*, U.S. Sen. Rep. no. 1654, 55th Cong., 3d Sess.; 31 *Cong. Rec.*, 6534; 31 *Cong. Rec.*, 6535; 33 *Cong. Rec.*, 1258–59.

10. 30 Stat. 750–51. For the debate over Hawaiian annexation, see Kauanui, *Hawaiian Blood*; Silva, *Aloha Betrayed*; Okihiro, *Pineapple Culture*; Love, *Race over Empire*; and MacLennon, *Sovereign Sugar*.

11. An Organic Act is a congressional measure to provide for the management of federal lands. Congress created an Organic Act for each of the territories, which served as a kind of constitution for each of them until they achieved statehood and were governed by the U.S. Constitution. In the case of territories not destined for statehood, the Organic Acts essentially created permanent civil governments.

12. 33 *Cong. Rec.*, Appendix, 200–201; 33 *Cong. Rec.*, 3863; 31 Stat. 150, 158–59.

13. Reprinted in Carroll, *Report on the Island of Porto Rico*, 778. For petitions from Puerto Ricans requesting free trade, see ibid., 144, 147, 390, 550, and 777–86. See also Go, *American Empire*, 59.

14. 33 *Cong. Rec.*, Appendix, 275. For the final Organic Act, see 31 Stat. 77. I have found no evidence of an attempt to implement Chinese exclusion in Puerto Rico. There were fewer than 100 Chinese people enumerated in the 1900 census, and none

had arrived as indentured laborers. Puerto Rico was included in the renewal of the overall exclusion policy in 1902; see 32 Stat. 176.

15. 33 *Cong. Rec.*, 4618–19; 33 *Cong. Rec.*, 4457; 33 *Cong. Rec.*, 4852. For the amendment to the Foraker Act, see 31 Stat. 715–16.

16. Ayala and Bernabe, *Puerto Rico in the American Century*, 36–37. Implications that sugar beet interests were behind colonial policy are quite common in the literature. See Perez, *Cuba between Empires*, 187; Mapes, *Sweet Tyranny*; and Lynch, "The U.S. Constitution and Philippine Colonialism," 354. Even Colorado Democratic senator Henry M. Teller, who sponsored the resolution prohibiting the annexation of Cuba in 1898, only began to defend the beet industry *after* 1900. Beet sugar was crucial to anti-imperialism, but not in the ways that scholars have assumed. It was about the principle more than about constituents' financial interests.

17. 35 *Cong. Rec.*, 1457–61, 3856. On reciprocity treaties and immigration, see Laughlin and Willis, *Reciprocity*, 79–80; and Coman, *History of Contract Labor*, 27. For Newlands's claims about Hawaiian labor conditions, see 35 *Cong. Rec.*, 4024; and Caspar Whitney, "Hawaiian-America; Part V—The Labor Question," *Harper's Weekly* 43, no. 2211 (1899): 464.

18. On nineteenth-century debates over Cuban annexation, see Love, *Race over Empire*; and Pérez, *On Becoming Cuban*. On the 1902 renewal of Chinese exclusion, see 32 Stat. 176. For Newlands's proposal to annex Cuba prior to the vote on Chinese exclusion, see 35 *Cong. Rec.*, 4417. On Chinese exclusion in Cuba, see "Admission of Chinese into Cuba," *FRUS*, 263–66; Salyer, *Laws Harsh as Tigers*, 102–3; and John B. Jackson to Secretary of State, June 9, 1911, *FRUS*, 110. For the final reciprocity treaty with Cuba, see 33 Stat. 4.

19. Taft, *Civil Government in the Philippines*, 103. For the images, see *The Philippine Islands Sugar Industry*.

20. Article I, Section 8, Clause 1, U.S. Constitution.

21. For Taft's views, see his *Civil Government in the Philippines*, 98. For debates over finance, see Go, *American Empire*; and Ayala and Bernabe, *Puerto Rico in the American Century*. Carroll, *Report on the Island of Porto Rico*, reports extensively on taxation and tariffs. See also "Levy and Collection of Taxes in Porto Rico," April 19, 1900, *Congressional Serial Set*, vol. 3868, 56th Cong., 1st Sess., 106. On the constitutionality of tax and tariff policy, see Sparrow, *Insular Cases*, 78; and Burnett and Marshall, *Foreign in a Domestic Sense*. On the political economy of Philippine industry, see Kramer, *Blood of Government*; Quirino, *History of the Philippine Sugar Industry*; and Lopez-Gonzaga, *Socio-politics of Sugar*. "Interstate commerce" is cited in the *Diamond Rings* ruling, 183 U.S. 176 (1901), 181. For the parallels between the Philippines and Indian policy, see Walter L. Williams, "United States Indian Policy." On the category of unincorporated territory, see Rivera Ramos, "Deconstructing Colonialism."

22. For Philippine tariff rates, see 32 Stat. 54. These rates were reconsidered in 1905–6 but not lowered until 1909. For a summary of Newlands's opposition to tariff concessions for the Philippines, see "A Democrat in the Philippines," *North American Review* 181, no. 589 (December 1905); and his testimony before the House Committee on Ways and Means on the Philippine Tariff in 1906. On Puerto Rico, see Report of Brigadier General George W. Davis on Civil Affairs in Porto Rico, U.S. House

Rep. no. 2, 56th Cong., 1st Sess. (1900); Carroll, *Report on the Island of Porto Rico*, 373–74; *Second Annual Report of the Governor of Porto Rico*, July 1, 1902, 9–10, 330–331; and Ayala, *American Sugar Kingdom*.

23. Advertisement for Pecos Irrigation and Improvement Co., Eddy, New Mexico, *Irrigation Age* 12, no. 1 (October 1897). The beet factory near to this land went bankrupt after two years. Newlands quoted in Taylor, "National Reclamation in Imperial Valley," 1; "The Progress of Western America," *Irrigation Age* 12, no. 1 (October 1897): 1; "The President and Irrigation," *Irrigation Age* 15, no. 8 (May 1901).

24. Worster, *Rivers of Empire*, 115–20, 131. On Newlands's association with Smythe, see Rowley, *Reclaiming the Arid West*, 121; and "The Progress of Western America," *Irrigation Age* 12, no. 1 (October 1897): 1. On the census, see Ethan Allen Hitchcock, "Federal Irrigation Talk," *Irrigation Age* 15, no. 6 (March 1901): 194, 192.

25. Worster, *Rivers of Empire*, 160–69; Rowley, *Reclaiming the Arid West*. Worster argues that Newlands and Roosevelt were "two minor, late-appearing, marginal voices on the water plateau." This interpretation does not take account of how well situated Newlands was to tie together issues of empire, economic development, and race. For Newlands's speech on reclamation, see 35 *Cong. Rec.*, 839, 841. For the longer history of land, race, and migration in California, see Almaguer, *Racial Fault Lines*; Street, *Beasts of the Field*; and Chan, *This Bittersweet Soil*.

26. For debates over public domain lands, see 35 *Cong. Rec.*, 841. For Philippine tariff reduction, see 32 Stat. 54; for corporate landholding, 32 Stat. 706, 709; for individual landholdings, 32 Stat. 709; for soil surveys, 32 Stat. 695; for water rights, 32 Stat. 697.

27. Shurts, *Indian Reserved Water Rights*, 5; *Proceedings of the Annual Meeting of the Lake Mohonk Conference of Friends of the Indian* (1904), 24; Campbell, "Newlands, Old Lands"; "Indian Labor Outside of Reservations," *Annual Report of the Commissioner of Indian Affairs* (Washington, D.C.: GPO, 1900), 15; *Thirty-ninth Annual Report of the Board of Indian Commissioners* (Washington, D.C.: GPO, 1907), 10; 47 *Cong. Rec.*, 3392 (1911); Alice M. Kingcade, "Demonstration Lessons: Sugar Beets," *Proceedings and Addresses of the Forty-sixth Annual Meeting* (1908), 1166–69.

28. Indian Appropriation Bill, March 9, 1910, 61–62, Report no. 357, *Congressional Serial Set*, Issue 5583, 19; Francis Leupp, Testimony, Senate Committee on Indian Affairs, April 1, 1908, 351, 593.

29. F. H. Newell, *Hawaii: Its Natural Resources and Opportunities for Home-Making* (Washington, D.C.: GPO, 1909), 45, 36–37, 24.

30. *Annual Report of the Governor of Porto Rico for the Fiscal Year Ending June 30 1907* (Washington, D.C.: GPO, 1907), 333.

31. *Report of the Commission of the Interior of Porto Rico, 1917* (Washington, D.C.: GPO, 1917), 510; "Division of Public Lands and Archives," *Annual Reports of the War Department for the Fiscal Year Ending June 30, 1919* (Washington, D.C.: GPO, 1919), 472.

32. "An Act to Provide for the Construction of an Irrigation System" and "An Act to Authorize the Issuance . . . of Bonds," September 18, 1908, *Fourth Legislative Assembly of Porto Rico*, 13–24.

33. W. L. Squire et al., "Irrigation in Porto Rico," *Water Power Chronicle* 2, no. 2 (January 1913); F. K. Knapp, "Notes in Connection with the Work in the Hydrographic Department of the Porto Rico Irrigation Service," *Cornell Civil Engineer* 23 (1915).

34. *Report of the Secretary of the Interior for the Fiscal Year Ending June 30, 1908* (Washington, D.C.: GPO, 1908), 49.

35. Gómez, *Manifest Destinies*, 125-27, 130; Deutsch, *No Separate Refuge*; Almaguer, *Racial Fault Lines*. See also Montejano, *Anglos and Mexicans*.

36. Ayala, *American Sugar Kingdom*, 67; Mapes, *Sweet Tyranny*.

37. Newlands to Erving Winslow, July 22, 1909, folder 177, box 18, series I, FGN Papers. On opposition to Philippines allotment, see 44 *Cong. Rec.*, 2184. Foster and Newlands traveled to the Philippines together in 1905 as part of Taft's delegation to the Philippines. See "Plans for Taft Party," *Washington Post*, March 26, 1905. Foster also opposed the reciprocity treaty with Cuba in 1903. See "Sectional Issue in Cuban Debate," *NYT*, December 13, 1903; and 44 *Cong. Rec.*, 2373.

38. 36 Stat. 11 exempted the Philippines from the act and positioned the Philippines as outside of the United States. The language used in this act had a long life afterward. 36 Stat. 83-84 (1909) provided for free trade between the Philippines and the United States, with limits. Export duties were authorized in 36 Stat. 130.

39. U.S. Congress, House Special Committee on Investigation of American Sugar Refining Co., 62nd Cong., 2nd Sess., February 17, 1912, Report 331, 18.

40. John Temple Graves, *Grasshopper Immigrants*, 1909, folder 776, box 76, series II, FGN Papers.

41. Balch et al., "Restriction of Immigration—Discussion," *American Economic Review* 2, no. 1 (March 1912): 71.

42. Taft, Special Message to Congress, June 16, 1909; Special Message to Congress, January 7, 1910, *Presidential Addresses and State Papers of William Howard Taft*, vol. 1 (New York: Doubleday, Page, and Company, 1910).

43. McCurdy, "The Knight Sugar Decision of 1895"; *United States v. E. C. Knight* (1895); "Senator Hoar's Trust Bill," *Baltimore American*, January 4, 1903, 6.

44. Hearings before the Special Committee on the Investigation of the American Sugar Refining Co. (1911), 2154; Hardwick Committee Report, 28.

45. Interestingly, the law asserted that businesses could choose their customers, thus discriminating among people to whom they would even offer *any* price. In other words, the law was designed specifically to not interfere with state segregation laws, thus enabling businesses to refuse to serve African American customers.

46. See Almaguer, *Racial Fault Lines*, on a 1903 strike organized jointly by Mexicans and Japanese. See also Coman, *History of Contract Labor*, 47; Matsumoto, *Farming the Homeplace*; and Barajas, "Resistance." Some Japanese did become sugar beet farmers in California and Colorado. On alien land laws generally, see Okihiro, *Pineapple Culture*, 68-69.

47. McKee, "The Chinese Boycott of 1905-1906 Reconsidered"; Gabaccia, *Foreign Relations*, 115.

48. Thomas, *Facts in a Nutshell about Immigration* (1912), 41, folder 776, box 76, series II, FGN Papers.

49. Okihiro, *Cane Fires*, 30-31.

50. Daniels, *The Politics of Prejudice*; A. M. Drew, "As to the Japanese Land Holders," *San Jose (California) Mercury News*, September 12, 1909, 2. On the Nevada law, see "To Exclude Japs," *Portland Oregonian*, February 8, 1909; and Nevada

Assembly Joint and Concurrent Resolution no. 4, February 27, 1909. For "the United States" quote, see Francis G. Newlands to Denver S. Dickerson, February 3, 1909, folder 704, box 69, series II, group 371, FGN Papers. See also correspondence between Newlands and his constituents on this topic, in folders 158–59, box 16, series I, FGN Papers. See also "the white race," Newlands, Speech on Senate Resolution no. 279, February 18, 1909, folder 704, box 69, series II, FGN Papers; and Newlands, "A Western View of the Race Question," *Annals of the American Academy of Political and Social Science.*

51. Department of Commerce, *Annual Report of the Chief of Bureau of Foreign and Domestic Commerce to the Secretary of Commerce for the Fiscal Year Ended June 30, 1916* (Washington, D.C.: GPO, 1916), 20.

52. A typical articulation of this theory is Frank C. Lowry, *Sugar at a Second Glance, 1913,* reprinted in 63d Cong., 1st Sess., Senate Doc. 23 (Washington, D.C.: GPO, 1923).

53. Aryan, *Aryans and Mongrelized America*, 29–32.

54. Helen Stewart Campbell to Francis G. Newlands, April 12, 1913, folder 358, box 35, series I, FGN Papers.

55. R. C. Bialy, Treasurer, Nevada Sugar Company, to Francis G. Newlands, April 30, 1913, folder 366, box 36, series I, FGN Papers; J. H. Kent to Francis G. Newlands, May 21, 1913, and May 26, 1913, folder 376, box 37, series I, FGN Papers; Rowley, *Reclaiming the Arid West*, 146. "The hope" quote is from Francis G. Newlands to President Woodrow Wilson, June 4, 1913, 7, folder 383, box 38, series I, FGN Papers. On Indian labor, see Campbell, "Newlands, Old Lands." There were some early attempts to hire Mexican and Japanese workers for beet production in 1913, a point upon which Newlands received criticism. See H. R. Cooke to Francis G. Newlands, May 24, 1913, folder 378, box 37, series I, FGN Papers.

56. 38 Stat. 114, 192 (1913).

57. 53 *Cong. Rec.*, 5778; Republican Party Platform (1896); Bernhardt, *The Tariff Commission*, 2, 9–10; Schnietz, "Democrats' 1916 Tariff Commission," 38.

58. Senator Furnifold Simmons (D-North Carolina), 53 *Cong. Rec.*, 5777; "To repeal the free-sugar provisions," February 28, 1916, *Congressional Serial Set*, vol. no. 6903, Sess. vol.1; "Tariff on Sugar," March 28, 1916, *Congressional Serial Set*, vol. no. 6898, Sess. vol.2; Brownlee, "Wilson and Financing the Modern State," 177. Brownlee shows that by mid-1915 there was consensus that the sugar duty should remain.

59. Dalton, *Sugar: A Case Study*, 290.

CHAPTER 2

1. Huntington and Cushing, *Rivalry*, 3–4.

2. "A Native Sugar Mill," no. 51375, Detroit Photographic Co. or Detroit Publishing Co., ca. 1901, Yale Collection of Western Americana, Beinecke Rare Book and Manuscript Library, Yale University. Thompson, in *An Eye for the Tropics*, 328 n19, attributes this image to William Henry Jackson and suggests 1903 as the date. See also "Sugar Cane," Image no. 43048, Ulrich B. Phillips Papers, Manuscripts and Archives, Sterling Library, Yale University; and Fuller and Petersham, *The Story Book*.

3. These images are part of a larger archive of racist memorabilia showing people engaged in stereotypical, happy, leisure activities, thereby naturalizing their labor and rendering their exploitation invisible. For an analysis of other visual tropes that circulated as postcard images of the Caribbean, see Thompson, *An Eye for the Tropics*, 276–77. On the tendency of nationalist narratives to naturalize commodity consumption, see McClintock, *Imperial Leather*, 358. On the cultural politics of the pickaninny and material culture, see Bernstein, *Racial Innocence*. On race and food in nineteenth-century literary and visual culture, see Tompkins, *Racial Indigestion*.

4. Bégin, "Partaking of Choice Poultry Cooked a la Southern Style"; Fitzgerald and Petrick, "In Good Taste"; Ferguson, "The Senses of Taste"; Norton, "Tasting Empire"; Mark M. Smith, *How Race Is Made*.

5. Brander Matthews, "Under an April Sky," *Harper's New Monthly Magazine* 98, no. 587 (April 1899): 770.

6. Grier, *Culture and Comfort*, 102.

7. Levenstein, *Revolution at the Table*, 60–61, 64; Woloson, *Refined Tastes*.

8. Kasson, *Rudeness and Civility*, 188–89; Grier, *Culture and Comfort*, 152, 157, 159. More generally, see Rosalind H. Williams, *Dream Worlds*, 24.

9. Oral History Interview with James and Nannie Pharis, December 5, 1978; January 8 and 30, 1979. Interview H-0039. Southern Oral History Program Collection (#4007) in the Southern Historical Collection, Wilson Library, University of North Carolina at Chapel Hill.

10. Hall et al., *Like a Family*, 157; Sharpless, *Cooking in Other Women's Kitchens*, 14, 175.

11. On this concept, see Roediger, *Wages of Whiteness*.

12. Levenstein, in *Revolution at the Table*, discusses the "servant problem" at length.

13. Kasson, *Rudeness and Civility*, 6–7, 211.

14. Springsteed, *The Expert Waitress*, 29; "Setting the Table for Breakfast," *Good Housekeeping* 35, no. 6 (December 1902); Harcourt, *Good Form for Women*, 147; Murphy, *The History of the Art of Tablesetting*, 40–43, 60–61; Sangster, *Good Manners for All Occasions*, 162; Parloa, *Home Economics*, 160; Hill, *The Up-to-Date Waitress*, 39, 67.

15. "Civilizing Negroes in Africa," *American Citizen*, June 13, 1902, 4. On African American engagement with German East Africa, see Zimmerman, *Alabama in Africa*.

16. Hopkins, *Contending Forces*, 103.

17. Ibid., 380. On Hopkins's imperial politics, see O'Brien, "Blacks in All Quarters of the Globe"; and Murphy, *Shadowing the White Man's Burden*.

18. For example, see Edwards, *The '98 Campaign*.

19. Albert Ernest Jenks, *Bontoc Igorot*, 148.

20. Wood, *Foods of the Foreign-Born*; Levenstein, *Revolution at the Table*; Veit, *Modern Food*.

21. John N. Tilden, "The Study of Commercial Geography in Common Schools," *Bulletin of the American Bureau of Geography* 2, no. 1 (March 1901): 8.

22. Harrington, *A First Book*, 111, 116.

23. Woloson, *Refined Tastes*, 54–62.

24. Emerson, *New Frontier*, 152.

25. Myers, *Language of America*, 80.

26. Hall, *Aspects of Child Life*, 58; Bederman, *Manliness and Civilization*, 48.

27. Woodruff, *Expansion of Races*, 296–97.

28. For example, in 1901 alone there were seven such requests reprinted in the *Annual Reports of the War Department*.

29. D. L. Brainerd to Adjutant-General, Manila, August 12, 1899; reprinted in *Annual Reports of the War Department* (1899), 231.

30. F. M. Munson, "The Ration in the Tropics," *Military Surgeon* 27 (1910): 45.

31. Woodruff, *Expansion of Races*, 296–97.

32. Woodhull, *Military Hygiene*, 139; Louis L. Seaman, "The Soldier's Ration in the Tropics—Its Use and Its Abuse," *Medical Record* (October 20, 1900).

33. Woodhull, *Military Hygiene*, 139.

34. Allan Stuart, "Tropical Hygiene in Reference to Clothing, Houses, Routine, and Diet," *Military Surgeon* 20, no. 2 (February 1907): 90.

35. Seaman, "The Soldier's Ration in the Tropics," 612.

36. Warwick Anderson, "The Trespass Speaks." Seaman elaborates on the digestibility of sugar in "The Soldier's Ration in the Tropics," 615. See also Woodruff, *Expansion of Races*, 294–95.

37. Aryan, *Aryans and Mongrelized America*, 29–32.

38. Fee, *A Woman's Impressions*, 258, 246.

39. Conger, *An Ohio Woman in the Philippines*, 99.

40. Green, *Fact Stranger Than Fiction*, 114.

41. "Reapportionment Vote in the House Today," *NYT*, January 8, 1901, 5.

42. "Democrats Unite on Reciprocity Policy," *NYT*, April 18, 1902, 1; "The Cuban Debate's Climax," *Outlook* 20, no. 17 (April 26, 1902): 985–86.

43. Green paraphrased in "Negro and the South," *Colored American* 10, no. 3 (April 26, 1902): 4. See also "Sold Again," *Wisconsin Weekly Advocate*, May 8, 1902, 1; "Colored Men Object," *Plaindealer*, June 20, 1902, 1; "B. Square's Blusters," *Freeman*, May 31, 1902, 7; and "Deeds of Omission," *Freeman*, August 9, 1902, 1.

44. Bruce Grit, "Gotham Notes," *Colored American*, July 26, 1902, 3.

45. "Sugar Is King," *Washington Bee*, May 3, 1902, 4.

46. "Pointers for the Cook," *Washington Bee*, August 9, 1902, 1.

47. On the trope of cannibalism and black bodies, see Brown, "Eating the Dead"; and Tompkins, *Racial Indigestion*.

48. Dunbar, *Lyrics of the Hearthside*, 139.

49. Daniel Webster Davis, *'Weh Down Souf*, 126.

50. Elam, "Dunbar's Children."

51. James Weldon Johnson, *Book of American Negro Poetry*, xli.

52. James, "Becoming the People's Poet." See also James Weldon Johnson, *Book of American Negro Poetry*, xliii.

53. Parks, *Sui Sin Far/Edith Maude Eaton*.

54. In addition to the songs discussed here, titles include "My Little Chocolate Cream" (1902); "By the Watermelon Vine: Lindy Lou" (1904); "Down among the Sugar-Cane" (1908); "Under the Swanee Moon" (1913); "Wrap Me in a Bundle, Dear, and Take Me Home with You" (1914); "Mammy's Chocolate Soldier" (1919); "Sweeter Than Sugar Is My Sweetie" (1919); "My Sugar-Coated Chocolate Boy" (1919); "Sugar" (1919); and "Mammy's Little Sugar Plum" (1920).

55. Hughes, *Not without Laughter*, 66, refers to Bon Bon Buddy.

56. "Molasses Candy Song" (1910), Eddie Leonard (lyrics) and J. J. Hill (music).

57. "Pickaninny Dreams" (1919), Sam Coslow (words) and Peter de Rose (music).

58. "Mammy's Lit'l Choc'late Cullud Chile" (1919), Noble Sissle (words), Eubie Blake (music).

CHAPTER 3

1. "Imaginative support" is from Hoover, Testimony before the Senate Committee on Agriculture and Forestry, May 7, 1917, *Production and Conservation of Food Supplies*, 65th Cong., 1st Sess. (Washington, D.C.: GPO, 1917), 385. "Essential food" is from Bernhardt, "Government Control," 4. "Fuel-food" is from USFA, *Sugar Questions* (Washington, D.C.: GPO, 1918). "Our soldiers" is from USFA Advertising Section, "In Who's Cup?," NARA-OPA; and Veit, *Modern Food*.

2. "The Necessity for Sugar Conservation," USFA Statistical Division Confidential Bulletin no. 1402, August 29, 1918, and "Sugar Distribution for the Years 1912–1917 by Months," USFA Statistical Division Confidential Bulletin no. 1447, September 23, 1918, Records of H. H. Bundy (1918–19), box 6, RG 6, NARA-II.

3. "Brooklyn Women, in Riots for Food, Wreck Pushcarts," *New York Tribune*, February 20, 1917, 1.

4. Hoover testimony, May 7, 1917, 381; Frank, "Housewives, Socialists, and the Politics of Food."

5. Kennedy, *Over Here*, 116–20; Dalton, *Sugar: A Case Study*, 34–39.

6. See Public Law 65-41, 40 Stat. 276 (1917–19); and Executive Order 2679-A (August 10, 1917). See also Mullendore, *History*; and Bernhardt, "Government Control."

7. Hoover, Introduction to Mullendore, *History*, 15.

8. The New York Sugar and Coffee Exchange began trading sugar futures in 1914 when the war forced the closure of the London and Hamburg exchanges. Roy G. Blakey, "Sugar Prices and Distribution under Food Control," *Quarterly Journal of Economics* 32, no. 4 (August 1918): 575.

9. USFA, *Annual Report, 1918*, 134–43.

10. USTC, *Costs of Production in the Sugar Industry*, 39.

11. Edgar Rickard and George Whitmarsh to George Zabriskie, January 19, 1920, Records of H. H. Bundy, entry 6, box 4, RG 6, NARA-II.

12. USTC, *Costs of Production in the Sugar Industry*, 38.

13. Kemper Simpson, "Price Fixing and the Theory of Profit," *Quarterly Journal of Economics* 34, no. 1 (November 1919): 139.

14. Hoover to Wilson, June 15, 1918, Sugar Equalization Board Minutes, 1918–19, entry 1, box 1, RG 6, NARA-II.

15. "Sugar Dealers Blame Labor for High Prices," *Christian Science Monitor*, February 19, 1917; "Philadelphia Refinery Strike," *Christian Science Monitor*, February 20, 1917; "1 Killed, 9 Hurt," *Chicago Daily Tribune*, February 22, 1917; "Women in Strike Riot," *NYT*, February 22, 1917; "Food Riots," *San Francisco Chronicle*, February 23, 1917, 1.

16. "Yiddish Papers Pledge Loyalty of Jews," *New York Tribune*, February 5, 1917, 4; "Jewish Women Pledge Services," *New York Tribune*, February 15, 1917; "Ostracize

Shirkers," *New York Tribune*, April 1, 1917, 8; "Yiddish Press Gives Pledges of Loyalty," *New York Tribune*, April 4, 1917, 4; "Jewish Food Commission," *(New York) Jewish Daily News*, July 25, 1917, 8; "Yom Kippur Is Celebrated by Jews with Prayers for Army and Navy," *New York Tribune*, September 17, 1918, 12; "Succoth and Food Conservation," *Reform Advocate*, November 10, 1917, 331; "Children Vote against Candy as Chanukah Gift," *(New York) Jewish Daily News*, December 17, 1917, 8; "East Side Digs Up Quarters in Rousing Thrift Stamp Drive," *New York Tribune*, May 14, 1918, 7; "The Hebrew National Orphan House," *(New York) Jewish Daily News*, December 12, 1918, 8. See also Veit, *Modern Food*.

17. Miss A. B. Macintosh to Arthur Williams, November 5, 1917, and Anonymous to Williams, November 21, 1917, entry 171-7, box 6, RG 4, NARA-NY.

18. Max Markowitz Case Affidavits, February and March 1918, entry 171-7, box 1, RG 4, NARA-NY.

19. Max Markowitz, Affidavit, February 26, 1918, New York, entry 171-7, box 1, RG 4, NARA-NY.

20. Chaim Schraub, Affidavit, February 5, 1918, entry 171-7, box 1, RG 4, NARA-NY; Samuel Ort Affidavit, ibid.

21. David Alperin to whom it may concern, February 16, 1918, Annie Markowitz to Hon. Mr. Schwartz, March 4, 1918, Max Markowitz to Federal Food Board, April 22, 1918, and Federal Food Board of New York to Max Markowitz, April 27, 1918, entry 171-7, box 1, RG 4, NARA-NY.

22. Samuel Epstein Affidavit, February 14, 1918, Max Solomon Affidavit, February 16, 1918, and Harris Farden Affidavit, February 19, 1918, entry 171-7, box 1, RG 4, NARA-NY.

23. Grant Jarvis, Report on Louis Steer, n.d., entry 171-7, box 1, RG 4, NARA-NY. See also Sam B. Zimmermann Affidavit, February 8, 1918, ibid.

24. Complaint against Hyman Sklamberg, December 7, 1917, entry 171-7, box 6, RG 4, NARA-NY.

25. Hyman Sklamberg, Affidavit, April 1, 1918, entry 171-7, box 6, RG 4, NARA-NY.

26. H. Sklamberg to USFA, November 28, 1917, entry 171-7, box 6, RG 4, NARA-NY.

27. Aaron Ashkanazy, Affidavit, April 1, 1918, entry 171-7, box 6, RG 4, NARA-NY.

28. Rabbi G. W. Magolies, Affidavit, April 1, 1918, entry 171-7, box 6, RG 4, NARA-NY.

29. Affidavits from David Marcus and Samuel Wolf, February 5, 1918, entry 171-7, box 1, RG 4, NARA-NY.

30. Charges in re: Max Markowitz, February 28, 1918, and Mitchell Williams to Herbert Hoover, February 28, 1918, entry 171-7, box 1, RG 4, NARA-NY; Memorandum for Mr. R. W. Boyden, re: Hyman Sklamberg, n.d., Cyrus C. Miller, Judgment, April 30, 1918, and Williams to R. W. Boyden, May 30, 1918, entry 171-7, box 6, RG 4, NARA-NY; *Report of New York State Food Administration*, New York Legislative Documents, vol. 15 (1919), 71.

31. Case of Joseph S. Schindel, November 6, 1918, entry 171-7, box 8, RG 4, NARA-NY.

32. Case of Meyer W. Taxan, November 6, 1918, entry 171-7, box 8, RG 4, NARA-NY.

33. Hoover to Pres. Wilson, June 15, 1918, Minute Book, 1918–19, entry 1, box 1, RG 6, NARA-II.

34. Rolph to Hoover, June 25, 1918, entry 9, box 28, RG 6, NARA-II.

35. On the smugglers, see Secretary of State to the Mexican Ambassador, May 1, 1918, *FRUS* (1930), 562. More generally, see Benjamin Johnson, *Revolution in Texas*; and St. John, *Line in the Sand*. On import/export restrictions, see "No Se Podrán Exportar," *La Prensa*, December 30, 1917, 4; "La Exportación De Víveres a México," *La Prensa*, July 14, 1917, 9; "Lo que puede llevarse a Mexico," *La Prensa*, January 27, 1918, 1; and USFA Press Release, April 14, 1918, entry 171-7, box 6, RG 4, NARA-NY.

36. T. Frothingham to George Rolph, January 14, 1918, box 51, RG 6, NARA-II.

37. J. M. Marroquin to G. F. Taylor, May 16, 1918, entry 33, box 53, RG 6, NARA-II. Manuel Z. Torreño, a San Antonio, Texas, soda bottler, briefly repurposed his factory to mold ersatz piloncillo. See advertisement in *El Cosmopolita*, November 8, 1919, 2; and advertisement in "Tres Carros de Piloncillo Mexicano Blanco," *La Prensa*, April 16, 1920, 3.

38. USFA to War Trade Board, January 25, 1918, and War Trade Board to USFA, January 14, 1918, entry 33, box 51, RG 6, NARA-II.

39. J. M. Marroquin to Chas. Bondies, Brokers, New York City, July 13, 1918, and USFA to W. R. Grace & Co., February 27, 1918, entry 33, box 52, RG 6, NARA-II.

40. Rolph, "Revised Temporary Rulings," February 27, 1918, entry 33, box 52, RG 6, NARA-II; USFA to War Trade Board, March 6, 1918, entry 33, box 53, RG 6, NARA-II; USFA Press Release, April 14, 1918, entry 171-7, box 6, RG 4, NARA-NY.

41. USFA to Sugar Division, May 6, 1918, entry 33, box 52, RG 6, NARA-II.

42. War Trade Board to George Rolph, August 20, 1918, entry 33, box 52, RG 6, NARA-II. See also Fred Taylor, Harvey L. Laughlin Company, to USFA, May 8, 1918, International Sugar Committee to USFA, May 3, 1918, and USFA to Sugar Division, May 6, 1918, entry 33, box 52, RG 6, NARA-II; and "Licenses—Export," entry 33, box 51, RG 6, NARA-II.

43. George Rolph to Herbert Hoover, June 25, 1918, entry 9, box 28, RG 6, NARA-II.

44. "Nuevamente Escasa el Azúcar en Laredo," *Evolucion*, June 22, 1918, 3; "Elevan Una Protesta Los Comerciantes Abarroteros," *La Prensa*, August 6, 1919, 8.

45. J. M. Marroquin to G. F. Taylor, May 16, 1918, entry 33, box 53, RG 6, NARA-II.

46. James Walker, Walker Manufacturing, Los Angeles, to USFA, May 15, 1918, entry 33, box 53, RG 6, NARA-II.

47. Emphasis in original. J. M. Marroquin (signed by S. B. Reachy, Jr., Secretary) to U.S. Food Administrator, July 18, 1918, and J. M. Marroquin to USFA, June 26, 1918, entry 33, box 52, RG 6, NARA-II. A customs broker whom Marroquin worked with occasionally made the same point in his appeal to the USFA: Chas. Bondies & Co. to the International Sugar Committee, July 18, 1918, and International Sugar Committee to Chas. Bondies & Co., July 20, 1918, entry 33, box 52, RG 6, NARA-II.

48. See, for example, Lamborn & Co., New York, to International Sugar Committee, July 20, 1918, entry 33, box 52, RG 6, NARA-II.

49. Thomas Witherspoon to George Rolph, May 15, 1918, and Head of Sugar Division to Hon. John M. Parker, Federal Food Administrator, New Orleans, May 30, 1918, entry 33, box 53, RG 6, NARA-II.

50. Thos. Witherspoon to George Rolph, May 31, 1918, and Federal Food Administrator for Texas to USFA, June 2, 1918, entry 33, box 53, RG 6, NARA-II.

51. USFA to Kwong Yuen Shing & Co., New York, February 14, 1918, box 48, RG 6, NARA-II.

52. Wm. A. Brown & Co. to USFA, February 15, 1918, box 48, RG 6, NARA-II.

53. USFA-NY to USFA, February 18, 1918, USFA to William A. Brown and Co., February 18, 1918, and USFA-NY to USFA, May 8, 1918, box 48, RG 6, NARA-II. Sugar Division to Ralph S. Merritt, August 2, 1918, and International Sugar Committee to Henry B. Endicott, August 14, 1918, box 48, RG 6, NARA-II.

54. USFA to Parrott & Company, September 20, 1918, box 48, RG 6, NARA-II.

55. Compiled from International Sugar Committee General Records, 1917–19, box 48, RG 6, NARA-II. On the preferences for sugar among Chinese consumers in China, see G. Roger Knight, *Commodities and Colonialism*, 34–35.

56. USFA to Sugar Division, Boston, October 28, 1918, Sugar Division to Ralph S. Merritt, USFA for California, September 9, 1918, and Merritt to USFA, October 18, 1918, box 48, RG 6, NARA-II.

57. 28 Stat. 7 (1893). On the Chinese middle class, see Ngai, *The Lucky Ones*. On labor brokers and merchants, see Chang, *Pacific Connections*.

58. For a discussion of Italian ethnic businessmen gaining an advantage in the wine industry during Prohibition, see Cinotto, *Soft Soil, Black Grapes*.

59. "Sugar Crops of the World," *Weekly Statistical Sugar Trade Journal*, January 6, 1916; cited in Roy G. Blakey, "Sugar Prices and Distribution under Food Control," *Quarterly Journal of Economics* 32, no. 4 (August 1918): 569. See also "Sugar Crops of the World," *Weekly Statistical Sugar Trade Journal*, January 6, 1921, 5.

60. Ministry of Food, Report for Week Ending Wednesday, April 25, 1917, CAB 24/11/82, 322, NA-UK.

61. Bernhardt, "Government Control," 8. See also "News Letter from Our Havana Office," *Louisiana Planter and Sugar Manufacturer* 57, no. 25 (December 23, 1916): 407–8.

62. Jacobs, *Pocketbook Politics*; Sklar, *Corporate Reconstruction*; Chandler, *The Visible Hand*.

63. Hardwick Committee Report, 32.

64. Letter to President Wilson, August 23, 1917, quoted in T. W. Gregory, Attorney General, to USFA, January 9, 1919, Correspondence (1918–20), entry 2, box 1, RG 6, NARA-II.

65. Hoover, Testimony before the Senate Committee on Agriculture and Forestry, May 7, 1917, *Production and Conservation of Food Supplies*, 65-1 (1917), 377.

66. Blakey, "Sugar Prices and Distribution," 575; Federal Trade Commission, *Report on the Beet Sugar Industry* (Washington, D.C.: GPO, 1917); Bernhardt, "Government Control," 26–27.

67. Confidential Report to Mr. Hoover, The Cost of Sugar Production in Cuba, Part I, August 16, 1918, Records of H. H. Bundy (1918–1919), Box 6, RG 6, NARA-II.

68. "The Food Situation," Memorandum by the Food Controller, December 1917, CAB 24/4/31, NA-UK.

69. Hoover to Wilson, June 15, 1918, Wilson to Hoover, June 16, 1918, and Hoover to Wilson, August 29, 1918, Minute Book, 1918–19, entry 1, box 1, RG 6, NARA-II; George Rolph to Herbert Hoover, May 20, 1918, George Rolph to Herbert Hoover, May 23,

1918, and Rolph to Davis Lewis, USTC, April 18, 1918, entry 9, box 28, RG 6, NARA-II; Bernhardt, "Government Control"; USTC, *Costs of Production in the Sugar Industry*; Simpson, "Price Fixing and the Theory of Profit," 141.

70. C. Herman Pritchett, "The Paradox of the Government Corporation," *Public Administration Review* 1, no. 4 (Summer 1941): 382; Van Dorn, *Government Owned Corporations*.

71. The Clayton Antitrust Act of 1914 prohibited such discrimination.

72. Adams, *Railways as Public Agents*, 137.

73. Bernhardt, "Government Control," 672–713. See also Sugar Equalization Board Minutes, Minutes Book, 1918–19, entry 1, box 1, RG 6, NARA-II.

74. Sugar Equalization Board Minutes, August 19, 1918, Minute Book, 1918–19, entry 1, box 1, RG 6, NARA-II; Bernhardt, "Government Control," 51.

75. George Zabriskie testimony, Sugar Shortage: Hearing before the Subcommittee on Senate Resolution 197 (1919), 6; see also Sugar Equalization Board Minutes, August 19, 1918, Minute Book, 1918–19, entry 1, box 1, RG 6, NARA-II.

76. See, for example, "Preliminary Tentative Draft for Submission to Subcommittee of the American Refiners' Committee," Correspondence, 1918–19, entry 2, box 1, RG 6, NARA-II.

77. T. W. Gregory, Attorney General, to USFA, January 9, 1919, entry 2, box 1, RG 6, NARA-II.

78. George Zabriskie to President Calvin Coolidge, November 10, 1923, entry 6, box 4, RG 6, NARA-II.

79. W. F. Willoughby, "The National Government as a Holding Corporation: The Question of Subsidiary Budgets," *Political Science Quarterly* 32, no. 4 (1917): 507, 519.

80. Pérez, *Intervention*, 100–101. See also *Annual Reports of the Navy Department for the Fiscal Year 1917*, 26–27, *Fiscal Year 1918*, 112, and *Fiscal Year 1921*, 128.

81. Sugar Equalization Board Minutes, August 19, 1918, Minute Book, 1918–19, entry 1, box 1, RG 6, NARA-II; Confidential Report to Mr. Hoover, "The Cost of Sugar Production in Cuba," pt. 1, August 16, 1918, box 6, RG 6, NARA-II.

82. Charles Winans, American Consul, Cuba, to Secretary of State, December 15, 1917, entry 9, box 28, RG 6, NARA-II; Henry Morgan, U.S. Consul General at Havana, Cuba, to Herbert Hoover, January 5, 1918, entry 9, box 28, RG 6, NARA-II; Correspondence in "Cuban Planters—Flour Supply," entry 9, box 49, RG 6, NARA-II.

83. International Sugar Committee Minutes, January 8, 1918, entry 9, box 36, RG 6, NARA-II. More broadly, see Rosenberg, *Financial Missionaries to the World*, 87–89; and Benjamin, *The United States & Cuba*.

84. *Annual Report of the Director*, Bureau of Standards, Fiscal Year Ending June 30, 1919 (Washington, D.C.: GPO, 1919), 126; Warner, *Sweet Stuff*.

85. USTC, *Summary of Tariff Information*, 1921 (Washington, D.C.: GPO, 1922), 593. G. Roger Knight discusses the Java equivalent, "factory whites," marketed throughout Asia, in his *Commodities and Colonialism*.

86. Rolph to William Glasgow, Chief Counsel, USFA, May 20, 1918, entry 9, box 30, RG 6, NARA-II; Federal Sugar Refining Company to Rolph, February 1, 1918, entry 9, box 30, RG 6, NARA-II; Rolph to Federal Sugar Refining Company, February 5, 1918, and April 26, 1918, entry 9, box 30, RG 6, NARA-II; Spreckles to Rolph, October 17,

1917, Spreckles to Hoover, October 31, 1917, Spreckles to Hoover, November 2, 1917, and Rolph to Federal Sugar Refining Company, May 9, 1918, entry 9, box 30, RG 6, NARA-II.

87. C. Lyman Spencer, *The Sugar Situation* (Drew Press, 1918). Emphasis in original.

88. Rolph, "Revised Temporary Rulings," February 27, 1918, entry 33, box 52, RG 6, NARA-II.

89. Albert E. Lee to Rolph, January 25, 1918, Lee to Rolph, February 6, 1918, Rolph to Lee, February 14, 1918, and "Resolution Fixing the Maximum Price for the Sale of Sugar at Retail in Porto Rico," April 20, 1917, entry 9, box 50, RG 6, NARA-II.

90. See correspondence in "Delivery Orders," entry 2, box 1, RG 6, NARA-II.

91. "Hawaiian Letter," *Louisiana Planter and Sugar Manufacturer* (September 2, 1916): 152.

92. George Fairchild to George Rolph, August 27, 1918, box 520, file 4122, RG 350, NARA-II.

93. George Rolph to James Post, Chairman, American Refiners Committee, September 16, 1918, entry 9, box 28, RG 6, NARA-II; Fairchild to Rolph, September 17, 1918, box 520, file 4122, RG 350, NARA-II.

94. Fairchild to Rolph, October 7, 1918, Fairchild to Rolph, October 11, 1918, and Walcutt to Fairchild, October 25, 1918, Records of George Rolph, entry 9, box 28, RG 6, NARA-II.

95. Correspondence with the Bureau of Insular Affairs (1915–17), box 520, file 4122, RG 350, NARA-II; Fairchild to Rolph, October 3, 1918, entry 9, box 28, RG 6, NARA-II; Quirino, *History of the Philippine Sugar Industry*, 56; Aguilar, *Clash of Spirits*, 201.

96. International Sugar Committee Correspondence, December 1918 through January 1919, entry 9, box 28, RG 6, NARA-II; Correspondence, November 1917 through November 1918, box 520, file 4122, RG 350, NARA-II; Correspondence, April–May 1919, entry 2, box 1, RG 6, NARA-II.

97. Bernhardt, "Government Control," 85–86.

98. Herbert Hoover to USFA, January 9, 1919, entry 9, box 28, RG 6, NARA-II.

99. Bernhardt, "Government Control," 99.

100. Investigation of the Scarcity of Sugar, Hearing before the House Committee on Interstate and Foreign Commerce, July 14, 1919, 66-1 (1919). See also Bernhardt, "Government Control," 114–15, 117.

101. Hoover, quoted in Bernhardt, "Government Control," vii.

CHAPTER 4

1. "Azúcar De Betabel," *Evolucion*, March 28, 1918, 3; "Haga usted su azúcar," *El democrata fronterizo*, April 13, 1918, 2; "Jardines de la libertad," *Evolucion*, May 19, 1918, 1.

2. C. O. Townsend and H. C. Gore, *Sugar-Beet Sirup*, USDA *Farmers' Bulletin* 823 (1917): 12. See also G. Holden, "Sugar Nation's Big Problem; A Sugar Beet Garden for Every Home," *Pueblo Chieftain*, 7 January 1918, 5.

3. Key literature on Mexican American sugar beet workers includes Deutsch, *No Separate Refuge*; Valdés, *Al Norte*; Vargas, *Labor Rights Are Civil Rights*; Norris, *North*

for the Harvest; and Mapes, *Sweet Tyranny*. On the guest worker program, see Alanís, *El Primer Programa Bracero*; and Hahamovitch, *Fruits of Their Labor*.

4. Arreola, *Tejano South Texas*; Gonzales, *Life along the Border*; Calleja Pinedo, "Los Empresarios." On the region more broadly, see St. John, *Line in the Sand*; Saragoza, *Monterrey Elite*; and Walsh, *Building the Borderlands*.

5. Gómez, *Manifest Destinies*; Montejano, *Anglos and Mexicans*; Deutsch, *No Separate Refuge*.

6. Haney López, *White by Law*; Almaguer, *Racial Fault Lines*; Foley, *White Scourge*.

7. Saragoza, *Monterrey Elite*; Alan Knight, *Counter-revolution and Reconstruction*.

8. Fred M. Rose to USFA, April 3, 1918, and USFA to War Trade Board, August 21, 1918, entry 33, box 52, RG 6, NARA-II; "Cubren los haberes con piloncillo," *Mexico City El Diario*, March 17, 1914, 5. See also Alan Knight, *Counter-revolution and Reconstruction*, 132.

9. Espinosa, "El Desarrollo," 21; Hart, *Empire and Revolution*; Hart, *Bitter Harvest*.

10. Bartra, "La Industria Cañero-Azucarera y la Revolución de 1910"; Aurrecoaches and Paredes, "El Nuevo Despegue"; Simpson, *Ejido*, 771; "Mexico Taxes Sugar," *Los Angeles Times*, July 31, 1920, I4; "Mexicans Want Sugar Duty," *Wall Street Journal*, March 15, 1921, 4; "Mexico Will Help Sugar Planters," *Los Angeles Times*, January 21, 1922, I2; "Mexican Duty on Sugar Increased," *Wall Street Journal*, February 17, 1922, I2; "Mexico Plans Returning Confiscated Sugar Lands," *Wall Street Journal*, November 27, 1926, 5.

11. Hamilton, "The State"; Crespo, *Historia*, 311–13; "Mexico Sugar Mill," *Wall Street Journal*, January 15, 1930, 20; "Mexican Sugar Central," *Wall Street Journal*, February 6, 1930; "Mexican Sugar Output Curbed," *Los Angeles Times*, December 26, 1932, A13; "To Construct a Sugar Central in Mexico," *Wall Street Journal*, May 7, 1928, 5; Servín, "Estudio económico fiscal de la industria del azúcar," *Revista de hacienda* (May 1938), 10, 17, 19. Mexican radicals singled Calles out for criticism in this regard. See articles in *El Machete Ilegal*, 1931–33.

12. Binford, "Peasants and Petty Capitalists." See also a series of articles in *Revista Mexicana de Sociologia* between 1940 and 1943 by Roberto Cerda de la Silva; Margaret Park Redfield, "Notes on the Cookery of Tepoztlan, Morelos," *Journal of American Folklore* 42, no. 164 (April–June 1929): 171–73, 184; "Sugar Factory for Acaponeta," *Los Angeles Times*, October 12, 1924, E12; Edmundo Mendieta Huerta, "La economía de los pueblos indígenas huastecos de San Luis Potosí," *Revista Mexicana de Sociología* 1, no. 2 (May–June 1939): 68; Chase, *Mexico*, 231; and "Seccion de consultas," *La Prensa*, August 19, 1918, 3.

13. Arce, *Sólo Tu*; Campos, *Home Grown*.

14. Lewis, "The Nation," 187; Francisco Rojas Gonzalez," Estudio historico-etnografico del alcoholismo entre los indios de México," *Revista Mexicana de Sociología*, 4, no. 2 (2nd quarter, 1942): 111–25; Mendieta Huerta, "La economía de los pueblos indígenas huastecos de San Luis Potosí," 59, 63, 68; Servín, "Estudio económico fiscal de la industria del azúcar" (pt. II); Lomnitz-Adler, *Exits from the Labyrinth*.

15. "Por si vas a ser pequeño agricultor," *La Prensa*, February 18, 1925, 9; R. Garcia Bravo y Olivera, "Sangre en el huarapo," *La Prensa*, October 20, 1935, 26.

16. Rochfort, "The Sickle"; Lewis, "The Nation"; Alan Knight, "Racism, Revolution, and *Indigenismo*"; Hedrick, *Mestizo Modernism*.

17. Tibol, *Los Murales*; Pilcher, *Que vivan los tamales!*

18. Treviño, "Prensa y patria"; Arredondo, *Mexican Chicago*; Benjamin Johnson, *Revolution in Texas*; Gutiérrez, *Walls and Mirrors*; Sánchez, *Becoming Mexican American*; Pilcher, *Planet Taco*; "Las Harinas De La 'Estrella'," *El Imparcial de Texas*, September 16, 1919, 11.

19. Paredes, *A Texas-Mexican Cancionero*, 155, 166; Herrera-Sobek, *Northward Bound*, 108, 121. Charamuscas and palanquetas are candies made from piloncillo.

20. "La exportacion de viveres a México," *La Prensa*, July 14, 1917, 9; advertisements in *La Prensa* and *El Heraldo De México*; "Productos Mexicanos en el mercado de EE. Unidos," *La Prensa*, June 28, 1920, 3; Gamio, *Life Story*, 55. On the overlap between retail and wholesale trade, see Calleja Pinedo, "Los empresarios," 324.

21. "La principal producción en el rico Municipio de Montemorelos, N. L.," *La Prensa*, February 3, 1925, 6; "Se han retardado la introduccion de frutas en Piedras Negras, Coah," *La Prensa*, October 28, 1926, 5; "Productos mexicanos," *La Prensa*, January 19, 1927, 4; "Viajeros," *La Prensa*, November 15, 1935, 4.

22. Advertisements in *La Prensa*, 1917–19; "Importadores por 26 años," *La Prensa*, December 20, 1939, 8.

23. "Las ventajas del cartón corrugado para el empaque," *La Prensa*, November 12, 1927, 6.

24. Advertisements in *La Prensa*, 1917–20; *El Heraldo De México*, 1919–22; *El Imparcial De Texas*, 1918. See also Cornelius Ferris, "Supply of Sugar at San Luis Potosi," *Sugar* 19, no. 1 (December 1917): 492; "Apunte sobre la fabricacion de panela," *La Prensa*, December 3, 1925, 6; Carlos Angurez Ruiz, "La quema de cañaverales," *La Prensa*, August 25, 1934, 2; "Como obtener panela blanca o dulce de mejor calidad," *La Prensa*, June 26, 1938, 13.

25. Advertisements in *La Prensa*, 1919–20. Gamio tabulated migrant remittances in *Mexican Immigration*, but he considered only postal money orders. Import-export companies that handled groceries were probably a common conduit for remittances. On Mexican American consumer cultures, see Gamio, *Mexican Immigration*; and McCrossen et al., *Land of Necessity*.

26. Advertisement in *El Cosmopolita*, November 8, 1919, 2.

27. Taylor, *Mexican Labor in the United States*; Mapes, *Sweet Tyranny*.

28. Albert Dakan to Edward P. Costigan, June 5, 1935, box 48, folder 14, EPC Papers; Taylor, *Mexican Labor in the United States*, 176–79, 191; Charles Gibbons, "Statement on Conditions Relating to Sugar Beet Workers in Colorado," submitted at the Hearing on the Sugar Stabilization Agreement, August 11, 1933, 7, box 49, folder 10, EPC Papers; Ellis, *Americanization through Homemaking*. See also Donato, *Mexicans and Hispanos*; Deutsch, *No Separate Refuge*; and Paul S. Taylor Interviews, Longmont, Colo., Field Notes, Set C, Transcript, November 1927, 54, 56, carton 11, folder 12, PST Papers. Grocers ran ads for mail-order food in all the Spanish-language papers in the 1920s. See also "Research on Kinds of Beans," *Greeley Tribune-Republican*, December 14, 1929, 6.

29. Gamio, *Life Story*, 64, 76, 143–44.

30. Ibid., 158. See also ibid., 22, 27, 44, 47, 53, 54, 65, 68, 103, 109, 126, 134, 161, 163, 166, 169, 208; Calleja Pinedo, "Los Empresarios"; and Pilcher, *Planet Taco*.

31. Advertisement in *El Amigo Del Hogar*, April 28, 1929, 4.

32. Paul S. Taylor Field Notes, Set D [typescript], 66, 1927, carton 11, folder 14, PST Papers.

33. Advertisement in *La Prensa*, October 21, 1925, 2; "Cartas a Juan de Afuera de La Capirotada y Otras Cosas," *La Prensa*, April 5, 1924, 3; "Sección de Consultas," *La Prensa*, May 2, 1918, 7.

34. Advertisement in "La Chapa Mercantile," *El Imparcial De Texas*, April 15, 1920, 7.

CHAPTER 5

1. Document Records has reissued recordings by Flo Johnson, Sister Harris, Lillian Harris, Hattie Garland, Lucille Hegamin, Monette Moore, Sara Martin, Alberta Hunter, Johnny Dunn, and Harry Reser, among others. See also Angela Y. Davis, *Blues Legacies*; and Carby, "The Sexual Politics of Women's Blues."

2. By comparison, in the thirty years between 1890 and 1920, the per capita increase was only about ten pounds per decade. See Ayala, *American Sugar Kingdom*; Woloson, *Refined Tastes*; and Bernhardt, "Government Control."

3. Schuyler Patterson, "The Sugar Industry: Its Past and Present," *Financial World* (May 31, 1920): 3–4; Federal Trade Commission, *Sugar Supply and Prices* (Washington, D.C.: GPO, 1920), 62; Brenner, *Emperors of Chocolate*; Dusselier, "Bon-Bons"; Bruegel, "How the French Learned to Eat Canned Food."

4. "Nature's Vindication of the Sweet Tooth," *Current Literature* (November 1909): 567.

5. "Selling Candy to Children," *WC* 8, no. 9 (June 1922): 78.

6. W. B. Stoddard, "Cashing in on Children's Parties," *WC* 8, no. 11 (August 1922): 43; Marie H. Anderson, "Feature 'Sensible Sweets for the Kiddies,'" *WC* 9, no. 9 (June 1923): 48; "Ideas Boost Sales to and through Children," *WC* 10, no. 6 (March 1924): 45; V. L. Price, "The Small 'Kid' as a Buyer," *WC* 10, no. 9 (June 1924): 44; Virginia Caldwell, "Candy Necessary in Well-Stocked Pantry," *WC* 13, no. 8 (May 1927): 41; William Bliss Stoddard, "Candy for the Kiddies," *WC* 13, no. 10 (July 1927): 35.

7. "New Ice Cream Confection Built on a Cartoon," *WC* 9, no. 1 (October 1922): 48; William Bliss Stoddard, "Watermelon on Ice Brings 'Em In," *WC* 12, no. 11 (August 1926): 33; "All Coons Look Alike to Me," *WC* 10, no. 12 (September 1924): 72a.

8. "Pickins from Portland," *WC* 9, no. 8 (May 1923): 54. On this imagery in the nineteenth century, see Tompkins, *Racial Indigestion*.

9. M. A. Ellis, "Treats to the Kiddies Make Great Publicity," *WC* 12, no. 6 (March 1926): 55; M. A. Ellis, "With the Trade in Denver and Colorado," *WC* 13, no. 11 (August 1927): 72; Nellye M. Graf, "And Popularity with the Kiddies Pays," *WC* 15, no. 11 (August 1929): 41.

10. "National Candy Week a Success in the West," *WC* 15, no. 2 (November 1928): 42.

11. BFDC, *Confectionery Distribution in the United States, 1927–1929* (1930): 12, 25; "J. N. Collins Company Announces New Philadelphia Factory," *WC* 10, no. 5 (February 1924): 84; "Peter Paul, Inc., Absorbs J. N. Collins Co. in Merger Deal," *WC* 15, no. 9 (June 1929): 91; "Loft Candy Merger Involves $20,000,000," *WC* 17, no. 1 (October 1930): 38.

12. E. E. Hemrich, "Industry's Campaign of Attrition," *WC* 13, no. 11 (August 1927): 47; "Confectioners Protest Lower Westbound Freight Rates on Candy," *WC* 13, no. 12 (September 1927): 29; "West Wins Recognition in Rate Case," *WC* 14, no. 3 (December

1927): 32; "Western Confectioners to Watch Traffic," *WC* 14, no. 5 (February 1928): 27; "Traffic Association Formed at Convention," *WC* 14, no. 6 (March 1928): 35.

13. M. A. Ellis, "Denver and the Rocky Mountain Country," *WC* 12, no. 6 (March 1926): 68.

14. Compiled from *1930 United States Federal Manuscript Census* and *City Directories of the United States, Meridian, MS* (1921–41). Little Rock, Ark., had a similar profile. See Schmand, *Sweet Side*. On southern confectioners more broadly, see correspondence between the BFDC and the Sophie Mae Candy Corporation, Atlanta, box 1386, RG 151, NARA-II; and "Atlanta Wholesale Confectioners Charged with Conspiracy to Restrain Trade," *WC* 12, no. 8 (May 1926): 37.

15. Statistics on syrup production by state are in E. W. Brandes et al., "Sugar," *Yearbook of Agriculture 1923*, 156, 160. On the development of cane syrup as a commodity, see Wiley, *Manufacture of Table Sirups*.

16. *FDA Notices of Judgment Collection, 1906-1964*, http://archive.nlm.nih.gov/fdanj/; "On Selecting Your Syrup," *(AAA) Consumer's Guide* 3, no. 24 (January 25, 1937): 8–9.

17. Du Bois, *The Souls of Black Folk*, 147; Washington, *Working with the Hands*, 26, 32, 206; Sharecroppers and Tenant Farmers Leaflet [1931], reel 191, delo 2538, 45, *Files of the CPUSA*; Soloman, *The Cry Was Unity*, 120.

18. Rosengarten, *All God's Dangers*, 475, 387.

19. Hughes, *Not without Laughter*, 127.

20. "Stop the Attack upon Negro Children!" [1931], reel 191, delo 2358, 46, *Files of the CPUSA*.

21. Roberts, *Anthracite Coal Communities*, 180. For further background, see Woloson, *Refined Tastes*, 39–40.

22. Buffalo, N.Y., City Directory, *City Directories of the United States, Segment IV, 1902-1935*.

23. On the intertwined histories of black women and food labor, see Williams-Forson, *Building Houses Out of Chicken Legs*; Witt, *Black Hunger*; and Sharpless, *Cooking in Other Women's Kitchens*.

24. Domosh, *American Commodities*; Glenn, *Female Spectacle*.

25. Walter Hawley, "Eat Chocolates to Keep Thin, Advises Film Star," *WC* 8, no. 3 (January 1922): 63; Virginia Caldwell, "Sidestepping the 'Fattening' Idea of Candy," *WC* 13, no. 7 (April 1927): 44; "Picture-Play Offers Publicity Hook-Up," *WC* 16, no. 2 (November 1929): 39; "Novel Experiment with Candies in Diet to Start May First," *WC* 16, no. 8 (May 1930): 40; "Modern Diet Calls for Candies," *WC* 16, no. 9 (June 1930): 34; "New School Teaches Commercial Dipping," *WC* 13, no. 2 (November 1926): 39.

26. Women's Bureau, *Wages of Candy Makers in Philadelphia in 1919* (Washington, D.C.: GPO, 1919), 35.

27. Commonwealth of Massachusetts, *Supplementary Report on the Wages of Women in Candy Factories in Massachusetts* (Boston: Wright & Potter, 1919); *Statement and Decree Concerning the Wages of Women Employed in the Minor Lines of Confectionery and Food Preparations Occupation in Massachusetts* (Boston: Massachusetts Department of Labor and Industries, 1921); U.S. Women's Bureau, *Women in Georgia Industries: A Study of Hours, Wages, and Working Conditions* (Washington, D.C.: GPO,

1922); U.S. Women's Bureau, *Women in the Candy Industry in Chicago and St. Louis* (Washington, D.C.: GPO, 1923); *Hours and Earnings of Women in Five Industries* (New York: Department of Labor, 1923); *Statement and Decree Concerning the Wages of Women Employed in the Candy Making Occupation in Massachusetts* (Boston: Massachusetts Department of Labor and Industries, 1926); *Behind the Scenes at Candy Factories* (New York: Consumers' League of New York, 1928).

28. Kessler-Harris, *Out to Work*; Hunter, *To 'Joy My Freedom*.

29. "Chocolate Dippers' School," *WC* 7, no. 1 (October 1920): 47; Factory Schedules, Women in Industry Survey by the U.S. Women's Bureau, Georgia, Alabama, Mississippi, Virginia, Kentucky, South Carolina, Arkansas [1920–25] , reel 17, *Black Workers in the Era of the Great Migration, 1916–1925*. University Publications of America, 1985. Microfilm edition.

30. "Among the Ice Cream Manufacturers," *WC* 17, no. 4 (January 1931): 46. On Japanese confectioners visiting the United States, see Kushner, "Sweetness and Empire"; and Imai, *Creating the Nisei Market*.

31. R. A. Roland, "Close-Up Views of Overseas Confectionery Markets," *WC* 7, no. 1 (October 1920): 52; H. B. Mills, "Seattle, Tacoma, and Spokane Gossip," *WC* 7, no. 1 (October 1920): 46; "Fountain Shipped to Mexico," *WC* 7, no. 9 (June 1921): 86; "Modern Soda Fountain in Mexico," *WC* 9, no. 5 (February 1923): 98; Charles D. Truman, "With the Trade in Hawaii," *WC* 9, no. 9 (June 1923): 85; C. M. Littlejohn, "Ice Cream for Java," *WC* 12, no. 9 (June 1926): 76; Ariel E. V. Dunn, "Hawaiian Islands Boast 200 Fountains," *WC* 13, no. 7 (April 1927): 56; "Among Our Subscribers," *WC* 14, no. 9 (June 1928): 34; "Philippine Confectionery Trade," *WC* 16, no. 8 (May 1930): 84; "Philippine Confectionery Market," *WC* 17, no. 12 (September 1931): 19.

32. Ngai, *The Lucky Ones*; Chang, *Pacific Connections*; Jung, *Reworking Race*; Glick, *Sojourners and Settlers*; Fuchs, *Hawaii Pono*; Shah, *Contagious Divides*; Adams, *Peoples of Hawaii*; Lind, *An Island Community*; Yu, *Thinking Orientals*.

33. Martha Jones et al., "Dental Disease in Hawaii," pt. III, *Dental Cosmos* 72, no. 7 (July 1930): 695.

34. "Candy for Hawaii," *WC* 7, no. 4 (January 1921): 40; Lawrence William Pedrose, "Seattle Gains in Export Candy Trade," *WC* 14, no. 3 (December 1927): 56; "More News of the Trade in San Francisco," *WC* 14, no. 1 (October 1927): 83.

35. "New Hilo Store Is Marvel of Beauty," *WC* 7, no. 3 (December 1920): 104; "Chinese Candy for Chinese Trade," *WC* 7, no. 11 (August 1921): 45; Ariel Dunn, "Hawaii Furnishes Candy Specialties," *WC* 13, no. 8 (May 1927): 69; Ann Barton Smith, "With the Trade in Los Angeles and the South," *WC* 13, no. 12 (September 1927): 66.

36. Thomas R. Taylor to Raymond G. Brown, September 11, 1924, box 1384, RG 151, NARA-II; Dunn, "Teaching the Hawaiians to Eat Ice Cream," *WC* 13, no. 7 (April 1927): 57; Theodore W. Johnson, "Ice Cream Business in Honolulu Large," *WC* 15, no. 1 (October 1928): 39.

37. On shaved ices competing with candy and ice cream in Puerto Rico, see R. L. Purdon to Joseph M. Smith, August 6, 1930, box 1385, RG 151, NARA-II; and BFDC, *Confectionery Distribution in the United States, 1929–1930* (1931), 16.

38. "Confectionery—General, 1919–1925," box 1384, RG 151, NARA-II; "Life Savers, 1924–1932," file 306, box 1385, RG 151, NARA-II; BFDC, *Foreign Markets for*

Confectionery I: Latin America and *Foreign Markets for Confectionery II: Far East* (1925); "The Government as Dictator," *WC* 18, no. 1 (October 1931): 18; "Export Sales Show Decline," *WC* 8, no. 7 (April 1922): 34; "Candy Exports Increase," *WC* 8, no. 8 (May 1922): 34; "Candy Exports Increasing," *WC* 9, no. 3 (December 1922): 48; de Grazia, *Irresistible Empire*.

39. "Sugar Consumption," *WC* 9, no. 8 (May 1923): 40; Charles H. Cunningham, Commercial Attache, Lima, Peru, to Director, Bureau of Foreign and Domestic Commerce, September 18, 1930, box 1385, RG 151, NARA-II.

40. R. L. Purdon to George C. Peck, Trade Commissioner, Panama City Office, September 16, 1926, and Purdon to Havana Office, January 10, 1927, box 1384, RG 151, NARA-II; W. B. Stoddard, "Candy and Fruit Merchants of Juarez," *WC* 11, no. 7 (April 1925): 78.

CHAPTER 6

1. 72 *Cong. Rec.*, 8242; "Hoover's Failure to Swap Sugar," *Literary Digest*, March 9, 1929, 16–17; "Washington's Battle of the Sugar Bowl," *Literary Digest*, May 11, 1929, 11–12; "The Sugar-Tariff Graft Again," *Nation*, May 29, 1929, 636; Albert Shaw, "The Progress of the World," *Review of Reviews*, September 1929, 31–34; "Bitterness in the Sugar-Bowl," *Literary Digest*, November 30, 1929, 12–13; "Cuban Sugar Lobby," *NYT*, October 29, 1929, 1, 4; "Beet Sugar Group Expended $500,000 on Lobby," *NYT*, October 17, 1929, 1, 16.

2. Wallace, "A 'Lucky' or a Sweet—or Both!" *Nation*, March 13, 1929, 305–7; Senator Reed Smoot, June 10, 1929, 71 *Cong. Rec.*, 2586–90; Walter H. Eddy, "May We Eat Candy?" *Good Housekeeping* (June 1929); "Sweets for Children," *American City* (June 1929); "Shall Children Eat Sweets?" *Hygeia* (July 1929).

3. Senate Committee on Finance Hearings, Tariff Schedule E, 62nd Cong., 2nd Sess., 484–86, 534–35; *The Child Workers of the Nation*, Proceedings of the Fifth Annual Conference, January 21–23, 1909 (New York: American Academy of Political and Social Science, 1909), 116–19, 226–27; "Colorado Children Worked 12 Hours in Beet Fields; Charge Made by Secretary of National Labor Conference in Chicago," *Rocky Mountain News*, January 22, 1909, 1.

4. Mapes, *Sweet Tyranny*; Trattner, *Crusade for the Children*; Sallee, *Whiteness of Child Labor Reform*.

5. Minutes, 1914–15, September 30, 1915, box 7, NCLC Papers. In 1910, census enumerators counted farm children "who materially assist their parents in the performance of work other than household work" as "farm laborers," whether they worked on a home farm or worked for wages.

6. Minutes, 1908–11, box 7, NCLC Papers; Sallee, *Whiteness of Child Labor Reform*, 124–30.

7. "Child Labor in Canneries, Truck Gardening, Tobacco, and Beet-Sugar Fields," *Child Employing Industries* (New York: NCLC, 1910); Owen Lovejoy, "Some Unsettled Questions about Child Labor," *Annals of the American Academy of Political and Social Science* 33 (March 1909): 59; *Twelfth Biennial Report of the Bureau of Labor Statistics of the State of Colorado, 1909–1910* (Denver: Smith-Brooks Printing Co., 1911).

8. NCLC Meeting Minutes, March 15, September 30, November 19, and November 22, 1915, box 7, NCLC Papers; Edward N. Clopper and Lewis W. Hine, "Child Labor in the Sugar-Beet Fields of Colorado," *Child Labor Bulletin* 4 (February 1916): 176–206; reprinted as Edward N. Clopper and Lewis W. Hine, *Child Labor in the Sugar-Beet Fields of Colorado*, NCLC Pamphlet 259 (New York: NCLC, 1916); and Clopper, "Beeters," *Survey* 35 (March 4, 1916): 655–60.

9. Hine, "Seven-Year-Old Alex Reiber Topping," Sterling, Colo., October 1915, NCLC Papers; Seixas, "Lewis Hine"; Lowry, "Lewis Hine's Family Romance."

10. Colorado Federation of Women's Clubs, "Child Labor in the Beet Fields of Colorado," enclosed in Mabel Costigan to Grace Abbott, September 27, 1917, file 6103, box 54, RG 102, NARA-II; Costin, *Two Sisters for Social Justice*; Greenbaum, *Fighting Progressive*; May, *Great Western Sugarlands*, 371–72.

11. L. A. Moorhouse et al., "Farm Practice in Growing Sugar Beets for Three Districts in Colorado, 1914–1915," USDA *Bulletin* 726 (1918); L. A. Moorhouse et al., "Farm Practice in Growing Sugar Beets for Three Districts in Utah and Idaho, 1914–15," USDA *Bulletin* 693 (1918); L. A. Moorhouse and T. H. Summers, "Saving Man Labor in Sugar-Beet Fields," USDA *Farmers' Bulletin* 1042 (1919); L. A. Moorhouse and S. B. Nuckols, "Cost of Producing Sugar Beets in Utah and Idaho, 1918–1919," USDA *Bulletin* 963 (1921); Fitzgerald, *Every Farm a Factory*; Taylor, *Story of Agricultural Economics*.

12. Lindenmeyer, *A Right to Childhood*, 132–36; Muncy, *Creating a Female Dominion*.

13. U.S. Children's Bureau, *Child Labor and the Work of Mothers in the Beet Fields of Colorado and Michigan* (1923). The findings were widely reported. A sampling includes Samuel Gompers, "Tax Child Labor Out of Beet Sugar," *American Federationist* 29, no. 1/7 (January/July 1922); "Child Labor and the Work of Mothers in the Beet-Sugar Industry," *School and Society* 17 (May 19, 1923); "Child with a Hoe," *Literary Digest* 77 (May 5, 1923); Arthur Evans, "Children Work in 'Home Shops' and Beet Fields," *Chicago Daily Tribune*, January 8, 1923; Arthur Evans, "Toil Cripples Child Workers in Beet Fields," *Chicago Daily Tribune*, February 28, 1924; Owen R. Lovejoy, "The Child Problem in the Beet-Sugar Industry," *Proceedings of the Ninth Annual Convention of the Association of Governmental Labor Officials of the United States and Canada* (1923).

14. "Farmers' States' Rights League Is Ferreted Out," *American Child* 7, no. 3 (March 1925); Helen V. Bary to Grace Abbott, January 25, 1923, and Wiley H. Swift to Grace Abbott, December 15, 1924, box 205, file 6-1-5-4, RG 102, NARA-II.

15. Alice K. McFarland, "Child Labor in Kansas Sugar-Beet Fields," box 205, file 6-1-5-4, RG 102, NARA-II; McFarland, "Child Labor in Sugar Beet Fields of Other States," *American Child* 5, no. 6 (June 1923).

16. "Caucasian Solidarity Urged to Insure Safety of World," *Christian Science Monitor*, August 17, 1923, 3; Culbertson, *International Economic Policies*, 487–88; Culbertson, *Raw Materials*; "Dimnet Says Debt Must Be Canceled," *NYT*, August 18, 1923; Cullather, *The Hungry World*.

17. See 42 Stat. 941 (1922); Wright, *Sugar in Relation to the Tariff*; and *J. W. Hampton v. United States* (1928), in which William Howard Taft wrote the unanimous opinion upholding the president's right to change duties to equalize foreign-versus-domestic costs of production.

18. "Report of the United States Tariff Commission to the President of the United States: Sugar," July 31, 1924 [typescript], file 147, reel 83, series 1, Coolidge Papers.

19. Both reports are available on file 147, reel 83, Coolidge Papers. The majority report was "Report of the United States Tariff Commission to the President of the United States: Sugar," July 31, 1924 [typescript]. It remained unpublished until 1928, when it was released as *Sugar: Report to the President* (1928).

20. 69 *Cong. Rec.*, 5209, 5212–13.

21. "Investigation of the Costs of Production of Sugar," Report Signed by Commissioners Marvin and Burgess of the U.S. Tariff Commission, August 1, 1924 [typescript], file 147, reel 83, Coolidge Papers; Goodykoontz, "Edward P. Costigan and the Tariff Commission"; Greenbaum, *Fighting Progressive*, 101–2.

22. Edward Costigan to Senator Joseph T. Robinson, Letter of Resignation, reprinted in 69 *Cong. Rec.*, 4734–35; "Chronological Outline in the Sugar Investigation," n.d., box 35, folder 1, EPC Papers; *Minutes of the Meetings of the United States Tariff Commission*, Serial Set vol. no. 8544, sess. vol. 6, 69th Cong., 1st sess.

23. Truman G. Palmer to Coolidge, August 20, 1924, and A. E. Carlton to Coolidge, August 21, 1924, reel 83, file 147, Coolidge Papers.

24. Editorial pages, *Nation*, April 4, 1923, 378; "New Sugar Boycott Is Planned Here as Prices Drop," *NYT*, May 1, 1923; "Women's Clubs Join in Boycott on Sugar," *NYT*, April 29, 1923; "25,000 to Parade in Sugar Protest," *NYT*, May 4, 1923; "Sugar Now 8 Cents," *NYT*, May 5, 1923; "Asks School Pupils to Boycott Sugar," *NYT*, May 6, 1923; "Women Ask Sugar Inquiry," *NYT*, June 6, 1923; "Child Labor in Michigan Sugar Beet Fields," *American Child* 5, no. 3 (March 1923); "Legislation Defeated, Colorado," *American Child* 5, no. 4 (April 1923); "Mr. Lovejoy's Work in Colorado," *American Child* 5, no. 4 (April 1923).

25. Owen R. Lovejoy to John W. Davis, September 21, 1923; Grace Abbott to Lovejoy, September 25, 1923, box 205, 6-1-5-4, RG 102, NARA-II; "Beet Complex," *American Child* 5, no. 6 (June 1923).

26. Frances B. Williams, "The Price of Sugar," *American Child* 5, no. 6 (June 1923); "Bitter-Sweets," *American Child* 5, no. 6 (June 1923); "Wlad of the Beets," *New Republic* 35 (August 8, 1923).

27. Owen R. Lovejoy, "Sugar Puzzle Picture—Find the Child," *American Child* 5, no. 10 (October 1923). *American Child* covered the controversy closely. See also Mapes, *Sweet Tyranny*.

28. A. E. Carlton to E. N. Mathews, December 21, 1923, box 205, 6-1-5-4, RG 102, NARA-II.

29. Carlton to Nelson Franklin, March 20, 1924, Carlton to Franklin, March 29, 1924, Roy Endicott to Carlton, February 6, 1924, M. W. Draper to Carlton, February 6, 1924, Fred G. Holmes to Carlton, February 6, 1924, F. J. Kaspar to Carlton, February 6, 1924, and Carlton to Grace Abbott, September 10, 1924, box 205, 6-1-5-4, RG 102, NARA-II.

30. Costigan to Grace Abbott, February 2, 1924, box 205, file 6-1-5-4, RG 102, NARA-II.

31. Testimonies and cross-examination of Hubert L. Shattuck, Harry A. Austin, E. F. Heckman, Howard Ottinger, Hon. Clifford R. Hope, F. H. Ross, and Hon. Charles B. Timberlake, *Immigration from Countries of the Western Hemisphere*, Hearings, 71st Cong., 2nd Sess. (Washington: D.C.: GPO, 1928).

32. J. C. Bailey, *Immigration from Countries of the Western Hemisphere*, 626.

33. Reisler, *By the Sweat of Their Brow*; Stern, *Eugenic Nation*; Foley, *White Scourge*; Gutiérrez, *Walls and Mirrors*.

34. "America's Stepchildren," *American Child* 8, no. 9 (September 1926); "The Front Line of the Fight," *American Child* 8, no. 4 (April 1926); Isabelle Alpers, "A Beet Speaks," *American Child* 8, no. 8 (August 1926); Owen Lovejoy, "'Democratic' Education," *American Child* 8, no. 2 (February 1926).

35. 71 *Cong. Rec.*, 1058, 1225–27, 1231–33, 1560, 1681–84, 1751–53, 2585, 8246, 8249–53.

36. U.S. Senate, *Lobby Investigation, Hearings before a Subcommittee of the Committee on the Judiciary*, 71st Congress, 2nd Session (Washington: D.C.: GPO, 1929), 388; *Lobbying and Lobbyists*, Sen. Rep. no. 43, pt. 5, January 6, 1930; "Lobby Committee Scored by Woman," *Washington Post*, January 11, 1930.

37. 71 *Cong. Rec.*, 1120, 1122, 1230, 1300–1302, 1371–75, 1455, 1546, 1581–82, 1587, 1691–93, 3918–19, 8255–56, 8315; "Labor Head Attacks Sugar Tariff in Bill," *Washington Post*, May 18, 1929; "An Indefensible Tax," *Washington Post*, May 18, 1929; "Unmasking the Tariff," *NYT*, May 20, 1929; "Mrs. Pratt Assails Sugar Duty," *NYT*, May 21, 1929; "Cuban Sugar Lobby Has Spent $75,000," *NYT*, October 29, 1929, 1, 4.

38. 71 *Cong. Rec.*, 1126–30, 1145, 1163–64, 1475–78, 1560, 1591.

39. Guerra y Sánchez, *Sugar and Society in the Caribbean*, 27, 71–72, 111, 142. It was first published as a serial in Cuban newspapers and then compiled into a book, *Azúcar y poblacion en los Antilles*, in 1927. That book was reissued in 1935 and 1944. The English translation is an adaptation of the third edition. See also Whitney, *State and Revolution*; McGillivray, *Blazing Cane*; and Ayala, *American Sugar Kingdom*.

40. Thomas Mahoney to Sidney Morgan, March 9, 1932, box 47, RG 81, NARA-II; Mahoney to Grace Abbott, December 1930, box 394, file 6-1-2-4, RG 102, NARA-II.

41. 71 *Cong. Rec.*, 8255; Schattschneider, *Politics, Pressures, and the Tariff*, 179–82, 202; Taussig, "The Tariff Act of 1930."

42. Bulosan, *America Is in the Heart*, 5, 19, 23, 24.

43. "Chronological Statement of Centrifugal Sugar Plants in the Philippine Islands," box 520, file 4122, RG 350, NARA-II; *Handbook of the Philippine Sugar Industry*, 114–15, 120; Quirino, *History of the Philippine Sugar Industry*, 50, 63; Bulosan, *America Is in the Heart*, 32, 44, 50; "Form Philippine Company," *Facts about Sugar*, January 29, 1921, 86. See also "Philippine Producers Form Sugar Association," *Facts about Sugar*, November 25, 1922, 430.

44. Steerage passengers on the U.S.S. *President McKinley* docked in Honolulu on May 5, 1928. NARA, series A3422, roll 97, Honolulu, Hawaii, Passenger Lists, 1900–1953, Ancestry.com.

45. Lawrence Judd to Roger Baldwin, December 15, 1933, reel 104, vol. 675a, ACLU Archives.

46. Frank McIntyre, Memorandum, October 23, 1922, box 521, file 4122, RG 350, NARA-II. For comparative work, see Giusti-Cordero, "Compradors or Compadres"; and Go, "Chains of Empire."

47. Serious proposals were made in 1922, 1926, 1927, and 1928. See Leonard Wood to Frank McIntyre, June 1, 1922, Ben F. Wright, "Memorandum on the Philippine National Bank Sugar Centrals," December 28, 1922, and McIntyre to Joseph H. Foley,

January 25, 1926, box 521, file 4122, RG 350, NARA-II; and Stimson Diary, reel 1, vol. viii, 107, June 6, 1928, HLS Papers.

48. Leonard Wood to John Weeks, August 25, 1923, and Frank McIntyre to D. Cowan, July 11, 1923, box 521, file 4122, RG 350, NARA-II.

49. Governor General Leonard Wood to Secretary of War John Weeks, August 25, 1923, box 521, file 4122, RG 350, NARA-II.

50. Frank McIntyre, Memorandum for the Secretary of War, Philippine National Bank and Sugar Centrals, October 23, 1922, box 521, file 4122, RG 350, NARA-II.

51. Ben F. Wright to Frank McIntyre, March 18, 1921, and Wright to E. W. Wilson, March 8, 1921, box 521, file 4122, RG 350, NARA-II; Wright to McIntyre, June 11, 1927, box 522, file 4122, RG 350, NARA-II.

52. McIntyre to Henry Stimson, January 27, 1928, and McIntyre, "Rumored Effort to Limit the Amount of Philippine Sugar," box 522, RG 350, NARA-II; Stimson Diaries, reel 1, vol. vii, 34, March 16, 1928, reel 2, vol. ix, 110–12, January 6, 1929, and reel 2, vol. ix, 114–16, January 7, 1929, HLS Papers.

53. This cartoon was published in the middle of the contentious 1929 sugar tariff debates in the *Manila Free Press*, May 18, 1929. The cartoon argued that the loss of laborers was a menace to the Philippines, but many read it as a menace to the United States. Reprinted in McCoy and Roces, *Philippine Cartoons*, 194–95.

54. Stimson Diary, reel 2, vol. x, 4–7, August 28, 1930, HLS Papers; Stimson, "Dangers of Tariff Restriction upon Imports from the Philippine Islands Particularly with Reference to Sugar," April 17, 1929, House Committee on Ways and Means, 71-1 (1929); USTC, *Colonial Tariff Policies.*

55. Friend, "The Philippine Sugar Industry"; Larkin, *Sugar*, 186.

56. The phrase is from "The Sugar Act of 1937," *Yale Law Journal* 47, no. 6 (April 1938): 982. Dalton, *Sugar: A Case Study*, 69, also uses the phrase "disproportionate share."

57. W. D. Hoover to Costigan, May 1932, box 48, folder 6, EPC Papers; Albert Daken to Costigan, March 6, 1934, box 48, folder 9, EPC Papers; Arthur Sears Henning, "Colorado May Send Democrat to U.S. Senate," *Chicago Daily Tribune*, October 11, 1930, 9; J. C. Bailey to Costigan, April 22, 1931, and July 7, 1931, box 48, folder 5, EPC papers.

58. W. D. Hoover, "Why Should the United States Impose a Tax of Two Cents a Pound or Forty Dollars a Ton on Sugar Shipped from Our Ward Cuba?" box 49, folder 8, EPC Papers; W. D. Hoover to Costigan, May 1932, box 48, folder 6, EPC Papers.

59. John L. Coulter to USTC, April 13, 1933, box 48, RG 81, NARA-II; London Conference, 1934, Instructions, box 498, file 3440-122, RG 350, NARA-II; Dalton, *Sugar: A Case Study*, 69–70, 198–200.

60. "Record Philippine Sugar Crop," *Wall Street Journal*, September 26, 1932, 7.

61. Robert L. O'Brien to USTC, April 7, 1933, box 48, RG 81, NARA-II.

62. Simpson, "Proposed Bounty on Sugar Beets," March 1932 [typescript], and Bernhardt, "Comments on Proposed Bill for Sugar Beet Subsidy," September 20, 1932 [typescript], box 49, folder 8, EPC Papers; Edminister to Costigan, December 1, 1932, Simpson to Costigan, December 11, 1932, Simpson to Costigan, December 22, 1932, and Bernhardt to Costigan, November 8, 1933, box 48, folder 7, EPC Papers.

63. John L. Coulter to USTC, March 16, 1932, and April 6, 1933, and Robert L. O'Brien to USTC, April 7, 1933, box 48, RG 81, NARA-II; Robert L. O'Brien to FDR,

April 11, 1933, box 51, RG 81, NARA-II; Mark A. Smith and C. O. Townsend to USTC, March 19, 1932, box 50, RG 81, NARA-II.

64. Stimson Diary, reel 3, vol. xv, 206–7, March 30, 1931, HLS Papers.

65. Stimson Diary, reel 4, vol. xx, 101–2, January 26, 1932, HLS Papers.

CHAPTER 7

1. Romeo L. Dougherty, "My Observations: Haitian Voodooism Brought Up to Date," *New York Amsterdam News*, September 21, 1932, 8; Renda, *Taking Haiti*, 226–27. Thanks to Alex Nemerov for suggesting the film. Thanks to Derek Merleaux for watching it with me, and for a remarkable feat of film still digitization.

2. Oswald Garrison Villard, "If I Were a Dictator," *Nation*, January 20, 1932; Luis Muñoz Marín, "Puerto Rico y el Partido Liberal," *El Mundo*, March 10, 1932, reprinted in Bothwell, *Puerto Rico*, vol. 2, 407.

3. Charles E. Gibbons, "The Price of Beet Sugar," *American Child* 15, no. 6 (September 1933); Dinwiddie to Mahoney, July 27, 1933, July 31, 1933, and August 3, 1933, Mahoney to Dinwiddie, August 4, 1933, Mexican Welfare Committee to Dinwiddie, August 5, 1933, Mahoney to Leo Rodriquez, August 6, 1933, and Dinwiddie to Mahoney, August 11, 1933, TFM Collection; Dinwiddie to Clara Beyers, August 1, 1933, box 529, file 6124, RG 102, NARA-II; Dinwiddie to Josephine Roche, August 17, 1933, box 48, EPC Papers; "Testimony of Leo Rodriguez on Behalf of Those Employed in Growing Sugar Beets," AAA, *Hearings*, reel 10, docket no. 22, August 11, 1933, 441–44. See also Deutsch, *No Separate Refuge*.

4. Gibbons, "The Price of Beet Sugar"; Leo Rodriguez to Thomas F. Mahoney, October 4, 1934, TFM Collection.

5. Jacobs, "Democracy's Third Estate"; Cohen, *Making a New Deal*.

6. Balderrama and Rodríguez, *Decade of Betrayal*; Vargas, *Labor Rights Are Civil Rights*; Jamieson, *Labor Unionism*; Gonzalez, *Mexican Consuls and Labor Organizing*; District Organizer #19 to Secretariat CC, January 15, 1932, reel 226, delo 2944, 4–5, *Files of the CPUSA*; Elinor Henderson, "Preliminary Report on the Agricultural Wage Workers of the U.S.A." (1928), reel 104, delo 1369, 27, *Files of the CPUSA*.

7. "TUUL Organization Bulletin," November 6, 1930, reel 163, delo 2175, 21, and reel 226, delo 2944, 145–46, *Files of the CPUSA*; Alberto Sanchez, "La explotación de los obreros Mexicanos en Colorado," *Vida Obrera* 3, no. 12 (November 17, 1930), in Exp. 3/510 (73-13), 39-9-53, SRE.

8. "La explotación en Los Estados Unidos," *El Machete Ilegal* 193 (March 1931): 2. These leaflets were collected by the Mexican consul in Denver, Y. N. Vazquez. See "Informe politico-economicos del consulado de Mexico en Denver, Colorado, EE.UU. de A., 1931," Exp. 3/510 (73-13), 39-9-53, SRE.

9. James Allander to CPUSA, October 13, 1930, reel 154, delo 1997, 25–26, and Jim Brooks, District 19 Report, n.d., reel 162, delo 2153, 35, *Files of the CPUSA*.

10. District Organizer #19 to Agrarian Dept., January 13, 1932, District Organizer #19 to Secretariat Central Committee, February 1, 1932, District Organizer 19 to W. Z. Foster, February 16, 1932, and Minutes of Secretariat Meeting, District 19, July 25, 1932, reel 226, delo 2944, 1–3, 8, 18, 30, 55, 150–55, *Files of the CPUSA*; Report of the Beet

Workers' Conference, n.d., reel 226, delo 2942, 57–59, *Files of the CPUSA*; Pat Toohey to Central Committee, July 23, 1932, reel 226, delo 2938, 16–17, *Files of the CPUSA*.

11. Bernhardt, *The Sugar Industry and the Federal Government*, 157–60.

12. Bernhardt, "Comments," September 20, 1932, and Thomas F. Mahoney to Edward P. Costigan, April 21, 1933, series I, box 14, TFM Collection; Edward P. Costigan to Charles M. Kearney, National Beet Growers' Association, January 7, 1936, box 48, folder 16, EPC Papers; Stimson Diary, reel 5, vol. xxvii, 40–41, May 18, 1934, HLS Papers; Alpers, *Dictators*.

13. "Diabetic octopus" is from Acosta, *La Zafra*, 130. See also Consul General L. J. Keena, Cuba, March 20, 1929, RG 166, NARA-II; Beals, *The Crime of Cuba*; Leland Hamilton Jenks, *Our Cuban Colony*; Whitney, *State and Revolution*; Pérez, *Cuba under the Platt Amendment*; and Pollitt, "The Cuban Sugar Economy."

14. "Proyecto de ley para amparar a la industria azucarera," *Gaceta Oficial* 4 (November 1925), reprinted in Rosell, *Luchas Obreras Contra Machado*, 104–5; Noble Brandon Judah to Secretary of State, January 19, 1928, RG 166, NARA-II; Willcox, *Can Industry Govern Itself?*, 24–25. On the Chadbourne plan, see Clifford L. James, "International Control of Raw Sugar Supplies," *American Economic Review* 21, no. 3 (1931): 481–97; and Kurt Wilk, "International Affaire: The International Sugar Regime," *American Political Science Review* 33, no. 5 (October 1939): 860–78.

15. Malwon Kaufman, "The Cuban Dictatorship," *Nation*, March 18, 1931, 309–11; "Cuba Revolts Again," *Nation*, August 26, 1931; "Secret Police Head Is Slain in Havana," *NYT*, July 10, 1932; "Cuba's Silent 'Reign of Terror,'" *Literary Digest* 114 (July 30, 1932); "Cuban Politics Goes Gangster," *Literary Digest* 114 (October 8, 1932); Russell Porter, "Machado Says Foes Stir Cuban Unrest," *NYT*, January 31, 1933; Russell Porter, "Terror in Cuba Laid to Broken Pledges," *NYT*, February 8, 1933; Pérez, *Essays on Cuban History*; Benjamin, "The Machadato and Cuban Nationalism"; Dur and Gilcrease, "U.S. Diplomacy."

16. Edward P. Costigan to Rudolph Johnson, February 7, 1934, box 48, folder 8, EPC Papers; Department of State Press Release, August 24, 1934, box 48, folder 11, EPC Papers; George and Mallory to Edward P. Costigan, April 24, 1933, box 48, folder 7, EPC Papers.

17. "Wallace Will Become Czar," *Greeley Tribune*, October 30, 1933; "Wallace Expected to Secure Cut on Cuban Sugar Tariff," *Greeley Tribune*, November 3, 1933; "New Sugar Head," *Greeley Tribune*, November 6, 1933; "Opponent of Beet Industry About to Quit," *Greeley Tribune*, November 13, 1933. See also constituent letters to Costigan, box 48, folders 7 & 9, EPC Papers.

18. Joshua Bernhardt to Edward P. Costigan, November 8, 1933, box 48, folder 7, EPC Papers; Pedro Guevara to Edward P. Costigan, April 14, 1934, box 48, folder 10, EPC Papers; and Dalton, *Sugar: A Case Study*, 101.

19. W. Lewis Abbott, "Report for the Committee on Labor Conditions in the Growing of Sugar Beets," March 1934 [typescript], box 44, folder 11, EPC Papers; W. Lewis Abbott to Edward P. Costigan, March 8, 1934, box 48, folder 9, EPC Papers; "Sugar Beet Inquiry," *American Child* 16, no. 2 (February 1934); "Beet Sugar Hearings," *American Child* 16, no. 8 (November 1934).

20. Correspondence between Helen W. Fischer and Clara Beyer, February–April 1934, John L. Shearer to Henry Wallace, March 21, 1934, and Ella Merritt to Clara Beyer, June 24, 1933, box 529, file 6124, RG 102, NARA-II.

21. 78 *Cong. Rec.*, 6019, 6020, 6041–42, 6929–33, 7242; "Sugar Control Bill Passed by Senate," *NYT*, April 20, 1934; "Sugar Bill Goes to the President," *NYT*, April 26, 1934.

22. Haggard, "Institutional Foundations of Hegemony"; Schnietz, "Institutional Foundation of U.S. Trade Policy"; Benjamin, "The New Deal, Cuba, and the Rise of a Global Foreign Economic Policy."

23. The shotgun metaphor was ubiquitous. See 78 *Cong. Rec.*, 6021, 6025–27, 6029, 6803, 6813.

24. Mordecai Ezekiel, "Who Benefits from High Tariffs?" [typescript], n.d. [1934], box 2080, RG 16, NARA-II; Bureau of Agricultural Economics, "Memorandum in Regard to Proposals for the Cuban Rate of Import Duty on Lard," April 12, 1934, box 2076, RG 16, NARA-II; "Considerations toward the Development of a Tariff Policy for Agriculture," December 29, 1934, box 2080, RG 16, NARA-II.

25. Frank Murphy, Radiogram to Secretary of War, December 14, 1933, box 523, file 4122, RG 350, NARA-II.

26. 48 Stat. 462.

27. Dalton, *Sugar: A Case Study*, 206.

28. On independence, see Kramer, *Blood of Government*; Ngai, *Impossible Subjects*; and Mapes, *Sweet Tyranny*.

29. "Hit Duty Free Sugar Imports," *Wall Street Journal*, December 8, 1932, 4; John H. Foley to Frank McIntyre and McIntyre to Foley, May 23, 1928, box 522, file 4122–346, RG 350, NARA-II; Stimson Diary, reel 1, vol. viii, 109, June 8, 1928, HLS Papers; Frank Parker to Secretary of War, box 523, file 4122, RG 350, NARA-II.

30. Allen V. De Ford to USTC, May 19, 1932, box 51, RG 81, NARA-II.

31. Millard Tydings to Henry Wallace, May 30, 1933, box 523, file 4122, RG 350, NARA-II; Tydings to USTC, February 29, 1932, Tydings to USTC, November 15, 1932, and Thomas Walker Page to Tydings, November 16, 1932, box 51, RG 81, NARA-II; Representative Peter A. Cavicchia (R-New Jersey) to Secretary of Agriculture, March 16, 1934, box 2076, RG 16, NARA-II.

32. 78 *Cong. Rec.*, 4991; Frank McIntyre, Memo, May 10, 1933, and Frank Murphy to Secretary of War, September 3, 1933, box 523, file 4122, RG 350, NARA-II; Costigan to Rudolph Johnson, February 7, 1934, box 48, folder 8, EPC Papers.

33. 48 Stat. 459, 460; Bernhardt, *The Sugar Industry and the Federal Government*, 164.

34. Frank Murphy to Creed Cox, October 19, 1933, box 523, file 4122, RG 350, NARA-II.

35. *Cincinnati Soap Co. v. U.S.*, 301 U.S. 308 (1937).

36. "Sugar Conference in Dr. Ezekiel's Office," May 8, 1934, box 523, file 4122, RG 350, NARA-II. See also H. A. Wallace to Franklin Roosevelt, November 29, 1935, box 2246, RG 16, NARA-II; and Memorandum for the Secretary of Agriculture from the [Agricultural Adjustment] Administrator, November 13, 1935, box 2246, RG 16, NARA-II.

37. For an especially cogent statement of the justification for the Sugar Act that hinges on the notion of worldwide overproduction, see Statement of Dr. Mordecai Ezekiel, *Include Sugar Beets and Sugarcane as Basic Commodities*, Hearing before the Committee on Agriculture, House of Representatives (1934), 68–84.

38. Dalton, *Sugar: A Case Study*, 104–5.

39. John Dalton, Draft Speech, n.d. [1935], box 2246, RG 16, NARA-II.

40. Harold Ickes to Pat Harrison, April 9, 1934, and Ickes to Wallace, May 12, 1934, box 620, RG 126, NARA-II.

41. Garfield, "Hawaii's Basic Reasons"; Jennings Bailey, Opinion in the Supreme Court of the District of Columbia, *Ewa Plantation Company v. Wallace* [1934], box 618, RG 126, NARA-II; Wallace to J. O. Fernandez, May 3, 1935, box 2247, RG 16, NARA-II.

42. Joshua Bernhardt to Ernest Gruening, March 11, 1936, box 888, RG 126, NARA-II; Dalton, *Sugar: A Case Study*, 219, 234.

43. J. A. Dickey, "Some Phases of the Puerto Rican Sugar Adjustment Program," January 22, 1936, box 888, RG 126, NARA-II. At the time Dickey wrote this memo, he worked as a lobbyist. However, he had been employed by the Sugar Division in Puerto Rico in 1935.

44. William H. Crozier Jr. to Edward P. Costigan, April 2, 1934, and Pedro N. Ortiz to Edward P. Costigan, April 2, 1934, box 48, folder 10, EPC Papers.

45. Rexford Tugwell to Governor General Murphy, Philippine Islands, June 9, 1934, box 2076, RG 16, NARA-II.

46. Creed Cox to Frank Murphy, June 23, 1934, box 523, file 4122, RG 350, NARA-II; Carl Rosenquist to John Dalton, May 17, 1935, box 2247, RG 16, NARA-II; *Report of the Governor General of the Philippine Islands* (1935), 42; *Report of the High Commissioner* (1936), 28; *Second Annual Report of the High Commissioner* (1937), 2, 180.

47. U.S. Bureau of Agricultural Economics, *The World Sugar Situation*, September 1943.

48. Vicente Laureano to Secretary of Agriculture, January 17, 1935, C. E. Davis to H. A. Nelson, February 21, 1935, and H. A. Wallace to Jose M. Garcia, March 11, 1935, box 2246, RG 16, NARA-II; Joshua Bernhardt to Carl Rosenquist, April 30, 1935, and Carl Rosenquist to John Dalton, May 15, 1935, box 2247, RG 16, NARA-II; Memorandum re: Mr. [Charles] Taussig's letter of June 17, 1935, July 9, 1935, box 3346, RG 16, NARA-II.

49. Carlos Chardón, *Report of the Puerto Rico Policy Commission* (San Juan, PR: Puerto Rico Policy Commission, 1934); Ayala and Bernabe, *Puerto Rico in the American Century*; McCook, *States of Nature*; Mathews, *Puerto Rican Politics*.

50. 49 Stat. 1135; Ernest Gruening, "Memorandum to the Comptroller General," [February 1936?], box 29, entry 1, box RG 323, NARA-NY.

51. H. A. Wallace to Santiago Iglesias, June 13, 1935, box 2247, RG 16, NARA-II; Memo, Conference between Officials, March 9, 1938, box 2881a, RG 16, NARA-II; Francis M. Shea, Memorandum, January 28, 1936, box 23, entry 1, box RG 323, NARA-NY; Rosenn, "Puerto Rican Land Reform"; García Colón, *Land Reform*.

52. M. L. Wilson to Homer Cummings, Attorney General, February 19, 1936, box 2425, RG 16, NARA-II.

53. Joshua Bernhardt to Ernest Gruening, March 11, 1936, box 888, RG 126, NARA-II.

54. Memorandum for the Secretary, USDA, December 23, 1936, and Memorandum on Sugar Policy, USDA, December 29, 1936, box 2425, RG 16, NARA-II; Gruening to Secretary of Interior, March 24, 1937, box 618, RG 126, NARA-II.

55. Bernhardt, Memorandum, "Notes for Reply to Senator O'Mahoney's Letter of July 16, 1937," box 93, RG 126, NARA-II; Gruening to Filipo I. de Hostos, July 8, 1937, box 888, RG 126, NARA-II.

56. Testimony of R. Menendez Ramos, House Committee on Agriculture, Hearings on Sugar, March 15, 1937, 115.

57. Bernhardt to Wallace, August 17, 1938, box 2881a, RG 16, NARA-II.

58. Bernhardt to R. M. Evans, September 12, 1938, and Wallace to Senator James F. Byrnes, October 6, 1938, box 2881a, RG 16, NARA-II.

CHAPTER 8

1. FDR to Harrison, August 11, 1937, reprinted in *1937 Public Papers and Addresses of Franklin D. Roosevelt* (1941), 321–22.

2. Ernest Gruening to Filipo I. de Hostos, July 8, 1937, box 888, RG 126, NARA-II.

3. "Memorandum of Approval of Sugar Bill," September 1, 1937, *1937 Public Papers and Addresses of Franklin D. Roosevelt* (1941), 347. See also Harold Ickes to Ellison D. Smith, January 31, 1938, and Harold Ickes to FDR, February 2, 1938, box 618, RG 126, NARA-II.

4. Mathews, *Puerto Rican Politics West*; Ayala and Bernabe, *Puerto Rico in the American Century*.

5. On the shift toward individualism, economic rights, and trade globalization, see Borgwardt, *A New Deal for the World*, 133–34; Brinkley, *End of Reform*, 164–70; and Cohen, *A Consumer's Republic*.

6. 71 *Cong. Rec.*, 3384.

7. 72 *Cong. Rec.*, 11240.

8. 48 Stat. 671.

9. Department of Interior Memorandum, August 7, 1937, box 93, RG 126, NARA-II.

10. Brief of Loring Farnum, Opposing Limitation of Refined Sugar from Puerto Rico, n.d. [1934], box 2076, RG 16, NARA-II.

11. FDR to Marvin Jones, April 11, 1940, box 93, RG 126, NARA-II; FDR to Jones, April 21, 1939, box 890, RG 126, NARA-II.

12. Harold Ickes to Fred C. Gilchrist, March 15, 1937, box 618, RG 126, NARA-II.

13. Ernest Gruening to Isador Feinstein, August 10, 1937, box 93, RG 126, NARA-II.

14. FDR to Jones, April 11, 1940, box 93, RG 126, NARA-II.

15. Chardón, *Report of the Puerto Rico Policy Commission*, June 14, 1934.

16. Harold Ickes to Mrs. C. P. Barry, New York Federation of Women's Clubs, Inc., March 21, 1940, box 93, RG 126, NARA-II.

17. Ayala and Bernabe, *Puerto Rico in the American Century*; Mathews, *Puerto Rican Politics*; Gattell, "Independence Rejected."

18. Luis Muñoz Marín to Roger Baldwin, March 24, 1937, reel 155, vol. 1062, ACLU Archives; Baldwin to Muñoz Marín, March 29, 1937, ibid..

19. Muñoz Marín, Memorandum for Secretary Ickes on Puerto Rican Independence, January 5, 1937, ibid.

20. Muñoz Marín to Roger Baldwin, January 20, 1937, ibid.; Baldwin to Harold Ickes, February 13, 1937, ibid.

21. Vito Marcantonio to Baldwin, February 24, 1937, ibid.

22. Ralston Hayden to Baldwin, May 6, 1937, reprinted in Bothwell, *Puerto Rico*, vol. 3, 26–29.

23. Ernest Gruening to Morris Ernst, February 28, 1938, and Gruening to Ernst, June 1, 1938, box 620, RG 126, NARA-II.

24. Ernst, "Opinion on Constitutionality of Direct-Consumption Provision in Sugar Act of 1937 Applicable to Hawaii," box 620, RG 126, NARA-II.

25. Alex Budge to Gruening, March 24, 1939, and Gruening to Budge, April 3, 1939, box 620, RG 126, NARA-II.

26. Acting Secretary of the Interior to Millard Tydings. April 13, 1939, box 93, RG 126, NARA-II; Joint Memorandum to the President, April 21, 1939, box 890, RG 126, NARA-II.

27. Gruening, Memorandum on the Ellender Sugar Bill, March 27, 1939, box 890, RG 126, NARA-II. For another comparison of the sugar industry with Germany, see Thurman Arnold, *The Folklore of Capitalism* (1937), chap. 11.

28. Confidential Memorandum on Sugar Policy, August 3, 1939, and Joshua Bernhardt, Memorandum to Paul Appleby, n.d., box 2881, RG 16, NARA-II.

29. Joshua Bernhardt, Memorandum for the Secretary, December 15, 1939, Confidential Memorandum re Sugar, December 6, 1939, and H. A. Wallace to FDR, December 27, 1939, box 3098, RG 16, NARA-II.

30. Wage Determination Hearings, San Juan, Puerto Rico, November 30, 1937, 128, box 890, RG 126, NARA-II.

31. "Apparent Civilian Per Capita Consumption from Bureau of the Census," U.S. Department of Commerce, *Historical Statistics of the United States, 1789-1945* (1949).

32. J. P. Cavin et al., "Agricultural Surpluses and Nutritional Deficits," *Yearbook of Agriculture 1940*, USDA (1940), 339.

33. "Food Patterns," *(AAA) Consumer's Guide* 14, no. 7 (June 14, 1937): 10.

34. Cavin et al., "Agricultural Surpluses and Nutritional Deficits," 338. See also Stella Stewart and Faith Williams, *Retail Prices of Food, 1923-36*, Bureau of Labor Statistics Bulletin no. 635 (1938): 165.

35. "Food Patterns," *(AAA) Consumer's Guide* 14, no. 7 (June 14, 1937): 10; Cavin et al., "Agricultural Surpluses and Nutritional Deficits," 338.

36. Albert S. Nemir, BFDC, *The Candy Industry*, July 1937.

37. "So You Have a Sweet Tooth!," *(AAA) Consumer's Guide* 5, no. 16 (January 30, 1939): 7.

38. Samuel Charles Miller and Isaac Neuwirth, "Tooth Decalcification Due to Hard Candies," *Dental Cosmos* 77 (May 1935).

39. "Food Patterns," *(AAA) Consumer's Guide* 14, no. 7 (June 14, 1937).

40. Morris Ernst, "Opinion on Constitutionality of Direct-Consumption Provision in Sugar Act of 1937 Applicable to Hawaii," box 620, RG 126, NARA-II.

41. Proposed Agreement to Be Entered Into between Employers and Employees of the Sugar Industry in Puerto Rico, as Approved by the Special Convention of the Agricultural and Factory Labor Unions of Puerto Rico, October 20-21, 1934, box 924, RG 126, NARA-II.

42. U.S. Bureau of Agricultural Economics, *The World Sugar Situation*, September 1943.

43. *Annual Report of the High Commissioner, 1937*, 151.

44. Carl Rosenquist to John Dalton, March 27, 1935, and Dalton to Rosenquist, March 28, 1935, box 2247, RG 16, NARA-II.

45. Vicente Laureano to Secretary of Agriculture, January 17, 1935, box 2246, RG 16, NARA-II.

46. H. A. Wallace, Administrative Ruling no. 3, Philippine Sugarcane Production Adjustment Contract, March 2, 1935, box 2247, RG 16, NARA-II.

47. J. D. Stubbe to Henry A. Wallace, March 4, 1939, box 891, RG 126, NARA-II.

48. Albert Dakan to Costigan, [1935], box 48, EPC Papers.

49. Charles Gibbons, "Statement on Conditions Relating to Sugar Beet Workers in Colorado," submitted at the Hearing on the Sugar Stabilization Agreement, August 11, 1933, 10–11, box 49, folder 10, EPC Papers.

50. Report of Beet Field Workers' Unions of Colorado Conference, held March 22, 1936, Denver, Colo., March 25, 1936, box 48, folder 16, EPC Papers; Vargas, *Labor Rights Are Civil Rights*.

51. M. L. Wilson to Edward P. Costigan, July 27, 1935, box 2247, RG 16, NARA-II.

52. Wallace to Perkins, June 4, 1935, and Perkins to Wallace, March 9, 1935, box 2247, RG 16, NARA-II.

53. Courtenay Dinwiddie to Edward P. Costigan, June 7, 1935, box 48, folder 14, EPC Papers.

54. Elizabeth S. Johnson, *Welfare of Families of Sugar-Beet Laborers: A Study of Child Labor and Its Relation to Family Work, Income, and Living Conditions in 1935*, Children's Bureau Publication no. 247 (1939).

55. For one complaint on this front, see Albert Dakan to Edward P. Costigan, June 5, 1935, forwarded by Costigan to Joshua Bernhardt, June 15, 1935, box 48, folder 14, EPC Papers.

56. Elizabeth S. Johnson, *Welfare of Families of Sugar-Beet Laborers*, 83.

57. "Cárdenas En La Cd. De Oaxaca Recibe Gran Número de Quejas Los Maestros," *La Prensa*, March 18, 1937, 1.

58. "Mexico Seizes Sugar Mill as Blow to Calles' Family," *Los Angeles Times*, February 19, 1939, 16; "Mexico Expropriates Sugar Property," *Wall Street Journal*, February 21, 1939, 2; "El Mante Sugar," *Wall Street Journal*, March 25, 1939, 10; "Mexican Sugar Mill," *Wall Street Journal*, March 4, 1938, 10; "Mexican Sugar Central," *Wall Street Journal*, January 17, 1938, 10; "Cardenas Called Truly Popular by Visiting Mexican Legislator," *Washington Post*, May 7, 1937, 10; Josephus Daniels to Ramón Beteta, 1940, "La Embajada Americana pide protección para los ciudadanos americanos," III-426-6, SRE.

59. Vicente Lombardo Toledano, "El veinte de Noviembre," *Futuro*, December 20, 1937, 4.

60. Servín, "Estudio económico fiscal de la industria del azúcar," 4.

61. On the discourse of degeneration in Mexico, see Campos, "Degeneration."

62. Frank Goodwyn, "Versos populares de los tejanos de habla española," *Anuario de la sociedad folklorica* (Mexico) 5 (1944): 415–33, reprinted in Herrera-Sobek, *Northward Bound*, 152–55. For a slightly different interpretation, see Schmidt Camacho, *Migrant Imaginaries*, 106–8.

63. Maria Enriqueta, "Para los niños: Pastillas de chocolate," *La Prensa*, January 31, 1931, 7, reprinted February 19, 1933, 18. This short story, intended for children, warns of taking things—figured here as irresistible sweets—that belong to others. The lesson is communicated via a female teacher to a Mexican boy, as in "La restrinción."

64. William Brady, "What's Wrong with Your Metabolism?," *Los Angeles Times*, July 10, 1939.

65. Brady, "Watch Too, Refined Sugar, Starch, Flour," *Atlanta Constitution*, June 13, 1939.

66. Brady, "The Atavist," *Los Angeles Times*, October 25, 1937.

67. Brady, "Speaking of Primitive Savages," *Los Angeles Times*, January 9, 1942.

68. This is not to say that sugar did not have its detractors earlier, which it did. See, for example, Tompkins, *Racial Indigestion*; and Levenstein, *Revolution at the Table*.

69. William Brady, "Teeth, Youth, and Beauty," *Los Angeles Times*, June 12, 1937; "Diet and Degeneration," *Atlanta Constitution*, May 24, 1937; "Deformed Race Being Produced by Modern Food," *Washington Post*, April 9, 1937; "Only 25% in U.S. Get Dental Care," *NYT*, May 14, 1936. Note that Price currently has a renewed following among food faddists.

70. Weston A. Price, "Resolved: 'That a Clean Tooth Does Not Decay and That Mouth Cleanliness Affords the Best Known Protection against Dental Caries.' Negative," *Dental Cosmos* 76, no. 8 (August 1934): 871.

71. Price, *Nutrition and Physical Degeneration*, 353.

72. Ibid., 263.

73. Raymond A. Bruner, "Dentist-Explorer Hunts the Health Secrets of Primitives," *Washington Post*, June 2, 1935, B5.

74. Price, *Nutrition and Physical Degeneration*, 127.

75. "Malnutrition Is Bad as Axis," *Atlanta Constitution*, November 18, 1942.

76. Price, *Nutrition and Physical Degeneration*, 285.

77. "A Dentist Writes of Diet and Death," *Pittsburgh Courier*, July 29, 1939, 11.

78. Martha R. Jones, "Our Changing Concept of an 'Adequate' Diet in Relation to Dental Disease," pt. II, *Dental Cosmos* 77, no. 7 (July 1935): 657. For reports on her initial studies, see Jones et al., "Dental Disease in Hawaii," pts. I, II, and III, *Dental Cosmos* 72, nos. 5, 6, and 7 (1930). On Japanese and Filipino candy consumption, see Imai, *Creating the Nisei Market*, 88, 111.

79. Martha Jones et al., "Taro and Sweet Potatoes versus Grain Foods in Relation to Health and Dental Decay in Hawaii," *Dental Cosmos* 76, no. 4 (April 1934): 397.

80. Martha Jones et al., "Report of Dietary Observations Carried on at Ewa Plantation, Territory of Hawaii, 1932–1933," H.S.P.A. Health Research Project, Bulletin no. 1.

81. Jones et al., "Taro and Sweet Potatoes," 400.

82. Rexford Tugwell to John Dalton, n.d. [1935], box 2247, RG 16, NARA-II.

83. Price responded to Jones by pointing out that the nutrients in molasses and syrups were more "safely" obtained from other foods. See Weston A. Price, "Acid-Base Balance of Diets Which Produce Immunity to Dental Caries among the South Sea Islanders and Other Primitive Races," *Dental Cosmos* 77, no. 9 (September 1935): 845–46.

84. Martha R. Jones, "Our Changing Concept of an 'Adequate' Diet in Relation to Dental Disease," pt. II, *Dental Cosmos*, 77, no. 7 (July 1935): 658. She mentions Filipino children chewing cane, in Jones et al., "Taro and Sweet Potatoes," 403.

85. Jones, "Our Changing Concept," pt. I, *Dental Cosmos* 77, no. 6 (June 1935): 549.

86. Martha R. Jones, "Sugar Sirup," applied for February 11, 1936, issued May 7, 1940, U.S. Patent #2199522.

87. Gilman, "Obesity, the Jews, and Psychoanalysis," 65.

88. Hilde Bruch, "Obesity in Childhood; V: The Family Frame of Obese Children," *Psychosomatic Medicine* 11, no. 2 (April 1940): 12–14, 17, 40, 43, 57, 62–64.

89. Ernest Gruening to Secretary of Interior, March 24, 1937, box 618, RG 126, NARA-II.

90. 54 Stat. 1178 (1940) and 55 Stat. 872 (1941).

EPILOGUE

1. Vasquez, "A Better Place to Live"; Gordon, "Dorothea Lange."

2. On the concept of "citizen consumer," see Cohen, *A Consumers' Republic.*

3. Dennis Chavez (D-New Mexico) and Millard Tydings (D-Maryland), *Economic and Social Conditions in Puerto Rico, Report of the Committee on Territories and Insular Affairs,* 78th Cong., 1st Sess., 24–25, 30, 38–39, 51; Ayala and Bernabe, *Puerto Rico in the American Century;* Valdés, *Al Norte,* 118–33. See also my forthcoming article, "Sweetness, Power, and Working Class Food Histories in America's Empire."

4. Ayala and Bernabe, *Puerto Rico in the American Century;* Valdés, *Al Norte,* 118–33.

5. Ngai, *Impossible Subjects,* 137–38.

6. Daniels, *Prisoners without Trial;* Okihiro, *Cane Fires.*

7. I am grateful to Alexis McCrossen for sharing her insights on this visual rhetoric in Lee's work at the 2009 Migration, Border, and the Nation-State conference at Texas Tech. See McCrossen et al., *Land of Necessity.*

8. Cohen, *Making a New Deal;* Jacobs, *Pocketbook Politics.*

9. John Dalton, Draft Speech, n.d. [1935], box 2246, RG 16, NARA-II.

10. Borgwardt, *A New Deal for the World.*

BIBLIOGRAPHY

MANUSCRIPT COLLECTIONS

Berkeley, Calif.
    Bancroft Library, University of California
        Paul Schuster Taylor Papers
Boulder, Colo.
    Western Historical Collections, Norlin Library, University of Colorado
        Edward P. Costigan Papers
College Park, Md., and New York, N.Y.
    National Archives and Records Administration
        Bureau of Insular Affairs General Records, Record Group 350
        Central Files of the Secretary of Agriculture, Record Group 16
        Puerto Rico Reconstruction Administration, Record Group 323
        Records of the Bureau of Foreign and Domestic Commerce, Record
            Group 151
        Records of the Children's Bureau, Record Group 102
        Records of the Foreign Agricultural Service, Record Group 166
        Records of the Office of Territories, Record Group 126
        Records of the U.S. Food Administration, Record Group 4
        Records of the U.S. Sugar Equalization Board, Inc., Record Group 6
        Records of the U.S. Tariff Commission, Record Group 81
Mexico City, Mexico
    Archivo Histórico del Agua, México, D.F.
    Dirección General del Acervo Histórico Diplomático, Secretaría de Relaciones
        Exteriores, México, D.F.
New Haven, Conn.
    Manuscripts and Archives, Sterling Memorial Library, Yale University
        Francis G. Newlands Papers
        Ulrich B. Phillips Papers
        Henry Lewis Stimson Papers
Notre Dame, Ind.
    University of Notre Dame Archives
        Thomas F. Mahoney Collection
Washington, D.C.
    Manuscript Division of the Library of Congress
        National Child Labor Committee Papers

ONLINE COLLECTIONS

Ancestry.com Library Edition Online Database
  Border Crossings: From Mexico to U.S., 1903–1957
  California Passenger and Crew Lists, 1893–1957
  Honolulu, Hawaii, Passenger Lists, 1900–1953
  New York Passenger Lists, 1820–1957
  U.S. Bureau of the Census. Thirteenth Census of the United States, 1910.
  U.S. Bureau of the Census. Fourteenth Census of the United States, 1920.
  U.S. Bureau of the Census. Fifteenth Census of the United States, 1930.
  U.S. Bureau of the Census. Sixteenth Census of the United States, 1940.

MICROFILM

The American Civil Liberties Union Archives. Princeton University. Microfilm edition.
Black Workers in the Era of the Great Migration, 1916–1925. University Publications of
  America, 1985. Microfilm edition.
Files of the Communist Party of the USA in the Comintern Archives (Moscow, Russia),
  IDC Publishers, 1999–2000. Microfilm edition.
Papers of Calvin Coolidge. Manuscript Division, Library of Congress, Washington,
  D.C. Microfilm edition.

NEWSPAPERS AND MAGAZINES

Actividad, El monitor del Comercio y de la Industria (Monterrey, Nuevo León, México)
American Child
American Citizen (Kansas City, Kans.)
Annals of the American Academy of Political and Social Science
Bulletin of the American Bureau of Geography
Chicago Daily Tribune
Child Labor Bulletin
Christian Science Monitor
Colorado Springs Gazette
Colored American
Daily Courier (Waterloo, Iowa)
Daily Telegraph (Macon, Ga.)
El Amigo Del Hogar (Indiana Harbor, Ind.)
El Cosmopolita (Kansas City, Mo.)
El Demócrata Fronterizo (Laredo, Tex.)
El Heraldo De México (Los Angeles, Calif.)
El Imparcial de Texas (San Antonio, Tex.)
El Machete (México, D.F.)
El Mundo (San Juan, Puerto Rico)
El Tucsonense (Tucson, Ariz.)
Evolución (Laredo, Tex.)

Facts about Sugar
Freeman (Indianapolis, Ind.)
Futuro (Universidad Obrera de México)
Good Housekeeping
Greeley Tribune (Colorado)
Harper's New Monthly Magazine
Harper's Weekly
Irrigation Age
La Prensa (San Antonio, Tex.)
Literary Digest
Los Angeles Times
Louisiana Planter and Sugar Manufacturer
Medical Record
Military Surgeon
Nation
New York Amsterdam News
New York Tribune
North American Review
Oakland Tribune (California)
Olympia Record (Washington)
Oregonian (Portland)
Outlook
Plaindealer (Topeka, Kans.)
Pueblo Chieftain (Colorado)
Quarterly Journal of Economics
Review of Reviews
Revista de Hacienda
Revista Mexicana de Sociología
Rising Son (Kansas City, Mo.)
San Francisco Chronicle
Telegram (Salt Lake City, Utah)
Wall Street Journal
Washington Bee
Washington Post
Weekly Statistical Sugar Trade Journal
Western Confectioner
Wisconsin Weekly Advocate
Yale Law Journal

GOVERNMENT DOCUMENTS

Congressional Record
Congressional Serial Set
Foreign Relations of the United States
Interstate Commerce Commission Reports

Treasury Decisions under Customs and Other Laws

U.S. Department of Agriculture, *Bulletin, Farmers' Bulletin,* and *Yearbook of Agriculture*

U.S. Department of Commerce, Bureau of Foreign and Domestic Commerce, *Commerce Reports*

U.S. Department of Labor, Children's Bureau, Bureau Publications

U.S. Department of Labor, Women's Bureau, *Bulletin of the Women's Bureau*

U.S. Statutes at Large

U.S. Tariff Commission, Tariff Information Series

PUBLISHED PRIMARY SOURCES

Agricultural Adjustment Administration. *The Hearings, Marketing Agreements, Codes, Licenses, and Processing Tax Matters of the Agricultural Adjustment Administration, 1931–1933.* Microfilm edition.

Arce, Miguel. *Sólo Tu: Una Novela.* San Antonio, Tex.: Editorial Lozano, 1928.

Aryan, Junius. *The Aryans and Mongrelized America: The Remedy.* Philadelphia: Eagle House, 1913.

Beals, Carleton. *The Crime of Cuba.* New York: J. B. Lippincott, 1933.

Bernhardt, Joshua. "Government Control of Sugar during the War." *Quarterly Journal of Economics* 33, no. 4 (August 1919): 672–713.

———. *The Sugar Industry and the Federal Government: A Thirty Year Record, 1917–1947.* Washington, D.C.: Sugar Statistics Service, 1947.

———. *The Tariff Commission: Its History, Activities, and Organization.* New York: D. Appleton, 1922.

Bothwell, Reece B., ed. *Puerto Rico, Cien Años De Lucha Política.* Río Piedras: Editorial Universitaria, Universidad de Puerto Rico, 1979.

Brown, Sara A. *Children Working in the Sugar Beet Fields of Certain Districts of the South Platte Valley, Colorado.* New York: National Child Labor Committee, 1925.

Bulosan, Carlos. *America Is in the Heart: A Personal History.* 1943. Seattle: University of Washington Press, 1974.

Carroll, Henry K. *Report on the Island of Porto Rico: Its Population, Civil Government, Commerce, Industries, Productions, Roads, Tariff, and Currency, with Recommendations.* Washington, D.C.: Government Printing Office, 1900.

Chase, Stuart. *Mexico: A Study of Two Americas.* New York: Macmillan, 1935.

Coen, B. F., W. E. Skinner, and D. Leach. *Children Working on Farms in Certain Sections of Northern Colorado Including Districts in the Vicinity of Windsor, Wellington, Fort Collins, Loveland, and Longmont.* Bulletin Series 27, No. 2. Fort Collins: Colorado Agricultural and Mechanical College, 1926.

Coman, Katharine. *The History of Contract Labor in the Hawaiian Islands.* Publications of the American Economic Association. New York: Macmillan, 1903.

Conger, Emily Bronson. *An Ohio Woman in the Philippines.* Akron, Ohio: Press of Richard H. Leighton, n.d.

Culbertson, William S. *International Economic Policies: A Survey of the Economics of Diplomacy.* New York: D. Appleton, 1925.

———. *Raw Materials and Foodstuffs in the Commercial Policies of Nations: With a Supplement Giving Papers Presented at the Round Table Conference.* Philadelphia: American Academy of Political and Social Science, 1924.

Dalton, John E. *Sugar: A Case Study of Government Control.* New York: Macmillan, 1937.

Davis, Daniel Webster. *'Weh Down Souf: And Other Poems.* Cleveland: Helman-Taylor Company, n.d.

Du Bois, W. E. B. *The Souls of Black Folk: Essays and Sketches.* Chicago: A. C. McClurg, 1903.

Dunbar, Paul Laurence. *Lyrics of the Hearthside.* New York: Dodd, Mead, 1899.

Dunn, Robert W. *American Foreign Investments.* New York: B. W. Huebsch/Viking Press, 1926.

Edwards, Frank E. *The '98 Campaign of the 6th Massachusetts, U. S. V.* Boston: Little, Brown, 1909.

Ellis, Pearl Idelia. *Americanization through Homemaking.* Los Angeles: Wetzel Publishing, 1929.

Emerson, Guy. *The New Frontier: A Study of the American Liberal Spirit, Its Frontier Origin, and Its Application to Modern Problems.* New York: H. Holt, 1920.

Fee, Mary Helen. *A Woman's Impressions of the Philippines.* Chicago: A. C. McClurg, 1910.

Fuller, Maud, and Miska Petersham. *The Story Book of Things We Use.* Chicago: John C. Winston, 1933.

Gamio, Manuel. *The Life Story of the Mexican Immigrant.* 1931. New York: Dover, 1971.

———. *Mexican Immigration to the United States.* 1930. New York: Arno Press, 1969.

Garfield, James R. "Hawaii's Basic Reasons for Contesting the Costigan-Jones Amendments to the Agricultural Adjustment Act." Address delivered to the Stockholders of Hawaiian Plantations, August 1, 1934, Honolulu, Hawaii.

Gibbons, Charles E., and Howard M. Bell. *Children Working on Farms in Certain Sections of the Western Slope of Colorado.* New York: National Child Labor Committee, 1925.

Green, John P. *Fact Stranger Than Fiction.* Cleveland: Rieal Printing Company, 1920.

Guerra y Sánchez, Ramiro. *Sugar and Society in the Caribbean: An Economic History of Cuban Agriculture.* New Haven: Yale University Press, 1964.

Hall, G. Stanley. *Aspects of Child Life and Education.* New York: D. Appleton, 1921.

Handbook of the Philippine Sugar Industry, Crop of 1926–27. Manila, Philippians: Sugar News Press, 1926.

Harrington, Walter Leo. *A First Book for Non-English-Speaking People.* Boston: Heath, 1904.

Hill, Janet McKenzie. *The Up-to-Date Waitress.* Boston: Little, Brown, 1908.

Hopkins, Pauline E. *Contending Forces: A Romance Illustrative of Negro Life North and South.* New York: Oxford University Press, 1988.

Hughes, Langston. *Not without Laughter.* 1930. New York: Scribner Paperback Fiction, 1995.

Jenks, Albert Ernest. *The Bontoc Igorot.* Manila, Philippines: Bureau of Public Printing, 1905.

Jenks, Leland Hamilton. *Our Cuban Colony*. New York: Vanguard, 1928.

Johnson, James Weldon. *The Book of American Negro Poetry*. New York: Harcourt, Brace, 1922.

Laughlin, J. Laurence, and H. Parker Willis. *Reciprocity*. New York: Baker and Taylor, 1903.

El Machete Ilegal, 1929-1934. Edición Facsimilar. Puebla, Mexico: Instituto de Ciencias Universidad Autónoma de Puebla, 1975.

Mautner, Bertram, and W. Lewis Abbott. *Child Labor in Agriculture and Farm Life in the Arkansas Valley of Colorado*. New York: National Child Labor Committee, 1929.

Murphy, Claudia Quigley. *The History of the Art of Tablesetting*. New York: De Vinne Press, 1921.

Myers, Caroline Clark. *The Language of America: Lessons in Elementary English and Citizenship for Adults*. New York: Newson, 1921.

Oliver, William H. *Roughing It with the Regulars*. New York: W. F. Parr, 1901.

Parloa, Maria. *Home Economics: A Guide to Household Management*. New York: Century, 1898.

The Philippine Islands Sugar Industry: Panama Pacific International Exposition, San Francisco, California. Manila, Philippines: Bureau of Public Printing, 1915.

Roberts, Peter. *Anthracite Coal Communities: A Study of the Demography, the Social, Educational and Moral Life of the Anthracite Regions*. New York: Macmillan, 1904.

Rosengarten, Theodore. *All God's Dangers: The Life of Nate Shaw*. New York: Random House, 1974.

Sangster, Margaret Elizabeth Munson. *Good Manners for All Occasions: A Practical Manual*. New York: Christian Herald, 1904.

Schattschneider, E. E. *Politics, Pressures and the Tariff*. New York: Prentice-Hall, 1935.

Siddall, John William. *Men of Hawaii: Being a Biographical Reference Library*. Honolulu: Honolulu Star-Bulletin, 1917.

Springsteed, Anne Frances. *The Expert Waitress: A Manual for the Pantry and Dining Room*. London: Harper, 1901.

Taft, William Howard. *Civil Government in the Philippines*. New York: Outlook Company, 1902.

Taussig, F. W. *Principles of Economics*. Vol. 1. New York: Macmillan, 1911.

——. "The Tariff Act of 1930." *Quarterly Journal of Economics* 45 (November 1930): 1-21.

——. *The Tariff History of the United States*. 8th ed. New York: G. P. Putnam's, 1931.

Taylor, Paul S. *Mexican Labor in the United States: Valley of the South Platte, Colorado*. University of California Publications in Economics, vol. 6, no. 2. Berkeley: University of California Press, 1929.

Van Dorn, Harold Archer. *Government Owned Corporations*. New York: Alfred Knopf, 1926.

Washington, Booker T. *Working with the Hands*. New York: Doubleday and Page, 1904.

Willcox, O. W. *Can Industry Govern Itself? An Account of Ten Directed Economies*. New York: W. W. Norton, 1936.

Wood, Bertha M. *Foods of the Foreign-Born in Relation to Health.* Boston: Whitcomb and Barrows, 1922.

Woodhull, Alfred Alexander. *Military Hygiene for Officers of the Line.* 4th ed. New York: John Wiley, 1909.

Woodruff, Charles Edward. *Expansion of Races.* New York: Rebman, 1909.

SECONDARY SOURCES

Agnew, Jean-Christophe. "Coming Up for Air: Consumer Culture in Historical Perspective." In *Consumption and the World of Goods,* edited by John Brewer and Roy Porter. New York: Routledge, 1993.

Aguilar, Filomeno V. *Clash of Spirits: The History of Power and Sugar Planter Hegemony on a Visayan Island.* Honolulu: University of Hawai'i Press, 1998.

Alanís, Fernando Saul. *El Primer Programa Bracero y el Gobierno de México, 1917–1918.* San Luis Potosí, Mexico: El Colegio de San Luis, 1999.

Almaguer, Tomás. *Racial Fault Lines: The Historical Origins of White Supremacy in California.* Berkeley: University of California Press, 1994.

Alpers, Benjamin. *Dictators, Democracy, and American Public Culture: Envisioning the Totalitarian Enemy, 1920s–1950s.* Chapel Hill: University of North Carolina Press, 2003.

Alvarez, Robert, Jr. *Mangos, Chiles, and Truckers: The Business of Transnationalism.* Minneapolis: University of Minnesota Press, 2005.

Anderson, Benedict. *Imagined Communities: Reflections on the Origin and Spread of Nationalism.* Rev. ed. New York: Verso, 1991.

Anderson, Warwick. "The Trespass Speaks: White Masculinity and Colonial Breakdown." *American Historical Review* 102, no. 5 (December 1, 1997): 1343–70.

Appadurai, Arjun, ed. *The Social Life of Things: Commodities in Cultural Perspective.* Cambridge: Cambridge University Press, 1986.

Arredondo, Gabriela F. *Mexican Chicago: Race, Identity, and Nation, 1916–1939.* Urbana: University of Illinois Press, 2008.

Arreola, Daniel D. *Tejano South Texas: A Mexican American Cultural Province.* Austin: University of Texas Press, 2002.

Aurrecoaches, Juan Manuel, and Lorena Paz Paredes. "El nuevo despegue de la agroindustria y la crisis de los años veintes." In *De haciendas, cañeros y paraestatales: Cien años de historia de la agroindustria cañero-azucarera en México: 1880–1980,* edited by Armando Bartra et al. Mexico, D.F.: Universidad Nacional Autonoma de México, Escuela Nacional de Estudios Profesionales Acatlan, 1993.

Ayala, César J. *American Sugar Kingdom: The Plantation Economy of the Spanish Caribbean, 1898–1934.* Chapel Hill: University of North Carolina Press, 1999.

Ayala, César J., and Rafael Bernabe. *Puerto Rico in the American Century: A History since 1898.* Chapel Hill: University of North Carolina Press, 2007.

Balderrama, Francisco E., and Raymond Rodríguez. *Decade of Betrayal: Mexican Repatriation in the 1930s.* Rev. ed. Albuquerque: University of New Mexico Press, 2006.

Balibar, Etienne, and Immanuel Maurice Wallerstein. *Race, Nation, Class: Ambiguous Identities*. New York: Verso, 1991.

Barajas, Frank P. "Resistance, Radicalism, and Repression on the Oxnard Plain: The Social Context of the Betabelero Strike of 1933." *Western Historical Quarterly* 35, no. 1 (2004): 29–52.

Bartra, Armando. "La industria cañero-azucarera y la revolución de 1910." In *De haciendas, cañeros y paraestatales: Cien años de historia de la agroindustria cañero-azucarera en México: 1880–1980*, edited by Armando Bartra et al. Mexico, D.F.: Universidad Nacional Autonoma de México, Escuela Nacional de Estudios Profesionales Acatlan, 1993.

Bederman, Gail. *Manliness and Civilization: A Cultural History of Gender and Race in the United States, 1880–1917*. Chicago: University of Chicago Press, 1995.

Bégin, Camille. " 'Partaking of Choice Poultry Cooked a la Southern Style': Taste and Race in the New Deal Sensory Economy." *Radical History Review* 2011, no. 110 (April 1, 2011): 127–53.

Benjamin, Jules R. "The Machadato and Cuban Nationalism, 1928–1932." *Hispanic American Historical Review* 55, no. 1 (February 1976): 66–91.

———. "The New Deal, Cuba, and the Rise of a Global Foreign Economic Policy." *Business History Review* 51, no. 1 (Spring 1977): 57–78.

———. *The United States and Cuba: Hegemony and Dependent Development, 1880–1934*. Pittsburgh: University of Pittsburgh Press, 1977.

Binford, Leigh. "Peasants and Petty Capitalists in Southern Oaxacan Sugar Cane Production and Processing, 1930–1980." *Journal of Latin American Studies* 24, no. 1 (February 1992): 50.

Briggs, Laura. *Reproducing Empire: Race, Sex, Science, and U.S. Imperialism in Puerto Rico*. Berkeley: University of California Press, 2002.

Brown, Vincent. "Eating the Dead: Consumption and Regeneration in the History of Sugar." *Food and Foodways: Explorations in the History and Culture of Human Nourishment* 16, no. 2 (2008): 117–26.

Brownlee, W. Elliot. "Wilson and Financing the Modern State: The Revenue Act of 1916." *Proceedings of the American Philosophical Society* 129, no. 2 (June 1985): 173–210.

Bruegel, Martin. "How the French Learned to Eat Canned Food, 1809–1930s." In *Food Nations: Selling Taste in Consumer Societies*, edited by Warren James Belasco and Philip Scranton. New York: Routledge, 2002.

Burbank, Jane, and Frederick Cooper. *Empires in World History: Power and the Politics of Difference*. Princeton: Princeton University Press, 2010.

Calleja Pinedo, Margarita. "Los empresarios en el comercio de frutas y hortalizas frescas de México a Estados Unidos." In *Empresarios migrantes Mexicanos en Estados Unidos*, edited by María Basilia Valenzuela Varela and Margarita Calleja Pinedo. Mexico, D.F.: Centro Universitario de Ciencias Económico Administrativas, Universidad de Guadalajara, 2009.

Campbell, Robert B. "Newlands, Old Lands: Native American Labor, Agrarian Ideology, and the Progressive-Era State in the Making of the Newlands Reclamation Project, 1902–1926." *Pacific Historical Review* 71, no. 2 (2002): 203–38.

Campos, Isaac. "Degeneration and the Origins of Mexico's War on Drugs." *Mexican Studies/Estudios Mexicanos* 26, no. 2 (August 2010): 379–408.

———. *Home Grown: Marijuana and the Origins of Mexico's War on Drugs.* Chapel Hill: University of North Carolina Press, 2013.

Carby, Hazel. "The Sexual Politics of Women's Blues." In *Cultures in Babylon: Black Britain and African America.* London: Verso, 1999.

Carr, Barry. "Identity, Class, and Nation: Black Immigrant Workers, Cuban Communism, and the Sugar Insurgency, 1925–1934." *Hispanic American Historical Review* 78, no. 1 (February 1998): 83–116.

Chan, Sucheng. *This Bittersweet Soil: The Chinese in California Agriculture, 1860–1910.* Berkeley: University of California Press, 1989.

Chang, Kornel S. *Pacific Connections: The Making of the U.S.-Canadian Borderlands.* Berkeley: University of California Press, 2012.

Cheng, Lucie, and Edna Bonacich, eds. *Labor Immigration under Capitalism: Asian Workers in the United States before World War II.* Berkeley: University of California Press, 1984.

Cinotto, Simone. *Soft Soil, Black Grapes: The Birth of Italian Winemaking in California.* New York: New York University Press, 2012.

Cohen, Lizabeth. *A Consumers' Republic: The Politics of Mass Consumption in Postwar America.* New York: Random House, 2003.

———. *Making a New Deal: Industrial Workers in Chicago, 1919–1939.* New York: Cambridge University Press, 1990.

Colby, Jason M. *Business of Empire: United Fruit, Race, and U.S. Expansion in Central America.* Ithaca: Cornell University Press, 2013.

———. "Race, Empire, and New England Capital in the Caribbean." *Massachusetts Historical Review* (September 2009): 1–25.

Connolly, Michael J. *Church Lands and Peasant Unrest in the Philippines: Agrarian Conflict in 20th-Century Luzon.* Manila, Philippines: Ateneo de Manila University Press, 1992.

Cook, Daniel T. *The Commodification of Childhood: The Children's Clothing Industry and the Rise of the Child Consumer.* Durham, N.C.: Duke University Press, 2004.

Costin, Lela B. *Two Sisters for Social Justice: A Biography of Grace and Edith Abbott.* Urbana: University of Illinois Press, 1983.

Crespo, Horacio. *Historia del azúcar en México.* Mexico, D.F.: Fondo de Cultura Económica, 1988.

Cronon, William. *Nature's Metropolis: Chicago and the Great West.* New York: W. W. Norton, 1992.

Cullather, Nick. *The Hungry World: America's Cold War Battle against Poverty in Asia.* Cambridge: Harvard University Press, 2010.

Daniels, Roger. *The Politics of Prejudice: The Anti-Japanese Movement in California and the Struggle for Japanese Exclusion.* Berkeley: University of California Press, 1962.

———. *Prisoners without Trial: Japanese Americans in World War II.* New York: Hill and Wang, 2004.

Davis, Angela Y. *Blues Legacies and Black Feminism: Gertrude "Ma" Rainey, Bessie Smith, and Billie Holiday.* New York: Vintage, 1999.

De Grazia, Victoria. *Irresistible Empire: America's Advance through Twentieth-Century Europe.* Cambridge: Harvard University Press, 2005.

Derby, Lauren, "Gringo Chickens with Worms: Food and Nationalism in the Dominican Republic." In *Close Encounters of Empire: Writing the History of U.S.-Latin American Relations,* edited by Gilbert M. Joseph et al. Durham, N.C.: Duke University Press, 1998.

Deutsch, Sarah. *No Separate Refuge: Culture, Class, and Gender on an Anglo-Hispanic Frontier, 1880–1940.* New York: Oxford University Press, 1987.

Diner, Hasia R. *Hungering for America: Italian, Irish, and Jewish Foodways in the Age of Migration.* Cambridge: Harvard University Press, 2003.

Domosh, Mona. *American Commodities in an Age of Empire.* New York: Routledge, 2006.

Donato, Rubén. *Mexicans and Hispanos in Colorado Schools and Communities, 1920–1960.* Albany: State University of New York Press, 2007.

Duany, Jorge. *The Puerto Rican Nation on the Move: Identities on the Island and in the United States.* Chapel Hill: University of North Carolina Press, 2002.

Duffy-Burnett, Christina, and Burke Marshall, eds. *Foreign in a Domestic Sense: Puerto Rico, American Expansion, and the Constitution.* Durham, N.C.: Duke University Press, 2001.

Dur, Philip, and Christopher Gilcrease. "U.S. Diplomacy and the Downfall of a Cuban Dictator: Machado in 1933." *Journal of Latin American Studies* 34 (2002): 255–82.

Dusselier, Jane. "Bon-Bons, Lemon Drops, and Oh! Henry Bars: Candy, Consumer Culture, and the Construction of Gender, 1895–1920." In *Kitchen Culture in America: Popular Representations of Food, Gender, and Race,* edited by Sherrie A. Inness. Philadelphia: University of Pennsylvania Press, 2001.

Eikelberner, George. *More American Glass Candy Containers.* S. Agadjanian, 1970.

Einhorn, Robin L. *American Taxation, American Slavery.* Chicago: University of Chicago Press, 2006.

Elam, Michele. "Dunbar's Children." *African American Review* 41, no. 2 (2007): 259–67.

Espinosa, Gisela D. "El desarrollo de la industria cañero-azucarera durante el Porfiriato." In *De haciendas, cañeros y paraestatales: Cien años de historia de la agroindustria cañero-azucarera en México, 1880–1980,* edited by Armando Bartra et al. Mexico, D.F.: Universidad Nacional Autonoma de México, Escuela Nacional de Estudios Profesionales Acatlan, 1993.

Ferguson, Priscilla Parkhurst. "The Senses of Taste." *American Historical Review* 116, no. 2 (April 2011): 371–84.

Fischer, Edward F., and Peter Benson. *Broccoli and Desire: Global Connections and Maya Struggles in Postwar Guatemala.* Stanford, Calif.: Stanford University Press, 2006.

Fitzgerald, Deborah. *Every Farm a Factory: The Industrial Ideal in American Agriculture.* New Haven: Yale University Press, 2003.

Fitzgerald, Gerard J., and Gabriella M. Petrick. "In Good Taste: Rethinking American History with Our Palates." *Journal of American History* 95, no. 2 (2008): 392–404.

Foley, Neil. *The White Scourge: Mexicans, Blacks, and Poor Whites in Texas Cotton Culture.* Berkeley: University of California Press, 1997.

Follett, Richard. *The Sugar Masters: Planters and Slaves in Louisiana's Cane World, 1820–1860.* Baton Rouge: Louisiana State University Press, 2005.

Fradera, Josep M. "Reading Imperial Transitions: Spanish Contraction, British Expansion, and American Irruption." In *Colonial Crucible: Empire in the Making of the Modern American State,* edited by Alfred W. McCoy and Francisco Scarano. Madison: University of Wisconsin Press, 2009.

Frank, Dana. *Buy American: The Untold Story of Economic Nationalism.* Boston: Beacon Press, 2000.

———. "Housewives, Socialists, and the Politics of Food: The 1917 New York Cost-of-Living Protests." *Feminist Studies* 11, no. 2 (Summer 1985): 255–85.

Friend, Theodore. "The Philippine Sugar Industry and the Politics of Independence, 1929–1935." *Journal of Asian Studies* 22, no. 2 (February 1963): 179–92.

Fuchs, Lawrence. *Hawaii Pono: A Social History.* New York: Harcourt, Brace and World, 1961.

Gabaccia, Donna R. *Foreign Relations: American Immigration in Global Perspective.* Princeton: Princeton University Press, 2012.

———. *We Are What We Eat: Ethnic Food and the Making of Americans.* Cambridge: Harvard University Press, 2000.

García Colón, Ismael. *Land Reform in Puerto Rico: Modernizing the Colonial State, 1941–1969.* Gainesville: University Press of Florida, 2009.

Gattell, Frank Otto. "Independence Rejected: Puerto Rico and the Tydings Bill of 1936." *Hispanic American Historical Review* 38, no. 1 (1958): 25–44.

Gilman, Sander. "Obesity, the Jews, and Psychoanalysis: On Shaping the Category of Obesity." *History of Psychiatry* 17, no. 1 (2006): 55–66.

Gilmore, Glenda Elizabeth. *Defying Dixie: The Radical Roots of Civil Rights.* New York: W. W. Norton, 2008.

———. *Gender and Jim Crow: Women and the Politics of White Supremacy in North Carolina, 1896–1920.* Chapel Hill: University of North Carolina Press, 1996.

Giusti-Cordero, Juan A. "Compradors or Compadres? 'Sugar Barons' in Negros (the Philippines) and Puerto Rico under American Rule." In *Sugarlandia Revisited: Sugar and Colonialism in Asia and the Americas, 1800 to 1940,* edited by Ulbe Bosma, G. Roger Knight, and Juan Giusti-Cordero. New York: Berghahn Books, 2007.

———. "Labour, Ecology, and History in a Puerto Rican Plantation Region: 'Classic' Rural Proletarians Revisited." *International Review of Social History* 41 (1996): 53–82.

Glick, Clarence E. *Sojourners and Settlers: Chinese Migrants in Hawaii.* Honolulu: University of Hawai'i Press, 1980.

Go, Julian. *American Empire and the Politics of Meaning: Elite Political Cultures in the Philippines and Puerto Rico during U.S. Colonialism.* Durham, N.C.: Duke University Press, 2008.

———. "Chains of Empire, Projects of State: Colonial State-Building in Puerto Rico and the Philippines." In *The American Colonial State in the Philippines: Global Perspectives,* edited by Julian Go and Anne L. Foster. Durham, N.C.: Duke University Press, 2003.

Gómez, Laura. *Manifest Destinies: The Making of the Mexican American Race*. New York: New York University Press, 2008.

Gomez Carpinteiro, Francisco Javier. *Gente de azúcar y agua: Modernidad y posrevolucion en el suroeste de Puebla*. Zamora, Mexico: El Colegio de Michoacan, 2003.

Gonzales, Jovita. *Life along the Border: A Landmark Tejana Thesis*. Edited and with an introduction by María Eugenia Cotera. College Station: Texas A&M Press, 2006.

Gonzalez, Gilbert G. *Mexican Consuls and Labor Organizing: Imperial Politics in the American Southwest*. Austin: University of Texas Press, 1999.

Goodykoontz, Colin B. "Edward P. Costigan and the Tariff Commission, 1917–1928." *Pacific Historical Review* 16, no. 4 (November 1947): 410–19.

Gootenberg, Paul. *Andean Cocaine: The Making of a Global Drug*. Chapel Hill: University of North Carolina Press, 2008.

Gordon, Linda. "Dorothea Lange: The Photographer as Agricultural Sociologist." *Journal of American History* 93, no. 3 (December 2006): 698–727.

Greenbaum, Fred. *Fighting Progressive: A Biography of Edward Costigan*. Washington, D.C.: Public Affairs Press, 1971.

Greene, Julie. *The Canal Builders: Making America's Empire at the Panama Canal*. New York: Penguin Books, 2009.

Gregory, James N. *The Southern Diaspora: How the Great Migrations of Black and White Southerners Transformed America*. Chapel Hill: University of North Carolina Press, 2005.

Grier, Katherine C. *Culture and Comfort: Parlor Making and Middle-Class Identity, 1850–1930*. Washington, D.C.: Smithsonian Institution Press, 1988.

Griffin, Farrah Jasmine. *"Who Set You Flowin'?" The African-American Migration Narrative*. New York: Oxford University Press, 1995.

Guthman, Julie. *Weighing In: Obesity, Food Justice, and the Limits of Capitalism*. Berkeley: University of California Press, 2011.

———. *Agrarian Dreams: The Paradox of Organic Farming in California*. Berkeley: University of California Press, 2004.

Gutiérrez, David. *Walls and Mirrors: Mexican Americans, Mexican Immigrants, and the Politics of Ethnicity*. Berkeley: University of California Press, 1995.

Gyory, Andrew. *Closing the Gate: Race, Politics, and the Chinese Exclusion Act*. Chapel Hill: University of North Carolina Press, 1998.

Haggard, Stephen. "The Institutional Foundations of Hegemony: Explaining the Reciprocal Trade Agreements Act of 1934." *International Organization* 42, no. 1 (Winter 1988): 91–119.

Hahamovitch, Cindy. *The Fruits of Their Labor: Atlantic Coast Farmworkers and the Making of Migrant Poverty, 1870–1945*. Chapel Hill: University of North Carolina Press, 1997.

Hall, Jacquelyn Dowd, et al. *Like a Family: The Making of a Southern Cotton Mill World*. Chapel Hill: University of North Carolina Press, 2000.

Hart, John Mason. *Empire and Revolution: The Americans in Mexico since the Civil War*. Berkeley: University of California Press, 2002.

Hart, Paul. *Bitter Harvest: The Social Transformation of Morelos, Mexico, and the Origins of the Zapatista Revolution, 1840–1910*. Albuquerque: University of New Mexico Press, 2007.

Harvey, David. "The Spatial Fix: Hegel, Von Thunen, and Marx." In *Spaces of Capital: Towards a Critical Geography*. New York: Routledge, 2001.

Heath, Elizabeth. "Creating Rural Citizens in Guadeloupe in the Early Third French Republic." *Slavery and Abolition* 32, no. 2 (2011): 289–307.

———. *Wine, Sugar, and the Making of Modern France: Global Economic Crisis and the Racialization of French Citizenship*. Cambridge: Cambridge University Press, 2014.

Hedrick, Tace. *Mestizo Modernism: Race, Nation, and Identity in Latin American Culture, 1900–1940*. New Brunswick: Rutgers University Press, 2003.

Heitmann, John Alfred. *The Modernization of the Louisiana Sugar Industry, 1830–1910*. Baton Rouge: Louisiana State University Press, 1987.

Herrera-Sobek, Maria. *Northward Bound: The Mexican Immigrant Experience in Ballad and Song*. Bloomington: Indiana University Press, 1993.

Higham, John. *Strangers in the Land: Patterns of American Nativism, 1860–1925*. New Brunswick: Rutgers University Press, 1994.

Hoganson, Kristin L. *Consumers' Imperium: The Global Production of American Domesticity, 1865–1920*. Chapel Hill: University of North Carolina Press, 2007.

Hollander, Gail M. *Raising Cane in the 'Glades: The Global Sugar Trade and the Transformation of Florida*. Chicago: University of Chicago Press, 2008.

Hunter, Tera W. *To 'Joy My Freedom: Southern Black Women's Lives and Labors after the Civil War*. Cambridge: Harvard University Press, 1997.

Imai, Shiho. *Creating the Nisei Market: Race and Citizenship in Hawai'i's Japanese American Consumer Culture*. Honolulu: University of Hawai'i Press, 2010.

Jacobs, Meg. *Pocketbook Politics: Economic Citizenship in Twentieth-Century America*. Princeton: Princeton University Press, 2005.

———. "New Deal Politics and the Construction of a 'Consuming Public.'" *International Labor and Working-Class History* 55 (April 1999): 27–51.

Jacobson, Matthew Frye. *Barbarian Virtues: The United States Encounters Foreign Peoples at Home and Abroad, 1876–1917*. New York: Hill and Wang, 2001.

———. *Special Sorrows: The Diasporic Imagination of Irish, Polish, and Jewish Immigrants in the United States*. Cambridge: Harvard University Press, 1995.

James, Winston. "Becoming the People's Poet: Claude McKay's Jamaican Years, 1889–1912." *Small Axe* 13 (March 2003): 17–45.

Jamieson, Stuart. *Labor Unionism in American Agriculture*. U.S. Department of Labor, Bureau of Labor Statistics, Bulletin No. 836. Washington, D.C.: Government Printing Office, 1945.

Johnson, Benjamin. *Revolution in Texas: How a Forgotten Rebellion and Its Bloody Suppression Turned Mexicans into Americans*. New Haven: Yale University Press, 2003.

Jung, Moon-Ho. *Coolies and Cane: Race, Labor, and Sugar in the Age of Emancipation*. Baltimore: Johns Hopkins University Press, 2006.

Jung, Moon-Kie. *Reworking Race: The Making of Hawaii's Interracial Labor Movement*. New York: Columbia University Press, 2010.

Kantrowitz, Stephen. *Ben Tillman and the Reconstruction of White Supremacy.* Chapel Hill: University of North Carolina Press, 2000.

Kasson, John F. *Rudeness and Civility: Manners in Nineteenth-Century Urban America.* New York: Hill and Wang, 1990.

Kennedy, David. *Freedom from Fear: The American People in Depression and War, 1929–1945.* New York: Oxford University Press, 2001.

———. *Over Here: The First World War and American Society.* New York: Oxford University Press, 2004.

Kessler-Harris, Alice. *Out to Work: A History of Wage-Earning Women in the United States.* Oxford: Oxford University Press, 1983.

Klein, Christina. *Cold War Orientalism: Asia in the Middlebrow Imagination, 1945–1961.* Berkeley: University of California Press, 2003.

Knight, Alan. *Counter-revolution and Reconstruction.* Vol. 2 of *The Mexican Revolution.* Lincoln: University of Nebraska Press, 1990.

———. "Racism, Revolution, and *Indigenismo*: Mexico, 1910–1940." In *The Idea of Race in Latin America, 1870–1940,* edited by Richard Graham. Austin: University of Texas Press, 1990.

Knight, G. Roger. *Commodities and Colonialism: The Story of Big Sugar in Indonesia, 1880–1942.* Leiden: Brill, 2013.

———. *Narratives of Colonialism: Sugar, Java, and the Dutch.* Huntington, N.Y.: Nova Science Publications, 2000.

Kramer, Paul. *The Blood of Government: Race, Empire, the United States, and the Philippines.* Chapel Hill: University of North Carolina Press, 2006.

———. "Power and Connection: Imperial Histories of the United States in the World." *American Historical Review* 116, no. 5 (2011): 1348–91.

Kushner, Barak. "Sweetness and Empire: Sugar Consumption in Imperial Japan." In *The Historical Consumer: Consumption and Everyday Life in Japan, 1850–2000,* edited by Janet Hunter and Penelope Francks. London: Palgrave Macmillan, 2011.

Larkin, John A. *Sugar and the Origins of Modern Philippine Society.* Berkeley: University of California Press, 1993.

Leach, William R. *Land of Desire: Merchants, Power, and the Rise of a New American Culture.* New York: Vintage, 1994.

Lee, Erika. *At America's Gates: Chinese Immigration during the Exclusion Era, 1882–1943.* Chapel Hill: University of North Carolina Press, 2003.

Levenstein, Harvey. *Paradox of Plenty: A Social History of Eating in Modern America.* Rev. ed. Berkeley: University of California Press, 2003.

———. *Revolution at the Table: The Transformation of the American Diet.* Berkeley: University of California Press, 2003.

Levine, Susan. *School Lunch Politics: The Surprising History of America's Favorite Welfare Program.* Princeton: Princeton University Press, 2010.

Lewis, Stephen E. "The Nation, Education, and the 'Indian Problem' in Mexico, 1920–1940." In *The Eagle and the Virgin: Nation and Cultural Revolution in Mexico, 1920–1940,* edited by Mary Kay Vaughan and Stephen E. Lewis. Durham, N.C.: Duke University Press, 2006.

Lindenmeyer, Kriste. *"A Right to Childhood": The U.S. Children's Bureau and Child Welfare, 1912–46.* Urbana: University of Illinois Press, 1997.

Lomnitz-Adler, Claudio. *Exits from the Labyrinth: Culture and Ideology in Mexican National Space.* Berkeley: University of California Press, 1992.

Look Lai, Walton. *Indentured Labor, Caribbean Sugar: Chinese and Indian Migrants to the British West Indies, 1838–1918.* Baltimore: Johns Hopkins University Press, 1993.

Lopez-Gonzaga, Violeta B. *The Socio-politics of Sugar: Wealth, Power Formation, and Change in Negros, 1899–1985.* Bacolod City, Philippines: Social Research Center, University of St. La Salle, 1989.

Love, Eric T. L. *Race over Empire: Racism and U.S. Imperialism, 1865–1900.* Chapel Hill: University of North Carolina Press, 2004.

Lowe, Lisa. *Immigrant Acts: On Asian American Cultural Politics.* Durham, N.C.: Duke University Press, 1999.

Lui, Mary Ting Yi. *The Chinatown Trunk Mystery: Murder, Miscegenation, and Other Dangerous Encounters in Turn-of-the-Century New York City.* Princeton: Princeton University Press, 2007.

MacLennan, Carol. *Sovereign Sugar: Industry and Environment in Hawai'i.* Honolulu: University of Hawai'i Press, 2014.

Mapes, Kathleen. *Sweet Tyranny: Migrant Labor, Industrial Agriculture, and Imperial Politics.* Urbana: University of Illinois Press, 2009.

Mathews, Thomas G. *Puerto Rican Politics and the New Deal.* Gainesville: University of Florida Press, 1960.

Mathias, Peter, and Sidney Pollard. *The Industrial Economies: The Development of Economic and Social Policies.* Vol. 8 of *The Cambridge Economic History of Europe.* Cambridge: Cambridge University Press, 1989.

Matsumoto, Valerie J. *Farming the Homeplace: A Japanese American Community in California, 1919–1982.* Ithaca: Cornell University Press, 1993.

May, William S. *The Great Western Sugarlands: The History of the Great Western Sugar Company and the Economic Development of the Great Plains.* New York: Garland, 1989.

McClintock, Anne. *Imperial Leather: Race, Gender, and Sexuality in the Colonial Contest.* New York: Routledge, 1995.

McCook, Stuart. *States of Nature: Science, Agriculture, and Environment in the Spanish Caribbean, 1760–1940.* Austin: University of Texas Press, 2010.

McCoy, Alfred, and Alfredo Roces. *Philippine Cartoons: Political Caricature of the American Era, 1900–1941.* Manila: Vera-Reyes, 1985.

McCoy, Alfred W., and Ed. C. de Jesus, eds. *Philippine Social History: Global Trade and Local Transformations.* Honolulu: University Press of Hawaii, 1982.

McCoy, Alfred W., and Francisco Antonio Scarano, eds. *Colonial Crucible: Empire in the Making of the Modern American State.* Madison: University of Wisconsin Press, 2009.

McCrossen, Alexis, et al., eds. *Land of Necessity: Consumer Culture in the United States–Mexico Borderlands.* Durham, N.C.: Duke University Press, 2009.

McCurdy, Charles W. "The Knight Sugar Decision of 1895 and the Modernization of American Corporation Law, 1869–1903." *Business History Review* 53, no. 03 (September 1979): 304–42.

McGillivray, Gillian. *Blazing Cane: Sugar Communities, Class, and State Formation in Cuba, 1868–1959*. Durham, N.C.: Duke University Press, 2009.

McKee, Delber L. "The Chinese Boycott of 1905–1906 Reconsidered: The Role of Chinese Americans." *Pacific Historical Review* 55, no. 2 (May 1986): 165–91.

McWilliams, Carey. *Factories in the Field: The Story of Migratory Farm Labor in California*. Berkeley: University of California Press, 2000.

Merleaux, April. "The Political Culture of Sugar Tariffs: Immigration, Race, and Empire, 1898–1930." *International Labor and Working-Class History* 81 (2012): 28–48.

Mintz, Sidney W. *Caribbean Transformations*. New York: Columbia University Press, 1989.

———. *Sweetness and Power: The Place of Sugar in Modern History*. New York: Penguin, 1986.

Montejano, David. *Anglos and Mexicans in the Making of Texas, 1836–1986*. Austin: University of Texas Press, 1987.

Mullendore, William Clinton. *History of the United States Food Administration, 1917–1919*. Stanford, Calif.: Stanford University Press, 1941.

Muncy, Robyn. *Creating a Female Dominion in American Reform, 1890–1935*. New York: Oxford University Press, 1991.

Murphy, Gretchen. *Shadowing the White Man's Burden: U.S. Imperialism and the Problem of the Color Line*. New York: New York University Press, 2010.

Ngai, Mae M. *Impossible Subjects: Illegal Aliens and the Making of Modern America*. Princeton: Princeton University Press, 2005.

———. *The Lucky Ones: One Family and the Extraordinary Invention of Chinese America*. Boston: Houghton Mifflin Harcourt, 2010.

Norris, Jim. *North for the Harvest: Mexican Workers, Growers, and the Sugar Beet Industry*. St. Paul: Minnesota Historical Society Press, 2009.

Norton, Marcy. "Tasting Empire: Chocolate and the European Internalization of Mesoamerican Aesthetics." *American Historical Review* 111, no. 3 (June 2006): 660–91.

O'Brien, Colleen C. "'Blacks in All Quarters of the Globe': Anti-Imperialism, Insurgent Cosmopolitanism, and International Labor in Pauline Hopkins's Literary Journalism." *American Quarterly* 61, no. 2 (2009): 245–70.

Okihiro, Gary Y. *Cane Fires: The Anti-Japanese Movement in Hawaii, 1865–1945*. Philadelphia: Temple University Press, 1992.

———. *Island World: A History of Hawai'i and the United States*. Berkeley: University of California Press, 2008.

———. *Margins and Mainstreams: Asians in American History and Culture*. Seattle: University of Washington Press, 1994.

———. *Pineapple Culture: A History of the Tropical and Temperate Zones*. Berkeley: University of California Press, 2010.

Omi, Michael, and Howard Winant. *Racial Formation in the United States: From the 1960s to the 1990s*. New York: Routledge, 1994.

Orenstein, Dara. "Foreign-Trade Zones and the Cultural Logic of Frictionless Production." *Radical History Review* (Winter 2011): 36–61.

Ortiz, Fernando. *Cuban Counterpoint: Tobacco and Sugar*. 1947. Durham, N.C.: Duke University Press, 1995.

Ortíz Cuadra, Cruz Miguel. *Eating Puerto Rico: A History of Food, Culture, and Identity*. Chapel Hill: University of North Carolina Press, 2013.

Paredes, Américo. *A Texas-Mexican Cancionero: Folksongs of the Lower Border*. Urbana: University of Illinois Press, 1976.

Parks, Annette White. *Sui Sin Far/Edith Maude Eaton: A Literary Biography*. Urbana: University of Illinois Press, 1995.

Pegler-Gordon, Anna. *In Sight of America: Photography and the Development of U.S. Immigration Policy*. Berkeley: University of California Press, 2009.

Pérez, Louis A. *Cuba under the Platt Amendment*. Pittsburgh: University of Pittsburgh Press, 1993.

———. *Essays on Cuban History: Historiography and Research*. Gainesville: University of Florida Press, 1995.

———. *Intervention, Revolution, and Politics in Cuba, 1913–1921*. Pittsburgh: University of Pittsburgh Press, 1979.

———. *On Becoming Cuban: Identity, Nationality, and Culture*. New York: HarperCollins, 1999.

———. *Cuba between Empires, 1878–1902*. Pittsburgh: University of Pittsburgh Press, 2007.

Phillips, Sarah T. *This Land, This Nation: Conservation, Rural America, and the New Deal*. New York: Cambridge University Press, 2007.

Pilcher, Jeffrey. *Planet Taco: A Global History of Mexican Food*. New York: Oxford University Press, 2012.

———. *Que vivan los tamales! Food and the Making of Mexican Identity*. Albuquerque: University of New Mexico Press, 1998.

Pitti, Stephen J. *The Devil in Silicon Valley: Northern California, Race, and Mexican Americans*. Princeton: Princeton University Press, 2004.

Pollitt, Brian. "The Cuban Sugar Economy in the 1930s." In *The World Sugar Economy in War and Depression, 1914–1945*, edited by Bill Albert and Adrian Graves. London: Routledge, 1988.

Powers, Richard. *Gain*. New York: Farrar, Straus & Giroux, 1998.

Pratt, Mary Louise. *Imperial Eyes: Travel Writing and Transculturation*. London: Routledge, 2007.

Quirino, Carlos. *History of the Philippine Sugar Industry*. Manila: Kalayaan Publishing, 1974.

Ramos, Efrén Rivera. "Deconstructing Colonialism: The 'Unincorporated Territory' as a Category of Domination." In *Foreign in a Domestic Sense: Puerto Rico, American Expansion, and the Constitution*, edited by Christina Duffy Burnett and Burke Marshall. Durham, N.C.: Duke University Press, 2001.

Reisler, Mark. *By the Sweat of Their Brow: Mexican Immigrant Labor in the United States, 1900–1940*. Westport, Conn.: Greenwood, 1976.

Renda, Mary. *Taking Haiti: Military Occupation and the Culture of U.S. Imperialism, 1915–1940*. Chapel Hill: University of North Carolina Press, 2001.

Rochfort, Desmond. "The Sickle, the Serpent, and the Soil: History, Revolution, Nationhood, and Modernity in the Murals of Diego Rivera, José Clemente Orozco, and David Alfaro Siqueiros." In *The Eagle and the Virgin: Nation and Cultural Revolution in Mexico, 1920-1940*, edited by Mary Kay Vaughan and Stephen E. Lewis. Durham, N.C.: Duke University Press, 2006.

Rodgers, Daniel T. *Atlantic Crossings: Social Politics in a Progressive Age*. Cambridge: Belknap Press of Harvard University Press, 2000.

Roediger, David. *Wages of Whiteness: Race and the Making of the American Working Class*. New York: Verso, 2007.

Rosenberg, Emily. *Financial Missionaries to the World: The Politics and Culture of Dollar Diplomacy, 1900-1930*. Durham, N.C.: Duke University Press, 2003.

Rosenn, Keith S. "Puerto Rican Land Reform: The History of an Instructive Experiment." *Yale Law Journal* 73, no. 2 (December 1963): 334–56.

Rowley, William. *Reclaiming the Arid West: The Career of Francis G. Newlands*. Bloomington: Indiana University Press, 1996.

Ruiz, Vicki L. *Cannery Women, Cannery Lives: Mexican Women, Unionization, and the California Food Processing Industry, 1930-1950*. Albuquerque: University of New Mexico Press, 1987.

Sackman, Douglas Cazaux. *Orange Empire: California and the Fruits of Eden*. Berkeley: University of California Press, 2007.

St. John, Rachel. *Line in the Sand: A History of the Western U.S.-Mexico Border*. Princeton: Princeton University Press, 2011.

Sallee, Shelley. *The Whiteness of Child Labor Reform in the New South*. Athens: University of Georgia Press, 2004.

Salyer, Lucy. *Laws Harsh as Tigers: Chinese Immigrants and the Shaping of Modern Immigration Law*. Chapel Hill: University of North Carolina Press, 1995.

Sánchez, George J. *Becoming Mexican American: Ethnicity, Culture, and Identity in Chicano Los Angeles, 1900-1945*. New York: Oxford University Press, 1993.

Sanders, Elizabeth. *Roots of Reform: Farmers, Workers, and the American State, 1877-1917*. Chicago: University of Chicago Press, 1999.

Saragoza, Alex M. *The Monterrey Elite and the Mexican State, 1880-1940*. Austin: University of Texas Press, 1988.

Schmand, Del. *The Sweet Side of Little Rock: A History of Candy Making in Arkansas*. Atlanta: August House Publishers, 1998.

Schmidt Camacho, Alicia. *Migrant Imaginaries: Latino Cultural Politics in the U.S.-Mexico Borderlands*. New York: New York University Press, 2008.

Schnietz, Karen. "Democrats' 1916 Tariff Commission: Responding to Dumping Fears and Illustrating the Consumer Costs of Protectionism." *Business History Review* 72, no. 1 (Spring 1998): 1–45.

———. "The Institutional Foundation of U.S. Trade Policy: Revisiting Explanations for the 1934 Reciprocal Trade Agreements Act." *Journal of Policy History* 12, no. 4 (2000): 417–44.

Scott, James C. *Seeing Like a State: How Certain Schemes to Improve the Human Condition Have Failed*. New Haven: Yale University Press, 1999.

Sedgewick, Augustine. "'The Spice of the Department Store': The 'Consumers' Republic,' Imported Knock-Offs from Latin America, and the Invention of

International Development, 1936–1941." *International Labor and Working-Class History* 81 (2012): 49–68.

Seigel, Micol. *Uneven Encounters: Making Race and Nation in Brazil and the United States.* Durham, N.C.: Duke University Press, 2009.

Shah, Nayan. *Contagious Divides: Epidemics and Race in San Francisco's Chinatown.* Berkeley: University of California Press, 2001.

Sharpless, Rebecca. *Cooking in Other Women's Kitchens: Domestic Workers in the South, 1865–1960.* Chapel Hill: University of North Carolina Press, 2010.

Shurts, John. *Indian Reserved Water Rights: The Winters Doctrine in Its Social and Legal Context.* Norman: University of Oklahoma Press, 2003.

Silva, Noenoe K. *Aloha Betrayed: Native Hawaiian Resistance to American Colonialism.* Durham, N.C.: Duke University Press, 2004.

Simpson, Eyler. *The Ejido: Mexico's Way Out.* Chapel Hill: University of North Carolina Press, 1937.

Sklar, Martin. *The Corporate Reconstruction of American Capitalism, 1890–1916.* Cambridge: Cambridge University Press, 1988.

Skocpol, Theda. *Protecting Soldiers and Mothers: The Political Origins of Social Policy in the United States.* Cambridge: Belknap Press of Harvard University Press, 1995.

Smith, Mark M. *How Race Is Made: Slavery, Segregation, and the Senses.* Chapel Hill: University of North Carolina Press, 2008.

Smith, Neil. *American Empire: Roosevelt's Geographer and the Prelude to Globalization.* Berkeley: University of California Press, 2003.

Smith, Shawn Michelle. *Photography on the Color Line: W. E. B. Du Bois, Race, and Visual Culture.* Durham, N.C.: Duke University Press, 2004.

Soloman, Mark I. *The Cry Was Unity: Communists and African Americans, 1917–1936.* Jackson: University Press of Mississippi, 1998.

Soluri, John. *Banana Cultures: Agriculture, Consumption, and Environmental Change in Honduras and the United States.* Austin: University of Texas Press, 2006.

Sparrow, Bartholomew H. *The Insular Cases and the Emergence of American Empire.* Lawrence: University Press of Kansas, 2006.

Stallybrass, Peter. "Marx's Coat." In *Border Fetishisms: Material Objects in Unstable Spaces*, edited by Patricia Spyer. New York: Routledge, 1998.

Stanley, Mary Louise. *A Century of Glass Toys: The Sweetest Memories of American Childhood.* Forward's Color Productions, 1976.

Stoll, Steven. *The Fruits of Natural Advantage: Making the Industrial Countryside in California.* Berkeley: University of California Press, 1998.

Streeby, Shelley. *American Sensations: Class, Empire, and the Production of Popular Culture.* Berkeley: University of California Press, 2002.

Striffler, Steve. *Chicken: The Dangerous Transformation of America's Favorite Food.* New Haven: Yale University Press, 2007.

Sutter, Paul S. "The Tropical Conquest and the Rise of the Environmental Management State: The Case of US Sanitary Efforts in Panama." In *Colonial Crucible: Empire in the Making of the Modern American State*, edited by Alfred W. McCoy and Francisco Scarano. Madison: University of Wisconsin Press, 2009.

Taussig, Michael T. *The Devil and Commodity Fetishism in South America*. Chapel Hill: University of North Carolina Press, 1980.

Taylor, Henry C. *The Story of Agricultural Economics in the United States, 1840-1932*. Ames: Iowa State College Press, 1952.

Taylor, Paul S. "National Reclamation in Imperial Valley: Law v. Policy." *Ecology Law Quarterly* 11 (1984): 125-34.

Tinsman, Heidi. *Buying into the Regime: Grapes and Consumption in Cold War Chile and the United States*. Durham, N.C.: Duke University Press, 2014.

Tompkins, Kyla Wazana. *Racial Indigestion: Eating Bodies in the Nineteenth Century*. New York: New York University Press, 2012.

Treviño, Roberto R. "Prensa y Patria: The Spanish-Language Press and the Biculturation of the Tejano Middle Class, 1920-1940." *Western Historical Quarterly* 22, no. 4 (1991): 451-72.

Valdés, Dionicio (Dennis). "Betabeleros: The Formation of an Agricultural Proletariat in the Midwest, 1897-1930." *Labor History* 30 (Fall 1989): 536-62.

——. *Al Norte: Agricultural Workers in the Great Lakes Region, 1917-1970*. Austin: University of Texas Press, 1991.

——. *Organized Agriculture and the Labor Movement before the UFW*. Austin: University of Texas Press, 2011.

——. "Settlers, Sojourners, and Proletarians: Social Formation in the Great Plains Sugar Beet Industry, 1890-1940." *Great Plains Quarterly* 10 (Spring 1990): 110-23.

Vargas, Zaragosa. *Labor Rights Are Civil Rights: Mexican American Workers in Twentieth-Century America*. Princeton: Princeton University Press, 2005.

Vasquez, Oscar E. "'A Better Place to Live': Government Agency Photography and the Transformations of the Puerto Rican Jibaro." In *Colonialist Photography: Imagining Race and Place*, edited by Gary Sampson et al. New York: Routledge, 2002.

Vaughan, Mary Kay. "Nationalizing the Countryside: Schools and Rural Communities in the 1930s." In *The Eagle and the Virgin: Nation and Cultural Revolution in Mexico, 1920-1940*, edited by Mary Kay Vaughan and Stephen E. Lewis. Durham, N.C.: Duke University Press, 2006.

Veit, Helen Zoe. *Modern Food, Moral Food: Self-Control, Science, and the Rise of Modern American Eating in the Early Twentieth Century*. Chapel Hill: University of North Carolina Press, 2013.

Villaronga, Gabriel. *Toward a Discourse of Consent: Mass Mobilization and Colonial Politics in Puerto Rico, 1932-1948*. Westport, Conn.: Greenwood, 2004.

Walsh, Casey. *Building the Borderlands: A Transnational History of Irrigated Cotton along the Mexico-Texas Border*. College Station: Texas A&M Press, 2008.

Warner, Deborah Jean. *Sweet Stuff: An American History of Sweeteners from Sugar to Sucralose*. Lanham, Md.: Rowman and Littlefield, 2011.

Weber, Devra. *Dark Sweat, White Gold: California Farm Workers, Cotton, and the New Deal*. Berkeley: University of California Press, 1994.

Weise, Julie M. "Mexican Nationalisms, Southern Racisms: Mexicans and Mexican Americans in the U.S. South, 1908-1939." *American Quarterly* 60, no. 3 (2008): 749-77.

Wexler, Laura. *Tender Violence: Domestic Visions in an Age of U.S. Imperialism.* Chapel Hill: University of North Carolina Press, 2000.

Whitney, Robert. *State and Revolution in Cuba: Mass Mobilization and Political Change, 1920–1940.* Chapel Hill: University of North Carolina Press, 2001.

Williams, Eric. *Capitalism and Slavery.* Chapel Hill: University of North Carolina Press, 2007.

Williams, Raymond. *Marxism and Literature.* New York: Oxford University Press, 1978.

Williams, Rosalind H. *Dream Worlds: Mass Consumption in Late Nineteenth-Century France.* Berkeley: University of California Press, 1982.

Williams, Walter L. "United States Indian Policy and the Debate over Philippine Annexation: Implications for the Origins of American Imperialism." *Journal of American History* 66, no. 4 (March 1980): 810–31.

Williams-Forson, Psyche. *Building Houses Out of Chicken Legs: Black Women, Food, and Power.* Chapel Hill: University of North Carolina Press, 2006.

Witt, Doris. *Black Hunger: Food and the Politics of U.S. Identity.* Oxford: Oxford University Press, 2004.

Woloson, Wendy A. *Refined Tastes: Sugar, Consumption, and Consumers in Nineteenth-Century America.* Baltimore: Johns Hopkins University Press, 2002.

Worster, Donald. *Rivers of Empire: Water, Aridity, and the Growth of the American West.* New York: Oxford University Press, 1985.

Wyckoff, William. *Creating Colorado: The Making of a Western American Landscape, 1860–1940.* New Haven: Yale University Press, 1999.

Yu, Henry. *Thinking Orientals: Migration, Contact, and Exoticism in Modern America.* New York: Oxford University Press, 2001.

Zimmerman, Andrew. *Alabama in Africa: Booker T. Washington, the German Empire, and the Globalization of the New South.* Princeton: Princeton University Press, 2012.

INDEX

Made in the USA
Middletown, DE
16 August 2019